Advanced Japanese

Written by
Mamori Sugita Hughes and Kumiko Ikeda Tsuji

Edited by
Suzanne McQuade

Published in the United States by Living Language, an imprint of Random House, Inc.

www.livinglanguage.com

Editor: Suzanne McQuade
Production Editor: Ciara Robinson
Production Manager: Tom Marshall
Interior Design: Sophie Chin
Illustrations: Sophie Chin

First Edition

ISBN: 978-0-307-97191-3

This book is available at special discounts for bulk purchases for sales promotions or premiums. Special editions, including personalized covers, excerpts of existing books, and corporate imprints, can be created in large quantities for special needs. For more information, write to Special Markets/ Premium Sales, 1745 Broadway, MD 3-1, New York, New York 10019 or e-mail specialmarkets@ randomhouse.com.

PRINTED IN THE UNITED STATES OF AMERICA

10 9

Acknowledgments

Thanks to the Living Language team: Amanda D'Acierno, Christopher Warnasch, Suzanne McQuade, Laura Riggio, Erin Quirk, Heather Dalton, Amanda Munoz, Fabrizio LaRocca, Siobhan O'Hare, Sophie Chin, Pat Stango, Sue Daulton, Alison Skrabek, Ciara Robinson, Andrea McLin, and Tom Marshall.

How to use this course   4

UNIT 1: Shopping   13

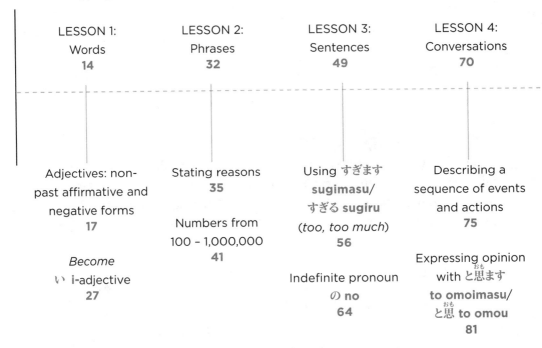

LESSON 1:
Words
14

LESSON 2:
Phrases
32

LESSON 3:
Sentences
49

LESSON 4:
Conversations
70

Adjectives: non-
past affirmative and
negative forms
17

Become
い **i-adjective**
27

Stating reasons
35

Numbers from
100 – 1,000,000
41

Using すぎます
sugimasu/
すぎる **sugiru**
(too, too much)
56

Indefinite pronoun
の **no**
64

Describing a
sequence of events
and actions
75

Expressing opinion
with と思ます
to omoimasu/
と思 **to omou**
81

C O U R S E

UNIT 2: At a Restaurant   104

LESSON 5:
Words
105

LESSON 6:
Phrases
125

LESSON 7:
Sentences
144

LESSON 8:
Conversations
166

Giving and
receiving verbs
107

Expressing the
completion of an
action and attempts
118

Adjectives: Past
tense, affirmative
and negative form
128

Before and *after*:
前に **mae ni** and
後で **ato de**
138

Polite expressions:
Honorific and
humble polite forms
of verbs
148

Expressing desires:
たい **tai** (past tense)
161

Inviting people:
Let's ... ,
Why don't we ... ?,
Shall we ... ?
171

Only X: X だけ **dake**
and X しか **shika** +
negative
179

OUTLINE

UNIT 3: Sports and Leisure   **202**

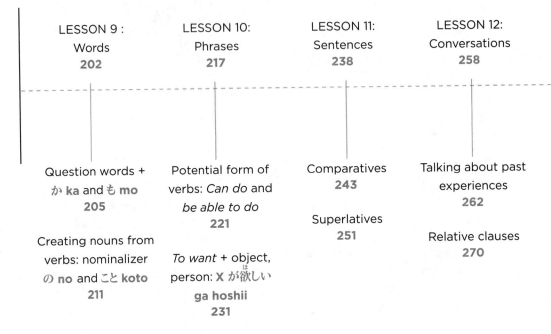

LESSON 9 :
Words
202

LESSON 10:
Phrases
217

LESSON 11:
Sentences
238

LESSON 12:
Conversations
258

Question words +
か ka and も mo
205

Creating nouns from
verbs: nominalizer
の no and こと koto
211

Potential form of
verbs: *Can do* and
be able to do
221

To want + object,
person: **X** が欲しい
ga hoshii
231

Comparatives
243

Superlatives
251

Talking about past
experiences
262

Relative clauses
270

C O U R S E

UNIT 4: Doctors and Health   290

LESSON 13:	LESSON 14:	LESSON 15:	LESSON 16:
Words	Phrases	Sentences	Conversations
291	307	326	343

Pronouns
294

Verb + ておきます
te okimasu
302

The て **te**-form of
adjectives
311

Giving and receiving
verbs 2
318

Asking for
permission
330

Negative request
338

Expressing
obligation
348

Giving advice
355

Glossary   379

How to Use This Course

Konnichi wa ! Welcome to *Living Language Advanced Japanese*! Ready to learn how to speak, read, and write even more Japanese?

Before we begin, let's go over what you'll see in this course. It's very easy to use, but this section will help you get started.

CONTENT

Advanced Japanese is a continuation of *Intermediate Japanese*.

Now that you've mastered the basics with *Essential* and *Intermediate Japanese*, you'll take your Japanese even further with a comprehensive look at more advanced Japanese grammar and complex sentences.

UNITS

There are four units in this course. Each unit has four lessons arranged in a "building block" structure: the first lesson will present essential *words*, the second will introduce longer *phrases*, the third will teach *sentences*, and the fourth will show how everything works together in everyday *conversations*.

At the beginning of each unit is an introduction highlighting what you'll learn in that unit. At the end of each unit you'll find the Unit Essentials, which reviews the key information from that unit, and a self-graded Unit Quiz, which tests what you've learned.

LESSONS

There are four lessons per unit for a total of 16 lessons in the course. Each lesson has the following components:

- **Introduction** outlining what you will cover in the lesson.

- **Word Builder 1** (first lesson of the unit) presenting key words and phrases.

- **Phrase Builder 1** (second lesson of the unit) introducing longer phrases and expressions.

- **Sentence Builder 1** (third lesson of the unit) teaching sentences.

- **Conversation 1** (fourth lesson of the unit) for a natural dialogue that brings together important vocabulary and grammar from the unit.

- **Take It Further** providing extra information about the new vocabulary you just saw, expanding on certain grammar points, or introducing additional words and phrases.

- **Word/Phrase/Sentence/Conversation Practice 1** practicing what you learned in Word Builder 1, Phrase Builder 1, Sentence Builder 1, or Conversation 1.

- **Grammar Builder 1** guiding you through important Japanese grammar that you need to know.

- **Work Out 1** for a comprehensive practice of what you saw in Grammar Builder 1.

- **Word Builder 2/Phrase Builder 2/Sentence Builder 2/Conversation 2** for more key words, phrases, or sentences, or a second dialogue.

- **Take It Further** for expansion on what you've seen so far and additional vocabulary.

- **Word/Phrase/Sentence/Conversation Practice 2** practicing what you learned in Word Builder 2, Phrase Builder 2, Sentence Builder 2, or Conversation 2.

- **Grammar Builder 2** for more information on Japanese grammar.

- **Work Out 2** for a comprehensive practice of what you saw in Grammar Builder 2.

- **Drive It Home** ingraining an important point of Japanese grammar for the long term.

- **Tip** or **Culture Note** for a helpful language tip or useful cultural information related to the lesson or unit.

- **Word Recall** reviewing important vocabulary and grammar from any of the previous lessons in *Advanced, Intermediate,* or *Essential Japanese.*

- **How Did You Do?** outlining what you learned in the lesson.

UNIT ESSENTIALS

You will see the **Unit Essentials** at the end of every unit. This section summarizes and reviews the key information from the unit, but with missing vocabulary information for you to fill in. In other words, each Unit Essentials works as both a study guide and a blank "cheat sheet." Once you complete it, you'll have your very own reference for the most essential vocabulary and grammar from the unit.

UNIT QUIZ

After each Unit Essentials, you'll see a **Unit Quiz**. The quizzes are self-graded so it's easy for you to test your progress and see if you should go back and review.

PROGRESS BAR

You will see a **Progress Bar** on each page that has course material. It indicates your current position within the unit and lets you know how much progress you're making. Each line in the bar represents a Grammar Builder section.

AUDIO

Look for the symbol ⊙ to help guide you through the audio as you're reading the book. It will tell you which track to listen to for each section that has audio. When you see the symbol, select the indicated track and start listening! If you don't see the symbol, then there isn't any audio for that section.

The audio can be used on its own—in other words, without the book—when you're on the go. Whether in your car or at the gym, you can listen to the audio on its own to brush up on your pronunciation or review what you've learned in the book.

GLOSSARY

At the back of this book you will find an extensive Japanese–English and English–Japanese glossary, including all of the essential words from all three levels of this Japanese course, as well as some additional vocabulary.

GUIDE TO READING AND WRITING JAPANESE

Three different types of characters are used to write Japanese: ひらがな hiragana, カタカナ katakana, and かんじ kanji. You will learn about each type gradually through this book and in the *Guide to Reading and Writing Japanese* included with this course. You'll also see the Japanese sounds transcribed into the Roman alphabet (also called romaji) throughout this course.

FREE ONLINE TOOLS

Go to **www.livinglanguage.com/languagelab** to access your free online tools. The tools are organized around the lessons in this course, with audiovisual flashcards, as well as interactive games and quizzes for each lesson, plus a grammar summary for all three levels. These tools will help you to review and practice the vocabulary and grammar that you've seen in the lessons, providing some extra words and phrases related to the lesson's topic as well.

Unit 1:
Shopping

Welcome to your first unit of *Advanced Japanese*! In Unit 1, you will learn some key expressions and vocabulary related to shopping for food and clothes. You will also learn how to use color words and numbers up to 1,000,000. By the end of the unit, you'll be able to:

☐ use key vocabulary related to clothes and grocery shopping

☐ conjugate adjectives in non-past tense

☐ use the verb *become* with い i-adjectives

☐ state reasons using し shi

☐ count up to 1,000,000

☐ express *too* and *too much*

☐ use indefinite pronoun *one*

☐ describe a sequence of events and actions

☐ state opinions with *I think that*

Lesson 1: Words

In this lesson you'll learn how to:

☐ use key vocabulary related to clothes and grocery shopping

☐ conjugate adjectives in non-past tense

☐ use the verb *become* with い i-adjectives

Word Builder 1

▶ 1A Word Builder 1 (CD 7, Track 1)

てんいん 店員	ten-in	*store clerk*
セーター	seetaa	*sweater*
シャツ	shatsu	*shirt*
ブラウス	burausu	*blouse*
ズボン、パンツ	zubon, pantsu	*pants*
ジーンズ	jiinzu	*jeans*
スカート	sukaato	*skirt*
ネクタイ	nekutai	*necktie*
ウール	uuru	*wool*
めん 綿	men	*cotton*
しま 縞	shima	*stripes*
む じ 無地	muji	*solid (color)*

Using すぎます sugimasu/
すぎる sugiru (too, too much)

Describing a sequence of events and actions

Indefinite pronoun の no

Expressing opinion with と思います
to omoimasu/と思う to omou

デザイン	dezain	design
サイズ	saizu	size
人気	ninki	popularity
（お）支払い	(o)shiharai (polite with o)	payment
現金	genkin	cash
カード、クレジットカード	kaado, kurejitto kaado	credit card
お釣り	otsuri	change
お返し	okaeshi (polite)	return, change
千円	sen en	1,000 yen
一万円	ichiman en	10,000 yen
赤、赤い	aka (noun), akai (adjective)	red
青、青い	ao (noun), aoi (adjective)	blue
緑	midori (noun)	green
黄色、黄色い	kiiro (noun), kiiroi (adjective)	yellow
茶色、茶色い	chairo (noun), chairoi (adjective)	brown
グレー	guree (noun)	grey
ピンク	pinku (noun)	pink
地味	jimi	sober, quiet (color)
派手	hade	showy, loud

あか 明るい	akarui	*bright*
くら 暗い	kurai	*dark*
かる 軽い	karui	*light*
おも 重い	omoi	*heavy*
あつ 暑い	atsui	*hot*
さむ 寒い	samui	*cold*
あたた 暖かい	atatakai	*warm*
すず 涼しい	suzushii	*cool*
おも おも 思います/思う	omoimasu/omou	*to think*
さが さが 探します/探す	sagashimasu/sagasu	*to look for*
あず あず 預かります/預かる	azukarimasu/azukaru	*to keep*
ございます	gozaimasu (*polite*)	*there is, to have, to exist*

Take It Further

Some Japanese equivalents of colors have both an い i-adjective form and a
noun form. For instance, *white sweater* can be either 白いセーター shiroi seetaa
(adjective + noun) or 白のセーター shiro no seetaa (noun + particle の no +
noun). Likewise, you can say either 茶色いスカート chairoi sukaato or 茶色
のスカートchairo no sukaato. However, many color names—such as *pink, gray,
green*—do not have adjective forms in Japanese. Thus, for such colors, you will
always need to use the second formula with の no: ピンクのセーター pinku no
seetaa (*pink sweater*), グレーのセーター guree no seetaa (*gray sweater*), 緑のセー
ター midori no seetaa (*green sweater*).

Using すぎます sugimasu/
すぎる sugiru (*too, too much*)

Describing a sequence of events and actions

Indefinite pronoun の no

Expressing opinion with と思います
to omoimasu/と思う to omou

✎ Word Practice 1

Translate the following words into Japanese.

1. *store clerk* _____

2. *cotton* _____

3. *stripes* _____

4. *solid (color)* _____

5. *popularity* _____

6. *payment* _____

7. *cash* _____

8. *change* _____

9. *return, change (polite)* _____

10. *sober, quiet (color)* _____

ANSWER KEY
1. 店員 ten-in; 2. 綿 men; 3. 縞 shima; 4. 無地 muji; 5. 人気 ninki; 6. (お) 支払い (o)shiharai; 7. 現金 genkin; 8. お釣り otsuri; 9. お返し okaeshi; 10. 地味 jimi

Grammar Builder 1

ADJECTIVES: NON-PAST AFFIRMATIVE AND NEGATIVE FORMS

▶ 1B Grammar Builder 1 (CD 7, Track 2)

Let's first look at the conjugation of い i-adjectives. The following chart shows both the polite and the plain form of the non-past tense.

PLAIN NON-PAST TENSE		POLITE NON-PAST TENSE	
Affirmative	Negative	Affirmative	Negative
高い takai *(expensive, high)*	高くない takaku nai	高いです takai desu	高く[ないです/あ りません] takaku [nai desu/ arimasen]
大きい ookii *(big)*	大きくない ookiku nai	大きいです ookii desu	大きく[ないです/ ありません] ookiku [nai desu/ arimasen]
面白い omoshiroi *(interesting)*	面白くない omoshiroku nai	面白いです omoshiroi desu	面白く[ないです/ ありません] omoshiroku [nai desu/arimasen]
明るい akarui *(bright)*	明るくない akaruku nai	明るいです akarui desu	明るく[ないです/ ありません] akaruku [nai desu/arimasen]
暖かい atatakai *(warm)*	暖かくない atatakaku nai	暖かいです atatakai desu	暖かく[ないです/ ありません] atatakaku [nai desu/arimasen]
いい ii *(good)*	良くない yoku nai	いいです ii desu	良く[ないです/ ありません] yoku [nai desu/ arimasen]

Using すぎます sugimasu/
すぎる sugiru (*too, too much*)

Describing a sequence of events and actions

Indefinite pronoun の no

Expressing opinion with と思います
to omoimasu/と思う to omou

In order to get the plain non-past negative form of an adjective, drop the final
い i and attach くない **ku nai**. For the polite form, drop the final い i and attach
くないです **ku nai desu** or くありません **ku arimasen**. Note that the negative
form of いい **ii** (*good*) is 良くない **yoku nai**.

A: このセーターは高いですか。

Kono seetaa wa takai desu ka.

Is this sweater expensive?

B: いいえ、高くないですよ。安いです。

Iie, takaku nai desu yo. Yasui desu.

No, it's not expensive. It's cheap.

A: そのピザはおいしいですか。

Sono piza wa oishii desu ka.

Is that pizza delicious?

B: いいえ、あまりおいしくありません。

Iie, amari oishiku arimasen.

No, it's not so delicious.

Next, let's look at the conjugation of な **na**-adjectives, which is the same as that
of nouns. In *Intermediate Japanese*, you were introduced to the conjugation of the
copula です **desu** and its plain form counterpart だ **da**. Once you're familiar with
the conjugation of です **desu** and だ **da**, it's easy to conjugate な **na**-adjectives.

PLAIN NON-PAST TENSE		POLITE NON-PAST TENSE	
Affirmative	Negative	Affirmative	Negative
きれいだ kiree da *(beautiful, clean)*	きれい[じゃ/では]ない kiree [ja/de wa] nai	きれいです kiree desu	きれい[じゃ/では][ないです/ありません] kiree [ja/de wa] [nai desu/ arimasen]
静かだ shizuka da *(quiet)*	静か[じゃ/では]ない shizuka [ja/de wa] nai	静かです shizuka desu	静か[じゃ/では][ないです/ありません] shizuka [ja/de wa] [nai desu/ arimasen]
有名だ yuumee da *(famous)*	有名[じゃ/では]ない yuumee [ja/de wa] nai	有名です yuumee desu	有名[じゃ/では][ないです/ありません] yuumee [ja/de wa] [nai desu/ arimasen]
便利だ benri da *(convenient)*	便利[じゃ/では]ない benri [ja/de wa] nai	便利です benri desu	便利[じゃ/では][ないです/ありません] benri [ja/de wa] [nai desu/ arimasen]

Using すぎます sugimasu/
すぎる sugiru (*too, too much*)

Describing a sequence of events and actions

Indefinite pronoun の no

Expressing opinion with と思います
to omoimasu/と思う to omou

地下鉄は便利です。

Chikatetsu wa benri desu.

The subway is convenient.

あの公園はあまり静かじゃありません。

Ano kooen wa amari shizuka ja arimasen.

That park is not so quiet.

そのデパートはとても有名です。

Sono depaato wa totemo yuumee desu.

That department store is very famous.

私の部屋はあまりきれいじゃありません。

Watashi no heya wa amari kiree ja arimasen.

My room is not so clean.

✎ Work Out 1

A. Fill in the blank with the appropriate い **i**-adjective from the list below, then
change them into their appropriate form (if necessary) to complete the sentences.
Use polite forms.
重い omoi, 面白い omoshiroi, 長い nagai, 高い takai, おいしい oishii, 広い
hiroi, 明るい akarui, 暖かい atatakai

1. *A:* その鞄は ＿＿＿＿＿＿＿＿ か。

   Sono kaban wa ＿＿＿＿＿＿＿＿＿＿＿＿ ka.

   Is that bag heavy?

1. *B:* いいえ、_____。軽<small>かる</small>いです。

   Iie, _____.

   Karui desu.

   No, it isn't heavy. It's light.

2. *A:* このは映画<small>えいが</small>は _____ か。

   Kono eega wa _____**ka.**

   Is this movie long?

   B: いいえ、_____。短<small>みじか</small>いですよ。

   Iie, _____.

   Mijikai desu yo.

   No, it isn't long. It's short.

3. *A:* そのセーターは _____ か。

   Sono seetaa wa _____ **ka.**

   Is that sweater expensive?

   B: いいえ、_____。安<small>やす</small>いですよ。

   Iie, _____.

   Yasui desu yo.

   No, it isn't expensive. It's cheap.

4. *A:* そのサラダは _____ か。

   Sono sarada wa _____**ka.**

   Is that salad delicious?

   B: いいえ、あまり _____。まずくありません
   けど。

Iie, amari _____

_____. Mazuku arimasen kedo.

No, it's not very delicious. It's not bad, though.

5. *A:* 居間は _____か。

Ima wa _____ka.

Is the living room bright?

B: いいえ、_____。ちょっと暗い
です。

Iie, _____

_____. Chotto kurai desu.

No, it isn't bright. It's a little dark.

B. Fill in the blank with the appropriate な na-adjective from the list below,
changing them into appropriate form [if necessary] based on the translation. Use
the polite form.
静か shizuka, 賑やか nigiyaka, 便利 benri, きれい kiree, 有名 yuumee

1. 新宿はとても _____ 。

Shinjuku wa totemo _____.

Shinjuku is very lively.

2. その会社はあまり _____

____。

Sono kaisha wa amari _____

_____ 。

That company is not so famous.

3. 私^{わたし}のアパートはあまり _____

_____ 。

Watashi no apaato wa amari _____

_____

My apartment is not so clean.

4. このコンピューターはとても _____ 。

Kono konpyuutaa wa totemo _____ 。

This computer is very convenient.

5. あの公園^{こうえん}はあまり _____ 。

Ano kooen wa amari _____ 。

That park is not so quiet.

ANSWER KEY

A: 1. 重^{おも}いです omoi desu, 重^{おも}く[ないです/ありません] omoku [nai desu/arimasen]; 2. 長^{なが}いです nagai desu, 長^{なが}く[ないです/ありません] nagaku [nai desu/arimasen]; 3. 高^{たか}いです takai desu, 高^{たか}く[ないです/ありません] takaku [nai desu/arimasen]; 4. おいしいです oishii desu, おいしく[ないです/ありません] oishiku [nai desu/arimasen]; 5. 明^{あか}るいです akarui desu, 明^{あか}るく[ないです/ありません] akaruku [nai desu/arimasen]

B: 1. 賑^{にぎ}やかです nigiyaka desu; 2. 有名^{ゆうめい}[じゃ/では][ありません/ないです] yuumee [ja/de wa] [arimasen/nai desu]; 3. きれい[じゃ/では][ありません/ないです] kiree [ja/de wa] [arimasen/nai desu]; 4. 便利^{べんり}です benri desu; 5. 静^{しず}か[じゃ/では][ありません/ないです] shizuka [ja/de wa] [arimasen/nai desu]

Using すぎます sugimasu/
すぎる sugiru (*too, too much*)

Describing a sequence of events and actions

Indefinite pronoun の no

Expressing opinion with と思います
to omoimasu/と思う to omou

Word Builder 2

▶ 1C Word Builder 2 (CD 7, Track 3)

ジュース	juusu	*juice, soft drink*
レタス	retasu	*lettuce*
キャベツ	kyabetsu	*cabbage*
きゅうり	kyuuri	*cucumber*
トマト	tomato	*tomato*
じゃがいも	jagaimo	*potato*
たまねぎ	tamanegi	*onion*
ハム	hamu	*ham*
卵	tamago	*egg*
ゆで卵	yudetamago	*boiled egg*
パン	pan	*bread*
チーズ	chiizu	*cheese*
バター	bataa	*butter*
ピザ	piza	*pizza*
調味料	choomiryoo	*seasoning*
胡椒	koshoo	*pepper*
塩	shio	*salt*
砂糖	satoo	*sugar*
ダース	daasu	*dozen*

カート	kaato	*shopping cart*
値段	nedan	*price*
物価	bukka	*prices (of commodities)*
同じ	onaji	*same*
全部	zenbu	*all*
もし	moshi	*if, in case*
作ります/作る	tsukurimasu/tsukuru	*to make*
足りません/足りない	tarimasen/tarinai	*be insufficient, be short*

✎ Word Practice 2

Translate the following words into Japanese.

1. *potato* _____

2. *egg* _____

3. *pepper* _____

4. *salt* _____

5. *sugar* _____

6. *dozen* _____

7. *price* _____

8. *prices (of commodities)* _____

9. *same* _____

10. *all* _____

ANSWER KEY

1. じゃがいも jagaimo; 2. 卵 tamago; 3. 胡椒 koshoo; 4. 塩 shio; 5. 砂糖 satoo; 6. ダース daasu; 7. 値段 nedan; 8. 物価 bukka; 9. 同じ onaji; 10. 全部 zenbu

Grammar Builder 2

BECOME い I-ADJECTIVE

▶ 1D Word Builder 2 (CD 7, Track 4)

You learned how to say *become a teacher* and *become famous* in *Intermediate Japanese. Teacher* is a noun, and *famous* in Japanese is a な na-adjective. Now, let's learn how to say, for instance, *become expensive* and *become cold. Expensive* and *cold* in Japanese are い i-adjectives. You can use the structure below.

> く ku-*form of*い i-*adjectives* + なります narimasu/なる naru

The く ku-form of adjectives is the form used in negatives, such as 高くない takaku nai and 大きくない ookiku nai. Let's look at some examples of this formula using other い i-adjectives.

高くなる	takaku naru	*become expensive*
大きくなる	ookiku naru	*become big*
暑くなる	atsuku naru	*become hot*
寒くなる	samuku naru	*become cold*
古くなる	furuku naru	*become old*
軽くなる	karuku naru	*become light*

最近物価は高くなりました。

Saikin bukka wa takaku narimashita.

Recently prices became high.

しちがつ
七月になると、暑くなります。

Shichigatsu ni naru to, atsuku narimasu.

When it becomes July, it becomes hot.

わたし   ふる   あたら   か
私のコンピューターは古くなったので、新しいコンピューターが買いたいです。

**Watashi no konpyuutaa wa furuku natta node, atarashii konpyuutaa ga kaitai
desu.**

My computer became old, so I want to buy a new computer.

✎ Work Out 2

Translate the following Japanese sentences into English.

わたし くるま ふる
1. 私の車は古くなりました。

   Watashi no kuruma wa furuku narimashita.

   _____

へ や あか
2. 部屋は明るくなりました。

   Heya wa akaruku narimashita.

   _____

ほん おもしろ
3. この本は面白くなりました。

   Kono hon wa omoshiroku narimashita.

   _____

はる あたた
4. 春になって、暖かくなりました。

   Haru ni natte, atatakaku narimashita.

   _____

Using すぎます sugimasu/
すぎる sugiru (*too, too much*)
Describing a sequence of events and actions

Indefinite pronoun の no

Expressing opinion with と思います
to omoimasu/と思う to omou

5. 十二月になると、寒くなります。

Juunigatsu ni naru to, samuku narimasu.

ANSWER KEY

1. *My car became old.* 2. *The room became bright.* 3. *This book became interesting.* 4. *Spring has come,
and it became warm.* 5. *When December comes (lit., when it becomes December), it becomes cold.*

✎ Drive It Home

Fill in the blanks with the appropriate words.

1. この映画は面白＿＿＿＿＿ないです。

Kono eega wa omoshiro _____ nai desu.

This movie is not interesting.

2. 私の部屋は明る＿＿＿＿＿ありません。

Watashi no heya wa akaru _____ arimasen.

My room is not bright.

3. 春になりましたが、暖か＿＿＿＿＿ないです。

Haru ni narimashita ga, atataka _____ nai desu.

Spring has come, but it's not warm.

4. 鞄が軽＿＿＿＿＿なりました。

Kaban ga karu _____ narimashita.

The bag became light.

5. とても寒＿＿＿＿＿なりました。

   Totemo samu ＿＿＿＿＿ narimashita.

   It became very cold.

6. コーヒーの値段は高＿＿＿＿＿なりました。

   Koohii no nedan wa taka ＿＿＿＿＿ narimashita.

   The price of coffee became high.

7. この町はあまり有名＿＿＿＿＿＿＿ないです。

   Kono machi wa amari yuumee ＿＿＿＿＿＿＿ nai desu.

   This town is not very famous.

8. この図書館はあまり静か＿＿＿＿＿＿ありません。

   Kono toshokan wa amari shizuka ＿＿＿＿＿＿＿ arimasen.

   This library is not very quiet.

9. この公園はあまりきれい＿＿＿＿＿ないです。

   Kono kooen wa amari kiree ＿＿＿＿＿＿＿ nai desu.

   This park is not very pretty/clean.

ANSWER KEY

1–6. く ku; 7–9. じゃ ja or では de wa

⊕ Culture Note

Department stores in Japan are much bigger than their American counterparts.
Many of them have five, six, seven, or even more floors, and you can buy almost
anything there. Usually they have groceries such as meat, fish, and vegetables,
and snack bars in the basement. Restaurants can be found on the upper floors,
and coffee shops may be found in the same building. Some stores even have

Using すぎます sugimasu/
すぎる sugiru (*too, too much*)

Describing a sequence of events and actions

Indefinite pronoun の no

Expressing opinion with と思います
to omoimasu/と思う to omou

playgrounds for children on the rooftop. Other stores convert the rooftop into a ビヤガーデン biyagaaden (*beer garden*) during summer, serving popular Japanese food such as 焼き鳥 yakitori (*skewered grilled chicken*), beer, and other drinks. These are popular after work and evening spots in larger cities.

How Did You Do?

Let's see how you did! By now, you should be able to:

☐ use key vocabulary related to clothes and grocery shopping (Still unsure? Jump back to page 14 or 25)

☐ conjugate adjectives in non-past tense (Still unsure? Jump back to page 17)

☐ use the verb *become* with い i-adjectives (Still unsure? Jump back to page 27)

✎ Word Recall

1. レポート repooto

2. 新幹線 shinkansen

3. カラー karaa

4. 五月 gogatsu

5. ソフト sofuto

6. 五階 gokai

7. 代わる kawaru

8. 待たせる mataseru

9. 道 michi

10. 右 migi

a. *hair dye, hair color*

b. *right*

c. *report*

d. *Japanese bullet train*

e. *to keep someone waiting*

f. *to transfer (a phone line)*

g. *May*

h. *fifth floor*

i. *street, road*

j. *software*

Become い i-adjective

Numbers from 100 – 1,000,000

ANSWER KEY

1. c; 2. d; 3. a; 4. g; 5. j; 6. h; 7. f; 8. e; 9. i; 10. b

Lesson 2: Phrases

In this lesson you'll learn how to:

☐ state reasons using し shi

☐ count up to 1,000,000

Phrase Builder 1

▶ 2A Phrase Builder 1 (CD 7, Track 5)

いらっしゃいませ。	Irasshaimase.	*Welcome (to our store).*
お待たせいたしました。	Omataseitashimashita.	*We have kept you waiting. (polite)*
いかがですか。	Ikaga desu ka.	*How is it? (polite)*
本当に	hontoo ni	*really*
これで	kore de	*with this*
エムでいい	emu de ii	*medium is okay*
どんなセーター	donna seetaa	*what kind of sweater*
ウール100パーセント	uuru hyakupaasento	*100% wool*
こちらの茶色いセーター	kochira no chairoi seetaa	*this brown sweater*

Using すぎます sugimasu/
すぎる sugiru (*too, too much*)

Describing a sequence of events and actions

Indefinite pronoun の no

Expressing opinion with と思います
to omoimasu/と思う to omou

そのグレーと赤の縞の	sono guree to aka no shima no	*that one with grey and red stripes*
茶色かグレー	chairo ka guree	*brown or grey*
もう少し明るい茶色	moo sukoshi akarui chairo	*a little brighter brown*
青かピンク	ao ka pinku	*blue or pink*
きれいな色	kiree na iro	*pretty color*
少し短い	sukoshi mijikai	*a little short*
ちょっと地味	chotto jimi	*a little sober*
無地のも	muji no mo	*the one in solid color, too*
いいデザイン	ii dezain	*good design*
人気があります/ある	ninki ga arimasu/aru	*is popular*
ジーンズにもパンツにも合います/合う	jiinzu ni mo pantsu ni mo aimasu/au	*match with both jeans and pants*
三千二百円のお返し	sanzen nihyaku en no okaeshi	*three thousand, two hundred yen change*
おいくらですか。	Oikura desu ka.	*How much is it?*
お安くなっています	oyasuku natte imasu	*has been priced down*
これ（を）ください。	Kore (o) kudasai.	*Please give me this.*

Take It Further

A か ka B means *A or B*. So, ワインかビール wain ka biiru means *wine or beer*, and 明日かあさって ashita ka asatte means *tomorrow* or *the day after tomorrow*.

The honorific prefix を o can be sometimes attached to adjectives like お安い oyasui (*cheap*) and おきれい okiree (*beautiful, pretty, clean*).

✎ Phrase Practice 1

Translate the expressions below into Japanese.

1. *Welcome (to our store).* _____

2. *How is it ?* _____

3. *really* _____

4. *with this* _____

5. *medium is okay* _____

6. *100% wool* _____

7. *brown or grey* _____

8. *a little sober* _____

9. *is popular* _____

10. *How much is it?* _____

ANSWER KEY

1. いらっしゃいませ。 **Irasshaimase.**; 2. いかがですか。 **Ikaga desu ka.**; 3. 本当に hontoo ni; 4. これ で kore de; 5. エムでいい emu de ii; 6. ウール100パーセント uuru hyakupaasento; 7. 茶色かグレー

chairo ka guree; 8. ちょっと地味 chotto jimi; 9. 人気があります (or 人気がある) ninki ga arimasu (or ninki ga aru); 10. おいくらですか。 Oikura desu ka.

Grammar Builder 1

STATING REASONS

▶ 2B Grammar Builder 1 (CD 7, Track 6)

You can state a reason using the following structure

A し, B し, Y。	A shi, B shi, Y.	*A, B, and so Y.*

In the above structure, A and B are expressing the reasons for Y. Let's see how this works in some example sentences.

このセーターは軽いし、暖かいし、とてもいいです。
Kono seetaa wa karui shi, atatakai shi, totemo ii desu.
This sweater is light and warm, and so very nice.

私のアパートは古いし、駅から遠いし、あまり良くありません。
Watashi no apaato wa furui shi, eki kara tooi shi, amari yoku arimasen.
My apartment is old, and furthermore, far from the station, and so not so good.

田中さんは親切だし、真面目だし、とてもいい人です。
Tanaka san wa shinsetsu da shi, majime (*earnest*) da shi, totemo ii hito desu.
Mr./Ms. Tanaka is kind and earnest, and so he/she is a very good person.

あの公園はきれいだし、静かだし、いいですよ。
Ano kooen wa kiree da shi, shizuka da shi, ii desu yo.
That park is clean and quiet, and so it's good.

そのレストランはおいしいし、あまり高_{たか}くないし、また行_いきたいです。

Sono resutoran wa oishii shi, amari takaku nai shi, mata ikitai desu.

That restaurant is delicious and not so expensive, and so I want to go there again.

As you can see, the plain form of verbs, い i-adjectives, and the copula appears before し shi.

Note that you can state three or more reasons using the same structure. It can also be used to give just one reason.

今日_{きょう}は雨_{あめ}だし、寒_{さむ}いし、風_{かぜ}が強_{つよ}いし、出掛_{でか}けたくないです。

Kyoo wa ame da shi, samui shi, kaze ga tsuyoi shi, dekaketaku nai desu.

Today it's raining, cold, and furthermore, the wind is strong, and so I don't want to go out.

雪_{ゆき}が降_ふっているし、今日_{きょう}は家_{うち}にいましょう。

Yuki ga futte iru shi, kyoo wa uchi ni imashoo.

It's snowing, and so let's stay at home.

✎ Work Out 1

Fill in the blanks with the appropriate words to complete the sentences.

1. 私_{わたし}の車_{くるま}は _____ し、_____ し、新_{あたら}しい車_{くるま}が買_かいたいです。

   Watashi no kuruma wa _____ shi, _____ shi, atarashii kuruma ga kaitai desu.

   My car is old and small, and so I want to buy a new car.

2. 山田さんは＿＿＿＿＿＿＿し、いい人です。

Yamada san wa _____ **shi, ii hito desu.**

Mr./Ms. Yamada is kind, and so he/she is a good person.

3. このセーターは＿＿＿＿＿し、＿＿＿＿＿し、買いません。

Kono seetaa wa _____ **shi,** _____ **shi, kaimasen.**

This sweater is large and expensive, and so I won't buy it.

4. 今日は＿＿＿＿＿し、いい日ですね。

Kyoo wa _____ **shi, ii hi desu ne.**

Today is warm, and so it's a nice day.

5. この本は＿＿＿＿＿し、＿＿＿＿＿＿＿し、読みません。

Kono hon wa _____ **shi,** _____ **shi,**

yomimasen.

This book is long and boring, and so I won't read it.

ANSWER KEY
1. 古い furui, 小さい chiisai; 2. 親切だ shinsetsu da or 優しい yasashii; 3. 大きい ookii, 高い takai;
4. 暖かい atatakai; 5. 長い nagai, つまらない tsumaranai

Phrase Builder 2

▶ 2C Phrase Builder 2 (CD 7, Track 7)

今日のパーティー	kyoo no paatii	*today's party*
何人ぐらい	nannin gurai	*about how many people*
ビールを3ダース	biiru o sandaasu	*three dozen bottles of beer*
ワインを六本	wain o roppon	*six bottles of wine*

白ワインと赤ワインを 三本ずつ	shiro wain to aka wain o sanbon zutsu	*white wine and red wine* *three bottles each*
日本のを2ダース	nihon no o nidaasu	*two dozen bottles of the* *Japanese one*
アメリカのを1ダース	amerika no o ichidaasu	*a dozen bottles of the* *American one*
日本のとアメリカの	nihon no to amerika no	*a Japanese one and an* *American one*
一本五千円	ippon gosen en	*five thousand yen for* *one bottle*
同じ値段	onaji nedan	*the same price*
同じ値段の赤ワイン	onaji nedan no aka wain	*red wine of the same price*
ちょっと高すぎます/ 高すぎる	chotto takasugimasu/ takasugiru	*a little too expensive*
もう少し安いの	moo sukoshi yasui no	*a little cheaper one*
サラダに入れます/ 入れる	sarada ni iremasu/ireru	*put into a salad*
全部でいくらぐらい	zenbu de ikura gurai	*about how much all* *together*
家を出ます/出る	uchi o demasu/deru	*leave home*
そうですね。	Soo desu ne.	*That's right.*

Using すぎます sugimasu/
すぎる sugiru (*too, too much*)

Describing a sequence of events and actions

Indefinite pronoun の no

Expressing opinion with と思います
to omoimasu/と思う to omou

Take It Further

Note the expressions 白ワイン shiro wain (*white wine*) and 赤ワイン aka wain (*red wine*). Here the color word precedes the noun directly without の no as one might expect. This is only allowed in well-established compound terms.

The word ずつ zutsu has no direct English translation, but it is used in a few set expressions: A と B を一つずつ買う A to B o hitotsu zutsu kau means *buy one A and one B each*, and 本を一冊ずつ読む hon o issatsu zutsu yomu means *read one book at a time*. Also, the phrase 少しずつ sukoshi zutsu means *little by little*.

✎ Phrase Practice 2

Fill in the missing words below.

1. 何人 _____

   nannin _____

   about how many people

2. ビールを _____

   biiru o 3 _____

   three dozen bottles of beer

3. 白ワインと赤ワインを _____

   shiro wain to aka wain o _____

   white wine and red wine three bottles each

Become い i-adjective

Numbers from 100 – 1,000,000

4. _____ と _____

_____ to _____

a Japanese one and an American one

5. _____ 値段
<ruby>ね だん</ruby>

_____ nedan

same price

6. もう少し _____
<ruby>すこ</ruby>

moo sukoshi _____

a little cheaper one

7. _____ いくらぐらい

_____ ikura gurai

about how much all together

8. 家を _____
<ruby>うち</ruby>

uchi o _____

leave home

ANSWER KEY

1. ぐらい gurai; 2. ダース daasu; 3. 三本ずつ sanbon zutsu; 4. 日本の nihon no, アメリカの amerika no; 5. 同じ onaji; 6. 安いの yasui no; 7. 全部で zenbu de; 8. 出ます (or 出る) demasu (or deru)

Using すぎます sugimasu/
すぎる sugiru (too, too much)

Describing a sequence of events and actions

Indefinite pronoun の no

Expressing opinion with と思います
to omoimasu/と思う to omou

Grammar Builder 2

NUMBERS FROM 100 – 1,000,000

▶ 2D Grammar Builder 2 (CD 7, Track 8)

You have already learned how to count to 100. Now, let's learn how to count to 1,000,000.

First, let's learn how to count from 100 to 999.

<ruby>百<rt>ひゃく</rt></ruby> hyaku	100
二百 nihyaku	200
三百 sanbyaku	300
四百 yonhyaku	400
五百 gohyaku	500
六百 roppyaku	600
七百 nanahyaku	700
八百 happyaku	800
九百 kyuuhyaku	900

100 is 百 hyaku, but note the variations in the word when it is combined with other elements, such as in the words for 300, 600 and 800. If you want to say 150, you just need to combine 百 hyaku and 五十 gojuu to get 百五十 hyaku gojuu. If you want to say *158*, you just need to combine 百 hyaku, 五十 gojuu, and 八 hachi. So, you will get 百五十八 hyaku gojuu hachi.

二百六十三 nihyaku rokujuu san	263
三百十二 sanbyaku juuni	312

よんひゃくはち 四百八 yonhyaku hachi	408
ご ひゃくなな じゅうきゅう 五百七十九 gohyaku nanajuu kyuu	579
ろっぴゃくさんじゅうさん 六百三十三 roppyaku sanjuu san	633
ななひゃくきゅうじゅういち 七百九十一 nanahyaku kyuujuu ichi	791
はっぴゃくさんじゅうご 八百三十五 happyaku sanjuu go	835
きゅうひゃくきゅうじゅうきゅう 九百九十九 kyuuhyaku kyuujuu kyuu	999

Next, let's learn how to count from 1000 to 9000.

せん 千 sen	1000
に せん 二千 nisen	2000
さんぜん 三千 sanzen	3000
よんせん 四千 yonsen	4000
ご せん 五千 gosen	5000
ろくせん 六千 rokusen	6000
ななせん 七千 nanasen	7000
はっせん 八千 hassen	8000
きゅうせん 九千 kyuusen	9000

1000 is 千 sen, but it is pronounced 千 zen in 3000. If you want to say 1600, you just need to combine 千 sen and 六百 roppyaku to get 千六百 sen roppyaku. If you want to say 1652, you just need to combine 千 sen, 六百 roppyaku, 五十 gojuu, and 二 ni to get 千六百五十二 sen roppyaku gojuu ni.

Using すぎます sugimasu/
すぎる sugiru (too, too much)

Describing a sequence of events and actions

Indefinite pronoun の no

Expressing opinion with と思います
to omoimasu/と思う to omou

に せんさんびゃくじゅう 二千三百十 nisen sanbyaku juu	2310
さんぜんはっぴゃくななじゅうご 三千八百七十五 sanzen happyaku nanajuu go	3875
よんせんきゅうひゃくろくじゅうろく 四千九百六十六 yonsen kyuuhyaku rokujuu roku	4966
ご せん に ひゃくよんじゅうご 五千二百四十五 gosen nihyaku yonjuu go	5245
ろくせんはっぴゃくいち 六千八百一 rokusen happyaku ichi	6801
ななせんよんひゃくさんじゅう に 七千四百三十二 nanasen yonhyaku sanjuu ni	7432
はっせんきゅうひゃくじゅうろく 八千九百十六 hassen kyuuhyaku juu roku	8916
きゅうせんきゅうひゃくきゅうじゅうきゅう 九千九百九十九 kyuusen kyuuhyaku kyuujuu kyuu	9999

Now, let's learn how to count from 10,000 to 1,000,000.

いちまん 一万 ichiman	10,000
にまん 二万 niman	20,000
さんまん 三万 sanman	30,000
よんまん 四万 yonman	40,000
ご まん 五万 goman	50,000
ろくまん 六万 rokuman	60,000
ななまん 七万 nanaman	70,000
はちまん 八万 hachiman	80,000

Become い i-adjective

Numbers from 100 – 1,000,000

きゅうまん 九万 kyuuman	90,000
じゅうまん 十万 juuman	100,000
にじゅうまん 二十万 nijuuman	200,000
さんじゅうまん 三十万 sanjuuman	300,000
よんじゅうまん 四十万 yonjuuman	400,000
ごじゅうまん 五十万 gojuuman	500,000
ろくじゅうまん 六十万 rokujuuman	600,000
ななじゅうまん 七十万 nanajuuman	700,000
はちじゅうまん 八十万 hachijuuman	800,000
きゅうじゅうまん 九十万 kyuujuuman	900,000
ひゃくまん 百万 hyakuman	1,000,000

To say 56,700, just combine 五万 goman, 六千 rokusen and 七百 nanahyaku to get 五万六千七百 goman rokusen nanahyaku. Likewise, to say 716,892, just combine 七十一万 nanajuuichiman, 六千 rokusen, 八百 happyaku, 九十 kyuujuu, and 二 ni to get 七十一万六千八百九十二 nanajuu ichiman rokusen happyaku kyuujuuni.

ろくじゅうまんせんさんびゃくにじゅういち 六十万千三百二十一 rokujuuman sen sanbyaku nijuu ichi	601,321
ななじゅういちまんご せんよんひゃくさんじゅう 七十一万五千四百三十 nanajuuichiman gosen yonhyaku sanjuu	715,430
きゅうじゅうきゅうまんきゅうせんきゅうひゃくきゅうじゅうきゅう 九十九万九千九百九十九 kyuujuukyuuman kyuusen kyuuhyaku kyuujuu kyuu	999,999

Advanced Japanese

Using すぎます sugimasu/
すぎる sugiru (too, too much)

Describing a sequence of events and actions

Indefinite pronoun の no

Expressing opinion with と思います
to omoimasu/と思う to omou

✏ Work Out 2

Write the following numbers in Japanese.

1. *303* _____

2. *685* _____

3. *899* _____

4. *971* _____

5. *1,320* _____

6. *2,007* _____

7. *3,866* _____

8. *8,682* _____

9. *11,100* _____

10. *24,318* _____

11. *83,688* _____

12. *90,877* _____

13. *101,134* _____

14. *265,359* _____

ANSWER KEY

1. 三百三 sanbyaku san; 2. 六百八十五 roppyaku hachijuu go; 3. 八百九十九 happyaku kyuujuu kyuu; 4. 九百七十一 kyuuhyaku nanajuu ichi; 5. 千三百二十 sen sanbyaku nijuu; 6. 二千七 nisen nana; 7. 三千八百六十六 sanzen happyaku rokujuu roku; 8. 八千六百八十二 hassen roppyaku hachijuu ni; 9. 一万千百 ichiman sen hyaku; 10. 二万四千三百十八 niman yonsen sanbyaku juu hachi; 11. 八万三千六百八十八 hachiman sanzen roppyaku hachijuu hachi; 12. 九万八百七十七 kyuuman happyaku nanajuu nana; 13. 十万千百三十四 juuman sen hyaku sanjuu yon; 14. 二十六万五千三百五十九 nijuu rokuman gosen sanbyaku gojuu kyuu

✎ Drive It Home

Fill in the blanks with the appropriate words.

1. このセーターは軽い _____、暖かい _____、とてもいいです。

   Kono seetaa wa karui_____, atatakai _____, totemo ii desu.

   This sweater is light and warm, and so very nice.

2. 私のアパートは古い _____、駅から遠い _____、あまり良くありません。

   Watashi no apaato wa furui _____, eki kara tooi _____, amari yoku arimasen.

   My apartment is old, and furthermore, far from the station, and so not so good.

3. 田中さんは親切だ _____、真面目だ _____、とてもいい人です。

   Tanaka san wa shinsetsu da _____, majime da _____, totemo ii hito desu.

   Mr./Ms. Tanaka is kind and earnest, and so he/she is a very good person.

4. あの公園はきれいだ _____、静かだ _____、いいですよ。

   Ano kooen wa kiree da _____, shizuka da _____, ii desu yo.

   That park is clean and quiet, and so it's good.

5. そのレストランはおいしい _____、あまり高くない _____、また行きたいです。

   Sono resutoran wa oishii _____, amari takaku nai _____, mata ikitai desu.

   That restaurant is delicious and not so expensive, and so I want to go there again.

6. 二^に___

ni _____

200

7. 三^{さん}___

san _____

300

8. 四^{よん}___

yon_____

4,000

9. 五^ご___

go _____

5,000

10. 六^{ろく}___

roku _____

60,000

ANSWER KEY

1–5. all し shi; 6. 百 hyaku; 7. 百 byaku; 8. 千 sen; 9. 千 sen; 10. 万 man

💡 Tip!

Check out the advertisement for automobiles, furniture stores, department stores, supermarkets, electric appliances stores, etc., in the newspaper, magazines or on the web, and try saying the prices out loud in Japanese. Also, you can check the advertisements by real estate companies, and try giving the prices of houses in Japanese. In this way, you can practice using a wide range of numbers. *Dollars* in

Japanese is ドル doru. So if you want to say *1,000 dollars*, you can say 千ドル sen doru.

How Did You Do?

Let's see how you did! By now, you should be able to:

☐ state reasons using し shi (Still unsure? Jump back to page 35)

☐ count up to 1,000,000 (Still unsure? Jump back to page 41)

✎ Word Recall

1. 左 hidari	a. *bed*
2. ビル biru	b. *sofa*
3. 曲がる magaru	c. *to run*
4. 歩く aruku	d. *to walk*
5. 走る hashiru	e. *to be able to be seen, to be visible*
6. 渡る wataru	f. *to cross*
7. 見える mieru	g. *to turn*
8. なる naru	h. *high-rise building*
9. ソファー sofaa	i. *to become*
10. ベッド beddo	j. *left*

ANSWER KEY

1. j; 2. h; 3. g; 4. d; 5. c; 6. f; 7. e; 8. i; 9. b; 10. a

Using すぎます sugimasu/
すぎる sugiru (*too, too much*)

Describing a sequence of events and actions

Indefinite pronoun の no

Expressing opinion with と思います
to omoimasu/と思う to omou

Lesson 3: Sentences

In this lesson you'll learn how to:

☐ express *too* and *too much*

☐ use indefinite pronoun *one*

Sentence Builder 1

▶ 3A Grammar Builder 1 (CD 7, Track 9)

セーターはどちらですか。

Seetaa wa dochira desu ka.

Where are the sweaters? (polite)

ネクタイはそちらにございます。

Nekutai wa sochira ni gozaimasu.

The neckties are there. (polite)

どんなセーターをお探しですか。

Donna seetaa o osagashi desu ka.

What kind of sweater are you looking for? (polite)

ウール 100 パーセントで、茶色かグレーのはありますか。

Uuru hyakupaasento de, chairo ka guree no wa arimasu ka.

Do you have one made of 100% wool and either brown or grey?

こちらの茶色いセーターはいかがですか。

Kochira no chairoi seetaa wa ikaga desu ka.

What about this brown sweater? (polite)

もう<ruby>少<rt>すこ</rt></ruby>し<ruby>明<rt>あか</rt></ruby>るい<ruby>茶色<rt>ちゃいろ</rt></ruby>がいいんですけど。

Moo sukoshi akarui chairo ga ii n desu kedo.

I prefer a little brighter brown, but…

そのグレーと<ruby>赤<rt>あか</rt></ruby>の<ruby>縞<rt>しま</rt></ruby>のはいいデザインですね。

Sono guree to aka no shima no wa ii dezain desu ne.

That one with grey and red stripes has a nice design, doesn't it?

このセーターは<ruby>人気<rt>にんき</rt></ruby>があるんですよ。

Kono seetaa wa ninki ga aru n desu yo.

This sweater is popular.

<ruby>軽<rt>かる</rt></ruby>いし、とても<ruby>暖<rt>あたた</rt></ruby>かいし、いいですよ。

Karuishi, totemo atatakaishi, ii desu yo.

It's light, very warm, and so, it's good.

<ruby>短<rt>みじか</rt></ruby>くありませんか。

Mijikaku arimasen ka.

Isn't it short?

<ruby>少<rt>すこ</rt></ruby>し<ruby>短<rt>みじか</rt></ruby>いかもしれません。

Sukoshi mijikai kamoshiremasen.

It may be a little short.

ジーンズにもパンツにも<ruby>合<rt>あ</rt></ruby>います。

Jiinzu ni mo pantsu ni mo aimasu.

It matches with both jeans and pants.

Using すぎます sugimasu/
すぎる sugiru (too, too much)

Describing a sequence of events and actions

Indefinite pronoun の no

Expressing opinion with と思います
to omoimasu/と思う to omou

スカートに合うと思います。

Sukaato ni au to omoimasu.

I think it matches with a skirt.

無地のもありますか。

Muji no mo arimasu ka.

Do you also have one in a solid color?

青かピンクだったらございます。

Ao ka pinku dattara gozaimasu.

If it's blue or pink, we have it. (polite)

青いのはきれいな色ですね。

Aoi no wa kiree na iro desu ne.

The blue one has a pretty color.

こちらは一万六千八百円です。

Kochira wa ichiman rokusen happyaku en desu.

This one is 16,800 yen.

二万円でしたが、セールなのでお安くなっています。

Niman en deshita ga, seeru na node oyasuku natte imasu.

It was 20,000 yen, but has been priced down because it's on sale.

サイズはエムでいいですか。

Saizu wa emu de ii desu ka.

As for size, is medium okay?

五万円持っています。

Goman en motte imasu.

I have 50,000 yen.

お支払いは現金ですか。

Oshiharai wa genkin desu ka.

Are you paying cash? (lit., As for payment, is it by cash?)

カードでお願いします。

Kaado de onegaishimasu.

With a card, please.

二万円お預かりします。

Niman en oazukarishimasu.

I'll keep 20,000 yen.

三千二百円のお返しです。

Sanzen nihyaku en no okaeshi desu.

It's 3,200 yen change.

Take It Further

You just learned the expression 五万円持っています Goman en motte imasu
(*I have 50,000 yen*). You learned in *Intermediate Japanese* that the structure
"verb + ています te imasu" results in the progressive form. So, you may have
wondered why 五万円持っています Goman en motte imasu does not have
a progressive meaning. In fact, not all ています te imasu forms of verbs yield
progressive meanings. The verb 持ちます mochimasu is one such example. One
of the meanings of the verb 持ちます mochimasu is *to hold*, and the ています te
imasu form of 持ちます mochimasu gives you a perfective meaning, the result

of holding something; i.e. *to have something with you*. The expression お<ruby>安<rt>やす</rt></ruby>くなっ
ています oyasuku natte imasu (*to have been priced down*) that you learned in
Lesson 2 is an another example. The verb なります narimasu means *to become*,
and its ています te imasu form yields the perfective *to have become*. So the literal
expression of お<ruby>安<rt>やす</rt></ruby>くなっています oyasuku natte imasu is *to have become cheap*.
Other examples of verbs that yield perfective meanings in the ています te imasu
form are listed in the following.

VERB		て TE FORM + います IMASU/いる IRU	
行きます/行く ikimasu/iku	*to go*	行っています/ 行っている itte imasu/itte iru	*to have gone*
来ます/来る kimasu/kuru	*to come*	来ています/ 来ている kite imasu/kite iru	*to have come, to be here*
戻ります/戻る modorimasu/ modoru	*to return*	戻っています/ 戻っている modotte imasu/ modotte iru	*to have returned*
出ます/出る demasu/deru	*to leave*	出ています/ 出ている dete imasu/dete iru	*to have left*
死にます/死ぬ shinimasu/shinu	*to die*	死んでいます/ 死んでいる shinde imasu/ shinde iru	*to be dead*

VERB		て TE **FORM** + います IMASU/いる IRU	
降<small>お</small>ります/降<small>お</small>りる orimasu/oriru	*to get off*	降<small>お</small>りています/ 降<small>お</small>りている orite imasu/orite iru	*to have gotten off, to be off*
借<small>か</small>ります/借<small>か</small>りる karimasu/kariru	*to borrow*	借<small>か</small>りています/ 借<small>か</small>りている karite imasu/ karite iru	*to have borrowed*
貸<small>か</small>します/貸<small>か</small>す kashimasu/kasu	*to lend*	貸<small>か</small>しています/ 貸<small>か</small>している kashite imasu/ kashite iru	*to have lent*
入<small>はい</small>ります/入<small>はい</small>る hairimasu/hairu	*to enter, to join*	入<small>はい</small>っています/ 入<small>はい</small>っている haitte imasu/ haitte iru	*to have entered, to belong*

At this point, don't worry about not being able to tell exactly which verbs yield progressive and which verbs yield perfective meanings. Whenever you see the expression 〜ています ... **te imasu** in a phrase or sentence list in this course, check its English translation. If the English does not look like progressive, you know it is perfective.

✎ Sentence Practice 1

Fill in the missing words in each of the following sentences.

1. セーターは _____ 。

   Seetaa wa _____.

   Where are the sweaters? (polite)

2. どんなセーターを _____ 。

   Donna seetaa o _____.

   What kind of sweater are you looking for? (polite)

3. こちらの茶色いセーターは _____ 。

   Kochira no chairoi seetaa wa _____.

   What about this brown sweater? (polite)

4. このセーターは _____ んですよ。

   Kono seetaa wa _____ **n desu yo.**

   This sweater is popular.

5. _____ 、とても _____ 、いいですよ。

   _____, **totemo** _____, **ii desu yo.**

   It's light, very warm, and so, it's good.

6. ジーンズにもパンツにも _____ 。

   Jiinzu ni mo pantsu ni mo _____.

   It matches with both jeans and pants.

7. スカートに合うと ＿＿＿＿＿＿ 。

Sukaato ni au to ＿＿＿＿＿＿＿＿＿.

I think it matches with a skirt.

8. ＿＿＿＿＿＿ ありますか。

＿＿＿＿＿＿＿＿＿ arimasu ka.

Do you also have one in a solid color?

ANSWER KEY

1. どちらですか dochira desu ka; 2. お探しですか osagashi desu ka; 3. いかがですか ikaga desu ka; 4. 人気がある ninki ga aru; 5. 軽いし Karuishi, 暖かいし atatakaishi; 6. 合います aimasu; 7. 思います omoimasu; 8. 無地のも Muji no mo

Grammar Builder 1

USING すぎます SUGIMASU/すぎる SUGIRU (*TOO, TOO MUCH*)

▶ 3B Grammar Builder 1 (CD 7, Track 10)

すぎます Sugimasu/すぎる sugiru (*too, too much*) is used in the following structure.

> *Stem of* い *i-adjective/*な *na-adjective/conjunctive form of the verb +* すぎます **sugimasu/**すぎる **sugiru**

The stem of い i-adjectives is the form without the final い i.

明るい akarui	明る akaru
優しい yasashii	優し yasashi
高い takai	高 taka

The stem of な na-adjectives is the form without the copula.

きれいです kiree desu	きれい kiree
有名_{ゆうめい}です yuumee desu	有名_{ゆうめい} yuumee
便利_{べんり}です benri desu	便利_{べんり} benri

The conjunctive form of verbs is the ます masu-form of verbs minus ます masu.

食_たべます tabemasu	食_たべ tabe
飲_のみます nomimasu	飲_のみ nomi
行_いきます ikimasu	行_いき iki

Now, let's see how these stems work with すぎます sugimasu/すぎる sugiru.

東京_{とうきょう}の映画館_{えいがかん}は高_{たか}すぎます。

Tookyoo no eegakan wa takasugimasu.

Movie theaters in Tokyo are too expensive.

この本_{ほん}は難_{むずか}しすぎます。

Kono hon wa muzukashisugimasu.

This book is too difficult.

このブラウスはちょっと派手_{はで}すぎますね。

Kono burausu wa chotto hadesugimasu ne.

This blouse is a little too showy, isn't it?

今_{いま}のアパートは不便_{ふべん}すぎますから、新_{あたら}しいアパートを探_{さが}しています。

Ima no apaato wa fubensugimasu kara, atarashii apaato o sagashite imasu.

The current apartment is too inconvenient, so I am looking for a new apartment.

日^{にち}曜^{よう}日^びはお昼^{ひる}まで寝^ねました。ちょっと寝^ねすぎました。

Nichiyoobi wa ohiru made nemashita. Chotto nesugimashita.

I slept until noon on Sunday. I slept a little too much.

昨^{きのう}日ビールを飲^のみすぎましたから、今^{きょう}日はお酒^{さけ}は飲^のみません。

Kinoo biiru o nomisugimashita kara, kyoo wa osake wa nomimasen.

I drank too much beer yesterday, so I won't drink alcohol today.

✎ Work Out 1

Complete the sentences using the expression すぎます **sugimasu**/すぎる **sugiru**.
Pay attention to the tense. Use the polite form with ます **masu** or です **desu**.

1. 今^{きょう}日の宿題^{しゅくだい}は _____。(簡単^{かんたん})

   Kyoo no shukudai wa _____. (kantan)

   Today's homework is too easy.

2. この雑誌^{ざっし}は _____。(つまらない)

   Kono zasshi wa _____.

   (tsumaranai)

   This magazine is too boring.

3. この公園^{こうえん}は _____。(静^{しず}か)

   Kono kooen wa _____. (shizuka)

   This park is too quiet.

4. 新宿_{しんじゅく}は_____。(賑_{にぎ}やか)

   Shinjuku wa _____. **(nigiyaka)**

   Shinjuku is too lively.

5. 昨日_{きのう}ワインを_____。(飲_のみます)

   Kinoo wain o _____. **(nomimasu)**

   I drank too much wine yesterday.

6. 今日_{きょう}は_____。(食_たべます)

   Kyoo wa _____. **(tabemasu)**

   I ate too much today.

7. 週末_{しゅうまつ}、に_____。(勉強_{べんきょう}します)

   Shuumatsu ni, _____.

   (benkyooshimasu)

   I studied too much on weekend.

8. _____。(買_かいます)

   _____. **(kaimasu)**

   I bought too much.

ANSWER KEY

1.簡単_{かんたん}すぎます kantansugimasu; 2. つまらなすぎます tsumaranasugimasu; 3.静_{しず}かすぎます
shizukasugimasu; 4.賑_{にぎ}やかすぎます nigiyakasugimasu; 5.飲_のみすぎました nomisugimashita;
6.食_たべすぎました tabesugimashita; 7.勉強_{べんきょう}しすぎました benkyooshisugimashita; 8.買_かいすぎました
Kaisugimashita

Take It Further

By now, you should be familar with the verb 勉強します benkyooshimasu (*to study*). This verb originally came from the noun 勉強 benkyoo (*study*) + the verb します shimasu (*to do*), but the combination is recognized as a single fixed verb. Instead of saying 勉強します **benkyooshimasu**, you may also break down the expression and say 勉強をします **benkyoo o shimasu**, which literally means *to do studying* (but you can just translate it to English as *to study*). However, if you want to specify the object of a studying activity as in *I study math* for example, you should use 勉強します **benkyooshimasu** rather than 勉強をします **benkyoo o shimasu**. This is because you want to avoid repeating the particle を o.

数学を勉強します。

Suugaku o bennkyoo shimasu.

I study math.

Other verbs similar to 勉強します **benkyooshimasu** in origin include 留学します **ryuugakushimasu** (*to study abroad*), 電話します **denwashimasu** (*to telephone*), 連絡します **renrakushimasu** (*to contact*), and 予約します **yoyakushimasu** (*to make an appointment/reservation*). Just as with 勉強します **benkyooshimasu**, these verbs can be expressed with an を o after the noun of Chinese origin: 留学をします **ryuugaku o shimasu**, 電話をします **denwa o shimasu**, 連絡をします **renraku o shimasu**, 予約をします **yoyaku o shimasu**.

Using **すぎます** sugimasu/
すぎる sugiru (*too, too much*)
Describing a sequence of events and actions

Indefinite pronoun の no

Expressing opinion with と思います
to omoimasu/と思う to omou

✎ Sentence Builder 2

▶ 3C Sentence Builder 2 (CD 7, Track 11)

今日ののパーティーは何人ぐらい来るんですか。

Kyoo no paatii wa nannin gurai kuru n desu ka.

As for today's party, about how many people are coming?

十人ぐらいだと思いますけど。

Juunin gurai da to omoimasu kedo.

I think about ten people, but …

ビールを3ダース買ったらいいですね。

Biiru o sandaasu kattara ii desu ne.

It will be okay if we buy three dozen bottles of beer, right?

ビールは日本のを2ダース買ったらどうですか。

Biiru wa nihon no o nidaasu kattara doo desu ka.

As for beer, what about buying two dozen bottles of Japanese (beer)?

それはいい考えですね。

Sore wa ii kangae desu ne.

That's a good idea.

この白ワインはどうですか。

Kono shiro wain wa doo desu ka.

What about this white wine?

それは一本五千円ですよ。

Sore wa ippon gosen en desu yo.

That's 5,000 yen for a bottle.

ちょっと高<small>たか</small>すぎると思<small>おも</small>います。

Chotto takasugiru to omoimasu.

I think it's a little too expensive.

もう少<small>すこ</small>し安<small>やす</small>いのはありませんか。

Moo sukoshi yasui no wa arimasen ka.

Isn't there one that's a little cheaper?

同<small>おな</small>じ値段<small>ねだん</small>の赤<small>あか</small>ワインもありますよ。

Onaji nedan no aka wain mo arimasu yo.

There's red wine at the same price, too.

その白<small>しろ</small>ワインとこの赤<small>あか</small>ワインを三本<small>さんぼん</small>ずつカートに入<small>い</small>れますね。

Sono shiro wain to kono aka wain o sanbon zutsu kaato ni iremasu ne.

I will put three bottles each of that white wine and this red wine into the cart.

レタスときゅうりとトマトとハムを買<small>か</small>って、サラダを作<small>つく</small>ったらどうですか。

Retasu to kyuuri to tomato to hamu o katte, sarada o tsukuttara doo desu ka.

What about if we buy lettuce, cucumbers, tomatos, and ham, and make a salad?

卵<small>たまご</small>も買<small>か</small>って、ゆで卵<small>たまご</small>を作<small>つく</small>って、サラダに入<small>い</small>れたらいいですね。

Tamago mo katte, yudetamago o tsukutte, sarada ni iretara ii desu ne.

It will be good if we also buy eggs, make boiled eggs, and put them into the salad, right?

すしとピザを買<small>か</small>いますから、全部<small>ぜんぶ</small>でいくらぐらいですか。

Sushi to piza o kaimasu kara, zenbu de ikura gurai desu ka.

Since we will buy sushi and pizza, about how much will it be all together?

Using **すぎます** sugimasu/
すぎる sugiru (*too, too much*)

Describing a sequence of events and actions

Indefinite pronoun の no

Expressing opinion with と思います
to omoimasu/と思う to omou

私は三万円ぐらい持っていますけど。

Watashi wa sanman en gurai motte imasu kedo.

I have about 30,000 yen, but…

もし足りなかったら、クレジットカードを使いますから、大丈夫ですよ。

Moshi tarinakattara, kurejitto kaado o tsukaimasu kara, daijoobu desu yo.

If it's not enough, I will use a credit card, so it will be okay.

✎ Sentence Practice 2

Fill in the missing words in each of the following sentences.

1. _____ と思いますけど。

   _____ to omoimasu kedo.

   I think about ten people, but …

2. _____ 買ったらいいですね。

   _____kattara ii desu ne.

   It will be okay if we buy three dozen bottles of beer, right?

3. ビールは日本のを2ダース買ったら _____。

   Biiru wa nihon no o nidaasu kattara _____.

   As for beer, what about buying two dozen bottles of Japanese (beer)?

4. それは _____ ね。

   Sore wa _____ **ne.**

   That's a good idea.

5. それは _____ ですよ。

Sore wa _____ desu yo.

That's 5,000 yen for a bottle.

6. _____ と思^{おも}います。

_____ to omoimasu.

I think it's a little too expensive.

7. すしとピザを買^かいますから、_____ ぐらいですか。

Sushi to piza o kaimasu kara, _____ gurai

desu ka.

Since we will buy sushi and pizza, about how much will it be all together?

8. もし足^たりなかったら、クレジットカードを使^{つか}いますから、_____ よ。

Moshi tarinakattara, kurejitto kaado o tsukaimasu kara,

_____ yo.

If it's not enough, I will use a credit card, so it will be okay.

ANSWER KEY

1. 十^{じゅう}人^{にん}ぐらいだ Juunin gurai da; 2. ビールを3ダース Biiru o sandaasu; 3. どうですか doo desu
ka; 4. いい考^{かんが}えです ii kangae desu; 5. 一^{いっ}本^{ぽん}五^ご千^{せん}円^{えん} ippon gosen en; 6. ちょっと高^{たか}すぎる Chotto
takasugiru; 7. 全^{ぜん}部^ぶでいくら zenbu de ikura; 8. 大^{だい}丈^{じょう}夫^ぶです daijoobu desu

Grammar Builder 2

INDEFINITE PRONOUN の NO

▶ 3D Grammar Builder 2 (CD 7, Track 12)

The indefinite pronoun の no usually corresponds to English *one* and replaces a
noun which has already been introduced. Note how this occurs in English:

Using すぎます sugimasu/
すぎる sugiru (*too, too much*)

Describing a sequence of events and actions

Indefinite pronoun の no

Expressing opinion with と思います
to omoimasu/と思う to omou

This red shirt is nice. But I don't like that blue one.

This sweater is short. Do you have a long one?

Now let's look at how this occurs in Japanese sentences with の no.

この赤いシャツはいいですね。でも、あの青いのは好きじゃありません。

Kono akai shatsu wa ii desu ne. Demo, ano aoi no wa suki ja arimasen.

This red shirt is nice. But I don't like that blue one.

このセーターは短いです。長いのはありますか。

Kono seetaa wa mijikai desu. Nagai no wa arimasu ka.

This sweater is short. Do you have a long one?

The indefinite pronoun の no, like the English *one*, is always accompanied by modifiers, such as an adjective or a demonstrative, or a combination of the two. Also, a possessor word can appear before の no.

スミスさんの車は新しいですが、リーさんのは古いです。

Sumisu san no kuruma wa atarashii desu ga, Rii san no wa furui desu.

Mr./Ms. Smith's car is new, but Mr./Ms. Lee's is old.

私の鞄は重いですが、妹のは軽いです。

Watashi no kaban wa omoi desu ga, imooto no wa karui desu.

My bag is heavy, but my younger sister's is light.

Note that の no cannot replace a noun referring to a person.

Also note that the possessive marker の no and the indefinite pronoun の no have the same form. As you can see in the last two examples above, when they appear next to each other in a sentence (as in リーさんののは古いです Rii san no no wa furui desu or 妹ののは軽いです imooto no no wa karui desu), they are combined to avoid repetition, so only one の no is actually used.

✎ Work Out 2

Translate the following Japanese sentences into English.

1. このグレーのズボンは長すぎますが、あの黒いのは短すぎます。

   Kono guree no zubon wa nagasugimasu ga, ano kuroi no wa mijikasugimasu.

   _____

2. 鈴木さんのコンピューターは新しいですが、森さんのは古いです。

   Suzuki san no konpyuutaa wa atarashii desu ga, Mori san no wa furui desu.

   _____

3. その赤いきれいなセーターを買いますが、あの茶色の地味なのは買いません。

   Sono akai kiree na seetaa o kaimasu ga, ano chairo no jimi na no wa kaimasen.

   _____

4. この小さいケーキはおいしいですが、その大きいのはあまりおいしくありません。

   Kono chiisai keeki wa oishii desu ga, sono ookii no wa amari oishiku

   arimasen.

   _____

5. そのオレンジのシャツはいいですけど、このピンクのはちょっと派手ですね。

   Sono orenji no shatsu wa ii desu kedo, kono pinku no wa chotto hade desu ne.

   _____

Using すぎます sugimasu/
すぎる sugiru (too, too much)

Describing a sequence of events and actions

Indefinite pronoun の no

Expressing opinion with と思います
to omoimasu/と思う to omou

ANSWER KEY

1. *These grey pants are too long, but those black ones are too short.* 2. *Mr./Ms. Suzuki's computer is new, but Mr./Ms. Mori's is old.* 3. *I will buy that red pretty sweater, but I won't buy that brown plain one over there.* 4. *This small cake is delicious, but that big one is not so delicious.* 5. *That orange shirt is nice, but this pink one is a little showy.*

✎ Drive It Home

Fill in the blanks with the appropriate words to complete the sentences. Use the polite form.

1. 東京の映画館は高 _____。

   Tookyoo no eegakan wa taka _____.

   Movie theaters in Tokyo are too expensive.

2. この本は難し _____。

   Kono hon wa muzukashi _____.

   This book is too difficult.

3. このブラウスはちょっと派手 _____ ね。

   Kono burausu wa chotto hade _____ ne.

   This blouse is a little too showy, isn't it?

4. 今のアパートは不便 _____。

   Ima no apaato wa fuben _____.

   The current apartment is too inconvenient.

5. 昨日ビールを飲み _____。

   Kinoo biiru o nomi _____.

   I drank too much beer yesterday.

6. この赤いシャツはいいですね。でも、あの青い _____ は好きじゃありません。

   Kono akai shatsu wa ii desu ne. Demo, ano aoi _____ wa suki ja arimasen.

   This red shirt is nice. But I don't like that blue one.

7. このセーターは短いです。長い _____ はありますか。

   Kono seetaa wa mijikai desu. Nagai _____ wa arimasu ka.

   This sweater is short. Do you have a long one?

8. スミスさんの車は新しいですが、リーさん _____ は古いです。

   Sumisu san no kuruma wa atarashii desu ga, Rii san _____ wa furui desu.

   Mr./Ms. Smith's car is new, but Mr./Ms. Lee's is old.

9. 私の鞄は重いですが、妹 _____ は軽いです。

   Watashi no kaban wa omoi desu ga, imooto _____ wa karui desu.

   My bag is heavy, but my younger sister's is light.

   ANSWER KEY

   1. すぎます sugimasu; 2. すぎます sugimasu; 3. すぎます sugimasu; 4. すぎます sugimasu; 5. すぎました sugimashita; 6. の no; 7. の no; 8. の no; 9. の no

🔆 Tip!

Look around your bedroom, living room, kitchen, yard, or another area of your house, and describe the objects you see using adjectives you've learned so far. For instance, you can describe sofa, table, bookshelf, refrigerator, flowers, and so on. Of course, you can also do this task at your workplace or school for more practice.

Using すぎます sugimasu/
すぎる sugiru (*too, too much*)

Describing a sequence of events and actions

Indefinite pronoun の no

Expressing opinion with と思います
to omoimasu/と思う to omou

How Did You Do?

Let's see how you did! By now, you should be able to:

☐ express *too* and *too much* (Still unsure? Jump back to page 56)

☐ use indefinite pronoun *one* (Still unsure? Jump back to page 64)

✎ Word Recall

1. フランス人 furansujin	a. *Chinese (person)*
2. カナダ人 kanadajin	b. *Spanish (language)*
3. スペイン人 supeinjin	c. *German (person)*
4. 中国人 chuugokujin	d. *English (language)*
5. ドイツ人 doitsujin	e. *English (person)*
6. イギリス人 igirisujin	f. *French (language)*
7. メキシコ人 mekishikojin	g. *French (person)*
8. フランス語 furansugo	h. *Canadian (person)*
9. スペイン語 supeingo	i. *Mexican (person)*
10. 英語 eego	j. *Spanish (person)*

ANSWER KEY

1. g; 2. h; 3. j; 4. a; 5. c; 6. e; 7. i; 8. f; 9. b; 10. d

Lesson 4: Conversations

In this lesson you'll learn how to:

☐ describe a sequence of events and actions

☐ state opinions with *I think that*

🔊 Conversation 1

▶ 4A Conversation 1 (Japanese: CD 7, Track 13; Japanese and English: CD 7, Track 14)

Ms. Mori came to the women's section of a department store in Tokyo to buy a sweater.

店員/Ten-in:	いらっしゃいませ。
	Irasshaimase.
森/Mori:	セーターはどちらですか。
	Seetaa wa dochira desu ka.
店員/Ten-in:	そちらにございますが、どんなセーターをお探しですか。
	Sochira ni gozaimasu ga, donna seetaa o osagashi desu ka.
森/Mori:	ウール 100 パーセントで、茶色かグレーのはありますか。
	Uuru hyaku paasento de, chairo ka guree no wa arimasu ka.
店員/Ten-in:	それでは、こちらの茶色いセーターはいかがですか。
	Soredewa, kochira no chairoi seetaa wa ikaga desu ka.
森/Mori:	えっと、もう少し明るい茶色がいいんですけど。ああ、その グレーと赤の縞のはいいデザインですね。
	Etto, moo sukoshi akarui chairo ga ii n desu kedo. Aah, sono guree to aka no shima no wa ii dezain desu ne.

Using すぎます sugimasu/
すぎる sugiru (too, too much)

Describing a sequence of events and actions

Indefinite pronoun の no

Expressing opinion with と思います
to omoimasu/と思う to omou

店員/Ten-in: こちらですか。このセーターは人気があるんですよ。軽
いし、とても暖かいし、いいですよ。

Kochira desu ka. Kono seetaa wa ninki ga aru n desu yo.

Karuishi, totemo atatakaishi, ii desu yo.

森/Mori: 短くありませんか。

Mijikaku arimasen ka.

店員/Ten-in: 少し短いかもしれませんが、ジーンズにもパンツにも合うと
思います。

Sukoshi mijikai kamoshiremasen ga, jiinzu ni mo

pantsu ni mo au to omoimasu.

森/Mori: 無地のもありますか。

Muji no mo arimasu ka.

店員/Ten-in: 青かピンクだったらございますが。こちらが青で、こちらが
ピンクです。

Ao ka pinku dattara gozaimasu ga. Kochira ga ao de,

kochira ga pinku desu.

森/Mori: 青いのはきれいな色ですね。これ、おいくらですか。

Aoi no wa kiree na iro desu ne. Kore, oikura desu ka.

店員/Ten-in: えっと、こちらは一万六千八百円です。二万円でした
が、セールなのでお安くなっています。

Etto, kochira wa ichiman rokusen happaku en desu.

Niman en deshita ga, seeru na node oyasuku natte

imasu.

森/Mori: じゃあ、これください。

Jaa, kore kudasai.

店員/Ten-in: サイズはエムでいいですか。

Saizu wa emu de ii desu ka.

森/Mori: はい。

Hai.

店員/Ten-in: お支払いは現金ですか。カードですか。

Oshiharai wa genkin desu ka. Kaado desu ka.

森/Mori:　　これでお願いします。

Kore de onegaishimasu.

店員/Ten-in:　はい、二万円お預かりします。少々お待ちください。

Hai. Niman en oazukarishimasu. Shooshoo omachi
kudasai.

(Three minutes later.)

店員/Ten-in:　お待たせいたしました。三千二百円のお返しです。どうも
ありがとうございました。

Omataseitashimashita. Sanzen nihyaku en no okaeshi
desu. Doomo arigatoo gozaimashita.

Sales person:	*Welcome to our store.*
Mori:	*Where are the sweaters?*
Sales person:	*Sweaters are there, but what kind of sweater are you looking for?*
Mori:	*Do you have one that's made of 100% wool, and brown or grey?*
Sales person:	*Then, what about this brown one?*
Mori:	*Well, I prefer a little brighter brown. Oh, that one with grey and red stripes has a nice design.*
Sales person:	*This one? This sweater is popular. It's light, very warm, and so it's good.*
Mori:	*Isn't it short?*
Sales person:	*It may be a little short, but I think it will match with both jeans and a pair of pants.*
Mori:	*Do you also have one in solid color?*
Sales person:	*If it's blue or pink, we have it. This is blue, and this is pink.*
Mori:	*The blue one has a pretty color, doesn't it? How much is this?*
Sales person:	*Well, this one is 16,800 yen. It was 20,000 yen, but has been priced down because it's on sale.*

Using すぎます sugimasu/
すぎる sugiru (*too, too much*)

Describing a sequence of events and actions

Indefinite pronoun の no

Expressing opinion with と思います
to omoimasu/と思う to omou

Mori:	*Then, please give me this one.*
Sales person:	*Is medium size okay?*
Mori:	*Yes.*
Sales person:	*As for the payment, is it by cash or by a credit card?*
Mori:	*With this one, please.*
Sales person:	*Okay, that's (lit., I'll keep) 20,000 yen. Please wait for a little moment.*
(Three minutes later.)	
Sales person:	*I'm sorry for keeping you waiting. It's 3,200 yen change. Thank you very much.*

Take It Further

When you enter stores and restaurants, sales people and waitresses/waiters will say いらっしゃいませ。Irasshaimase. (*welcome*) to you. You will also often hear どんなのを お探しですか。Donna no o osagashi desu ka. (*What (kind of item) are you looking for?*) and お待ちください。Omachi kudasai. (*Please wait*).

You may have noticed that the last line of the dialogue, どうもありがとうございました。Doomo arigatoo gozaimashita. *Thank you*, is in the past tense. This can be used if something has already been done for you, but this form of the expression is optional. If you're unsure, you can always rely on the non-past ありがとうございます。Arigatoo gozaimasu to express your thanks.

✎ Conversation Practice 1

Fill in the blanks in the following sentences with the missing words. If you're unsure of the answer, listen to the conversation one more time.

1. 森さんは、＿＿＿＿＿＿＿＿ を買いに来ました。

   Mori san wa ＿＿＿＿＿＿＿＿ o kai ni kimashita.

2. 森さんは、ウール 100 パーセントで ＿＿＿＿＿＿ か ＿＿＿＿＿＿ のセーターを探しています

   Morisan wa uuru hayku paasento de ＿＿＿＿＿＿＿＿ ka

   ＿＿＿＿＿＿＿＿ no seetaa o sagashite imasu.

3. グレーと赤の縞のセーターは ＿＿＿＿＿＿＿ があります。

   Guree to aka no shima no seetaa wa ＿＿＿＿＿＿＿ ga arimasu.

4. グレーと赤の縞のセーターは、＿＿＿＿＿＿＿ にも ＿＿＿＿＿＿ にも合います。

   Guree to aka no shima no seetaa wa, ＿＿＿＿＿＿＿ ni mo

   ＿＿＿＿＿＿＿＿ ni mo aimasu.

5. 青いセーターは ＿＿＿＿＿＿＿＿＿＿ 円です。

   Aoi seetaa wa ＿＿＿＿＿＿＿＿＿＿＿＿＿＿＿＿＿＿＿＿＿

   ＿＿＿＿＿＿＿＿＿＿ en desu.

ANSWER KEY

1. セーター seetaa; 2. 茶色 chairo, グレー guree; 3. 人気 ninki; 4. ジーンズ jiinzu, パンツ pantsu;
5. 一万六千八百 ichiman rokusen happaku

Using すぎます sugimasu/
すぎる sugiru (*too, too much*)

Describing a sequence of events and actions

Indefinite pronoun の no

Expressing opinion with と思います
to omoimasu/と思う to omou

Grammar Builder 1

DESCRIBING A SEQUENCE OF EVENTS AND ACTIONS

▶ 4B Grammar Builder 1 (CD 7, Track 15)

The て te-form of verbs was introduced in *Intermediate Japanese*, where you
learned about two structures that use this form: the progressive form and
requests. The て te-form of verbs is also used to describe a sequence of events
and actions.

スーパーへ行って、レタスときゅうりを買いました。

Suupaa e itte, retasu to kyuuri o kaimashita.

I went to a supermarket and bought lettuce and cucumbers.

日本へ行って、一年間日本語を勉強しました。

Nihon e itte, ichinenkan nihongo o benkyooshimashita.

I went to Japan and studied Japanese for a year.

You can theoretically connect any number of events or actions using the て te-
form of verbs, but very long sequences would be difficult to process, and they
are usually divided up into two or more sentences. For instance, if you want
to describe your daily routine, you would need several sentences to list all the
activities you engage in every day.

六時半に起きて、朝ご飯を食べて、新聞を読んで、八時に家を出て、会社に行
きます。十二時まで仕事をして、昼ご飯を食べて、一時にミーティングに出ます。
それから、レポートを書いて、六時に会社を出て、七時に家に着きます。晩ご飯
を食べて、テレビを見て、お風呂に入って、十一時半に寝ます。

**Rokuji han ni okite, asagohan o tabete, shinbun o yonde, hachiji ni uchi o dete,
kaisha ni ikimasu. Juuniji made shigoto o shite, hirugohan o tabete, ichiji ni**

miitingu ni demasu. Sorekara, repooto o kaite, rokuji ni kaisha o dete, shichiji ni uchi ni tsukimasu. Bangohan o tabete, terebi o mite, ofuro ni haitte (*take a bath*), juuichiji han ni nemasu.

I wake up at six thirty, eat breakfast, read a newspaper, leave home at eight, and go to work (lit., the company). I work until twelve, eat lunch and attend the meeting at one. After that, I write a report, leave the company at six, and arrive home at seven. I eat dinner, watch TV, take a bath, and go to bed at eleven thirty.

Note that the て te-form of verbs cannot appear at the end of a sentence. Also, since tense isn't expressed in the て te-form, tense is determined by the final verb in a sequence—the verb that appears at the end of each sentence.

✎ Work Out 1

Choose the appropriate verbs from the list below and fill in the blanks with their て te-form.

勉強する benkyoosuru, 留学する ryuugakusuru, 卒業する sotsugyoosuru, 話す hanasu, 会う au, 買う kau, 読む yomu, 見る miru, 聞く kiku, 食べる taberu, 行く iku

1. 先生と_____、ここに来ました。

   Sensee to _____, **koko ni kimashita.**

   I talked with a teacher and then came here.

2. ワインを二本_____、パーティーに行きました。

   Wain o nihon _____, **paatii ni ikimashita.**

   I bought two bottles of wine and then went to a party.

Using すぎます sugimasu/
すぎる sugiru (*too, too much*)

Describing a sequence of events and actions

Indefinite pronoun の no

Expressing opinion with と思います
to omoimasu/と思う to omou

3. 雑誌を _____ 、音楽を _____ 、それから寝ました。

Zasshi o _____, ongaku o _____, sorekara nemashita.

I read a magazine, listened to the music, and then went to bed.

4. 銀座で友達に _____ 、映画を _____ 、それからレストランへ _____ 、
晩ご飯を食べました。

Ginza de tomodachi ni _____, eega o _____, sorekara

resutoran e _____, bangohan o tabemashita.

I met my friend in Ginza, saw a movie, and then went to a restaurant, and had

dinner.

5. 大学を _____ 、日本に _____ 、二年間日本語を
_____ 、それから英語を教えました。

Daigaku o _____, nihon ni

_____, ninenkan nihongo o

_____, sorekara eego o oshiemashita.

I graduated from a university, studied abroad in Japan, studied Japanese for two

years, and then taught English.

ANSWER KEY
1. 話して hanashite; 2. 買って katte; 3. 読んで yonde, 聞いて kiite; 4. 会って atte, 見て mite, 行って
itte; 5. 卒業して sotsugyooshite, 留学して ryuugakushite, 勉強して benkyooshite

🔊 Conversation 2

▶ 4C Conversation 2 (Japanese: CD 7, Track 16; Japanese and English: CD 7, Track 17)

Mr. Collins is at a supermarket with his new Japanese roommate Mr. Hayashi in
order to get some food and beverages for their house party.

コリンズ/Korinzu: 今日のパーティーは何人ぐらい来るんですか。

Kyoo no paatii wa nannin gurai kuru n desu ka.

林/Hayashi: えっと、十人ぐらいだと思いますけど。

Etto, juunin gurai da to omoimasu kedo.

コリンズ/Korinzu: じゃあ、ビールを3ダースとワインを六本買ったらいいですね。

Jaa, biiru o sandaasu to wain o roppon kattara ii desu ne.

林/Hayashi: そうですね。ビールは日本のを2ダースとアメリカのを1ダース買ったらどうですか。

Soo desu ne. Biiru wa nihon no o nidaasu to amerika no o ichidaasu kattara doo desu ka.

コリンズ/Korinzu: それはいい考えですね。それから、ワインは白と赤を三本ずつ買ったらいいですね。

Sore wa ii kangae desu ne. Sorekara, wain wa shiro to aka o sanbon zutsu kattara ii desu ne.

林/Hayashi: ええ。じゃあ、そのじゃあ、この白ワインはどうですか。

Ee. Jaa, kono shiro wain wa doo desu ka.

コリンズ/Korinzu: でも、それは一本五千円ですよ。ちょっと高すぎると思います。もう少し安いのはありませんか。

Demo, sore wa ippon gosen en desu yo. Chotto takasugiru to omoimasu. Moo sukoshi yasui no wa arimasen ka.

林/Hayashi: じゃあ、これはどうですか。一本千二百円ですよ。同じ値段の赤ワインもありますよ。

Jaa, kore wa doo desu ka. Ippon sennihyaku en desu yo. Onaji nedan no aka wain mo arimasu yo.

Using すぎます sugimasu/
すぎる sugiru (*too, too much*)

Describing a sequence of events and actions

Indefinite pronoun の no

Expressing opinion with と思います
to omoimasu/と思う to omou

コリンズ/Korinzu: ええ。じゃあ、その白ワインとこの赤ワインを三本ずつ
カートに入れますね。

Ee. Jaa, sono shiro wain to kono aka wain o sanbon

zutsu kaato ni iremasu ne.

林/Hayashi: それから、レタスときゅうりとトマトとハムを買って、
サラダを作ったらどうですか。

Sorekara, retasu to kyuuri to tomato to hamu o katte,

sarada o tsukuttara doo desu ka.

コリンズ/Korinzu: ええ。じゃあ、卵も買って、ゆで卵を作って、サラダに入
れたらいいですね。

Ee. Jaa, tamago mo katte, yudetamago o tsukutte,

sarada ni iretara ii desu ne.

林/Hayashi: それから、すしとピザを買いますから、全部でいくらぐ
らいですか。

Sorekara, sushi to piza o kaimasu kara, zenbu de

ikuragurai desu ka.

コリンズ/Korinzu: 僕は九千円ぐらい持っていますけど。

Boku wa kyuusen en gurai motte imasu kedo.

林/Hayashi: 僕は一万二千円ぐらいです。もし足りなかったら、クレジッ
トカードを使いますから大丈夫ですよ。

Boku wa ichiman nisen en gurai desu. Moshi

tarinakattara, kurejitto kaado o tsukaimasu kara

daijoobu desu yo.

コリンズ/Korinzu: そうですね。

Soo desu ne.

Collins: *About how many people are coming to today's party?*
Hayashi: *Well, I think about ten people, but…*
Collins: *Then, it will be good if we buy three dozen bottles of beer and
six bottles of wine, right?*

Hayashi:	Yes. As for beer, what about buying two dozen bottles of Japanese beer and one dozen bottles of American beer?
Collins:	That's a good idea. And then, as for wine, it will be good if we buy three bottles of white wine and three bottles of red wine, right?
Hayashi:	Yes. Then, what about this white wine?
Collins:	But, that's five thousand yen for a bottle. That's a little too expensive. Isn't there a slightly cheaper one?
Hayashi:	Then, what about this? It's one thousand two hundred yen for one. There is also red wine at the same price.
Collins:	Okay. Then, I will put that white wine and this red wine, three bottles each, into the cart.
Hayashi:	And then, what about buying lettuce, cucumber, tomato, and ham and making a salad?
Collins:	Okay. Then, it will be good if we also buy eggs, make boiled eggs, and put them in the salad.
Hayashi:	And, since we will buy sushi and pizza, how much will it be all together?
Collins:	I have about 9,000 yen.
Hayashi:	As for me, about 12,000 yen. If it's not enough, I will use a credit card, so it's okay.
Hayashi:	That's right.

✎ Conversation Practice 2

Fill in the blanks in the following sentences with the missing words. If you're unsure of the answer, listen to the conversation one more time.

1. 今日のパーティーには、 ＿＿ 人ぐらい来ます。

   Kyoo no paatii ni wa ＿＿＿＿＿＿ nin gurai kimasu.

Using すぎます sugimasu/
すぎる sugiru (*too, too much*)

Describing a sequence of events and actions

Indefinite pronoun の no

Expressing opinion with と思います
to omoimasu/と思う to omou

2. 林さんとコリンズさんは日本のビールを ＿＿＿＿＿＿＿ダースとアメリカのビールを ＿＿＿＿＿＿ダース買いました。

Hayashi san to Korinzu san wa nihon no biiru o _____ daasu to amerika no biiru o _____ daasu kaimashita.

3. 林さんとコリンズさんは白ワインと赤ワインを ＿＿＿＿＿＿ ずつ買いました。

Hayashi san to Korinzu san wa shiro wain to aka wain o _____ zutsu kaimashita.

4. 林さんとコリンズさんは一本 ＿＿＿＿＿＿ 円のワインを買いました。

Hayashi san to Korinzu san wa ippon _____ en no wain o kaimashita.

5. 林さんとコリンズさんはレタスときゅうりとトマトとハムと卵で ＿＿＿＿＿＿ を作ります。

Hayashi san to Korinzu san wa retasu to kyuuri to tomato to hamu to tamago de _____ o tsukurimasu.

ANSWER KEY
1. 十 juu; 2. 2 ni, 1 ichi; 3. 三本 sanbon; 4. 千二百 sennihyaku; 5. サラダ sarada

Grammar Builder 2
EXPRESSING OPINION WITH と思います TO OMOIMASU/と思う TO OMOU

▶ 4D Grammar Builder 2 (CD 7, Track 18)

If you want to express your opinion by saying *I think that* you will use the following formula:

> *Plain form of verbs/adjectives/copula +* と思います to omoimasu/と思う to
> omou

Note that the plain form appears before と思います to omoimasu/と思う to
omou.

このすしはどうですか。
Kono sushi wa doo desu ka.
How's this sushi?

とてもおいしいと思います。
Totemo oishii to omoimasu.
I think it's very delicious.

佐藤さんは大学生ですか。
Satoo san wa daigakusee desu ka.
Is Mr./Ms. Sato a college student?

いいえ、大学生じゃないと思います。去年大学を卒業したと思います。
**Iie, daigakusee ja nai to omoimasu. Kyonen daigaku o sotsugyooshita to
omoimasu.**
No, I think he/she is not a college student. I think he/she graduated last year.

今日林さんが会社に来ると思いますか。
Kyoo Hayashi san ga kaisha ni kuru to omoimasu ka.
Do you think Mr./Ms. Hayashi will come to the office (lit., company) today?

ええ、来ると思います。
Ee, kuru to omoimasu.
Yes, I think he/she will come.

Using すぎます sugimasu/
すぎる sugiru (*too, too much*)

Describing a sequence of events and actions

Indefinite pronoun の no

Expressing opinion with と思います
to omoimasu/と思う to omou

高橋さんは今日忙しいと思いますか。

Takahashi san wa kyoo isogashii to omoimasu ka.

Do you think Mr./Ms. Takahashi is busy today?

いいえ、忙しくないと思いますけど。

Iie, isogashiku nai to omoimasu kedo.

No, I think he/she is not busy, but…

山田さんは昨日ミーティングに出ましたか。

Yamada san wa kinoo miitingu ni demashita ka.

Did Mr./Ms. Yamada attend the meeting yesterday?

ええ、出たと思いますけど。

Ee, deta to omimasu kedo.

Yes, I think he/she attended, but…

In negative sentences, you can negate either the verb 思う **omou** or the other verb, as in English, but the latter is more common in Japanese.

ロペスさんはアメリカ人じゃないと思います。

Ropesu san wa amerikajin ja nai to omoimasu.

I think Mr./Ms. Lopez is not an American.

ロペスさんはアメリカ人だと思いません。

Ropesu san wa amerikajin da to omoimasen.

I don't think Mr./Ms. Lopez is an American.

このセーターは安くないと思います。

Kono seetaa wa yasukunai to omoimasu.

I think this sweater is not cheap.

このセーターは安いと思いません。

Kono seetaa wa yasui to omoimasen.

I don't think this sweater is cheap.

チェンさんは車を買わなかったと思います。

Chen san wa kuruma o kawanakatta to omoimasu.

I think Mr./Ms. Chen didn't buy a car.

チェンさんは車を買ったと思いません。

Chen san wa kuruma o katta to omoimasen.

I don't think Mr./Ms. Chen bought a car.

✎ Work Out 2

Translate the following Japanese sentences into English.

1. リーさんは中国人だと思いますか。

   Rii san wa chuugokujin da to omoimasu ka.

   _____

2. このワインはあまり高くないと思います。

   Kono wain wa amari takakunai to omoimasu.

   _____

3. 川村さんは今日学校へ行かなかったと思います。

   Kawamura san wa kyoo gakkoo e ikanakatta to omoimasu.

   _____

Using すぎます sugimasu/
すぎる sugiru (*too, too much*)

Describing a sequence of events and actions

Indefinite pronoun の no

Expressing opinion with と思います
to omoimasu/と思う to omou

4. 私のアパートはちょっと不便だと思います。

Watashi no apaato wa chotto fuben da to omoimasu.

5. その映画は面白いと思いません。

Sono eega wa omoshiroi to omoimasen.

6. この本は長すぎると思います。

Kono hon wa nagasugiru to omoimasu.

7. このケーキは甘すぎると思いませんか。

Kono keeki wa amasugiru to omoimasen ka.

8. そのカレーは辛くないと思います。

Sono karee (*curry*) wa karaku nai to omoimasu.

ANSWER KEY

1. Do you think Mr./Ms. Lee is Chinese? 2. I think this wine is not so expensive. 3. I think Mr./Ms. Kawamura didn't go to school today. 4. I think my apartment is slightly inconvenient. 5. I don't think that movie is interesting. 6. I think this book is too long. 7. Don't you think this cake is too sweet? 8. I think that curry is not spicy.

✎ Drive It Home

Fill in the blanks with appropriate words.

1. スーパーへ行っ＿＿＿＿＿、レタスときゅうりを買いました。

   Suupaa e it＿＿＿＿＿, retasu to kyuuri o kaimashita.

   I went to a supermarket and bought lettuce and cucumbers.

2. 日本へ行っ＿＿＿＿＿、一年間日本語を勉強しました。

   Nihon e it＿＿＿＿＿, ichinenkan nihongo o benkyooshimashita.

   I went to Japan and studied Japanese for a year.

3. 六時半に起き＿＿＿＿＿、朝ご飯を食べ＿＿＿＿＿、新聞を読んで、八時に家を出
   ＿＿＿＿＿、会社に行きます。

   Rokuji han ni oki＿＿＿＿＿, asagohan o tabe ＿＿＿＿＿, shinbun o yon de, hachiji

   ni uchi o de ＿＿＿＿＿, kaisha ni ikimasu.

   I wake up at six thirty, eat breakfast, read a newspaper, leave home at eight, and go

   to work (lit., the company).

4. 十二時まで仕事をし＿＿＿＿、昼ご飯を食べ＿＿＿＿＿、一時にミーティングに出
   ます。

   Juuniji made shigoto o shi ＿＿＿＿＿, hirugohan o tabe ＿＿＿＿＿, ichiji ni

   miitingu ni demasu.

   I work until twelve, eat lunch and attend the meeting at one.

5. とてもおいしいと ＿＿＿＿＿＿＿＿＿＿。

   Totemo oishii to ＿＿＿＿＿＿＿＿＿＿＿＿＿＿.

   I think it's very delicious.

6. 去年大学を卒業したと ＿＿＿＿＿＿＿。

Kyonen daigaku o sotsugyooshita to ＿＿＿＿＿＿＿＿＿.

I think he/she graduated last year.

7. 高橋さんは今日忙しいと ＿＿＿＿＿＿か。

Takahashi san wa kyoo isogashii to ＿＿＿＿＿＿＿ **ka.**

Do you think Mr./Ms. Takahashi is busy today?

8. ロペスさんはアメリカ人じゃないと ＿＿＿＿＿＿。

Ropesu san wa amerikajin ja nai to ＿＿＿＿＿＿＿.

I think Mr./Ms. Lopez is not an American.

9. ロペスさんはアメリカ人だと ＿＿＿＿＿＿＿。

Ropesu san wa amerikajin da to ＿＿＿＿＿＿＿.

I don't think Mr./Ms. Lopez is an American.

ANSWER KEY

1–4. all て te; 5–8. all 思います omoimasu; 9. 思いません omoimasen

How Did You Do?

Let's see how you did! By now, you should be able to:

☐ describe a sequence of events and actions (Still unsure? Jump back to page 75)

☐ state opinions with *I think that* (Still unsure? Jump back to page 81)

✏ Word Recall

1. きれい kiree   a. *quiet*

2. 便利 benri   b. *have a lot of free time*
   べんり

3. 親切 shinsetsu   c. *kind, generous*
   しんせつ

4. 賑やか nigiyaka   d. *beautiful, pretty, clean*
   にぎ

5. 暇 hima   e. *easy, simple*
   ひま

6. 有名 yuumee   f. *inconvenient*
   ゆうめい

7. 不便 fuben   g. *lively*
   ふべん

8. 簡単 kantan   h. *convenient*
   かんたん

9. 静か shizuka   i. *famous*
   しず

10. 大切 taisetsu   j. *important*
    たいせつ

ANSWER KEY

1. d; 2. h; 3. c; 4. g; 5. b; 6. i; 7. f; 8. e; 9. a; 10. j

Don't forget to practice and reinforce what you've learned by visiting **www.livinglanguage.com/languagelab** for flashcards, games, and quizzes for Unit 1!

Unit 1 Essentials

Vocabulary Essentials

Test your knowledge of the key material in this unit by filling in the blanks in the following charts. Once you've completed these pages, you'll have tested your retention, and you'll have your own reference for the most essential vocabulary.

SHOPPING

	store clerk
	popularity
	payment
	cash
	credit card
	change
	return, change (polite)
	price
	prices (of commodities)
	all
	1,000 yen
	10,000 yen
	Welcome (to our store).
	How much is it?
	Please give me this.

CLOTHES

	sweater
	shirt
	blouse
	pants
	jeans
	skirt
	necktie
	wool
	cotton
	stripes
	solid (color)
	design
	size

COLORS

	red
	blue
	green
	yellow
	brown
	grey
	pink

Advanced Japanese

GROCERY

	juice, soft drink
	lettuce
	cabbage
	cucumber
	tomato
	potato
	onion
	ham
	egg
	boiled egg
	bread
	cheese
	butter
	pizza
	seasoning
	pepper
	salt
	sugar
	dozen
	shopping cart

VERBS

	to think
	to look for

	to keep
	to be, to exist (polite)
	to make
	be insufficient, be short

ADJECTIVES

	sober, quiet (color)
	showy, loud
	bright
	dark
	light
	heavy
	hot
	cold
	warm
	cool
	same

CONJUNCTION

	if, in case

NUMBERS

	100
	200

	300
	400
	500
	600
	700
	800
	900
	1,000
	2,000
	3,000
	4,000
	5,000
	6,000
	7,000
	8,000
	9,000
	10,000
	20,000
	30,000
	40,000
	50,000
	60,000
	70,000
	80,000
	90,000

	100,000
	200,000
	300,000
	400,000
	500,000
	600,000
	700,000
	800,000
	900,000
	1,000,000

Grammar Essentials

Here is a reference of the key grammar that was covered in Unit 1. Make sure you understand the summary and can use all of the grammar it covers.

ADJECTIVES: NON-PAST AFFIRMATIVE AND NEGATIVE FORMS

PLAIN NON-PAST TENSE		POLITE NON-PAST TENSE	
Affirmative	Negative	Affirmative	Negative
たか 高い takai *(expensive or high)*	たか 高くない takaku nai	たか 高いです takai desu	たか 高く[ないです/ ありません] takaku [nai desu/ arimasen]
おお 大きい ookii *(big)*	おお 大きくない ookiku nai	おお 大きいです ookii desu	おお 大きく[ないです/ ありません] ookiku [nai desu/ arimasen]

PLAIN NON-PAST TENSE		POLITE NON-PAST TENSE	
Affirmative	Negative	Affirmative	Negative
<ruby>面白<rt>おもしろ</rt></ruby>い omoshiroi *(interesting)*	<ruby>面白<rt>おもしろ</rt></ruby>くない omoshiroku nai	<ruby>面白<rt>おもしろ</rt></ruby>いです omoshiroi desu	<ruby>面白<rt>おもしろ</rt></ruby>く[ないです/ ありません] omoshiroku [nai desu/arimasen]
<ruby>明<rt>あか</rt></ruby>るい akarui *(bright)*	<ruby>明<rt>あか</rt></ruby>るくない akaruku nai	<ruby>明<rt>あか</rt></ruby>るいです akarui desu	<ruby>明<rt>あか</rt></ruby>るく[ないです/ ありません] akaruku [nai desu/arimasen]
<ruby>暖<rt>あたた</rt></ruby>かい atatakai *(warm)*	<ruby>暖<rt>あたた</rt></ruby>かくない atatakaku nai	<ruby>暖<rt>あたた</rt></ruby>かいです atatakai desu	<ruby>暖<rt>あたた</rt></ruby>かく[ないです/ ありません] atatakaku [nai desu/arimasen]
いい ii *(good)*	<ruby>良<rt>よ</rt></ruby>くない yoku nai	いいです ii desu	<ruby>良<rt>よ</rt></ruby>く[ないです/ ありません] yoku [nai desu/ arimasen]

PLAIN NON-PAST TENSE		POLITE NON-PAST TENSE	
Affirmative	Negative	Affirmative	Negative
きれいだ kiree da *(beautiful or clean)*	きれい[じゃ/では] ない kiree [ja/de wa] nai	きれいです kiree desu	きれい[じゃ/では] [ないです/ありま せん] kiree [ja/de wa] [nai desu/ arimasen]

PLAIN NON-PAST TENSE		POLITE NON-PAST TENSE	
Affirmative	Negative	Affirmative	Negative
静<ruby>しず</ruby>かだ shizuka da (quiet)	静<ruby>しず</ruby>か[じゃ/では] ない shizuka [ja/de wa] nai	静<ruby>しず</ruby>かです shizuka desu	静<ruby>しず</ruby>か[じゃ/では] [ないです/あります せん] shizuka [ja/de wa] [nai desu/ arimasen]
有名<ruby>ゆうめい</ruby>だ yuumee da (famous)	有名<ruby>ゆうめい</ruby>[じゃ/では] ない yuumee [ja/de wa] nai	有名<ruby>ゆうめい</ruby>です yuumee desu	有名<ruby>ゆうめい</ruby>[じゃ/では] [ないです/あります せん] yuumee [ja/de wa] [nai desu/ arimasen]
便利<ruby>べんり</ruby>だ benri da (convenient)	便利<ruby>べんり</ruby>[じゃ/では] ない benri [ja/de wa] nai	便利<ruby>べんり</ruby>です benri desu	便利<ruby>べんり</ruby>[じゃ/では] [ないです/あります せん] benri [ja/de wa] [nai desu/ arimasen]

"BECOME" い I-ADJECTIVE

く ku-form of い i-adjectives + なります narimasu/ なる naru

高<ruby>たか</ruby>くなります	takaku narimasu	become expensive

STATING REASONS

A し、B し、Y。	A shi, B shi, Y.	*A, B, and so Y.*

The plain form of verbs, い i-adjectives, and the copula appears before し shi.

すぎます SUGIMASU/すぎる SUGIRU (*TOO, TOO MUCH*)

Stem of い *i-adjective/* な *na-adjective/conjunctive form of the verb +*すぎます sugimasu/すぎる sugiru

INDEFINITE PRONOUN の NO

このセーターは短いで す。長いのはあります か。	Kono seetaa wa mijikai desu. Nagai no wa arimasu ka.	*This sweater is short. Do you have a long one?*

DESCRIBING A SEQUENCE OF EVENTS AND ACTIONS
The て te-form of verbs is used to describe a sequence of events and actions.

スーパーへ行って、レタ スときゅうりを買いまし た。	Suupaa e itte, retasu to kyuuri o kaimashita.	*I went to a supermarket and bought lettuce and cucumbers.*

STATING ONE'S OPINION WITH と思います TO OMOIMASU/と思う TO OMOU (*I THINK THAT*)

Plain form of verbs/adjectives/copula + と思います to omoimasu/と思う to omou

Unit 1 Quiz

Let's put the most essential Japanese words and grammar points you've learned so far to practice in a few exercises. It's important to be sure that you've mastered this material before you move on. Score yourself at the end of the review and see if you need to go back for more practice, or if you're ready to move on to Unit 2.

A. Fill in the blanks with adjectives in their appropriate form.

1. *A:* 弟さんの部屋は ＿＿＿＿＿＿＿＿＿＿ か。

   Otooto san no heya wa ＿＿＿＿＿＿＿＿＿＿ ka.

   Is your brother's room clean?

   B: いいえ、あまり ＿＿＿＿＿＿ 。

   Iie, amari ＿＿＿＿＿＿.

   No, it isn't very clean.

2. *A:* この映画は ＿＿＿＿＿＿＿＿ か。

   Kono eega wa ＿＿＿＿＿＿＿＿ ka.

   Is this movie good?

   B: いいえ、あまり ＿＿＿＿ 。

   Iie, amari ＿＿＿＿＿＿.

   No, it isn't very good.

3. *A:* そのピザは ＿＿＿＿＿＿＿＿＿＿ か。

   Sono piza wa ＿＿＿＿＿＿＿＿＿＿ ka.

   Is that pizza delicious?

B: いいえ、あまり _____ 。

Iie, amari _____.

No, it isn't very delicious.

4. *A:* そのデパートは _____ か。

Sono depaato wa _____ **ka.**

Is that department store famous?

B: いいえ、あまり _____ 。

Iie, amari _____.

No, it isn't very famous.

B. Fill in the blanks with adjectives and the verb *become*.

1. 七月^{しちがつ}になると、 _____ 。

Shichigatsu ni naru to, _____.

When it becomes July, it becomes hot.

2. 私^{わたし}のコンピューターは _____ 。

Watashi no konpyuutaa wa _____

_____.

My computer became old.

C. Fill in the blanks with the appropriate words + し shi.

1. 今日^{きょう}は _____ 、 _____ 、風^{かぜ}が _____ 、出掛^{で か}けたくないです。

Kyoo wa _____ , _____ , **kaze ga**

_____ , **dekaketaku nai desu.**

Today it's raining, cold, and furthermore, the wind is strong, and so I don't want to go out.

2. 私のアパートは _____ 、駅から _____ 、あまり良くありません。

Watashi no apaato wa _____, eki kara _____

_____, amari yoku arimasen.

My apartment is old, and furthermore, far from the station, and so not so good.

D. Write the following numbers in Japanese.

1. 773,823 _____

2. 859,754 _____

3. 999,999 _____

E. Complete the sentences using the appropriate words + the expression すぎます sugimasu. Pay attention to the tense.

1. この色は _____ 。

Kono iro wa _____.

This color is too bright.

2. 映画は _____ 。

Eega wa _____.

The movie was too short.

F. Fill in the blanks using the appropriate words + the indefinite pronoun の no.

1. 私のセーターは赤いですが、_____ は青いです。

Watashi no seetaa wa akai desu ga, _____

wa aoi desu.

My sweater is red but Mr./Mrs. Tanaka's is blue.

2. この高い（たか）セーターはきれいですが、あの ＿＿＿＿＿＿＿＿はあまりきれいじゃありません。

Kono takai seetaa wa kiree desu ga, ano ＿＿＿＿＿＿＿＿＿＿＿＿＿＿＿＿＿＿ wa amari kiree ja arimasen.

This expensive sweater is pretty but that cheap one is not very pretty.

G. Fill in the blanks with the appropriate verbs in their て te-form.

1. 六時（ろくじ）に ＿＿＿＿＿＿＿＿、コーヒーを ＿＿＿＿＿＿＿＿、新聞（しんぶん）を読（よ）みます。

Rokuji ni ＿＿＿＿＿＿＿＿＿＿＿＿＿, koohii o ＿＿＿＿＿＿＿＿＿＿＿＿＿, shinbun o yomimasu.

I wake up at six, drink coffee, and read a newspaper.

2. 晩（ばん）ご飯（はん）を ＿＿＿＿＿＿＿＿、テレビを ＿＿＿＿＿＿、十一時（じゅういちじ）に寝（ね）ます。

Bangohan o ＿＿＿＿＿＿＿＿＿＿＿＿＿, terebi o ＿＿＿＿＿＿＿＿＿＿＿, juuichiji ni nemasu.

I eat dinner, watch TV, and go to sleep at eleven.

H. Fill in the blanks with the appropriate words + と思（おも）います to omoimasu or と思（おも）いません to omoimasen.

1. リーさんは ＿＿＿＿＿＿＿＿＿＿＿＿＿＿＿＿＿＿＿＿ 。

Rii san wa ＿＿＿＿＿＿＿＿＿＿＿＿＿＿＿＿＿＿＿＿＿

＿＿＿＿＿＿＿＿＿＿＿＿＿＿＿.

I think Mr./Ms. Lee is an American.

2. このセーターは ＿＿＿＿＿＿＿＿＿＿＿＿＿＿＿＿ 。

Kono seetaa wa ＿＿＿＿＿＿＿＿＿＿＿＿＿＿＿＿＿＿＿

＿＿＿＿＿＿＿＿＿＿＿＿＿＿＿.

I think this sweater is not cheap.

3. このセーターは _____ 。

Kono seetaa wa _____.

I don't think this sweater is cheap.

How Did You Do?

Give yourself a point for every correct answer, then use the following key to tell whether you're ready to move on:

0-7 points: It's probably a good idea to go back through the lesson again. You may be moving too quickly, or there may be too much "down time" between your contact with Japanese. Remember that it's better to spend 30 minutes with Japanese three or four times a week than it is to spend two or three hours just once a week. Find a pace that's comfortable for you, and spread your contact hours out as much as you can.

8-12 points: You would benefit from a review before moving on. Go back and spend a little more time on the specific points that gave you trouble. Re-read the Grammar Builder sections that were difficult, and do the work out one more time. Don't forget about the online supplemental practice material, either. Go to **www.livinglanguage.com/languagelab** for games and quizzes that will reinforce the material from this unit.

13-17 points: Good job! There are just a few points that you could consider reviewing before moving on. If you haven't worked with the games and quizzes on **www.livinglanguage.com/languagelab**, please give them a try.

18-20 points: Great! You're ready to move on to the next unit.

points

Giving and receiving verbs

Adjectives: Past tense, affirmative
and negative form

Expressing the completion
of an action and attempts

Before and *after*: 前に mae
ni and 後で ato de

Unit 2:
At a Restaurant

In Unit 2, you'll learn some expressions you can use when dining out at a restaurant. You will also learn how to describe food. Honorific and humble polite forms of verbs will be also introduced. By the end of the unit, you'll be able to:

☐ use key vocabulary related to food and dining

☐ use giving and receiving verbs

☐ express a completion of an action and an attempt

☐ use adjectives in their past tense forms

☐ express *before …* and *after …*

☐ use honorific and humble polite forms of verbs

☐ express *wanted to …*

☐ express *Let's …* , *Why don't we …?*, *Shall we …?*

☐ express *only*

Polite expressions: Honorific and
humble polite forms of verbs

Inviting people: *Let's . . . .*
Why don't we . . . ?, Shall we . . . ?

Expressing desires:
たい tai (past tense)

Only X: X だけ dake and
X しか shika + negative

Lesson 5: Words

In this lesson you'll learn how to:

☐ use key vocabulary related to food and dining

☐ use giving and receiving verbs

☐ express a completion of an action and an attempt

Word Builder 1

▶ 5A Word Builder 1 (CD 7, Track 19)

二名様	nimeesama	*two people (polite)*
天ぷら	tenpura	*tempura (fried shrimp, vegetables, etc.)*
うなぎ	unagi	*eel*
うな重	unajuu	*broiled eel on rice*
コロッケ	korokke	*croquette*
かつ	katsu	*cutlet*
カレー	karee	*curry*
味噌	miso	*soy bean paste*
(お)味噌汁	(o)misoshiru (*polite with o*)	*miso soup*
ご飯	gohan	*cooked rice, meal*

おかず	okazu	dish eaten with cooked rice
食べ物	tabemono	food
ドレッシング	doresshingu	dressing
量	ryoo	amount
半分	hanbun	half
煙草	tabako	tobacco, cigarette
塩辛い	shiokarai	salty
一度	ichido	once
注文します/注文する	chuumonshimasu/ chuumonsuru	to order
あげます/あげる	agemasu/ageru	to give
もらいます/もらう	moraimasu/morau	to receive
いただきます/いただく	itadakimasu/itadaku (humble polite)	to eat, to drink, to receive

Take It Further

二名様 Nimeesama is a polite form of 二名 nimee and is used to talk about customers in restaurants, clubs, or bars. 二名 Nimee means *two people*, and 様 sama, the polite form of さん san (*Mr./Ms.*), is added to it. At a restaurant, waitresses and waiters usually use 一名様 ichimeesama (*one person*), 二名様 nimeesama (*two people*), 三名様 sanmeesama (*three people*), 四名様 yonmeesama (*four people*), 五名様 gomeesama (*five people*), and so on.

✎Word Practice 1

Translate the following words into Japanese.

1. *miso soup* _____

2. *cooked rice, meal* _____

3. *dish eaten with cooked rice* _____

4. *food* _____

5. *amount* _____

6. *half* _____

7. *tobacco, cigarette* _____

8. *salty* _____

9. *once* _____

10. *to order* _____

ANSWER KEY

1. (お)味噌汁 (o)misoshiru; 2. ご飯 gohan; 3. おかず okazu; 4. 食べ物 tabemono; 5. 量 ryoo; 6. 半分 hanbun; 7. 煙草 tabako; 8. 塩辛い shiokarai; 9. 一度 ichido; 10. 注文します (or 注文する) chuumonshimasu (or chuumonsuru)

Grammar Builder 1

GIVING AND RECEIVING VERBS

▶ 5B Grammar Builder 1 (CD 7, Track 20)

あげます Agemasu (*to give*), もらいます moraimasu (*to receive*), and くれます kuremasu (*to give*) are called the "giving and receiving verbs." They are special in that they can either be used as main verbs or can be attached to the て te-form

Giving and receiving verbs

Adjectives: Past tense, affirmative
and negative form

Expressing the completion
of an action and attempts

Before and *after*: 前に mae
ni and 後で ato de

of other verbs. In this lesson, we'll look at how the giving and receiving verbs function as main verbs.

First, let's look at あげます agemasu.

A [が/は] B に X を [あげます/あげる] 。
A [ga/wa] B ni X o [agemasu/ageru].
A gives B X./A gives X to B.

私は母にスカーフをあげました。

Watashi wa haha ni sukaafu o agemashita.

I gave my mother a scarf.

リーさんは渡辺さんにチョコレートをあげました。

Rii san wa Watanabe san ni chokoreeto o agemashita.

Mr./Ms. Lee gave Mr./Ms. Watanabe chocolates.

森田さんにこの本をあげたいんですが。

Morita san ni kono hon o agetai n desu ga.

I want to give Mr./Ms. Morita this book, but…

If the receiver is an animal or a plant, you can use やります **yarimasu** instead of あげます **agemasu.**

私は犬にクッキーを [あげます/やります]。

Watashi wa inu ni kukkii o [agemasu/yarimasu].

I give cookies to a dog/dogs.

花に水を [あげます/やります]。

Hana ni mizu o [agemasu/yarimasu].

I give water to plants.

Polite expressions: Honorific and
humble polite forms of verbs

Inviting people: *Let's …,
Why don't we … ?, Shall we … ?*

Expressing desires:
たい tai (past tense)

Only X: X だけ dake and
X しか shika + negative

やります **Yarimasu** is less polite than あげます **agemasu**. Even though やります **yarimasu** may be used in informal situations when the receiver is a person, it is always better to use it only when the receiver is an animal or a plant. さしあげます **Sashiagemasu** is a humble polite form of あげます **agemasu**, and it is used when the receiver is someone you need or want to pay respect to.

A [が/は] B に X を [さしあげます/さしあげる] 。
A [ga/wa] B ni X o [sashiagemasu/sashiageru].
A gives B X./A gives X to B.

わたし せんせい
私は先生にボールペンをさしあげました。
Watashi wa sensee ni boorupen o sashiagemashita.
I gave a teacher a ballpoint pen.

はは やま だ せんせい
母は山田先生にワインをさしあげました。
Haha wa Yamada sensee ni wain o sashiagemashita.
My mother gave Professor Yamada a bottle of wine.

ぶ ちょう
部長にネクタイをさしあげたらどうですか。
Buchoo (*division manager*) ni nekutai o sashiagetara doo desu ka.
What about if you give a necktie to the division manager?

Note that when さしあげます **sashiagemasu** is used, the giver is always a speaker or a member of the speaker's in-group, such as a family member. Also, it is important to remember that the humble polite form, さしあげます **sashiagemasu**, cannot be used if the receiver is a family member. So, even if you want to pay respect to your parents, you cannot use さしあげます **sashiagemasu** in the following sentence, あげます **agemasu** is used instead.

Giving and receiving verbs

Adjectives: Past tense, affirmative
and negative form

Expressing the completion
of an action and attempts

Before and *after*: 前に mae
ni and 後で ato de

私は父と母にセーターをあげました。

Watashi wa chichi to haha ni seetaa o agemashita.

I gave a sweater to my father and mother.

Next, let's look もらいます **moraimasu** (*to receive*).

B [が/は] A [に/から] X を [もらいます/もらう] 。
B [ga/wa] A [ni/kara] X o [moraimasu/morau].
B receives X from A.

私は兄に古いコンピューターをもらいました。

Watashi wa ani ni furui konpyuutaa o moraimashita.

I received an old computer from my older brother.

加藤さんは山本さんからきれいな花をもらいました。

Katoo san wa Yamamoto san kara kiree na hana o moraimashita.

Mr./Ms. Kato received beautiful flowers from Mr./Ms. Yamamoto.

私は友達に赤い鞄をもらいました。

Watashi wa tomodachi ni akai kaban o moraimashita.

I received a red bag from my friend.

If the giver is someone you need or want to pay respect to, いただきます
itadakimasu, the humble polite form of もらいます **moraimasu**, is used.

B [が/は] A [に/から] X を [いただきます/いただく] 。
B [ga/wa] A [ni/kara] X o [itadakimasu/itadaku].
B receives X from A.

Polite expressions: Honorific and
humble polite forms of verbs

Inviting people: *Let's . . . ,*
Why don't we . . . ?, Shall we . . . ?

Expressing desires:
たい tai (past tense)

Only X: X だけ dake and
X しか shika + negative

私は先生にこの本をいただきました。

Watashi wa sensee ni kono hon o itadakimashita.

I received this book from my teacher.

妹は英語の先生から辞書をいただきました。

Imooto wa eego no sensee kara jisho o itadakimashita.

My younger sister received a dictionary from her English teacher.

私は部長からビール券をいただきました。

Watashi wa buchoo kara biiru ken o itadakimashita.

I received beer gift coupons from the division manager.

It is important to remember that when いただきます itadakimasu is used,
the receiver has to be a speaker or a speaker's in-group member, such as a
family member. Also, you cannot use the humble polite form いただきます
itadakimasu if the giver is your in-group member. So, again, even if you want
to pay respect to your parents, you cannot use いただきます itadakimasu in the
following sentence.

私は父と母に新しいカメラをもらいました。

Watashi wa chichi to haha ni atarashii kamera o moraimashita.

I received a new camera from my father and mother.

Finally, let's discuss くれます kuremasu (*to give*). Both あげます agemasu and
くれます kuremasu are translated as *to give*, but in case of くれます kuremasu,
the receiver is always a speaker or a member of the speaker's in-group.

Giving and receiving verbs

Adjectives: Past tense, affirmative
and negative form

Expressing the completion
of an action and attempts

Before and *after*: 前に mae
ni and 後で ato de

A [が/は] B に X を [くれます/くれる]。
A [ga/wa] B ni X o [kuremasu/kureru].
A gives B X./A gives X to B. (B is a speaker or a speaker's in-group member, e.g., family.)

矢野さんが私にこの本をくれました。

Yano san ga watashi ni kono hon o kuremashita.

Mr./Ms. Yano gave me this book.

林さんは妹にきれいなノートをくれました。

Hayashi san wa imooto ni kiree na nooto o kuremashita.

Mr./Ms. Hayashi gave my younger sister a pretty notebook.

森さんは私と弟にペンを一本ずつくれました。

Mori san wa watashi to otooto ni pen o ippon zutsu kuremashita.

Mr./Ms. Mori gave me and my younger brother one pen for each.

If the subject of a sentence is someone you need or want to pay respect to, くださいます kudasaimasu, the honorific form of くれます kuremasu, is used.

A [が/は] B に X を [くださいます/くださる]。
A [ga/wa] B ni X o [kudasaimasu/kudasaru].
A gives B X./A gives X to B. *(B is a speaker or a speaker's in-group member, e.g., family.)*

スミス先生が私とクラスメートに辞書をくださいました。

Smisu sensee ga watashi to kurasumeeto ni jisho o kudasaimashita.

Professor Smith gave me and my classmates a dictionary.

Polite expressions: Honorific and
humble polite forms of verbs

Inviting people: *Let's . . . ,*
Why don't we . . . ?, Shall we . . . ?

Expressing desires:
たい tai (past tense)

Only X: X だけ dake and
X しか shika + negative

<ruby>課<rt>か</rt></ruby><ruby>長<rt>ちょう</rt></ruby>が<ruby>私<rt>わたし</rt></ruby>にフランスの<ruby>赤<rt>あか</rt></ruby>ワインをくださいました。

Kachoo (*section manager*) **ga watashi ni furansu no aka wain o kudasaimashita.**

The section manager gave me a French red wine.

<ruby>山<rt>やま</rt></ruby><ruby>田<rt>だ</rt></ruby><ruby>先<rt>せん</rt></ruby><ruby>生<rt>せい</rt></ruby>が<ruby>兄<rt>あに</rt></ruby>にその<ruby>辞<rt>じ</rt></ruby><ruby>書<rt>しょ</rt></ruby>をくださいました。

Yamada sensee ga ani ni sono jisho o kudasaimashita.

Professor Yamada gave that dictionary to my older brother.

Take It Further

The choice of が ga and は wa after the subject roughly corresponds to a difference in intonation in the English.

<ruby>山<rt>やま</rt></ruby><ruby>田<rt>だ</rt></ruby><ruby>先<rt>せん</rt></ruby><ruby>生<rt>せい</rt></ruby>が<ruby>兄<rt>あに</rt></ruby>にその<ruby>辞<rt>じ</rt></ruby><ruby>書<rt>しょ</rt></ruby>をくださいました。

<u>**Yamada sensee ga**</u> **ani ni sono jisho o kudasaimashita.**

Professor Yamada gave that dictionary to my older brother. (accent on *Professor Yamada*)

<ruby>山<rt>やま</rt></ruby><ruby>田<rt>だ</rt></ruby><ruby>先<rt>せん</rt></ruby><ruby>生<rt>せい</rt></ruby>は<ruby>兄<rt>あに</rt></ruby>にその<ruby>辞<rt>じ</rt></ruby><ruby>書<rt>しょ</rt></ruby>をくださいました。

Yamada sensee wa <u>**ani ni sono jisho o**</u> **kudasaimashita.**

Professor Yamada gave that dictionary to my older brother. (accent on either *that dictionary* or *to my older brother.*)

The first sentence can be an answer to the question, <ruby>誰<rt>だれ</rt></ruby>がお<ruby>兄<rt>にい</rt></ruby>さんにこの<ruby>辞<rt>じ</rt></ruby><ruby>書<rt>しょ</rt></ruby>をあげましたか。**Dare ga oniisan ni kono jisho o agemashita ka.** *Who gave this dictionary to your older brother?* In other words, <ruby>山<rt>やま</rt></ruby><ruby>田<rt>だ</rt></ruby><ruby>先<rt>せん</rt></ruby><ruby>生<rt>せい</rt></ruby> **Yamada sensee** in the first sentence is treated as "new information" because the particle が ga is attached to it. On the other hand, <ruby>山<rt>やま</rt></ruby><ruby>田<rt>だ</rt></ruby><ruby>先<rt>せん</rt></ruby><ruby>生<rt>せい</rt></ruby> **Yamada sensee** in the second sentence is marked with the topic particle は wa. So *Professor Yamada* is a given piece of information shared by the participants in the conversation. The second sentence can be an answer to the question, <ruby>山<rt>やま</rt></ruby><ruby>田<rt>だ</rt></ruby><ruby>先<rt>せん</rt></ruby><ruby>生<rt>せい</rt></ruby>は<ruby>誰<rt>だれ</rt></ruby>にこの<ruby>辞<rt>じ</rt></ruby><ruby>書<rt>しょ</rt></ruby>をあげま

したか。**Yamada sensee wa dare ni kono jisho o agemashita ka.** *To whom did Professor Yamada give this dictionary?* or 山田先生はお兄さんに何をあげました たか。**Yamada sensee wa oniisan ni nani o agemashita ka.** *What did Professor Yamada give to your older brother?* The different effects of は **wa** and が **ga** here are sometimes summarized as "old information" vs. "new information". They apply to many Japanese sentences and are not restricted to sentences with giving and receiving verbs. Acquiring a full understanding of the differences between は **wa** and が **ga** is not an easy task, however, so don't worry too much about it for now.

✎ Work Out 1

Fill in the blanks with the appropriate giving and receiving verbs listed below. Change them into their appropriate forms as necessary.

あげます **agemasu**, さしあげます **sashiagemasu**, もらいます **moraimasu**, いただ きます **itadakimasu**, くれます **kuremasu**, くださいます **kudasaimasu**

1. 私は弟に古いコンピューターを _____ 。

   Watashi wa otooto ni furui konpyuutaa o _____.

   I gave my younger brother an old computer.

2. この辞書は小林先生に _____ んです。

   Kono jisho wa Kobayashi sensee ni _____ **n desu.**

   As for this dictionary, I received it from Professor Kobayashi.

3. 鈴木さんが妹にチョコレートを _____ 。

   Suzuki san ga imooto ni chokoreeto o _____.

   Mr./Ms. Suzuki gave my younger sister chocolates.

Expressing desires:
たい tai (past tense)

Only X: X だけ dake and
X しか shika + negative

4. 明日私とクラスメートは先生に花を _____ 。

Ashita watashi to kurasumeeto wa sensee ni hana o

_____.

I and my classmates will give our teacher flowers tomorrow.

5. 部長にこのワインを _____ 。

Buchoo ni kono wain o _____.

I received this wine from a division manager.

6. このボールペンは課長が _____ んです。

Kono boorupen wa kachoo ga _____ **n desu.**

As for this ballpoint pen, a section manager gave it to me.

ANSWER KEY

1. あげました agemashita; 2. いただいた itadaita; 3. くれました kuremashita; 4. さしあげます
sashiagemasu; 5. いただきました itadakimashita; 6. くださった kudasatta

Word Builder 2

▶ 5C Word Builder 2 (CD 7, Track 21)

焼き魚	yakizakana	*broiled fish*
煮魚	nizakana	*boiled fish*
刺身	sashimi	*sliced raw fish*
えび	ebi	*shrimp*
いか	ika	*cuttlefish, squid*
たこ	tako	*octpus*
帆立	hotate	*scallop*

Giving and receiving verbs

Adjectives: Past tense, affirmative
and negative form

Expressing the completion
of an action and attempts

Before and *after*: 前に mae
ni and 後で ato de

貝	kai	shellfish
ムール貝	muurugai	mussel
和風	wafuu	Japanese style
洋風	yoofuu	Western style
機会、チャンス	kikai, chansu	chance
デザート	dezaato	dessert
アイスクリーム	aisukuriimu	ice cream
シャーベット	shaabetto	sherbet
チョコレートケーキ	chokoreeto keeki	chocolate cake
カプチーノ	kapuchiino	cappuccino
カフェオレ	kafeore	café au lait
社長	shachoo	president of a company
部長	buchoo	division manager
課長	kachoo	section manager
冷たい	tsumetai	cold
召し上がります/ 召し上がる	meshiagarimasu/ meshiagaru (*honorific polite*)	to eat, to drink
お目にかかります/ お目にかかる	ome ni kakarimasu/ ome ni kakaru (*humble polite*)	to see, to meet

Take It Further

You just learned the adjective 冷たい tsumetai (*cold*). You also learned the adjective 寒い samui in Lesson 1, which also means *cold*. The adjective 寒い samui is used to describe the weather or the temperature of a room. On the other hand, 冷たい tsumetai is used for something cold to the touch; for example, food and drinks. The same kind of contrast apply to the adjectives that mean *hot*. 暑い atsui and 熱い atsui both mean *hot*, but 暑い atsui is used for the weather while 熱い atsui is used for something that is hot to the touch. Note that 暑い atsui and 熱い atsui have the identical pronunciation and the only difference is in the kanji.

✎ Word Practice 2

Translate the following words or phrases into Japanese.

1. *broiled fish* _____

2. *shrimp* _____

3. *shellfish* _____

4. *Japanese style* _____

5. *Western style* _____

6. *chance* _____

7. *president of a company* _____

8. *division manager* _____

9. *section manager* _____

10. *cold* _____

ANSWER KEY
1. 焼き魚 yakizakana; 2. えび ebi; 3. 貝 kai; 4. 和風 wafuu; 5. 洋風 yoofuu; 6. 機会 kikai or チャンス chansu; 7. 社長 shachoo; 8. 部長 buchoo; 9. 課長 kachoo; 10. 冷たい tsumetai

Grammar Builder 2

EXPRESSING THE COMPLETION OF AN ACTION AND ATTEMPTS

▶ 5D Grammar Builder 2 (CD 7, Track 22)

First, let's learn how to express a completion of an action. Take a look at the following structure.

て te-*form of verb* + しまいました shimaimashita/しまった shimatta

Note that the adverb, もう moo (*already*), is often used with this structure.

宿題をしてしまいましたから、音楽を聞きます。

Shukudai o shite shimaimashita kara, ongaku o kikimasu.

I finished homework, so I will listen to music.

もう昼ご飯を食べてしまいました。

Moo hirugohan o tabete shimaimashita.

I have already eaten lunch.

In negative sentences, a combination of the て te-form of verbs and いません imasen is used.

もうこの映画は見てしまいましたか。

Moo kono eega wa mite shimaimashita ka.

Have you already seen this movie?

Polite expressions: Honorific and
humble polite forms of verbs

Inviting people: *Let's . . . ,*
Why don't we . . . ?, Shall we . . . ?

Expressing desires:
たい tai (past tense)

Only X: X だけ dake and
X しか shika + negative

いいえ、まだ見ていません。

Iie, mada mite imasen.

No, I haven't seen it yet.

もうその小説は読んでしまいましたか。

Moo sono shoosetsu wa yonde shimaimashita ka.

Have you already read that novel?

いいえ、まだ読んでいません。

Iie, mada yonde imasen.

No, I haven't read it yet.

Note that the adverb まだ **mada** is often used in negative sentences. まだ **Mada** is translated as *not yet* in negative sentences and as *still* in affirmative sentences

まだ食べています。

Mada tabete imasu.

I'm still eating.

In some contexts, the combination of the て **te**-form of verbs and しまいました **shimaimashita** expresses the speaker's regret.

昨日はビールを１ダース飲んでしまいました。

Kinoo wa biiru o ichi daasu nonde shimaimashita.

I ended up drinking one dozen bottles of beer yesterday.

お昼まで寝てしまいました。

Ohiru made nete shimaimashita.

I regrettably slept until noon.

Giving and receiving verbs

Adjectives: Past tense, affirmative
and negative form

Expressing the completion
of an action and attempts

Before and *after*: 前に mae
ni and 後で ato de

チョコレートケーキを三つ食べてしまいました。

Chokoreeto keeki o mittsu tabete shimaimashita.

I ended up eating three slices of chocolate cake.

Next, let's learn how to express attempt. Use the following structure to express an attempt to do something.

て te-*form of verbs* + みます mimasu/みる miru

日本人の友達と日本語で話してみました。

Nihonjin no tomodachi to nihongo de hanashite mimashita.

I tried speaking with my Japanese friend(s) in Japanese (to see how it goes).

週末、新しいカメラを使ってみます。

Shuumatsu, atarashii kamera o tsukatte mimasu.

I will try using a new camera on weekends (to see how it is).

家ですしを作ってみましたが、あまりおいしくありませんでした。

Uchi de sushi o tsukutte mimashita ga, amari oishiku arimasen deshita.

I tried making sushi at home (to see how it goes), but it was not so good.

✎ Work Out 2

Translate the following Japanese sentences into English.

1. 昨日カレーを作ってみましたが、ちょっと辛すぎました。

   Kinoo karee o tsukutte mimashita ga, chotto karasugimashita.

   _____

Expressing desires:
たい tai (past tense)

Only X: X だけ dake and
X しか shika + negative

2. クレジットカードで十五万円のカメラを買ってしまいました。

Kurejitto kaado de juugoman en no kamera o katte shimaimashita.

_____

3. この本をもう読んでしまったので、妹にあげます。

Kono hon o moo yonde shimatta node, imooto ni agemasu.

_____

4. 来年スペインへ行ってみたいです。

Rainen supein e itte mitai desu.

_____

5. パーティーへ行って、お酒を飲みすぎてしまいました。

Paatii e itte, osake o nomisugite shimaimashita.

_____

ANSWER KEY

1. *I tried making curry yesterday, but it was a little too spicy. 2. I ended up buying a camera of 150,000 yen by credit card. 3. Since I have already read this book, I will give it to my younger sister. 4. I want to try going to Spain next year. 5. I went to a party and ended up drinking too much alcohol.*

✎ Drive It Home

A. Fill in the blanks by choosing appropriate verbs from the word bank.

あげます agemasu, さしあげます sashiagemasu, もらいます moraimasu,
いただきます itadakimasu, くれます kuremasu

1. 私は父にカードを _____ 。

Watashi wa chichi ni kaado o _____.

I give a card to my father.

Expressing the completion
of an action and attempts

Before and *after*: 前に mae
ni and 後で ato de

2. 私は山田先生にカードを _____ 。

Watashi wa Yamada sensee ni kaado o _____.

I give a card to Professor Yamada.

3. 私は父から本を _____ 。

Watashi wa chichi kara hon o _____.

I receive a book from my father.

4. 私は山田先生から本を _____ 。

Watashi wa Yamada sensee kara hon o _____.

I receive a book from Professor Yamada.

5. 田中さんは弟に本を _____ 。

Tanaka san wa otooto ni hon o _____.

Mr./Ms. Tanaka gives a book to my younger brother.

B. Fill in the blanks with しまいます **shimaimasu** in the past tense form.

1. 宿題をして _____。

Shukudai o shite _____.

I finished homework.

2. 昼ご飯を食べて _____。

Hirugohan o tabete _____.

I have already eaten lunch.

3. お昼まで寝て _____ 。

Ohiru made nete _____.

I regrettably slept until noon.

Polite expressions: Honorific and
humble polite forms of verbs

Inviting people: *Let's ... ,*
Why don't we ... ?, Shall we ... ?

Expressing desires:
たい tai (past tense)

Only X: X だけ dake and
X しか shika + negative

C. Fill in the blanks with みます mimasu in the past tense form.

1. 日本人の友達と日本語で話して _____ 。

   Nihonjin no tomodachi to nihongo de hanashite _____ .

   I tried speaking with my Japanese friend(s) in Japanese (to see how it goes).

2. 新しいカメラを使って _____ 。

   Atarashii kamera o tsukatte _____ .

   I tried using a new camera (to see how it is).

3. 家ですしを作って _____ 。

   Uchi de sushi o tsukutte _____ .

   I tried making sushi at home (to see how it goes).

ANSWER KEY

A: 1. あげます agemasu; 2. さしあげます sashiagemasu; 3. もらいます moraimasu; 4. いただきます itadakimasu; 5. くれます kuremasu

B: 1.-3. all しまいました shimaimashita

C: 1.-3. all みました mimashita

⊕ Culture Note

The service you receive in restaurants and cafes is generally very good, even though you don't have to leave any tip. When you are seated, you are immediately served water, or water and Japanese tea, together with a wet napkin for your hands. Customers usually pay for their food at the cashier.

How Did You Do?

Let's see how you did! By now, you should be able to:

☐ use key vocabulary related to food and dining (Still unsure? Jump back to page 105 or 115)

☐ use giving and receiving verbs (Still unsure? Jump back to page 107)

☐ express the completion of an action and attempts (Still unsure? Jump back to page 118)

✎ Word Recall

1. 優しい yasashii

2. 難しい muzukashii

3. 近い chikai

4. 遠い tooi

5. おいしい oishii

6. 面白い omoshiroi

7. 新しい atarashii

8. まずい mazui

9. つまらない tsumaranai

10. 低い hikui

a. *interesting*

b. *far*

c. *difficult*

d. *near*

e. *delicious*

f. *boring*

g. *new*

h. *low*

i. *kind, gentle*

j. *bad (taste)*

ANSWER KEY

1. i; 2. c; 3. d; 4. b; 5. e; 6. a; 7. g; 8. j; 9. f; 10. h

olite expressions: Honorific and   Inviting people: *Let's … ,*
humble polite forms of verbs   *Why don't we … ?, Shall we … ?*

Expressing desires: *Only X*: X だけ dake and
たい tai (past tense)   X しか shika + negative

Lesson 6: Phrases

In this lesson you'll learn how to:

☐ use adjectives in the past tense

☐ express *before …* and *after …*

Phrase Builder 1

▶ 6A Phrase Builder 1 (CD 8, Track 1)

きれいなレストラン	kiree na resutoran	*pretty restaurant*
どんな料理	donna ryoori	*what kind of meal*
混んでいます	konde imasu	*be crowded*
天ぷら定食かコロッケ定食	tenpura teishoku ka korokke teishoku	*prix fixe tempura meal or prix fixe croquette meal*
うな重かすし定食	unajuu ka sushi teeshoku	*unajuu or sushi prix fixe meal*
コーヒーでも	koohii demo	*coffee or something like that*
ご飯の上	gohan no ue	*on top of cooked rice*
ご飯の上にうなぎが載っています/載っている	gohan no ue ni unagi ga notte imasu/notte iru	*eel is put on cooked rice*
実は	jitsu wa	*actually*
後で	ato de	*later*

Giving and receiving verbs

Adjectives: Past tense, affirmative
and negative form

Expressing the completion
of an action and attempts

Before and *after*: 前に mae
ni and 後で ato de

レストランを出た後で	resutoran o deta ato de	*after leaving a restaurant*
コロッケ定食にします/する	korokke teeshoku ni shimasu/suru	*have a prix fixe croquette meal (lit., make it a prix fixe croquette meal)*
そうします/そうする	soo shimasu/soo suru	*do so*
もし良かったら	moshi yokattara	*if it's okay*
半分あげます/あげる	hanbun agemasu/ageru	*give half*
煙草を吸います/吸う	tabako o suimasu/suu	*smoke a cigarette*

Take It Further

When attached to a noun, でも demo means *something like that*. For instance, コーヒーでも koohii demo and 森さんでも Mori san demo mean *coffee or something like that* and *Mr./Ms. Mori or someone like him/her* respectively. でも demo is used to make speech less direct, and more polite, even if a speaker is actually thinking about a specific thing or person.

もし Moshi (*if*) can be used in conditional sentences, such as the たら tara- and と to-conditional. Adding もし moshi does not change the meaning of a sentence, but rather, emphasizes its meaning.

Polite expressions: Honorific and
humble polite forms of verbs

Inviting people: *Let's . . . ,
Why don't we . . . ?, Shall we . . . ?*

Expressing desires:
たい tai (past tense)

Only X: X だけ dake and
X しか shika + negative

✎ Phrase Practice 1

Fill in the missing words below.

1. _____ レストラン

   _____ resutoran

   pretty restaurant

2. _____ 料理
   （りょうり）

   _____ ryoori

   what kind of meal

3. _____ います

   _____ imasu

   be crowded

4. うな重 _____ すし定食
   （じゅう）（ていしょく）

   unajuu _____ sushi teeshoku

   unajuu or sushi prix fixe meal

5. コーヒー _____

   koohii _____

   coffee or something like that

6. _____ は

   _____ wa

   actually

Giving and receiving verbs

Adjectives: Past tense, affirmative
and negative form

Expressing the completion
of an action and attempts

Before and *after*: 前に mae
ni and 後で ato de

7. コロッケ定食 _____

   korokke teeshoku _____

   have a prix fixe croquette meal (lit., make it a prix fixe croquette meal)

8. もし _____

   moshi _____

   if it's okay

ANSWER KEY

1. きれいな **kiree na**; 2. どんな **donna**; 3. 混んで **konde**; 4. か **ka**; 5. でも **demo**; 6. 実 **jitsu**; 7. にします (or にする) **ni shimasu** (or **ni suru**); 8. 良かったら **yokattara**

Grammar Builder 1

ADJECTIVES: PAST TENSE, AFFIRMATIVE AND NEGATIVE FORM

▶ 6B Grammar Builder 1 (CD 8, Track 2)

In Lesson 1, you learned the non-past tense form of adjectives. Now, let's learn their past tense form. First, let's look at いい **i**-adjectives.

POLITE FORM, PAST TENSE		PLAIN FORM, PAST TENSE	
Affirmative	Negative	Affirmative	Negative
良かったです **yokatta desu** *(was/were good)*	良く[なかったです/ありませんでした] **yoku [nakatta desu/arimasen deshita]**	良かった **yokatta**	良くなかった **yoku nakatta**

POLITE FORM, PAST TENSE		PLAIN FORM, PAST TENSE	
Affirmative	Negative	Affirmative	Negative
甘かったです amakatta desu *(was/were sweet)*	甘く[なかったです/ありませんでした] amaku [nakatta desu/arimasen deshita]	甘かった amakatta	甘くなかった amaku nakatta
辛かったです karakatta desu *(was/were spicy)*	辛く[なかったです/ありませんでした] karaku [nakatta desu/arimasen deshita]	辛かった karakatta	辛くなかった karaku nakatta
広かったです hirokatta desu *(was/were spacious)*	広く[なかったです/ありませんでした] hiroku [nakatta desu/arimasen deshita]	広かった hirokatta	広くなかった hiroku nakatta
難しかったです muzukashikatta desu *(was/were difficult)*	難しく[なかったです/ありませんでした] muzukashiku [nakatta desu/arimasen deshita]	難しかった muzukashikatta	難しくなかった muzukashiku nakatta

Giving and receiving verbs

Adjectives: Past tense, affirmative
and negative form

Expressing the completion
of an action and attempts

Before and *after*: 前に mae
ni and 後で ato de

For the plain affirmative form, drop the final い i and attach かった katta, and for the polite affirmative form, just add です desu. For the plain negative form, replace the final い i with く ku and add なかった nakatta. For the polite negative form, replace the final い i with く ku and add either なかったです nakatta desu or ありませんでした arimasen deshita.

このカレーはとても辛かったので、水をたくさん飲みました。
Kono karee wa totemo karakatta node, mizu o takusan nomimashita.
This curry was very spicy, so I drank a lot of water.

チョコレートケーキは甘かったですけど、チーズケーキはあまり甘くなかったです。
Chokoreeto keeki wa amakatta desu kedo, chiizu keeki wa amari amaku nakatta desu.
The chocolate cake was sweet, but the cheesecake was not so sweet.

その映画はとても良かったので、もう一度見たいです。
Sono eega wa totemo yokatta node, moo ichido mitai desu.
That movie was very good, so I want to see it again.

Next, let's look at the past tense form of な na-adjectives, which is the same as that of nouns.

Polite expressions: Honorific and
humble polite forms of verbs

Inviting people: *Let's …,*
Why don't we … ?, Shall we … ?

Expressing desires:
たい tai (past tense)

Only X: X だけ dake and
X しか shika + negative

POLITE FORM, PAST TENSE		PLAIN FORM, PAST TENSE	
Affirmative	Negative	Affirmative	Negative
暇 ひま でした **hima deshita** *(had a lot of free time)*	暇 ひま [じゃ/では][な かったです/ありま せんでした] **hima [ja/de wa] [nakatta desu/arimasen deshita]**	暇 ひま だった **hima datta**	暇 ひま [じゃ/では]な かった **hima [ja/de wa] nakatta**
きれいでした **kiree deshita** *(was beautiful, was clean)*	きれい[じゃ/では] [なかったです/あ りませんでした] **kiree [ja/de wa] [nakatta desu/arimasen deshita]**	きれいだった **kiree datta**	きれい[じゃ/では] なかった **kiree [ja/de wa] nakatta**
親切 しんせつ でした **shinsetsu deshita** *(was kind, was generous)*	親切 しんせつ [じゃ/では] [なかったです/あ りませんでした] **shinsetsu [ja/ de wa] [nakatta desu/arimasen deshita]**	親切 しんせつ だった **shinsetsu datta**	親切 しんせつ [じゃ/では] なかった **shinsetsu [ja/de wa] nakatta**

Giving and receiving verbs

Adjectives: Past tense, affirmative
and negative form

Expressing the completion
of an action and attempts

Before and *after*: 前に mae
ni and 後で ato de

POLITE FORM, PAST TENSE		PLAIN FORM, PAST TENSE	
Affirmative	Negative	Affirmative	Negative
不便でした fuben deshita *(was inconvenient)*	不便[じゃ/では] [なかったです/あ りませんでした] fuben [ja/de wa] [nakatta desu/arimasen deshita]	不便だった fuben datta	不便[じゃ/では] なかった fuben [ja/de wa] nakatta

As long as you know the conjugation of です desu and its plain form counterpart だ da, you won't have any problems conjugating the past tense form as well as the non-past tense form of な na-adjectives.

週末銀座はとても賑やかでしたが、今日は静かですね。

Shuumatsu ginza wa totemo nigiyaka deshita ga, kyoo wa shizuka desu ne.

Ginza was very lively on weekends, but it's quiet today, isn't it?

部長はあまり親切じゃありませんでしたが、最近はとても親切です。

Buchoo wa amari shinsetsu ja arimasen deshita ga, saikin wa totemo shinsetsu desu.

The division manager used to be not so kind, but recently he/she is very kind.

去年までその歌手は有名じゃありませんでしたが、今はとても有名です。

Kyonen made sono kashu (*singer*) wa yuumee ja arimasen deshita ga, ima wa totemo yuumee desu.

That singer was not famous until last year, but now he/she is very famous.

✎ Work Out 1

Fill in the blanks with the appropriate form of the adjectives below. Use the polite form.

難しい muzukashii, 便利 benri, いい ii, うるさい urusai (*noisy*), 不便 fuben, 静か shizuka, おいしい oishii

1. この本はとても _____ よ。読んでみたらいかがですか。

   Kono hon wa totemo _____ yo. Yonde mitara ikaga desu ka.

   This book was very good. How about if you try reading it?

2. A:図書館は _____ か。

   Toshokan wa _____ ka.

   Was the library quiet?

3. B: いいえ、_____。少し _____ 。

   Iie, _____. Sukoshi _____

   _____

   No, it was not quiet. It was a little noisy.

4. 近くにスーパーがあった時は _____ が、今はスーパーがありませんから

   _____ 。

   Chikaku ni suupaa ga atta toki wa _____ ga,

   ima wa suupaa ga arimasen kara _____.

   When there was a supermarket nearby, it was convenient, but now it's inconvenient

   because there's no supermarket.

Giving and receiving verbs

Adjectives: Past tense, affirmative
and negative form

Expressing the completion
of an action and attempts

Before and *after*: 前に mae
ni and 後で ato de

5. あのレストランは＿＿＿＿＿＿＿＿＿＿＿＿＿＿が、このレストランはあまり

＿＿＿＿＿＿＿＿。

Ano resutoran wa ＿＿＿＿＿＿＿＿＿＿＿ **ga, kono**

resutoran wa amari ＿＿＿＿＿＿＿＿**.**

That restaurant was excellent (lit., delicious), but this restaurant was not so excellent.

6. その会社の面接は＿＿＿＿＿＿＿＿が、この会社の面接は全然＿＿＿＿

＿＿＿＿＿。

Sono kaisha no mensetsu wa ＿＿＿＿＿＿＿＿＿＿＿＿＿＿＿

＿＿＿＿＿＿ **ga, kono kaisha no mensetsu wa zenzen**

＿＿＿＿＿＿＿＿＿＿＿＿**.**

The interview at that company was difficult, but the interview at this company was

not difficult at all.

ANSWER KEY

1. 良かったです yokatta desu; 2. 静かでした shizuka deshita, 静か [じゃ/では] [ありませんでした/なかったです] shizuka [ja/de wa] [arimasen deshita/nakatta desu], うるさかったです urusakatta desu; 3. 便利でした benri deshita, 不便です fuben desu; 4. おいしかったです oishikatta desu, おいしく [なかったです/ありませんでした] oishiku [nakatta desu/arimasen deshita]; 5. 難しかったです muzukashikatta desu, 難しく [なかったです/ありませんでした] muzukashiku [nakatta desu/arimasen deshita]

Phrase Builder 2

▶ 6C Phrase Builder 2 (CD 8, Track 3)

その魚料理	sono sakana ryoori	*that fish dish*
この和風サラダ	kono wafuu sarada	*this Japanese-style salad*

Polite expressions: Honorific and
humble polite forms of verbs

Inviting people: *Let's . . . ,
Why don't we . . . ?, Shall we . . . ?*

Expressing desires:
たい tai (past tense)

Only X: X だけ dake and
X しか shika + negative

その帆立の料理	sono hotate no ryoori	*that scallop dish*
冷たいデザート	tsumetai dezaato	*cold dessert*
デザートとコーヒーでも	dezaato to koohii demo	*dessert and coffee or something like that*
いかがでしたか。	Ikaga deshita ka. (*polite*)	*How was it?*
どうでしたか。	Doo deshita ka.	*How was it?*
一度来てみたかった	ichido kite mitakatta	*wanted to try and come once*
見てみましょう。	Mite mimashoo.	*Let's try seeing it.*
なかなかチャンスがなかった	nakanaka chansu ga nakatta	*didn't have an opportunity*
ムール貝も入っています/入っている	muurugai mo haitte imasu/haitte iru	*mussels are also added to it*
量が多かった	ryoo ga ookatta	*it was a lot (lit., the amount was a lot)*
全部食べてしまった	zenbu tabete shimatta	*finished eating everything*
飲みすぎてしまった	nomisugite shimatta	*ended up drinking too much*
少しいただいた	sukoshi itadaita (*humble polite*)	*ate a little, received a little*

Giving and receiving verbs

Adjectives: Past tense, affirmative
and negative form

Expressing the completion
of an action and attempts

Before and *after*: 前に mae
ni and 後で ato de

少し召し上がりませんか。	Sukoshi meshiagarimasen ka. (*honorific polite*)	*Would you like to eat/ drink a little?*
ホテルの近くで	hoteru no chikaku de	*near the hotel*
部長にお目にかかります/ かかる	buchoo ni ome ni kakarimasu/kakaru (*humble polite*)	*meet a division manager*
部長にお目にかかった 時に	buchoo ni ome ni kakatta toki ni (*humble polite*)	*when I met a division manager*
もう一度	moo ichido	*one more time*
コーヒーだけでいい	koohii dake de ii	*okay with only coffee*
それで	sorede	*so, for that reason*
是非	zehi	*by all means, at any cost*
喜んで	yorokonde	*be glad to*

Take It Further

なかなか Nakanaka, used in a negative clause, means *not easily* or *not readily*. So, なかなかチャンスがない nakanaka chansu ga nai and なかなか来ない nakanaka konai mean *not have an easy opportunity* and *not come readily* respectively. In an affirmative context, なかなか nakanaka means *quite*; なかなかいい nakanaka ii and なかなかおいしい nakanaka oishii mean *quite good* and *quite delicious* respectively.

Polite expressions: Honorific and
humble polite forms of verbs

Inviting people: *Let's . . . ,*
Why don't we … ?, Shall we … ?

Expressing desires:
たい tai (past tense)

Only X: X だけ dake and
X しか shika + negative

✎ Phrase Practice 2

Fill in the missing words below.

1. _____ でしたか。

   _____ **deshita ka.**

   How was it? (polite)

2. _____でしたか。

   _____ **deshita ka.**

   How was it?

3. _____ 来_きてみたかった

   _____ **kite mitakatta**

   wanted to try and come

4. 見_みて _____ 。

   Mite _____.

   Let's try seeing it.

5. _____ チャンスがなかった

   _____ **chansu ga nakatta**

   didn't have an opportunity

6. 少_{すこ}し _____

   sukoshi _____

   ate a little, received a little (humble polite)

7. _____ 一度

_____ ichido

one more time

8. コーヒー _____ でいい

koohii _____ de ii

okay with only coffee

ANSWER KEY

1. いかが Ikaga; 2. どう Doo; 3. 一度 ichido; 4. みましょう mimashoo; 5. なかなか nakanaka; 6. いただいた itadaita; 7. もう moo; 8. だけ dake

Grammar Builder 2
BEFORE AND *AFTER*: 前に MAE NI AND 後で ATO DE

▶ 6D Grammar Builder 2 (CD 8, Track 4)

You can describe a sequence of events or actions using 前 mae (*before*) and 後 ato (*after*). に Ni follows 前 mae, and 前に mae ni follows either a noun + の no or the plain, non-past, affirmative form of a verb (regardless of the tense in the main clause). 後 ato follows either a noun + の no or the plain, past, affirmative form of a verb (regardless of the tense in the main clause). で de follows 後 ato, but it is optional. The following chart summarizes these structures.

Noun + の no/verb (plain non-past affirmative) + に mae ni	before ...
Noun + の no/verb (plain past affirmative) + 後 (で) ato (de)	after ...

Polite expressions: Honorific and
humble polite forms of verbs

Inviting people: *Let's ... ,
Why don't we ... ?, Shall we ... ?*

Expressing desires:
たい tai (past tense)

Only X: X だけ dake and
X しか shika + negative

パーティーの前<ruby>前<rt>まえ</rt></ruby>にワインを買<ruby>買<rt>か</rt></ruby>いました。

Paatii no mae ni wain o kaimashita.

I bought wine before the party.

パーティーへ行<ruby>行<rt>い</rt></ruby>く前<ruby>前<rt>まえ</rt></ruby>にワインを買<ruby>買<rt>か</rt></ruby>いました。

Paatii e iku mae ni wain o kaimashita.

I bought wine before going to the party.

晩<ruby>晩<rt>ばん</rt></ruby>ご飯<ruby>飯<rt>はん</rt></ruby>の前<ruby>前<rt>まえ</rt></ruby>に宿題<ruby>宿題<rt>しゅくだい</rt></ruby>をしてしまいました。

Bangohan no mae ni shukudai o shite shimaimashita.

I have done my homework before dinner.

晩<ruby>晩<rt>ばん</rt></ruby>ご飯<ruby>飯<rt>はん</rt></ruby>を食<ruby>食<rt>た</rt></ruby>べる前<ruby>前<rt>まえ</rt></ruby>に宿題<ruby>宿題<rt>しゅくだい</rt></ruby>をしてしまいました。

Bangohan o taberu mae ni shukudai o shite shimaimashita.

I have done my homework before eating dinner.

ミーティングの後<ruby>後<rt>あと</rt></ruby>、昼<ruby>昼<rt>ひる</rt></ruby>ご飯<ruby>飯<rt>はん</rt></ruby>を食<ruby>食<rt>た</rt></ruby>べました。

Miitingu no ato, hirugohan o tabemashita.

After the meeting, I ate lunch.

ミーティングに出<ruby>出<rt>で</rt></ruby>た後<ruby>後<rt>あと</rt></ruby>、昼<ruby>昼<rt>ひる</rt></ruby>ご飯<ruby>飯<rt>はん</rt></ruby>を食<ruby>食<rt>た</rt></ruby>べました。

Miitingu ni deta ato, hirugohan o tabemashita.

After attending the meeting, I ate lunch.

映画<ruby>映画<rt>えいが</rt></ruby>を見<ruby>見<rt>み</rt></ruby>た後<ruby>後<rt>あと</rt></ruby>で家<ruby>家<rt>うち</rt></ruby>へ帰<ruby>帰<rt>かえ</rt></ruby>ります。

Eega o mita ato de uchi e kaerimasu.

I will go home after seeing a movie.

Giving and receiving verbs

Adjectives: Past tense, affirmative
and negative form

Expressing the completion
of an action and attempts

Before and *after*: 前に mae
ni and 後で ato de

森さんの後でこのコンピューターを使います。

Mori san no ato de kono konpyuutaa o tsukaimasu.

I will use this computer after Mr./Ms. Mori.

大学を卒業した後、銀行で働きます。

Daigaku o sotsugyooshita ato, ginkoo de hatarakimasu.

I will work at a bank after graduating from the university.

Note that に ni and で de are both dropped before the copula です desu or だ da.

テストの前ですから、たくさん勉強します。

Tesuto no mae desu kara, takusan benkyooshimasu.

Since it's before the test, I study a lot.

ジョギングをした後ですから、水が飲みたいです。

Jogingu o shita ato desu kara, mizu ga nomitai desu.

Since it's after I jogged, I want to drink water.

✎ Work Out 2

Fill in the blanks with the appropriate Japanese expressions.

1. _____ 友達に電話にします。

_____ tomodachi ni

denwashimasu.

I will call my friend before dinner.

Polite expressions: Honorific and
humble polite forms of verbs

Inviting people: *Let's ... ,*
Why don't we ... ?, Shall we ... ?

Expressing desires:
たい tai (past tense)

Only X: X だけ dake and
X しか shika + negative

2. _____ コーヒーを飲みます。

_____ koohii o nomimasu.

I drink coffee after getting up.

3. _____ 日本語を勉強しました。

_____ nihongo o

benkyooshimashita.

I studied Japanese before going to Japan.

4. _____喫茶店へ行きました。

_____ kissaten e ikimashita.

I went to a café after lunch.

5. _____本を読みます。

_____ hon o yomimasu.

I read a book before going to bed.

ANSWER KEY

1. [晩ご飯/夕飯/夕食] の前に [Bangohan/Yuuhan/Yuushoku] no mae ni; 2. 起きた後 (で) Okita
ato (de); 3. 日本 [へ/に] 行く前に Nihon [e/ni] iku mae ni; 4. [昼ご飯/昼食] の後 (で) [Hirugohan/
Chuushoku] no ato (de); 5. 寝る前に Neru mae ni

✎ Drive It Home

A. Fill in the blanks with the appropriate form of the adjectives in parentheses.

1. この本は _____ です。(難しい)

Kono hon wa _____ **desu. (muzukashii)**

This book was difficult.

Giving and receiving verbs

Adjectives: Past tense, affirmative
and negative form

Expressing the completion
of an action and attempts

Before and *after*: 前に mae
ni and 後で ato de

2. この本は ＿＿＿＿＿＿＿＿＿＿＿＿＿＿＿ です。(難しい)

   Kono hon ＿＿＿＿＿＿＿＿＿＿＿＿＿＿＿＿＿＿＿＿＿＿＿＿＿＿ **desu.**

   (muzukashii)

   This book was not difficult.

3. 昨日は ＿＿＿＿＿＿＿＿＿。(暇)

   Kinoo wa ＿＿＿＿＿＿＿＿＿＿＿＿＿＿＿＿. **(hima)**

   I had a lot of free time yesterday.

4. 昨日は ＿＿＿＿＿＿＿＿＿＿＿＿＿＿＿＿＿ です。(暇)

   Kinoo ＿＿＿＿＿＿＿＿＿＿＿＿＿＿＿＿＿＿＿＿＿ **nakatta] desu. (hima)**

   I didn't have a lot of free time yesterday.

B. Fill in the blanks with the appropriate words to complete the sentences.

1. パーティーの ＿＿＿＿ ワインを買いました。

   Paatii no ＿＿＿＿＿＿＿＿＿＿ **wain o kaimashita.**

   I bought wine before the party.

2. パーティーへ行く ＿＿＿＿ ワインを買いました。

   Paatii e iku ＿＿＿＿＿＿＿＿＿＿ **wain o kaimashita.**

   I bought wine before going to the party.

3. ミーティングの ＿＿＿＿＿＿、昼ご飯を食べました。

   Miitingu no ＿＿＿＿＿＿＿＿＿＿, **hirugohan o tabemashita.**

   After the meeting, I ate lunch.

Polite expressions: Honorific and
humble polite forms of verbs

Inviting people: *Let's ... ,*
Why don't we ... ?, Shall we ... ?

Expressing desires:
たい tai (past tense)

Only X: X だけ dake and
X しか shika + negative

4. ミーティングに出た _____ 、昼ご飯を食べました。

   Miitingu ni deta _____, hirugohan o tabemashita.

   After attending the meeting, I ate lunch.

ANSWER KEY
A: 1. 難しかった muzukashikatta; 2. 難しくなかった muzukashiku nakatta; 3. 暇でした hima deshita; 4. 暇 [じゃ/では]なかった hima [ja/de wa] nakatta
B: 1. 前に mae ni; 2. 前に mae ni; 3. 後 (で) ato (de); 4. 後 (で) ato (de)

💡 Tip!

Keeping a diary in Japanese is a good way to improve your Japanese language skills. You can write about things you do and experience every or almost every day using several sentences. Challenge yourself by going beyond simple sentences; try putting together more complex sentences using structures such as the て te-form of verbs, the と to and たら tara-conditionals, 時 toki, の前に no mae ni and の 後 (で) no ato (de), as well as conjunctions like が ga, けど kedo, から kara, and ので node.

How Did You Do?

Let's see how you did! By now, you should be able to:

☐ use adjectives in their past tense forms (Still unsure? Jump back to page 128)

☐ express *before ...* and *after ...* (Still unsure? Jump back to page 138)

✏️ Word Recall

1. 店員 ten-in   a. *wool*

2. シャツ shatsu   b. *cash*

Giving and receiving verbs
Adjectives: Past tense, affirmative
and negative form

Expressing the completion
of an action and attempts

Before and *after*: 前に mae
ni and 後で ato de

3. ズボン zubon   c. *store clerk*

4. スカート sukaato   d. *popularity*

5. ウール uuru   e. *design*

6. 縞 shima   f. *shirt*

7. デザイン dezain   g. *pants*

8. 人気 ninki   h. *skirt*

9. 現金 genkin   i. *change*

10. お釣り otsuri   j. *stripes*

ANSWER KEY

1. c; 2. f; 3. g; 4. h; 5. a; 6. j; 7. e; 8. d; 9. b; 10. i

Lesson 7: Sentences

In this lesson you'll learn how to:

☐ use honorific and humble polite forms of verbs

☐ express *wanted to ...*

Sentence Builder 1

▶ 7A Sentence Builder 1 (CD 8, Track 5)

このレストランは人気があるから、いつも混んでいます。

Kono resutoran wa ninki ga aru kara, itsumo konde imasu.

This restaurant is very popular, so it's always crowded.

Polite expressions: Honorific and
humble polite forms of verbs

Inviting people: *Let's ...,*
Why don't we ... ?, Shall we ... ?

Expressing desires:
たい tai (past tense)

Only X: X だけ dake and
X しか shika + negative

何が食べたいですか。

Nani ga tabetai desu ka.

What would you like (lit., do you want) to eat?

天ぷら定食かコロッケ定食がいいかしら。

Tenpura teeshoku ka korokke teeshoku ga ii kashira.

I wonder if the prix fixe tempura meal or the croquette meal are good.

うな重はどんな料理ですか。

Unajuu wa donna ryoori desu ka.

What kind of meal is unajuu?

ご飯の上にうなぎが載っています。

Gohan no ue ni unagi ga notte imasu.

It's eel placed over cooked rice.

先週ここでうな重を食べたんですが、とてもおいしかったですよ。

Senshuu koko de unajuu o tabeta n desu ga, totemo oishikatta desu yo.

I ate unajuu here last week, and it was very delicious.

一度食べてみたらどうですか。

Ichido tabete mitara doo desu ka.

How about if you try it out once? (lit., How about if you eat it once?)

今日はうな重にします。

Kyoo wa unajuu ni shimasu.

Today I will have unajuu. (lit., I will make it unajuu.)

うな重は定食じゃないから、お味噌汁を注文したらどうですか。

Unajuu wa teeshoku ja nai kara, omisoshiru o chuumonshitara doo desu ka.

Unit 2 Lesson 7: Sentences

145

Giving and receiving verbs

Adjectives: Past tense, affirmative
and negative form

Expressing the completion
of an action and attempts

Before and *after*: 前に mae
ni and 後で ato de

Since unajuu is not a prix fixe meal, would you like to order (lit., how about if you order) a miso soup?

サラダも注文しましょうか。

Sarada mo chuumonshimashoo ka.

Shall I order a salad, too?

もし良かったら、私のを半分あげます。

Moshi yokattara, watashi no o hanbun agemasu.

If it's okay with you, I will give you half of mine.

先週サラダを注文したら、とても量が多かったです。

Senshuu sarada o chuumonshitara, totemo ryoo ga ookatta desu.

When I ordered a salad last week, it was quite large (lit., the amount was a lot).

ここは混んでいるから、後で喫茶店に行きましょう。

Koko wa konde iru kara, ato de kissaten ni ikimashoo.

It's crowded here, so afterwards let's go to a café.

時間があったら、このレストランを出た後で、喫茶店でコーヒーでも飲みませんか。

Jikan ga attara, kono resutoran o deta ato de, kissaten de koohii demo nomimasen ka.

If we have time, after leaving this restaurant, why don't we have coffee or something like that at a café?

じゃあ、注文しましょうか。

Jaa, chuumonshimashoo ka.

Then, shall we order?

olite expressions: Honorific and
humble polite forms of verbs

Inviting people: *Let's ... ,
Why don't we ... ?, Shall we ... ?*

Expressing desires:
たい tai (past tense)

Only X: X だけ dake and
X しか shika + negative

ええ、注文しましょう。

Ee, chuumonshimashoo.

Yes, let's order!

✎ Sentence Practice 1

Fill in the missing words in each of the following sentences.

1. このレストランは人気があるから、_____ 。

   Kono resutoran wa ninki ga arukara, _____

   _____.

   This restaurant is very popular, so it's always crowded.

2. うな重は _____ 。

   Unajuu wa _____.

   What kind of meal is unajuu?

3. 一度 _____ どうですか。

   Ichido _____ **doo desu ka.**

   How about if you try it out once? (lit., How about if you eat it once?)

4. 今日はうな重 _____ 。

   Kyoo wa unajuu _____.

   Today I will have unajuu. (lit., I will make it unajuu.)

5. _____ 、私のを半分あげます。

   _____, **watashi no o hanbun agemasu.**

   If it's okay with you, I will give you half of mine.

Giving and receiving verbs

Adjectives: Past tense, affirmative
and negative form

Expressing the completion
of an action and attempts

Before and after: 前に mae
ni and 後で ato de

6. _____ 、このレストランを出た後で、喫茶店でコーヒーでも飲み

ませんか。

_____ , kono resutoran o deta ato de,

kissaten de koohii demo nomimasen ka.

If we have time, after leaving this restaurant, why don't we have coffee or something

like that at a café?

7. じゃあ、 _____ 。

Jaa, _____ .

Then, shall we order?

8. ええ、 _____ 。

Ee, _____ .

Yes, let's order!

ANSWER KEY

1. いつも混んでいます itsumo konde imasu; 2. どんな料理ですか donna ryoori desu ka;
3. 食べてみたら tabete mitara; 4. にします ni shimasu; 5. もし良かったら Moshi yokattara;
6. 時間があったら Jikan ga attara; 7. 注文しましょうか chuumonshimashoo ka; 8. 注文しましょう
chuumonshimashoo

Grammar Builder 1

POLITE EXPRESSIONS: HONORIFIC AND HUMBLE POLITE
FORMS OF VERBS

▶ 7B Grammar Builder 1 (CD 8, Track 6)

Some polite expressions were already introduced in *Intermediate Japanese*. Now,
let's look at the honorific and humble polite form of verbs.

Polite expressions: Honorific and
humble polite forms of verbs

Inviting people: *Let's ... ,
Why don't we ... ?, Shall we ... ?*

Expressing desires:
たい tai (past tense)

Only X: X だけ dake and
X しか shika + negative

ます MASU-FORM	HONORIFIC FORM	HUMBLE FORM
行_いきます ikimasu *(go)* *and* 来_きます kimasu *(come)*	いらっしゃいます irasshaimasu いらっしゃる irassharu	参_{まい}ります mairimasu 参_{まい}る mairu
います imasu *(exist)*	いらっしゃいます irasshaimasu いらっしゃる irassharu	おります orimasu おる oru
します shimasu *(do)*	なさいます nasaimasu なさる nasaru	いたします itashimasu いたす itasu
食_たべます tabemasu *(eat)* *or* 飲_のみます nomimasu *(drink)*	召_めし上_あがります meshiagarimasu 召_めし上_あがる meshiagaru	いただきます itadakimasu いただく itadaku
見_みます mimasu *(see, look,watch)*	ご覧_{らん}になります goran ni narimasu ご覧_{らん}になる goran ni naru	拝見_{はいけん}します haikenshimasu 拝見_{はいけん}する haikensuru

Giving and receiving verbs

Adjectives: Past tense, affirmative
and negative form

Expressing the completion
of an action and attempts

Before and *after*: 前に mae
ni and 後で ato de

ます MASU-FORM	HONORIFIC FORM	HUMBLE FORM
言います iimasu (*say*)	おっしゃいます osshaimasu おっしゃる ossharu	申します mooshimasu 申す moosu

Not all verbs have special honorific and humble polite forms; in these cases, honorific and humble polite forms can be formed using the following rules.

Honorific form	お o + *conjunctive form of verb* + になり ます ni narimasu/になる ni naru
Humble form	お o + *conjunctive form of verb* + しま す shimasu/する suru *or* いたします itashimasu/いたす itasu

Note that you can use either します shimasu or いたします itashimasu to form a humble polite form such as お書きします okakishimasu or お書きいた します okakiitashimasu (*to write*), because いたします itashimasu is actually the humble polite form of します shimasu, it is even more polite than します shimasu. Here are some examples.

ます MASU-FORM	HONORIFIC FORM	HUMBLE FORM
読みます yomimasu (*read*)	お読みになります oyomi ni narimasu お読みになる oyomi ni naru	お読みします oyomi shimasu お読みする oyomi suru *or* お読みいたします oyomi itashimasu お読みいたす oyomi itasu

ます MASU-FORM	HONORIFIC FORM	HUMBLE FORM
聞きます kikimasu *(listen)*	お聞きになります okiki ni narimasu お聞きになる okiki ni naru	お聞きします okiki shimasu お聞きする okiki suru *or* お聞きいたします okiki itashimasu お聞きいたす okiki itasu
作ります tsukurimasu *(make)*	お作りになります otsukuri ni narimasu お作りになる otsukuri ni naru	お作りします otsukuri shimasu お作りする otsukuri suru *or* お作りいたします otsukuri itashimasu お作りいたす otsukuri itasu
使います tsukaimasu *(use)*	お使いになります otsukai ni narimasu お使いになる otsukai ni naru	お使いします otsukai shimasu お使いする otsukai suru *or* お使いいたします otsukai itashimasu お使いいたす otsukai itasu

Giving and receiving verbs

Adjectives: Past tense, affirmative
and negative form

Expressing the completion
of an action and attempts

Before and *after*: 前に mae
ni and 後で ato de

ます MASU-FORM	HONORIFIC FORM	HUMBLE FORM
出掛ける dekakeru *(go out)*	お出掛けになります odekake ni narimasu お出掛けになる odekake ni naru	お出掛けします odekake shimasu お出掛けする odekake suru *or* お出掛けいたします odekake itashimasu お出掛けいたす odekake itasu

There are also verbs which have a special honorific form but do not have a special humble polite form, or vice versa. For instance, the verb 会います aimasu (*meet*) has a special humble polite form, お目にかかります ome ni kakarimasu, but its honorific form, お会いになります oai ni narimasu, is formed following the regular rules you've just learned.

Now, let's look at how the honorific and humble polite forms of verbs are used. As pointed out in *Intermediate Japanese*, an honorific form is used when describing actions taken by someone you need to or want to pay respect to, such as a superior at work, a teacher or a customer. On the other hand, a humble form is used when describing actions taken by the speaker himself/herself or members of his/her in-group, such as a family member. Take a look at the following example mini-dialogues. Assume that A is 部長 buchoo (*division manager*) and B is 社員 shain (*company employee*).

A: 鈴木さん、明日何時に会社に来ますか。

Suzuki san, ashita nanji ni kaisha ni kimasu ka.

Mr./Ms. Suzuki, what time are you coming to the office (lit., company) tomorrow?

Polite expressions: Honorific and humble polite forms of verbs

Inviting people: *Let's . . . ,*
Why don't we . . . ?, Shall we . . . ?

Expressing desires:
たい tai (past tense)

Only X: X だけ dake and
X しか shika + negative

B: 八時頃参ります。部長は何時にいらっしゃいますか。

Hachi ji goro mairimasu. Buchoo wa nanji ni irasshaimasu ka.

I'll come around eight. What time are you coming, Division Manager?

A: 私は八時半頃来ると思います。

Watashi wa hachiji han goro kuru to omoimasu.

I think I'll come around eight-thirty.

B: 部長、もう少しビールを召し上がりませんか。

Buchoo, moo sukoshi biiru o meshiagarimasen ka.

Wouldn't you like to have a little more beer, Division Manager?

A: じゃあ、もう少し。林さんももう少しどうですか。

Jaa, moo sukoshi. Hayashi san mo moo sukoshi doo desu ka.

Well, a little more. Would you also like a little more, Mr./Ms. Hayashi?

B: では、私ももう少しいただきます。

Dewa, watashi mo moo sukoshi itadakimasu.

Okay, I will have a little more, too.

B: 部長はゴルフをなさいますか。

Buchoo wa gorufu o nasaimasu ka.

Division Manager, do you play golf?

A: うん、時々ね。

Un, tokidoki ne.

Yes, sometimes.

Giving and receiving verbs

Adjectives: Past tense, affirmative
and negative form

Expressing the completion
of an action and attempts

Before and *after*: 前に mae
ni and 後で ato de

B: 明日のミーティングで部長がこのレポートをお読みになりますか。

Ashita no miitingu de buchoo ga kono repooto o oyomi ni narimasu ka.

Division Manager, will you read this report at tomorrow's meeting?

A: そうだなあ。

Soo da naa.

Let me see.

B: よろしかったら、私がお読みいたしますが。

Yoroshikattara, watashi ga oyomi itashimasu ga.

If it's okay, I will read it, but …

A: じゃあ、お願いします。

Jaa, onegaishimasu.

Please do. (lit., Then, please.)

✎ Work Out 1

A. Choose the appropriate honorific polite form from the list below to complete the sentences. Change them into their appropriate form if necessary.

召し上がります **meshiagarimasu**, いらっしゃいます **irasshaimasu**, お書きになります **okaki ni narimasu**, なさいます **nasaimasu**, お読みになります **oyomi ni narimasu**, おっしゃいます **osshaimasu**, ご覧になります **goran ni narimasu**

1. 小田先生がこの本を _____。

Oda sensee ga kono hon o _____

_____.

Professor Oda wrote this book.

Expressing desires:
たい tai (past tense)

Only X: X だけ dake and
X しか shika + negative

2. 部長は明日アメリカへ _____ 。

Buchoo wa ashita amerika e _____ .

The division manager will come to the U.S.A. tomorrow.

3. 社長は天ぷらが好きですから、たくさん _____ と思います。

Shachoo wa tenpura ga suki desu kara, takusan

_____ to omoimasu.

The president likes tempura, so I think he/she'll eat a lot.

4. 週末課長はテニスを _____ 。

Shuumatsu kachoo wa tenisu o _____ .

The section manager plays tennis on weekends.

5. 部長、この映画を _____ か。

Buchoo, kono eega o _____

_____ ka.

Division Manager, did you see this movie?

B. Choose the appropriate humble polite form from the list below to complete the
sentences. Change them into their appropriate form if necessary.
お話しします ohanashishimasu, いただきます itadakimasu, 拝見します
haikenshimasu, 参ります mairimasu, お書きします okakishimasu, 申します
mooshimasu, いたします itashimasu, お目にかかります ome ni kakarimasu

1. 部長、それは私が _____ 。

Buchoo, sore wa watashi ga _____ .

Division Manager, I'll do it.

Giving and receiving verbs

Adjectives: Past tense, affirmative
and negative form

Expressing the completion
of an action and attempts

Before and *after*: 前に mae
ni and 後で ato de

2. 先生の写真を ＿＿＿＿＿＿＿＿ が、とても良かったです。

Sensee no shashin (*photography*) **o**

＿＿＿＿＿＿＿＿＿＿＿＿＿＿＿ **ga, totemo yokatta desu.**

I saw the professor's photography, and it was very good.

3. パーティーで課長の料理を ＿＿＿＿＿＿＿＿＿ が、とてもおいしかっ
たです。

Paatii de kachoo no ryoori o ＿＿＿＿＿＿＿＿＿＿ **ga,
totemo oishikatta desu.**

I ate a meal (cooked) by the section manager, and it was very delicious.

4. 社長、明日の四時頃また ＿＿＿＿＿＿ 。

Shachoo, ashita no yoji goro mata ＿＿＿＿＿＿＿＿ **.**

President, I'll come again tomorrow around four o'clock.

5. 部長、ちょっと ＿＿＿＿＿＿＿ んですが。

Buchoo, chotto ＿＿＿＿＿＿＿＿＿＿＿ **n desu ga.**

Division Manager, I'd like to speak with you for a little while.

ANSWER KEY

A: 1. お書きになりました okaki ni narimashita; 2. いらっしゃいます irasshaimasu; 3. 召し上がる
meshiagaru; 4. なさいます nasaimasu; 5. ご覧になりました goran ni narimashita

B: 1. いたします itashimasu; 2. 拝見しました haikenshimashita; 3. いただきました itadakimashita;
4. 参ります mairimasu; 5. お話ししたい ohanashishitai

olite expressions: Honorific and
humble polite forms of verbs

Inviting people: *Let's . . . ,
Why don't we . . . ?, Shall we . . . ?*

Expressing desires:
たい tai (past tense)

Only X: X だけ dake and
X しか shika + negative

Sentence Builder 2

▶ 7C Sentence Builder 2 (CD 8, Track 7)

その魚料理はいかがでしたか。

Sono sakana ryoori wa ikaga deshita ka.

How was that fish dish? (polite)

その帆立の料理はどうでしたか。

Sono hotate no ryoori wa doo deshita ka.

How was that scallop dish?

この和風サラダもおいしかったです。

Kono wafuu sarada mo oishikatta desu.

This Japanese-style salad was also good.

それは良かった。

Sore wa yokatta.

That's good. (referring to something that happened in the past)/*I'm glad to hear that.*

一度このレストランへ来てみたかったんです。

Ichido kono resutoran e kite mitakatta n desu.

I wanted to try and come to this restaurant once.

えびやいかやムール貝も入っていて、量が多かったんですが、全部食べてしまいました。

Ebi ya ika ya muurugai mo haitte ite, ryoo ga ookatta n desu ga, zenbu tabete shimaimashita.

Among other things, shrimp, cuttlefish, mussels are also in it, and it was a lot, but I finished it all.

Giving and receiving verbs

Adjectives: Past tense, affirmative
and negative form

Expressing the completion
of an action and attempts

Before and *after*: 前に mae
ni and 後で ato de

私も加藤さんの料理を少しいただきましたから。

Watashi mo Kato san no ryoori o sukoshi itadakimashita kara.

I also had a little bit of Mr. Kato's dish, so …

ワインをもう少し召し上がりませんか。

Wain o moo sukoshi meshiagarimasen ka.

Would you like to have a little more wine?

実は昨日少し飲みすぎてしまったんです。

Jitsu wa kinoo sukoshi nomisugite shimatta n desu.

Actually, I ended up drinking a little too much yesterday.

小田部長にお目にかかった時に、部長がビール券をくださいました。

Oda buchoo ni ome ni kakatta toki ni, buchoo ga biiruken o kudasaimashita.

When I saw the Division Manager Oda, he/she gave me a beer gift certificate.

それで、ホテルの近くでビールを1ダース買って、全部飲んでしまいました。

Sorede, hoteru no chikaku de biiru o ichi daasu katte, zenbu nonde shimaimashita.

So, I bought a dozen bottles of beer near the hotel and ended up drinking them all.

デザートとコーヒーでも注文しませんか。

Dezaato to koohii demo chuumonshimasen ka.

Why don't we order a dessert and coffee or something like that?

冷たいデザートが食べたいです。

Tsumetai dezaato ga tabetai desu.

I want to eat a cold dessert.

olite expressions: Honorific and
humble polite forms of verbs

Inviting people: *Let's . . . ,
Why don't we . . . ?, Shall we . . . ?*

Expressing desires:
たい tai (past tense)

Only X: X だけ dake and
X しか shika + negative

もう一度メニューを見てみましょう

Moo ichido menu o mite mimashoo.

Let's try looking at the menu one more time.

ケーキしかないですね。

Keeki shika nai desu ne.

There are only cakes.

アイスクリームかシャーベットが食べたかったです。

Aisukuriimu ka shaabetto ga tabetakatta desu.

I wanted to eat ice cream or sherbet.

コーヒーだけでいいです。

Koohii dake de ii desu.

I'm fine with only coffee.

チョコレートケーキと紅茶にします。

Chokoreeto keeki to koocha ni shimasu.

I will have chocolate cake and tea. (lit., I will make it chocolate cake and tea.)

✎ Sentence Practice 2

Fill in the missing words in each of the following sentences.

1. その魚料理は _____。

   Sono sakana ryoori wa _____.

   How was that fish dish? (polite)

2. それは ＿＿＿＿＿＿＿＿ 。

Sore wa ＿＿＿＿＿＿＿＿＿＿.

That's good. (referring to something that happened in the past)

3. 一度このレストランへ ＿＿＿＿＿＿＿＿＿＿ んです。

Ichido kono resutoran e ＿＿＿＿＿＿＿＿＿＿ n desu.

I wanted to try and come to this restaurant once.

4. ワインをもう少し ＿＿＿＿＿＿＿＿＿＿ 。

Wain o moo sukoshi ＿＿＿＿＿＿＿＿＿＿.

Would you like to have a little more wine?

5. デザートとコーヒー ＿＿＿＿＿＿＿＿＿＿ 。

Dezaato to koohii ＿＿＿＿＿＿＿

＿＿＿＿＿＿＿＿＿＿.

Why don't we order a dessert and coffee or something like that?

6. ＿＿＿＿＿＿＿＿＿＿ メニューを見てみましょう。

＿＿＿＿＿＿＿＿＿＿ menu o mite mimashoo.

Let's try looking at the menu one more time.

7. ケーキ ＿＿＿＿＿＿＿ ですね。

Keeki ＿＿＿＿＿＿＿ desu ne.

There are only cakes.

8. コーヒー ＿＿＿＿＿＿＿ です。

Koohii ＿＿＿＿＿＿＿ desu.

I'm fine with only coffee.

Polite expressions: Honorific and humble polite forms of verbs

Inviting people: *Let's . . . ,*
Why don't we . . . ?, Shall we . . . ?

Expressing desires:
たい tai (past tense)

Only X: X だけ dake and
X しか shika + negative

ANSWER KEY

1. いかがでしたか ikaga deshita ka; 2. 良かった yokatta; 3. 来てみたかった kite mitakatta; 4. 召し上がりませんか meshiagarimasen ka; 5. でも注文しませんか demo chuumonshimasen ka; 6. もう一度 Moo ichido; 7. しかない shika nai; 8. だけでいい dake de ii

Grammar Builder 2

EXPRESSING DESIRES: たい TAI (PAST TENSE)

▶ 7D Grammar Builder 2 (CD 8, Track 8)

In *Intermediate Japanese*, the non-past tense from of たい tai (*want to*) was introduced. Now let's learn the past tense form of たい tai. The conjugation of たい tai is the same as that of い i-adjectives. Since you just learned the past tense form of い i-adjectives in Lesson 6, forming the past tense of たい tai should be simple.

POLITE FORM, PAST TENSE		PLAIN FORM, PAST TENSE	
Affirmative	Negative	Affirmative	Negative
たかったです takatta desu (*wanted to*)	たくなかったです taku nakatta desu *or* たくありませんでした taku arimasen deshita	たかった takatta	たくなかった taku nakatta

ミーティングに出たくありませんでしたが、社長もお出になったので、出ました。

Miitingu ni detaku arimasen deshita ga, shachoo mo ode ni natta node, demashita.

I didn't want to attend the meeting, but I did (lit., attended) because the president also attended.

Giving and receiving verbs

Adjectives: Past tense, affirmative
and negative form

Expressing the completion
of an action and attempts

Before and *after*: 前に mae
ni and 後で ato de

グレーのセーターが買いたかったですが、なかったので、茶色のを買いました。

Guree no seetaa ga kaitakatta desu ga, nakatta node, chairo no o kaimashita.

I wanted to buy a gray sweater, but they didn't have one, so I bought a brown one.

✎ Work Out 2

Fill in the blanks with the appropriate expressions to complete the sentences.

1. 昨日は魚料理が ＿＿＿＿＿＿＿＿＿＿＿ が、今日は肉料理が食べたいで
す。

   Kinoo wa sakana ryoori ga ＿＿＿＿＿＿＿＿＿＿＿＿＿＿＿＿＿＿

   ga, kyoo wa nikuryoori ga tabetai desu.

   I wanted to eat fish yesterday, but today I want to eat meat.

2. 日曜日にテニスが ＿＿＿＿＿＿＿＿＿＿＿ んですが、月曜日にテストがあったの
   で、家で勉強しました。

   Nichiyoobi ni tenisu ga ＿＿＿＿＿＿＿＿＿＿＿＿＿＿ n desu ga, getsuyoobi

   ni tesuto ga atta node, uchi de benkyoo shimashita.

   I wanted to play tennis on Sunday, but since there was a test on Monday, I studied at

   home.

3. その映画は ＿＿＿＿＿＿＿＿＿ けど、この映画は ＿＿＿＿＿＿＿＿＿＿＿＿。

   Sono eega wa ＿＿＿＿＿＿＿＿＿＿＿＿＿＿ kedo, kono eega wa

   ＿＿＿＿＿＿＿＿＿＿＿＿＿＿＿＿＿＿.

   I wanted to see that movie; I didn't want to see this movie.

Polite expressions: Honorific and
humble polite forms of verbs

Inviting people: *Let's ...*,
Why don't we ... ?, Shall we ... ?

Expressing desires:
たい tai (past tense)

Only X: X だけ dake and
X しか shika + negative

4. イタリアへ＿＿＿＿＿＿＿＿んですが、友達がいるので、スペインへ行きました。

Itaria e ＿＿＿＿＿＿＿＿ n desu ga, tomodachi ga iru node,

supein e ikimashita.

I wanted to go to Italy, but I went to Spain because I had a friend there.

5. その本は長いし、難しいし、＿＿＿＿＿＿＿＿んですが、読んだらなかなか良かったです。

Sono hon wa nagai shi, muzukashii shi, ＿＿＿＿＿＿＿＿

＿＿＿＿＿＿＿＿ n desu ga, yondara nakanaka yokatta desu.

That book was long and diffcult, and so I didn't want to read it (at first), but I liked it

(lit., it was quite good) when I read it.

ANSWER KEY

1. 食べたかったです tabetakatta desu; 2. したかった shitakatta; 3. 見たかった mitakatta, 見たくなかった mitaku nakatta; 4. 行きたかった ikitakatta; 5. 読みたくなかった yomitaku nakatta

✎ Drive It Home

A. Fill in the blanks by choosing the approriate words from the word bank.

いただきます itadakimasu, 召し上がります meshiagarimasu, お出掛けになります odekake ni narimasu, 参ります mairimasu.

1. 部長は＿＿＿＿＿＿＿＿。

Buchoo wa ＿＿＿＿＿＿＿＿.

The division manager is going out.

Giving and receiving verbs

Adjectives: Past tense, affirmative
and negative form

Expressing the completion
of an action and attempts

Before and *after*: 前に mae
ni and 後で ato de

2. 私_{わたし}が _____ 。

   Watashi ga _____.

   I'm going.

3. 部長_{ぶちょう}はビールを _____ 。

   Buchoo wa biiru o _____.

   The division manager drinks beer.

4. 私_{わたし}はビールを _____ 。

   Watashi wa biiru o _____.

   I drink beer.

B. Fill in the blanks with the appropriate words.

1. ビールが飲_のみ _____ です。

   Biiru ga nomi _____ **desu.**

   I wanted to drink beer.

2. ビールは飲_のみ _____ です。

   Biiru wa nomi _____**desu.**

   I didn't want to drink beer.

3. すしが食_たべ _____ です。

   Sushi ga tabe _____ **desu.**

   I wanted to eat sushi.

4. すしは食_たべ _____ です。

   Sushi wa tabe _____ **desu.**

   I didn't want to eat sushi.

Expressing desires:
たい tai (past tense)

ANSWER KEY

A: 1. お出掛けになります odekake ni narimasu; 2. 参ります mairimasu; 3. 召し上がります
meshiagarimasu; 4. いただきます itadakimasu

B: 1. たかった takatta; 2. たくなかった taku nakatta; 3. たかった takatta; 4. たくなかった taku
nakatta

Tip!

Japanese food is well-known and well-liked in the United States and around
the world. Many Japanese restaurants exist in big cities. Even in small towns,
you're likely to find at least one Japanese restaurant. If there's one in your town,
visit it and see if you can read the names of dishes in Japanese. The names of the
dishes are probably written both in Japanese and English. Also, try ordering your
food in Japanese. Maybe you can even have a little chat with Japanese waiters
and waitresses.

How Did You Do?

Let's see how you did! By now, you should be able to:

☐ use honorific and humble polite forms of verbs (Still unsure? Jump back to
page 148)

☐ express *wanted to . . .* (Still unsure? Jump back to page 161)

✎ Word Recall

1. 千円 sen en   a. *bright*

2. 一万円 ichiman en   b. *1,000 yen*

3. 地味 jimi   c. *to keep*

Expressing the completion
of an action and attempts

Before and *after*: 前に mae
ni and 後で ato de

4. 明るい akarui

d. *warm*

5. 軽い karui

e. *sober, quiet (color)*

6. 暑い atsui

f. *10,000 yen*

7. 暖かい atatakai

g. *light*

8. 思う omou

h. *hot*

9. 探す sagasu

i. *to look for*

10. 預かる azukaru

j. *to think*

ANSWER KEY

1. b; 2. f; 3. e; 4. a; 5. g; 6. h; 7. d; 8. j; 9. i; 10. c

Lesson 8: Conversations

In this lesson you'll learn how to:

☐ express *Let's . . . , Why don't we . . . ?, Shall we . . . ?*

☐ express *only*

Conversation 1

▶ 8A Conversation 1 (Japanese: CD 8, Track 9; Japanese and English: CD 8, Track 10)

Ms. Taylor is having lunch with her Japanese colleague Ms. Takahashi at a
Japanese restaurant.

ウェイトレス/Weitoresu:　いらっしゃいませ。二名様ですか。
　　　　　　　　　　　　　Irasshaimase. Nimeesama desu ka.

高橋/**Takahashi:** はい。

Hai.

ウェイトレス/**Weitoresu:** お煙草はお吸いになりますか。

Otabako wa osui ni narimasu ka.

高橋/**Takahashi:** いいえ。

Iie.

ウェイトレス/**Weitoresu:** では、こちらへどうぞ。メニューでございます。

Dewa, kochira e doozo. Menyuu de gozaimasu.

テイラー/**Teiraa:** 小さいけど、きれいなレストランですね。このレストランはとても人気があるから、いつも混んでいるんですよ。

Chiisai kedo, kiree na resutoran desu ne. Kono resutoran wa totemo ninki ga aru kara, itsumo konde iru n desu yo.

高橋/**Takahashi:** ええ。テイラーさんは何が食べたいですか。

Ee. Teiraa san wa nani ga tabetai desu ka.

テイラー/**Teiraa:** ううん、天ぷら定食かコロッケ定食がいいかしら。

Uun, tenpura teishoku ka korokke teishoku ga ii kashira.

高橋/**Takahashi:** 私はうな重かすし定食がいいかなあ?

Watashi wa unajuu ka sushi teishoku ga ii ka naa?

テイラー/**Teiraa:** うな重はどんな料理ですか。

Unajuu wa donna ryoori desu ka.

高橋/**Takahashi:** ご飯の上にうなぎが載っているんですよ。実は先週ここでうな重を食べたんですけど、とてもおいしかったです。一度食べてみたらどうですか。

Gohan no ue ni unagi ga notte iru n desu yo. Jitsu wa senshuu koko de unajuu o tabeta n desu kedo, totemo oishikatta desu. Ichido tabete mitara doo desu ka.

テイラー/**Teiraa:** そうですね。じゃあ、今日はうな重にします。

Soo desu ne. Jaa, kyoo wa unajuu ni shimasu.

Unit 2 Lesson 8: Conversations

Giving and receiving verbs

Adjectives: Past tense, affirmative
and negative form

Expressing the completion
of an action and attempts

Before and *after*: 前に mae
ni and 後で ato de

高橋/Takahashi:	私は今日はすし定食にします。うな重は定食じゃないか ら、お味噌汁を注文したらどうですか。
	Watashi wa kyoo wa sushi teeshoku ni shimasu. Unajuu wa teeshoku ja nai kara, omisoshiru o chuumon shitara doo desu ka.
テイラー/Teiraa:	そうですね。サラダも注文しましょうか。
	Soo desu ne. Sarada mo chuumon shimashoo ka.
高橋/Takahashi:	サラダは、もし良かったら、私のを半分あげます。先週 サラダを注文したら、とても量が多かったんです。
	Sarada wa, moshi yokattara, watashi no o hanbun agemasu. Senshuu sarada o chuumonshitara, totemo ryoo ga ookatta n desu.
テイラー/Teiraa:	じゃあ、そうします。飲み物も注文しますか。
	Jaa, soo shimasu. Nomimono mo chuumon shimasu ka.
高橋/Takahashi:	えっと、時間があったら、このレストランを出た後で、 喫茶店でコーヒーでも飲みませんか。
	Etto, jikan ga attara, kono resutoran o deta ato de, kissaten de koohii demo nomimasen ka.
テイラー/Teiraa:	そうですね。ここは混んでいるから、後で喫茶店に行きま しょう。
	Soo desu ne. Koko wa konde iru kara, ato de kissaten ni ikimashoo.
高橋/Takahashi:	じゃあ、注文しましょうか。
	Jaa, chuumonshimashoo ka.
テイラー/Teiraa:	ええ、注文しましょう。
	Ee, chuumonshimashoo.

Waitress:	*Welcome. Two people?*
Takahashi:	*Yes.*
Waitress:	*Do you (lit., will you) smoke?*
Takahashi:	*No.*

Expressing desires:
たい tai (past tense)

Waitress:	*Then, this way, please. Here is the menu.*
Taylor:	*It's a small but pretty restaurant, isn't it? This restaurant is very popular, so it's always crowded.*
Takahashi:	*Yes. What do you want to eat, Ms. Taylor?*
Taylor:	*Well, I wonder if prix fixe tempura or croquette meals are good.*
Takahashi:	*I wonder if the prix fixe unajuu or sushi meals are good.*
Taylor:	*What kind of dish is unajuu?*
Takahashi:	*It's eel placed over rice. Actually, I ate unajuu here last week, and it was very delicious. How about if you try it once?*
Taylor:	*Yes, then I will have unajuu today.*
Takahashi:	*I will have the prix fixe sushi meal today. Since unajuu is not a prix fixe meal, how about ordering a miso soup?*
Taylor:	*Yes, right. Should I order a salad, too?*
Takahashi:	*As for the salad, if you'd like (lit., it's okay with you), I'll give you half of mine. When I ordered the salad last week, it was pretty big.*
Taylor:	*Yes, then I will do so. Are we going to order drinks, too?*
Takahashi:	*Well, if we have time, after (lit., we leave) the restaurant, why don't we have coffee or something like that at a café?*
Taylor:	*That's good. It's crowded here, so let's go to a café later.*
Takahashi:	*Then, shall we order?*
Taylor:	*Yes, let's order.*

✎ Conversation Practice 1

Fill in the blanks in the following sentences with the missing words. If you're
unsure of the answer, listen to the conversation one more time.

1. このレストランは小さいですが、＿＿＿＿＿＿＿ です。

    Kono resutoran wa chiisai desu ga ＿＿＿＿＿＿＿ **desu.**

Expressing the completion
of an action and attempts

Before and *after*: 前に mae
ni and 後で ato de

2. このレストランはとても _____ から、いつも混んでいます。

Kono resutoran wa totemo _____ kara, itsumo

konde imasu.

3. 高橋さんは _____ を注文します。

Takahashi san wa _____ o chuumon

shimasu.

4. テイラーさんはうな重と _____ を注文します。

Teiraa san wa unajuu to _____ o chuumon

shimasu.

5. 高橋さんとテイラーさんはレストランを出た後で、_____ に行きます。

Takahashi san to Teiraa san wa resutoran o deta ato de

_____ ni ikimasu.

ANSWER KEY

1. きれい kiree; 2. 人気がある ninki ga aru; 3. すし定食 sushi teeshoku; 4. (お)味噌汁
(o) misoshiru; 5. 喫茶店 kissaten

Take It Further

かな ka na, かなあ ka naa or かしら kashira are often added to sentences in the
course of a conversation. They can be translated as *I wonder*. They are attached
to the plain-form of verbs, copula です desu and だ da, and their past tense
counterpart でした deshita and だった datta. The expression かしら kashira is
used only by female speakers.

Polite expressions: Honorific and
humble polite forms of verbs

Inviting people: *Let's . . . ,*
Why don't we . . . ?, Shall we . . . ?

Expressing desires:
たい tai (past tense)

Only X: X だけ dake and
X しか shika + negative

Grammar Builder 1

INVITING PEOPLE: *LET'S . . . , WHY DON'T WE . . . ?, SHALL WE . . . ?*

▶ 8B Grammar Builder 1 (CD 8, Track 11)

You already learned how to say *Let's . . .* and *Why don't we . . . ?* in *Essential Japanese*. Let's review these expressions as well as adding the expression *Shall we . . . ?*

Conjunctive form of the verb + ません か **masen ka**	*Why don't we . . . ?*
Conjunctive form of the verb + ましょう か **mashoo ka**	*Shall we . . . ?*
Conjunctive form of the verb + ましょう **mashoo**	*Let's . . . !*

A: 土曜日に一緒に映画を見ませんか。

Doyoobi ni issho ni eega o mimasen ka.

Why don't we see a movie together on Saturday?

B: いいですね。何を見ましょうか。

Ii desu ne. Nani o mimashoo ka.

That's good. What shall we see?

A: この新しい映画はどうですか。

Kono atarashii eega wa doo desu ka.

What about this new movie?

B: ええ、じゃあそれを見ましょう。

Ee, jaa sore o mimashoo.

Yes, then let's see it!

A: 一緒に昼ご飯を食べませんか。

Issho ni hirugohan o tabemasen ka.

Why don't we eat lunch together?

B: ええ、是非。どこで食べましょうか。

Ee, zehi. Doko de tabemashoo ka.

Yes, by all means. Where shall we eat?

A: 会社の前のイタリアレストランはどうですか。

Kaisha no mae no itaria resutoran wa doo desu ka.

What about the Italian restaurant in front of the company?

B: そうですね。じゃあ、そこに行きましょう。

Soo desu ne. Jaa, soko ni ikimashoo.

Yes. Then, let's go there.

A: 明日一緒にテニスをしませんか。

Ashita issho ni tenisu o shimasen ka.

Why don't we play tennis together tomorrow?

B: ええ、喜んで。どこでしましょうか。

Ee, yorokonde. Doko de shimashoo ka.

Yes, I'm glad to. Where shall we play?

Expressing desires:
たい tai (past tense)

Only X: X だけ dake and
X しか shika + negative

A: 駅の向かいの公園はどうですか。

Eki no mukai no kooen wa doo desu ka.

What about the park across from the station?

B: そうですね。そうしましょう。

Soo desu ne. Soo shimashoo.

Yes. Let's do so!

Question words such as 何 nani, どこ doko, 誰 dare, and いつ itsu can be combined with ましょうか mashoo ka (*shall we*), but not with ませんか masen ka (*why don't we*) and ましょう mashoo (*let's*), just as in English. Also, ましょうか mashoo ka can be translated as *Shall I ... ?* depending on the context.

A: 部長、そのレポートは私がお書きいたしましょうか。

Buchoo, sono repooto wa watashi ga okakiitashimashoo ka.

Division Manager, shall I write that report?

B: じゃあ、お願いします。

Jaa, onegaishimasu.

Sure, please.

✎ Work Out 1

Translate the following sentences into Japanese using the words inside the parentheses. You will also need to add the appropriate particles.

1. *Why don't we listen to the music together?*
   (音楽 ongaku, 一緒に issho ni, 聞きませんか kikimasen ka)

---

2. *What kind of music shall we listen to?*

（音楽 ongaku, どんな donna, 聞きましょうか kikimashoo ka）

3. *Let's listen to Japanese music!*

（聞きましょう kikimashoo, 音楽 ongaku, 日本 nihon）

4. *Why don't we talk at a café?*

（喫茶店 kissaten, 話しませんか hanashimasen ka）

5. *Which café shall we go?*

（行きましょうか ikimashoo ka, 喫茶店 kissaten, どの dono）

6. *Let's go to the café next to the university.*

（大学 daigaku, 行きましょう ikimashoo, 喫茶店 kissaten, 隣 tonari）

7. *Why don't we make sushi together?*

（すし sushi, 作りませんか tsukurimasen ka, 一緒に issho ni）

8. *When shall we make it?*

（作りましょうか tsukurimashoo ka, いつ itsu）

Expressing desires:
たい tai (past tense)

Only X: X だけ dake and
X しか shika + negative

9. *Let's make sushi on Sunday!*

(作りましょう tsukurimashoo, すし sushi, 日曜日 nichiyoobi)

10. *Why don't we buy a new TV?*

(テレビ terebi, 買いませんか kaimasen ka, 新しい atarashii)

11. *Where shall we buy it?*

(買いましょうか kaimashoo ka, どこ doko)

12. *Let's buy a TV at the department store!*

(テレビ terebi, デパート depaato, 買いましょう kaimashoo)

ANSWER KEY

1. 一緒に音楽を聞きませんか。Issho ni ongaku o kikimasen ka. 2. どんな音楽を聞きましょうか。
Donna ongaku o kikimashoo ka. 3. 日本の音楽を聞きましょう。Nihon no ongaku o kikimashoo.
4. 喫茶店で話しませんか。Kissaten de hanashimasen ka. 5. どの喫茶店[へ/に]行きましょうか。
Dono kissaten [e/ni] ikimashoo ka. 6. 大学の隣の喫茶店[へ/に]行きましょう。Daigaku no tonari
no kissaten [e/ni] ikimashoo. 7. 一緒にすしを作りませんか。Issho ni sushi o tsukurimasen ka.
8. いつ作りましょうか。Itsu tsukurimashoo ka. 9. 日曜日にすしを作りましょう。Nichiyoobi ni
sushi o tsukurimashoo. 10. 新しいテレビを買いませんか。Atarashii terebi o kaimasen ka.
11. どこで買いましょうか。Doko de kaimashoo ka. 12. デパートでテレビを買いましょう。Depaato
de terebi o kaimashoo.

◀ Conversation 2

▶ 8C Conversation 2 (Japanese: CD 8, Track 12; Japanese and English: CD 8, Track 13)

Mr. Kato has brought his business partner Mr. Smith to a seafood restaurant in
Tokyo. They have just finished their meal.

Giving and receiving verbs

Adjectives: Past tense, affirmative
and negative form

Expressing the completion
of an action and attempts

Before and *after*: 前に mae
ni and 後で ato de

加藤/Katoo:
その魚料理はいかがでしたか。

Sono sakana ryoori wa ikaga deshita ka.

スミス/Sumisu:
とてもおいしかったですよ。この和風サラダもおいしか
ったです。

Totemo oishikatta desu yo. Kono wafuu sarada mo
oishikatta desu.

加藤/Katoo:
それは良かった。一度このレストランへ来てみたかったん
ですが、なかなかチャンスがなかったんです。

Sore wa yokatta. Ichido kono resutoran e kite mitakatta n
desu ga, nakanaka chansu ga nakatta n desu.

スミス/Sumisu:
そうですか。その帆立の料理はどうでしたか。

Soo desu ka. Sono hotate no ryoori wa doo deshita ka.

加藤/Katoo:
この帆立の料理もおいしかったですよ。えびやいかやムー
ル貝も入っていて、量が多かったんですが、全部食べてし
まいました。

Kono hotate no ryoori mo oishikatta desu yo. Ebi ya ika
ya muurugai mo haitte ite, ryoo ga ookatta n desu ga,
zenbu tabete shimaimashita.

スミス/Sumisu:
でも、私も加藤さんの料理を少しいただきましたから。

Demo, watashi mo Kato san no ryoori o sukoshi
itadakimashita kara.

加藤/Katoo:
ワインをもう少し召し上がりませんか。

Wain o moo sukoshi meshiagarimasen ka.

スミス/Sumisu:
実は昨日少し飲みすぎてしまったんです。昨日、小田部長
にお目にかかった時に、部長がビール券をくださったんで
す。それで、ホテルの近くでビールを1ダース買って、全部
飲んでしまいました。

Jitsu wa kinoo sukoshi nomisugite shimatta n desu.
Kinoo, Oda buchoo ni omenikakatta toki ni, buchoo ga
biiruken o kudasatta n desu. Sorede, hoteru no chikaku
de biiru o ichi daasu katte, zenbu nonde shimaimashita.

olite expressions: Honorific and
humble polite forms of verbs

Inviting people: *Let's ...* ,
Why don't we ... ?, Shall we ... ?

Expressing desires:
たい tai (past tense)

Only X: X だけ dake and
X しか shika + negative

加藤/Katoo:
そうですか。じゃあ、デザートとコーヒーでも注文しま
せんか。

Soo desu ka. Jaa, dezaato to koohii demo
chuumonshimasen ka.

スミス/Sumisu:
ええ、冷たいデザートが食べたいですね。

Ee, tsumetai dezaato ga tabetai desu ne.

加藤/Katoo:
えっと、もう一度メニューを見てみましょう。ケーキし
かないですね。

Etto, moo ichido menyuu o mite mimashoo. Keeki shika
nai desu ne.

スミス/Sumisu:
ううん、アイスクリームかシャーベットが食べたかったんで
すけど。それじゃあ、私はコーヒーだけ注文します。

Uun, aisukuriimu ka shaabetto ga tabetakatta
n desu kedo. Sore jaa, watashi wa koohii dake
chuuomonshimasu.

加藤/Katoo:
じゃあ、私はチョコレートケーキと紅茶にします。

Jaa, watashi wa chokoreeto keeki to koocha ni shimasu.

Kato:	How was that fish dish?
Smith:	It was really delicious. This Japanese-style salad was also delicious.
Kato:	That's good. I wanted to try and come to this restaurant once, but I didn't have a chance (until now).
Smith:	I see. How was that scallop dish?
Kato:	The scallop dish was also good. Shrimp, cuttlefish and mussels were also in the dish, among other things; and it was a big dish, but I finished eating all.
Smith:	But, I also had a little bit of your dish, so...
Kato:	Wouldn't you like to have a little more wine?

Giving and receiving verbs

Adjectives: Past tense, affirmative
and negative form

Expressing the completion
of an action and attempts

Before and *after*: 前に mae
ni and 後で ato de

Smith:	Actually, I had a little too much to drink yesterday. When I saw the Division Manager Oda, he/she gave me a beer gift certificate, so I bought a dozen bottles of beer near the hotel and ended up drinking everything.
Kato:	I see. Then, why don't we order dessert and coffee or something like that?
Smith:	Yes, I'd like (lit., to eat) a cold dessert.
Kato:	Well, let's take a look at the menu again. There are only cakes.
Smith:	Well, I wanted to eat ice cream or sorbet, but… Then, I will order only coffee.
Kato:	Then, I will have a chocolate cake and tea.

✎ Conversation Practice 2

Fill in the blanks in the following sentences with the missing words. If you're unsure of the answer, listen to the conversation one more time.

1. スミスさんは _____ と和風サラダを食べました。

   Sumisu san wa _____ to wafuu sarada o
   tabemashita.

2. 加藤さんの帆立の料理は _____ が多かったです。

   Katoo san no hotate no ryoori wa _____ ga ookatta desu.

3. 昨日、スミスさんは _____ を1ダース買って飲みました。

   Kinoo, sumisu san wa _____ o ichi daasu katte nomimashita.

4. ケーキしかないので、スミスさんは _____ だけ注文します。

   Keeki shika nainode, Sumisu san wa _____ dake chuumon
   shimasu.

olite expressions: Honorific and
humble polite forms of verbs

Inviting people: *Let's . . . ,
Why don't we . . . ?, Shall we . . . ?*

Expressing desires:
たい tai (past tense)

Only X: X だけ dake and
X しか shika + negative

5. 加藤^{か とう}さんはチョコレートケーキと ＿＿＿＿＿＿＿＿＿ を注文^{ちゅうもん}します。

Katoo san wa chokoreeto keeki o to ＿＿＿＿＿＿＿＿＿ o chuumon

shimasu.

ANSWER KEY
1. 魚料理^{さかなりょうり} sakana ryoori; 2. 量^{りょう} ryoo; 3. ビール biiru; 4. コーヒー koohii; 5. 紅茶^{こうちゃ} koocha

Grammar Builder 2

ONLY X: X だけ DAKE AND X しか SHIKA + NEGATIVE

▶ 8D Grammar Builder 2 (CD 8, Track 14)

Let's learn how to say *only X*. There are two different expressions you can use:

X だけ dake	*only X*
X しか shika + *negative*	*only X, nothing/no one but X*

It is important to know that だけ dake and しか shika replace particles が ga, は wa and を o, but do not replace other particles such as へ e, に ni, で de, and と to.

野菜^{や さい}だけ食^たべます。

Yasai dake tabemasu.

I eat only vegetables.

野菜^{や さい}しか食^たべません。

Yasai shika tabemasen.

I eat nothing but vegetables.

五人^{ご にん}だけパーティーに来^きました。

Gonin dake paatii ni kimashita.

Only five people came to the party.

Unit 2 Lesson 8: Conversations   179

Giving and receiving verbs

Adjectives: Past tense, affirmative
and negative form

Expressing the completion
of an action and attempts

Before and *after*: 前に mae
ni and 後で ato de

五人しかパーティーに来ませんでした。

Gonin shika paatii ni kimasen deshita.

No one else but five people came to the party.

月曜日と水曜日と金曜日にだけ働きます。

Getsuyoobi to suiyoobi to kin-yoobi ni dake hatarakimasu.

I work only on Mondays, Wednesday, and Fridays.

月曜日と水曜日と金曜日にしか働きません。

Getsuyoobi to suiyoobi to kin-yoobi ni shika hatarakimasen.

I work on no other days but on Mondays, Wednesdays and Fridays.

昨日高橋さんとだけ話しました。

Kinoo Takahashi san to dake hanashimashita.

Yesterday, I only talked with Mr./Ms. Takahashi.

昨日高橋さんとしか話しませんでした。

Kinoo Takahashi san to shika hanashimasen deshita.

Yesterday, I talked with no one but Mr./Ms. Takahashi.

Even though the two expressions can usually be used interchangeably, there is a slight difference in the nuance. In most cases, when X しか **shika** + negative is used there is an implication that the speaker thinks the amount insufficient, whereas in the case of だけ **dake** a speaker is just stating fact, and there is no such implication. For instance, the sentence, 五人しかパーティーに来ませんでした。**Gonin shika paatii ni kimasen deshita.** (*No one else but five people came to the party*), implies that the speaker thinks having only five people at a party was not enough. On the other hand, the sentence, 五人だけパーティーに来ました。**Gonin dake paatii ni kimashita.** (*Only five people came to the party*), is just stating the fact that five people came to the party.

Polite expressions: Honorific and humble polite forms of verbs

Inviting people: *Let's ... ,*
Why don't we ... ?, Shall we ... ?

Expressing desires:
たい tai (past tense)

Only X: X だけ dake and
X しか shika + negative

✎ Work Out 2

Rephrase the following sentences using the construction しか shika + negative.

1. ミーティングに田中さんだけ来ました。

   Miitingu ni Tanaka san dake kimashita.

   _____

2. スポーツはテニスだけします。

   Supootsu wa tenisu dake shimasu.

   _____

3. 兄は英語だけ話します。

   Ani wa eego dake hanashimasu.

   _____

4. 日本へ行った時、京都へだけ行きました。

   Nihon e itta toki, kyooto e dake ikimashita.

   _____

5. 今日は経済の勉強だけしました。

   Kyoo wa keezai no benkyoo dake shimashita.

   _____

6. 部長にだけお目にかかりました。

   Buchoo ni dake ome ni kakarimashita.

   _____

7. 今週 林さんとだけテニスをしました。

Konshuu Hayashi san to dake tenisu o shimashita.

_____

8. 居間にだけテレビがあります。

Ima ni dake terebi ga arimasu.

_____

ANSWER KEY

1. ミーティングに田中さんしか来ませんでした。**Miitingu ni Tanaka san shika kimasen deshita.**
2. スポーツはテニスしかしません。**Supootsu wa tenisu shika shimasen.** 3. 兄は英語しか話しません。 **Ani wa eego shika hanashimasen.** 4. 日本へ行った時、京都へしか行きませんでした。**Nihon e itta toki, kyooto e shika ikimasen deshita.** 5. 今日は経済の勉強しかしませんでした。**Kyoo wa keezai no benkyoo shika shimasen deshita.** 6. 部長にしかお目にかかりませんでした。**Buchoo ni shika ome ni kakarimasen deshita.** 7. 今週 林さんとしかテニスをしませんでした。**Konshuu Hayashi san to shika tenisu o shimasen deshita.** 8. 居間にしかテレビがありません。**Ima ni shika terebi ga arimasen.**

✎ Drive It Home

Fill in the blanks with the appropriate words to complete the following sentences.

1. テニスをし _____。

Tenisu o shi _____.

Why don't we play tennis?

2. テニスをし _____。

Tenisu o shi _____.

Shall we play tennis?

Expressing desires:
たい tai (past tense)

Only X: X だけ dake and
X しか shika + negative

3. テニスをし _____ 。

   Tenisu o shi _____ .

   Let's play tennis.

4. 音楽を聞き _____ 。

   Ongaku o kiki _____ .

   Why don't we listen to music?

5. 音楽を聞き _____ 。

   Ongaku o kiki _____ .

   Shall we listen to music?

6. 音楽を聞き _____ 。

   Ongaku o kiki _____ .

   Let's listen to music.

7. 野菜 _____ 食べます。

   Yasai _____ **tabemasu.**

   I eat only vegetables.

8. 野菜 _____ 食べません。

   Yasai _____ **tabemasen.**

   I eat nothing but vegetables.

9. 五人 _____ パーティーに来ました。

   Gonin _____ **paatii ni kimashita.**

   Only five people came to the party.

10. 五人（ごにん）＿＿＿＿＿＿ パーティーに来（き）ませんでした。

Gonin ＿＿＿＿＿＿＿ paatii ni kimasen deshita.

No one else but five people came to the party.

ANSWER KEY

1. ませんか masen ka; 2. ましょうか mashoo ka; 3. ましょう mashoo; 4. ませんか masen ka; 5. ましょうか mashoo ka; 6. ましょう mashoo; 7. だけ dake; 8. しか shika; 9. だけ dake; 10. しか shika

How Did You Do?

Let's see how you did! By now, you should be able to:

☐ express *Let's ...* , *Why don't we ... ?*, *Shall we ... ?* (Still unsure? Jump back to page 171)

☐ express *only* (Still unsure? Jump back to page 179)

Polite expressions: Honorific and
humble polite forms of verbs

Inviting people: *Let's ...* ,
Why don't we ... ?, Shall we ... ?

Expressing desires:
たい tai (past tense)

Only X: X だけ dake and
X しか shika + negative

✎ Word Recall

1. グレー guree	a. *pink*
2. 茶色 chairo	b. *red*
3. 黄色 kiiro	c. *yellow*
4. 緑 midori	d. *blouse*
5. ピンク pinku	e. *green*
6. 青 ao	f. *pants*
7. 赤 aka	g. *blue*
8. セーター seetaa	h. *sweater*
9. ブラウス burausu	i. *grey*
10. パンツ pantsu	j. *brown*

ANSWER KEY

1. i; 2. j; 3. c; 4. e; 5. a; 6. g; 7. b; 8. h; 9. d; 10. f

Don't forget to practice and reinforce what you've
learned by visiting **www.livinglanguage.com/
languagelab** for flashcards, games, and quizzes for
Unit 2!

Unit 2 Essentials

Vocabulary Essentials

Test your knowledge of the key material in this unit by filling in the blanks in the following charts. Once you've completed these pages, you'll have tested your retention, and you'll have your own reference for the most essential vocabulary.

FOOD AND DRINKS

	tempura (fried shrimp, vegetables, etc.)
	eel
	broiled eel on rice
	croquette
	cutlet
	curry
	soy bean paste
	miso soup
	cooked rice, meal
	dish eaten with cooked rice
	food
	dressing
	broiled fish
	boiled fish
	sliced raw fish
	shrimp
	cuttlefish, squid

	octpus
	scallop
	shellfish
	mussel
	dessert
	ice cream
	sherbet
	chocolate cake
	cappuccino
	café au lait

AT A RESTAURANT

	two people (polite)
	tobacco, cigarette
	Japanese style
	Western style
	what kind of meal
	coffee or something like that
	How was it? (polite)
	How was it?

VERBS

	to order
	to give
	to receive

187

	to eat, to drink, to receive (humble polite)
	to eat, to drink (honorific polite)
	to see, to meet (humble polite)
	to be crowded
	to smoke a cigarette
	to be glad to

ADJECTIVES

	cold
	salty

ADVERBS

	actually
	later
	once
	one more time

OTHER USEFUL EXPRESSONS

	chance
	amount
	half
	president of a company
	division manager

	section manager
	if it's okay
	so, for that reason
	by all means, at any cost

Grammar Essentials

Here is a reference of the key grammar that was covered in Unit 2. Make sure you understand the summary and can use all of the grammar it covers.

GIVING AND RECEIVING VERBS

A [が/は] B に X を [あげます/あげる] 。 *(humble polite form:* [さしあげます/さしあげる]*)*
A [ga/wa] B ni X o [agemasu/ageru]. *(humble polite form:* [sashiagemasu/sashiageru]*)*
A gives B X./A gives X to B.
B [が/は] A [に/から] X を [もらいます/もらう] 。 *(humble polite form:* [いただきます/いただく]*)*
B [ga/wa] A [ni/kara] X o [moraimasu/morau]. *(humble polite form:* [itadakimasu/itadaku]*)*
B receives X from A.
A [が/は] B に X を [くれます/くれる] 。 *(honorific form:* [くださいます/くださる]*)* *(B is a speaker or a speaker's in-group member, e.g., family.)*
A [ga/wa] B ni X o [kuremasu/kureru]. *(honorific form:* [kudasaimasu/kudasaru]*)* *(B is a speaker or a speaker's in-group member, e.g., family.)*
A gives B X./A gives X to B.

EXPRESSING THE COMPLETION OF AN ACTION

て Te-*form of verb* + しまいました shimaimashita/しまった shimatta

EXPRESSING AN ATTEMPT

て te-*form of verbs* + みます mimasu/みる miru

ADJECTIVES: PAST TENSE, AFFIRMATIVE AND NEGATIVE FORM

い i-adjectives

POLITE FORM, PAST TENSE		PLAIN FORM, PAST TENSE	
Affirmative	Negative	Affirmative	Negative
良^よかったです yokatta desu (*was/were good*)	良^よく [なかったです/ ありませんでした] yoku [nakatta desu/ arimasen deshita]	良^よかった yokatta	良^よくなかった yoku nakatta
甘^{あま}かったです amakatta desu (*was/were sweet*)	甘^{あま}く [なかったです/ ありませんでした] amaku [nakatta desu/arimasen deshita]	甘^{あま}かった amakatta	甘^{あま}くなかった amaku nakatta
辛^{から}かったです karakatta desu (*was/were spicy*)	辛^{から}く [なかったです/ ありませんでした] karaku [nakatta desu/arimasen deshita]	辛^{から}かった karakatta	辛^{から}くなかった karaku nakatta

POLITE FORM, PAST TENSE		PLAIN FORM, PAST TENSE	
Affirmative	Negative	Affirmative	Negative
広^{ひろ}かったです hirokatta desu *(was/were spacious)*	広^{ひろ}く [なかったです/ありませんでした] hiroku [nakatta desu/arimasen deshita]	広^{ひろ}かった hirokatta	広^{ひろ}くなかった hiroku nakatta
難^{むずか}しかったです muzukashi katta desu *(was/were difficult)*	難^{むずか}しく [なかったです/ありませんでした] muzukashiku [nakatta desu/arimasen deshita]	難^{むずか}しかった muzukashi katta	難^{むずか}しくなかった muzukashiku nakatta

な na-adjectives

POLITE FORM, PAST TENSE		PLAIN FORM, PAST TENSE	
Affirmative	Negative	Affirmative	Negative
暇^{ひま}でした hima deshita *(had a lot of free time)*	暇^{ひま} [じゃ/では] [なかったです/ありませんでした] hima [ja/de wa] [nakatta desu/arimasen deshita]	暇^{ひま}だった hima datta	暇^{ひま} [じゃ/では]なかった hima [ja/de wa] nakatta
きれいでした kiree deshita *(was beautiful, was clean)*	きれい [じゃ/では] [なかったです/ありませんでした] kiree [ja/de wa] [nakatta desu/arimasen deshita]	きれいだった kiree datta	きれい [じゃ/では]なかった kiree [ja/de wa] nakatta

POLITE FORM, PAST TENSE		PLAIN FORM, PAST TENSE	
Affirmative	Negative	Affirmative	Negative
しんせつ 親切でした shinsetsu deshita *(was kind, was generous)*	しんせつ 親切 [じゃ/では] [なかったです/ ありませんでした] shinsetsu [ja/ de wa] [nakatta desu/arimasen deshita]	しんせつ 親切だった shinsetsu datta	しんせつ 親切 [じゃ/では] なかった shinsetsu [ja/de wa] nakatta
ふ べん 不便でした fuben deshita *(was inconvenient)*	ふ べん 不便 [じゃ/では] [なかったです/ ありませんでした] fuben [ja/de wa] [nakatta desu/ arimasen deshita]	ふ べん 不便だった fuben datta	ふ べん 不便 [じゃ/では] なかった fuben [ja/de wa] nakatta

BEFORE AND *AFTER*: 前に MAE NI AND 後で ATO DE

Noun + の *no/verb (plain non-past* まえ *affirmative) +* 前に *mae ni*	*before …*
Noun + の *no/verb (plain past* あと *affirmative) +* 後 *(*で*) ato (de)*	*after …*

POLITE EXPRESSIONS: HONORIFIC AND HUMBLE POLITE FORMS OF VERBS

Verbs with special polite forms:

ます MASU-FORM	HONORIFIC FORM	HUMBLE FORM
行きます ikimasu (*go*) *and* 来ます kimasu (*come*)	いらっしゃいます irasshaimasu いらっしゃる irassharu	参ります mairimasu 参る mairu
います imasu (*exist*)	いらっしゃいます irasshaimasu いらっしゃる irassharu	おります orimasu おる oru
します shimasu (*do*)	なさいます nasaimasu なさる nasaru	いたします itashimasu いたす itasu
食べます tabemasu (*eat*) *or* 飲みます omimasu (*drink*)	召し上がります meshiagarimasu 召し上がる meshiagaru	いただきます itadakimasu いただく itadaku
見ます mimasu (*see, look, watch*)	ご覧になります goran ni narimasu ご覧になる goran ni naru	拝見します haikenshimasu 拝見する haikensuru

ます MASU-FORM	HONORIFIC FORM	HUMBLE FORM
言います iimasu (say)	おっしゃいます osshaimasu おっしゃる ossharu	申します mooshimasu 申す moosu

Other verbs:

Honorific form	お o + conjunctive form of verb + になります ni narimasu/になる ni naru
Humble form	お o + conjunctive form of verb + します shimasu/する suru or いたします itashimasu/いたす itasu

EXPRESSING DESIRES: たい TAI (PAST TENSE)

POLITE FORM, PAST TENSE		PLAIN FORM, PAST TENSE	
Affirmative	Negative	Affirmative	Negative
たかったです takatta desu (wanted to)	たくなかったです taku nakatta desu たくありませんでした taku arimasen deshita	たかった takatta	たくなかった taku nakatta

INVITING PEOPLE: LET'S ... , WHY DON'T WE ... ?, SHALL WE ... ?

Conjunctive form of the verb + ません か masen ka	Why don't we ...?
Conjunctive form of the verb + ましょう か mashoo ka	Shall we ...?
Conjunctive form of the verb + ましょう mashoo	Let's ...!

ONLY X: だけ DAKE AND X しか SHIKA + NEGATIVE

X だけ dake	only X
X しか shika + negative	only X, nothing/no one but X

Unit 2 Quiz

Let's put the most essential Japanese words and grammar points you've learned so far to practice in a few exercises. It's important to be sure that you've mastered this material before you move on. Score yourself at the end of the review and see if you need to go back for more practice, or if you're ready to move on to Unit 3.

A. Fill in the blanks with the appropriate giving and receiving verbs that are listed below. Change them into their appropriate forms as necessary.

あげます agemasu, さしあげます sashiagemasu, もらいます moraimasu, いただきます itadakimasu, くれます kuremasu, くださいます kudasaimasu

1. 私は先生にボールペンを _____ 。

   Watashi wa sensee ni boorupen o

   _____ .

   I gave a teacher a ballpoint pen.

2. 私は友達に赤い鞄を _____ 。

   Watashi wa tomodachi ni akai kaban o_____ .

   I received a red bag from my friend.

3. 山田先生が兄にその辞書を _____ 。

やまだ せんせい あに じしょ

Yamada sensee ga ani ni sono jisho o

_____.

Professor Yamada gave that dictionary to my older brother.

4. リーさんは渡辺さんにチョコレートを _____ 。

わたなべ

Rii san wa Watanabe san ni chokoreeto o _____.

Mr./Ms. Lee gave Mr./Ms. Watanabe chocolates.

5. 妹は英語の先生から辞書を _____ 。

いもうと えいご せんせい じしょ

Imooto wa eego no sensee kara jisho o

_____.

My younger sister received a dictionary from her English teacher.

B. Based on the English translation, complete the following sentences by using the verbs or adjectives in parentheses.

1. チョコレートケーキを三つ _____ 。(食べる)

みっ た

Chokoreeto keeki o mittsu _____

_____. (taberu)

I ended up eating three slices of chocolate cake.

2. 日本人の友達と日本語で _____ 。(話す)

に ほんじん ともだち に ほん ご はな

Nihonjin no tomodachi to nihongo de _____

_____. (hanasu)

I tried speaking with my Japanese friend(s) in Japanese (to see how it goes).

3. チョコレートケーキは＿＿＿＿＿＿ですけど、チーズケーキはあまり＿＿＿＿＿

   ＿＿＿＿＿です。(<ruby>甘<rt>あま</rt></ruby>い)

   Chokoreeto keeki wa ＿＿＿＿＿＿＿＿ desu kedo, chiizu keeki wa

   amari ＿＿＿＿＿＿＿＿＿ desu. (amai)

   The chocolate cake was sweet, but the cheesecake was not so sweet.

4. グレーのセーターが＿＿＿＿＿＿です。(<ruby>買<rt>か</rt></ruby>う)

   Guree no seetaa ga ＿＿＿＿＿＿＿＿ desu. (kau)

   I wanted to buy a gray sweater.

5. ミーティングに＿＿＿＿＿＿でした。(<ruby>出<rt>で</rt></ruby>る)

   Miitingu ni ＿＿＿＿＿＿＿＿ deshita. (deru)

   I didn't want to attend the meeting.

6. <ruby>土曜日<rt>どようび</rt></ruby>に<ruby>一緒<rt>いっしょ</rt></ruby>に<ruby>映画<rt>えいが</rt></ruby>を＿＿＿＿＿＿。(<ruby>見<rt>み</rt></ruby>る)

   Doyoobi ni issho ni eega o ＿＿＿＿＿＿＿＿. (miru)

   Why don't we see a movie together on Saturday?

7. いいですね。<ruby>何<rt>なに</rt></ruby>を＿＿＿＿＿＿。(<ruby>見<rt>み</rt></ruby>る)

   Ii desu ne. Nani o ＿＿＿＿＿＿＿＿. (miru)

   That's good. What shall we see?

8. この<ruby>新<rt>あたら</rt></ruby>しい<ruby>映画<rt>えいが</rt></ruby>を＿＿＿＿＿＿。(<ruby>見<rt>み</rt></ruby>る)

   Kono atarashii eega o ＿＿＿＿＿＿＿＿. (miru)

   Let's see this new movie!

C. Fill in the blanks with either だけ dake or しか shika.

1. <ruby>昨日高橋<rt>きのうたかはし</rt></ruby>さんと＿＿＿＿＿<ruby>話<rt>はな</rt></ruby>しました。

   Kinoo Takahashi san to ＿＿＿＿＿ hanashimashita.

   Yesterday, I only talked with Mr./Ms. Takahashi.

2. 昨日高橋さんと _____ 話しませんでした。

きのう たかはし はな

Kinoo Takahashi san to _____ hanashimasen deshita.

Yesterday, I talked with no one but Mr./Ms. Takahashi.

D. Fill in the blanks with the appropriate phrases based on the English translation.

1. _____ 宿題をしてしまいました。

しゅくだい

_____ shukudai o shite shimaimashita.

I have done my homework before dinner.

2. _____ 宿題をしてしまいました。

しゅくだい

_____ shukudai o shite shimaimashita.

I have done my homework before eating dinner.

3. _____ 家へ帰ります。

うち かえ

_____ uchi e kaerimasu.

I will go home after the movie.

4. _____ 家へ帰ります。

うち かえ

_____ uchi e kaerimasu.

I will go home after watching the movie.

E. Read the following short dialogue and fill in the blanks with either いらっしゃいます irasshaimasu or おります orimasu.

1. 社員: 部長はお子さんは _____ か。

しゃいん ふちょう こ

Buchoo wa okosan wa _____ ka.

Do you have children, Division Manager?

2. 部長: ええ。息子が一人いますよ。田中さんは？
<small>ぶちょう</small> <small>むすこ</small> <small>ひとり</small> <small>たなか</small>

Ee. Musuko ga hitori imasu yo. Tanaka san wa?

Yes. I have one son. What about you, Mr. Tanaka?

3. 社員: 私は娘が二人 ＿＿＿＿＿＿＿＿＿＿＿＿＿＿。
<small>しゃいん</small> <small>わたし</small> <small>むすめ</small> <small>ふたり</small>

Watashi wa musume ga futari ＿＿＿＿＿＿＿＿＿＿＿＿.

I have two daughters.

ANSWER KEY

A. 1. さしあげました sashiagemashita; 2. もらいました moraimashita; 3. くださいました kudasaimashita; 4. あげました agemashita; 5. いただきました itadakimashita

B. 1. 食べてしまいました tabete shimaimashita; 2. 話してみました hanashite mimashita; 3. 甘かった amakatta, 甘くなかった amaku nakatta; 4. 買いたかった kaitakatta; 5. 出たくありません detaku arimasen; 6. 見ませんか mimasen ka; 7. 見ましょうか mimashoo ka; 8. 見ましょう mimashoo

C. 1. だけ dake; 2. しか shika

D. 1. [晩ご飯/夕飯/夕食] の前に [Bangohan/Yuuhan/Yuushoku] no mae ni; 2. [晩ご/夕飯/夕食] を食べる前に [Bangohan/Yuuhan/Yuushoku] o taberu mae ni; 3. 映画の後 (で) Eega no ato (de); 4. 映画を見た後 (で) Eega o mita ato (de)

E. 1. いらっしゃいます irasshaimasu, 3. おります orimasu

How Did You Do?

Give yourself a point for every correct answer, then use the following key to tell whether you're ready to move on:

0-7 points: It's probably a good idea to go back through the lesson again. You may be moving too quickly, or there may be too much "down time" between your contact with Japanese. Remember that it's better to spend 30 minutes with Japanese three or four times a week than it is to spend two or three hours just once a week. Find a pace that's comfortable for you, and spread your contact hours out as much as you can.

8-12 points: You would benefit from a review before moving on. Go back and spend a little more time on the specific points that gave you trouble. Re-read the Grammar Builder sections that were difficult, and do the work out one more time. Don't forget about the online supplemental practice material, either. Go to **www.livinglanguage.com/languagelab** for games and quizzes that will reinforce the material from this unit.

13-17 points: Good job! There are just a few points that you could consider reviewing before moving on. If you haven't worked with the games and quizzes on **www.livinglanguage.com/languagelab**, please give them a try.

18-20 points: Great! You're ready to move on to the next unit.

[ ][ ] points

Question words
+ か ka and も mo

Potential form of verbs:
Can do and *be able to do*

Creating nouns from verbs:
nominalizer の no and こと koto

To want + object, person:
X が欲しい ga hoshii

Unit 3:
Sports and Leisure

In Unit 3, you will learn how to talk about your favorite sports and hobbies. Also, you'll learn some key expressions you can use when asking other people questions about their favorite sports and hobbies. By the end `of the unit, you'll be able to:

- ☐ use key vocabulary related to sports and hobbies
- ☐ express *something, someone, somewhere* and *nothing, nobody* and *nowhere*
- ☐ create nouns out of verbs
- ☐ express *can do* and *be able to do*
- ☐ express *to want X*
- ☐ compare two items using *A is more X than B*
- ☐ compare three or more items using *A is the most X among D*
- ☐ talk about past experiences
- ☐ use relative clauses

Lesson 9: Words

- ☐ In this lesson you'll learn how to:
- ☐ use key vocabulary related to sports and hobbies

☐ express *something, someone, somewhere* and *nothing, nobody* and *nowhere*

☐ create nouns out of verbs

Word Builder 1

▶ 9A Word Builder 1 (CD 8, Track 15)

うんどう 運動	undoo	*exercise(s)*
サッカー	sakkaa	*soccer*
バレーボール	bareebooru	*volleyball*
すいえい 水泳	suiee	*swimming*
じゅうどう 柔道	juudoo	*judo*
けんどう 剣道	kendoo	*kendo*
テニスコート	tenisu kooto	*tennis court*
クラブ	kurabu	*club*
し あい 試合	shiai	*game (sports)*
こん ど 今度	kondo	*next time, this time, shortly*
だい す 大好き	daisuki	*like a lot*
じょうず 上手	joozu	*skillful*
へ た 下手	heta	*unskillful*
とく い 得意	tokui	*to be good at*
にが て 苦手	nigate	*to be bad at*
やっぱり	yappari	*after all, as expected*

Question words
+ か ka and も mo

Potential form of verbs:
Can do and *be able to do*

Creating nouns from verbs:
nominalizer の no and こと koto

To want + object, person:
X が欲しい ga hoshii

うんどう うんどう 運動します/運動する	undooshimasu/ undoosuru	*to exercise*
およ およ 泳ぎます/泳ぐ	oyogimasu/oyogu	*to swim*
なら なら 習います/習う	naraimasu/narau	*to take lessons on*
やります/やる	yarimasu/yaru	*to do*

✎ Word Practice 1

Translate the following words or phrases into Japanese.

1. *exercise(s)* _____

2. *swimming* _____

3. *game (of sport)* _____

4. *next time, this time, shortly* _____

5. *like a lot* _____

6. *skillful* _____

7. *unskillful* _____

8. *to be good at* _____

9. *to be bad at* _____

10. *after all, as expected* _____

ANSWER KEY
うんどう すいえい しあい こんど だいす じょうず へた
1. 運動 undoo; 2. 水泳 suiee; 3. 試合 shiai; 4. 今度 kondo; 5. 大好き daisuki; 6. 上手 joozu; 7. 下手
とくい にがて
heta; 8. 得意 tokui; 9. 苦手 nigate; 10. やっぱり yappari

Take It Further

やります Yarimasu (*do*) is less polite than します shimasu (*do*). As discussed in Lesson 5, やります yarimasu can be used in the sense of *give*, but only when the indirect object refers to animals and plants. The use of やります yarimasu in the sense of *do* is not so limited, and やります yarimasu and します shimasu are often used interchangeably.

Grammar Builder 1

QUESTION WORDS + か KA AND も MO

▶ 9B Grammar Builder 1 (CD 8, Track 16)

Let's learn how to say *something, someone, somewhere* and *nothing, nobody* and *nowhere*.

何^{なに}か	nani ka	*something*
誰^{だれ}か	dare ka	*someone*
どこか	doko ka	*somewhere*
何^{なに}も + *negative*	nani mo + *negative*	*nothing*
誰^{だれ}も + *negative*	dare mo + *negative*	*no one, nobody*
どこも + *negative*	doko mo + *negative*	*nowhere*

Let's look at how these expressions are used. Notice that the particles か ka and も mo replace particles が ga, は wa, and を o.

A: 何^{なに}か特技^{とくぎ}がありますか。

Nani ka tokugi (*special skills*) ga arimasu ka.

Do you have any special skills?

Question words
+ か ka and も mo

Potential form of verbs:
Can do and *be able to do*

Creating nouns from verbs:
nominalizer の no and こと koto

To want + object, person:
X が欲しい ga hoshii

B: いいえ、何もありません。

Iie, nani mo arimasen.

No, I don't have any.

A: 何か食べたいですか。

Nani ka tabetai desu ka.

Do you want to eat anything?

B: いいえ、何も食べたくありません。

Iie, nani mo tabetaku arimasen.

No, I don't want to eat anything.

A: 昨日誰か来ましたか。

Kinoo dare ka kimashita ka.

Did anyone come yesterday?

B: いいえ、誰も来ませんでした。

Iie, dare mo kimasen deshita.

No, no one came.

The particles か ka and も mo do not replace any particles other than が ga, は wa, and を o. Pay special attention to the position of particles in affirmative and negative sentences.

A: 週末にどこかへ行きましたか。

Shuumatsu ni doko ka e ikimashita ka.

Did you go anywhere on weekends?

B: いいえ、どこへも行きませんでした。

Iie, doko e mo ikimasen deshita.

No, I didn't go anywhere.

A: 昨日誰かに会いましたか。

Kinoo dare ka ni aimashita ka.

Did you meet anyone yesterday?

B: いいえ、誰にも会いませんでした。

Iie, dare ni mo aimasen deshita.

No, I didn't meet anyone.

A: 今誰かと話したいですか。

Ima dare ka to hanashitai desu ka.

Do you want to talk with someone now?

B: いいえ、誰とも話したくありません。

Iie, dare to mo hanashitaku arimasen.

No, I don't want to talk with anyone.

As you can see, the particles へ e, に ni, and と to follow か ka in affirmative sentences (e.g., 誰かと話しましたか。Dare ka to hanashimashita ka.), but come between the question word and particle も mo in negative sentences (e.g., 誰とも話しませんでした。Dare to mo hanashimasen deshita.).

✎ Work Out 1

Fill in the blanks with the appropriate expressions to complete the sentences.

1. ＿＿＿＿＿＿＿映画が見たいですか。

   ＿＿＿＿＿＿＿＿ eega ga mitai desu ka.

   Do you want to see any movies?

2. ＿＿＿＿＿＿＿見たくありません。

   ＿＿＿＿＿＿＿＿ mitaku arimasen.

   I don't want to see any.

3. 昨日＿＿＿＿＿＿＿＿行きましたか。

   Kinoo ＿＿＿＿＿＿＿＿＿＿ ikimashita ka.

   Did you go anywhere yesterday?

4. いいえ、＿＿＿＿＿＿＿＿行きませんでした。

   Iie, ＿＿＿＿＿＿＿＿＿＿ ikimasen deshita.

   No, I didn't go anywhere.

5. 明日＿＿＿＿＿＿＿会いますか。

   Ashita ＿＿＿＿＿＿＿＿＿＿ aimasu ka.

   Will you see anyone tomorrow?

6. いいえ、＿＿＿＿＿＿＿会いません。

   Iie, ＿＿＿＿＿＿＿＿＿＿ aimasen.

   No, I won't see anyone.

ANSWER KEY
1. 何か Nani ka; 2. 何も Nani mo; 3. どこか [へ/に] doko ka [e/ni]; 4. どこ [へ/に]も doko [e/ni] mo;
5. 誰か [に/と] dare ka [ni/to]; 6. 誰 [に/と] も dare [ni/to] mo

Word Builder 2

▶ 9C Word Builder 2 (CD 8, Track 17)

趣味	shumi	hobby
特技	tokugi	special ability, special skill
絵	e	painting, drawing
読書	dokusho	reading books
映画鑑賞	eega kanshoo	seeing movies (lit., movie appreciation)
写真	shashin	photography, photograph
楽器	gakki	musical instrument
ピアノ	piano	piano
バイオリン	baiorin	violin
チェロ	chero	cello
フルート	furuuto	flute
クラリネット	kurarinetto	clarinet
コンサート	konsaato	concert
持ちます/持つ	mochimasu/motsu	to own, to hold
演奏します/演奏する	ensooshimasu/ensoosuru	to perform (a musical instrument)

Creating nouns from verbs:
nominalizer の no and こと koto

To want + object, person:
X が欲しい ga hoshii

弾きます/弾く	hikimasu/hiku	to play (a string instrument)
吹きます/吹く	fukimasu/fuku	to play (a wind instrument)
たたきます/たたく	tatakimasu/tataku	to play (a percussion instrument)
欲しいです	hoshii desu	to want

✎ Word Practice 2

Translate the following words into Japanese.

1. *hobby* _____

2. *special ability, special skill* _____

3. *painting, drawing* _____

4. *reading books* _____

5. *seeing movies (lit., movie appreciation)* _____

6. *photography, photograph* _____

7. *musical instrument* _____

8. *concert* _____

9. *to own, to hold* _____

10. *to perform (a musical instrument)* _____

ANSWER KEY

1. 趣味 shumi; 2. 特技 tokugi; 3. 絵 e; 4. 読書 dokusho; 5. 映画鑑賞 eega kanshoo; 6. 写真 shashin; 7. 楽器 gakki; 8. コンサート konsaato; 9. 持ちます(or 持つ) mochimasu (or motsu); 10. 演奏します (or 演奏する) ensooshimasu (or ensoosuru)

Grammar Builder 2

CREATING NOUNS FROM VERBS: NOMINALIZER の NO AND こと KOTO

▶ 9D Grammar Builder 2 (CD 8, Track 18)

You can create nouns out of verbs in Japanese by adding the nominalizers の no and こと koto to them. These Japanese nouns usually correspond to English nouns ending in *–ing*; e.g. *knitting.* の No and こと koto follow the plain form of verbs as described in the following formula.

> *Plain form of verbs +* の no or こと koto

In most cases の no and こと koto are interchangeable, but there are also some differences between the two. の No is preferred when talking about personal matters, such as what you like doing or what you are good at. Also, の no is more colloquial, while こと koto sounds a little more bookish.

食べるのと寝るのが好きです。

Taberu no to neru no ga suki desu.

I like eating and sleeping.

勉強するのはあまり好きじゃありません。

Benkyoosuru no wa amari suki ja arimasen.

I don't like studying so much.

Creating nouns from verbs:
nominalizer の no and こと koto

ピアノを弾くのが上手です。

Piano o hiku no ga joozu desu.

I'm good at playing the piano.

日本語を話すのは簡単です。

Nihongo o hanasu no wa kantan desu.

Speaking Japanese is easy.

絵を描くのが苦手です。

E o kaku no ga nigate desu.

I'm bad at (and dislike) painting.

本を読むことは楽しいです。

Hon o yomu koto wa tanoshii desu.

Reading books is fun.

人に会って話すことは大切です。

Hito ni atte hanasu koto wa taisetsu desu.

Meeting and talking to people is important.

趣味は料理することです。

Shumi wa ryoorisuru koto desu.

My hobby is cooking.

の No cannot appear before the copula, です desu and だ da; you must use こと koto instead.

趣味は映画を見ることです。

Shumi wa eega o miru koto desu.

My hobby is watching movies.

特技<ruby>とくぎ</ruby>はクラリネットを吹<ruby>ふ</ruby>くことです。

Tokugi wa kurarinetto o fuku koto desu.

My special skill is playing the clarinet.

✎ Work Out 2

Translate the following Japanese sentences into English.

1. 漢字<ruby>かんじ</ruby>を書<ruby>か</ruby>くのは難<ruby>むずか</ruby>しいです。

   Kanji o kaku no wa muzukashii desu.

   _____

2. 趣味<ruby>しゅみ</ruby>はバイオリンを弾<ruby>ひ</ruby>くことです。

   Shumi wa baiorin o hiku koto desu.

   _____

3. 友達<ruby>ともだち</ruby>と出掛<ruby>でか</ruby>けるのは楽<ruby>たの</ruby>しいです。

   Tomodachi to dekakeru no wa tanoshii desu.

   _____

4. 映画<ruby>えいが</ruby>を見<ruby>み</ruby>るのが好<ruby>す</ruby>きです。

   Eega o miru no ga suki desu.

   _____

5. 特技<ruby>とくぎ</ruby>はフルートを吹<ruby>ふ</ruby>くことです。

   Tokugi wa furuuto o fuku koto desu.

   _____

Question words
+ か ka and も mo

Potential form of verbs:
Can do and *be able to do*

Creating nouns from verbs:
nominalizer の no and こと koto

To want + object, person:
X が欲しい ga hoshii

6. 好きな食べ物しか食べないのは良くありません。

Sukina tabemono shika tabenai no wa yoku arimasen.

_____

7. サッカーをするのが苦手です。

Sakkaa o suru no ga nigate desu.

_____

ANSWER KEY

1. *Writing Kanji is difficult.* 2. *My hobby is playing the violin.* 3. *It's enjoyable/fun to go out with friends.*
4. *I like watching movies.* 5. *My special skill is playing the flute.* 6. *It's not good to eat only food you like.*
7. *I'm poor at playing soccer.*

✎ Drive It Home

A. Fill in the blanks with appropriate particles.

1. 何 _____ 特技がありますか。

   Nani _____ tokugi ga arimasu ka.

   Do you have any special skills?

2. 昨日誰 _____ 来ましたか。

   Kinoo dare _____ kimashita ka.

   Did anyone come yesterday?

3. 誰 _____ 来ませんでした。

   Dare _____ kimasen deshita.

   No one came.

4. 週末にどこ _____ へ行きましたか。

   Shuumatsu ni doko _____ e ikimashita ka.

   Did you go anywhere on weekends?

5. どこへ _____ 行きませんでした。

   Doko e _____ ikimasen deshita.

   I didn't go anywhere.

B. Fill in the blanks with appropriate words.

1. 食べる _____と寝る _____が好きです。

   Taberu _____ to neru _____ ga suki desu.

   I like eating and sleeping.

2. 勉強する _____はあまり好きじゃありません。

   Benkyoosuru _____ wa amari suki ja arimasen.

   I don't like studying so much.

3. ピアノを弾く _____が上手です。

   Piano o hiku _____ ga joozu desu.

   I'm good at playing the piano.

4. 日本語を話す _____は簡単です。

   Nihongo o hanasu _____ wa kantan desu.

   Speaking Japanese is easy.

ANSWER KEY

A. 1. か ka; 2. か ka; 3. も mo; 4. か ka; 5. も mo

B. 1.-4. all の no or こと koto

Question words
+ か ka and も mo

Potential form of verbs:
Can do and *be able to do*

Creating nouns from verbs:
nominalizer の no and こと koto

To want + object, person:
X が欲しい ga hoshii

⊕ Culture Note

Sumo is considered to be the national sport of Japan, even though there aren't many people who actually practice the sport. Still, many Japanese, especially the older generation, enjoy watching sumo competitions on TV. There are also women's sumo competitions—at the college level for instance—but women are prohibited from becoming professional sumo wrestlers. Recently the number of foreign professional sumo wrestlers has been increasing, whereas the number of young Japanese men who want to practice the sport on a professional level is decreasing. Baseball, on the other hand, is a popular sport in Japan with a much wider audience. Recently more and more famous Japanese players have left for the United States to join major league baseball teams, and some of the major league games are broadcast in Japan. After the establishment of the Japanese professional soccer league (J League) in 1992, soccer became very popular, too, and many become especially interested in the sport during the World Cup.

How Did You Do?

Let's see how you did! By now, you should be able to:

☐ use key vocabulary related to sports and hobbies (Still unsure? Jump back to page 203 or 209)

☐ express *something*, *someone*, *somewhere* and *nothing*, *nobody* and *nowhere* (Still unsure? Jump back to page 205)

☐ create nouns out of verbs (Still unsure? Jump back to page 211)

✎ Word Recall

1. ジーンズ jiinzu   a. *necktie*

2. ネクタイ nekutai   b. *solid (color)*

3. 綿 men   c. *dark*

4. 無地 muji   d. *heavy*

5. サイズ saizu   e. *showy, loud*

6. 支払い shiharai   f. *return, change (polite)*

7. お返し okaeshi   g. *cotton*

8. 派手 hade   h. *jeans*

9. 暗い kurai   i. *payment*

10. 重い omoi   j. *size*

ANSWER KEY

1. h; 2. a; 3. g; 4. b; 5. j; 6. i; 7. f; 8. e; 9. c; 10. d

Lesson 10: Phrases

In this lesson you'll learn how to:

☐ express *can do* and *be able to do*

☐ express *to want X*

Question words
+ か ka and も mo

Potential form of verbs:
Can do and *be able to do*

Creating nouns from verbs:
nominalizer の no and こと koto

To want + object, person:
X が欲しい ga hoshii

Phrase Builder 1

▶ 10A Phrase Builder 1 (CD 8, Track 19)

どんなスポーツ	donna supootsu	*what kind of sports*
柔道のクラブ	juudoo no kurabu	*judo club*
野球とサッカー	yakyuu to sakkaa	*baseball and soccer*
柔道か剣道	juudoo ka kendoo	*judo or kendo*
学生の時	gakusee no toki	*when I was a student*
試合がある時	shiai ga aru toki	*when there's a game*
家の近くのテニスコート	ie no chikaku no tenisu kooto	*tennis court near my house*
平日使っているコート	heejitsu tsukatte iru kooto	*the tennis court I'm using on weekdays*
二時間ぐらい	nijikan gurai	*for about two hours*
特に	toku ni	*especially*
何度か	nando ka	*several times*
テニスが上手です	tenisu ga joozu desu	*be good at tennis*
テニスが下手です	tenisu ga heta desu	*be bad at tennis*
数学が得意です	suugaku ga tokui desu	*be good at (and like) mathematics*
数学が苦手です	suugaku ga nigate desu	*be poor at (and dislike) mathematics*
バスケットボールをやっています/やっている	basukettobooru o yatte imasu/yatte iru	*be playing basketball*

クラブに入っています/ 入っている	kurabu ni haitte imasu/haite iru	*belong to a club*
何かスポーツをします/す る	nanika supootsu o shimasu/suru	*play some sports*
何もスポーツはしません/ しない	nanimo supootsu wa shimasen/shinai	*play no sports*
全然スポーツはしません/ しない	zenzen supootsu wa shimasen/shinai	*don't play sports at all*
まあまあです。	Maa maa desu.	*So so.*

Take It Further

While 上手です joozu desu and 得意です tokui desu both translate as *be good at*, 上手です joozu desu is used when describing one's skills and cannot be used when referring to certain academic subjects, such as mathematics, physics, or history. 得意です Tokui desu can be used when talking about playing sports, instruments, or having good skills in other areas, including academic subjects. The same distinction exists between 下手です heta desu and 苦手です nigate desu.

✎ Phrase Practice 1

Fill in the missing words below.

1. 柔道 _____ 剣道

   juudoo _____ kendoo

   judo or kendo

Creating nouns from verbs:
nominalizer の no and こと koto

To want + object, person:
X が欲しい ga hoshii

2. 二^に時^じ間^{かん}_____

nijikan _____

for about two hours

3. _____ に

_____ ni

especially

4. _____ か

_____ ka

several times

5. テニスが _____ です

tenisu ga _____ desu

be good at tennis

6. テニスが _____ です

tenisu ga _____ desu

be bad at tennis

7. 数^{すう}学^{がく}が _____ です

suugaku ga _____ desu

be good at (and like) mathematics

8. 数^{すう}学^{がく}が _____ です

suugaku ga _____ desu

be poor at (and dislike) mathematics

ANSWER KEY

1. か ka; 2. ぐらい gurai; 3. 特 toku; 4. 何度 nando; 5. 上手 joozu; 6. 下手 heta; 7. 得意 tokui;
8. 苦手 nigate

Grammar Builder 1

POTENTIAL FORM OF VERBS: *CAN DO* AND *BE ABLE TO DO*

▶ 10B Grammar Builder 1 (CD 8, Track 20)

The potential form of verbs is used to express the meaning of the English *can/to be able to* + verb. Let's first look at how the potential form of Class I and Class II verbs is formed.

Class I (う u-verbs)	Drop the final -u from the dictionary form and add -eru.
Class II (る ru-verbs)	Drop the final る -ru from the dictionary form and add られる -rareru.

Now, let's look at the conjugation of the potential form of some verbs.

CLASS I (う U-VERBS)

DICTIONARY FORM	POTENTIAL FORM OF VERBS (PLAIN FORM)			
	Non-past affirmative	Non-past negative	Past affirmative	Past negative
書く kaku (to write)	書ける kakeru	書けない kakenai	書けた kaketa	書けなかった kakenakatta

Question words
+ か ka and も mo

Potential form of verbs:
Can do and *be able to do*

Creating nouns from verbs:
nominalizer の no and こと koto

To want + object, person:
X が欲しい ga hoshii

DICTIONARY FORM	POTENTIAL FORM OF VERBS (PLAIN FORM)			
	Non-past affirmative	Non-past negative	Past affirmative	Past negative
読む yomu (to read)	読める yomeru	読めない yomenai	読めた yometa	読めなかった yomenakatta
聞く kiku (to listen)	聞ける kikeru	聞けない kikenai	聞けた kiketa	聞けなかった kikenakatta
使う tsukau (to use)	使える tsukaeru	使えない tsukaenai	使えた tsukaeta	使えなかった tsukaenakatta
行く iku (to go)	行ける ikeru	行けない ikenai	行けた iketa	行けなかった ikenakatta

CLASS II (る RU-VERBS)

DICTIONARY FORM	POTENTIAL FORM OF VERBS (PLAIN FORM)			
	Non-past affirmative	Non-past negative	Past affirmative	Past negative
食べる taberu (to eat)	食べられる taberareru	食べられない taberarenai	食べられた taberareta	食べられなかった taberarenakatta
見る miru (to see)	見られる mirareru	見られない mirarenai	見られた mirareta	見られなかった mirarenakatta

DICTIONARY FORM	POTENTIAL FORM OF VERBS (PLAIN FORM)			
	Non-past affirmative	Non-past negative	Past affirmative	Past negative
起きる okiru *(to get up)*	起きられる okirareru	起きられない okirarenai	起きられた okirareta	起きられなかった okirarenakatta
寝る neru *(to sleep)*	寝られる nerareru	寝られない nerarenai	寝られた nerareta	寝られなかった nerarenakatta
教える oshieru *(to teach)*	教えられる oshierareru	教えられない oshierarenai	教えられた oshierareta	教えられなかった oshierarenakatta

And here are the conjugations of the two Class III verbs する suru (*to do*) and
来る kuru (*to come*).

CLASS III

DICTIONARY FORM	POTENTIAL FORM OF VERBS (PLAIN FORM)			
	Non-past affirmative	Non-past negative	Past affirmative	Past negative
する suru (*to do*)	できる dekiru	できない dekinai	できた dekita	できなかった dekinakatta
来る kuru (*to come*)	来られる korareru	来られない korarenai	来られた korareta	来られなかった korarenakatta

Question words
+ か ka and も mo

Potential form of verbs:
Can do and *be able to do*

Creating nouns from verbs:
nominalizer の no and こと koto

To want + object, person:
X が欲しい ga hoshii

Now, let's look at how the potential form of verbs are used in sentences. Note that the logical direct object of potential form of verbs is marked by the particle が **ga** instead of を **o** in affirmative sentences and questions with question words. For yes/no questions and negative sentences, you can keep using the particle は **wa** as you're used to.

A: 日本語の本は読めますか。

Nihongo no hon wa yomemasu ka.

Can you read Japanese books?

B: ええ、少し読めます。/いいえ、全然読めません。

Ee, sukoshi yomemasu./Iie, zenzen yomemasen.

Yes, I can read a little./No, I cannot read at all.

A: 明日午前五時に起きられますか。

Ashita gozen goji ni okiraremasu ka.

Can you get up at 5:00 a.m. tomorrow?

B: 多分起きられるでしょう。/多分起きられないでしょう。

Tabun okirareru deshoo./Tabun okirarenai deshoo.

I can probably get up./I probably can't get up.

A: お刺身は食べられますか。

Osashimi wa taberaremasu ka.

Can you eat sliced raw fish?

B: いいえ、食べられません。でも、おすしは食べられます。

Iie, taberaremasen. Demo, osushi wa taberaremasu.

No, I cannot eat it. But, I can eat sushi.

A: 何語が話せますか。

Nanigo ga hanasemasu ka.

What languages can you speak ?

B: 英語とスペイン語が話せます。

Eego to supeingo ga hanasemasu.

I can speak English and Spanish.

A: 数学の宿題はできましたか。

Suugaku no shukudai wa dekimashita ka.

Were you able to do the mathematics homework?

B: はい、できました。/いいえ、難しすぎましたから、できませんでした。

Hai, dekimashita./Iie, muzukashisugimashita kara, dekimasen deshita.

Yes, I was able to do it./No, it was too difficult, so I couldn't do it.

A: 日曜日に会社に来られますか。

Nichiyoobi ni kaisha ni koraremasu ka.

Can you come to the company on Sunday?

B: はい、来られると思います。/いいえ、来られないと思います。

Hai, korareru to omoimasu./Iie, korarenai to omoimasu.

Yes, I think I can come./No, I think I can't come.

There is another expression which corresponds to the English *can/be able to*; it is used in the following structure.

> *Dictionary form of a verb* + ことができる **koto ga dekiru**

こと **Koto** is the nominalizer you saw introduced in Lesson 9, and できる **dekiru** is the potential form of する **suru** (*to do*). Let's look at how this expression is used.

Creating nouns from verbs:
nominalizer の no and こと koto

To want + object, person:
X が欲しい ga hoshii

川田さんはドイツ語とフランス語を話すことができます。

Kawada san wa doitsugo to furansugo o hanasu koto ga dekimasu.

Mr./Ms. Kawada is able to speak German and French.

昨日そのコンピューターを使うことはできませんでした。

Kinoo sono konpyuutaa o tsukau koto wa dekimasen deshita.

I was unable to use that computer yesterday.

友達に券をもらったので、野球の試合を見ることができました。

Tomodachi ni ken (*ticket*) o moratta node, yakyuu no shiai o miru koto ga dekimashita.

I got a ticket from my friend, so I was able to see a baseball game.

あさっては会社に来ることはできないと思います。

Asatte wa kaisha ni kuru koto wa dekinai to omoimasu.

I think I am not able to come to the office the day after tomorrow.

何か楽器を演奏することはできますか。

Nani ka gakki o ensoosuru koto wa dekimasu ka.

Can you play any musical instruments?

✎ Work Out 1

A. Complete the sentences using the appropriate form of the verbs given in parentheses.

1. パーティーに _____ か。(行く)

   Paatii ni _____ ka. (iku)

   Can you go to the party?

2. 中田さんと _____ 。(話す)

   Nakata san to _____.

   (hanasu)

   I couldn't talk with Mr. Nakata.

3. 明日学校に _____。(来る)

   Ashita gakkoo ni _____. (kuru)

   I cannot come to school tomorrow.

4. ミーティングに _____ か。(出る)

   Miitingu ni _____ ka. (deru)

   Can you attend the meeting?

5. 有名な絵は _____ 。(見る)

   Yuumee na e wa _____.

   (miru)

   I couldn't see the famous painting.

6. 何かスポーツは _____ か。(する)

   Nanika supootsu wa _____ ka. (suru)

   Can you play any sports?

B. Translate the following Japanese sentences into English.

1. 姉はピアノとバイオリンを弾くことができます。

   Ane wa piano to baiorin o hiku koto ga dekimasu.

   _____

Question words
+ か ka and も mo

Potential form of verbs:
Can do and *be able to do*

Creating nouns from verbs:
nominalizer の no and こと koto

To want + object, person:
X が欲しい ga hoshii

2. 父は料理することはできません。

Chichi wa ryoorisuru koto wa dekimasen.

3. 今日先生に会うことはできませんでした。

Kyoo sensee ni au koto wa dekimasen deshita.

4. おとといセミナーに出ることはできませんでした。

Ototoi seminaa ni deru koto wa dekimasen deshita.

5. これは大切な物ですから、誰にもあげることができません。

Kore wa taisetsu na mono desu kara, dare ni mo ageru koto ga dekimasen.

ANSWER KEY

A: 1. 行けますか ikemasu ka; 2. 話せませんでした hanasemasen deshita; 3. 来られません koraremasen; 4. 出られます deraremasu; 5. 見られませんでした miraremasen deshita; 6. できます dekimasu

B: 1. *My older sister is able to play the piano and the violin.*; 2. *My father is unable to cook.*; 3. *I was not able to see my teacher today.*; 4. *I was not able to attend the seminar the day before yesterday.*; 5. *This is an important thing, so I am not able to give it to anyone.*

Phrase Builder 2

▶ 10C Phrase Builder 2 (CD 8, Track 21)

バイオリンとチェロとピアノ	baiorin to chero to piano	*the violin, the cello, and the piano*
銀座のレストラン	ginza no resutoran	*a restaurant in Ginza*

今度の土曜日 （こんど の どようび）	kondo no doyoobi	*next Saturday*
絵を描くことと読書 （え を かく ことと どくしょ）	e o kaku koto to dokusho	*painting and reading books*
写真を撮るの （しゃしん を とる）	shashin o toru no	*taking photos*
ロペスさんが書いた絵 （か え）	Ropesu san ga kaita e	*the painting that Ms. Lopez painted*
今使っているバイオリン （いま つか）	ima tsukatte iru baiorin	*the violin I am using now*
新しいの （あたら）	atarashii no	*new one*
新しいのが欲しい （あたら ほ）	atarashii no ga hoshii	*want a new one*
実は （じつ）	jitsu wa	*actually*
今までに （いま）	ima made ni	*up to now*
コンサートで	konsaato de	*at a concert*
一週間に二冊ぐらい （いっしゅうかん に さつ）	isshuukan ni nisatsu gurai	*about two books a week*
何か楽器が演奏できます / できる （なに がっき えんそう）	nanika gakki ga ensoodekimasu/dekiru	*can play some musical instruments*
何も楽器は演奏できません / できない （なに がっき えんそう）	nanimo gakki wa ensoodekimasen/ dekinai	*can play no musical instruments*
〜を習っています / 習っている （なら）（なら）	… o naratte imasu/ naratte iru	*be taking lessons on…*
カメラを持って出掛けます / 出掛ける （も でか）（でか）	kamera o motte dekakemasu/dekakeru	*go out with a camera*

なかなか上手に吹けません / 吹けない	nakanaka joozu ni fukemasen/fukenai	*cannot play (a wind instrument) well*
すごいですね。	Sugoi desu ne.	*That's amazing.*

✎ Phrase Practice 2

Complete the following by inserting appropriate particles.

1. バイオリン _____ チェロ _____ピアノ

   baiorin _____ chero _____ piano

   the violin, the cello, and the piano

2. 銀座_____レストラン

   ginza _____ resutoran

   a restaurant in Ginza

3. 今度 _____ 土曜日

   kondo _____ doyoobi

   next Saturday

4. 写真 _____ 撮る _____

   shashin _____ toru _____

   taking photos

5. ロペスさん _____ 書いた絵

   Ropesu san _____ kaita e

   the painting that Ms. Lopez painted

6. 新しい^{あたら} _____

   atarashii _____

   new one

7. 今^{いま}まで _____

   ima made _____

   up to now

8. コンサート _____

   konsaato _____

   at a concert

ANSWER KEY

1. と to, と to; 2. の no; 3. の no; 4. を o,の no; 5. が ga; 6. の no; 7. に ni; 8. で de

Grammar Builder 2

TO WANT + OBJECT, PERSON: X が欲^ほしい GA HOSHII

▶ 10D Grammar Builder 2 (CD 8, Track 22)

You learned how to express the wish to do something, i.e., to engage in an activity, in *Intermediate Japanese*, and also in Lesson 7 of this course. Now, let's learn how to say you'd like to get something or someone, like an object or a person.

> X が欲^ほしい (です) ga hoshii (desu).

Just as with たい **tai** (*want to*), the conjugation of 欲^ほしい **hoshii** is the same as that of い **i**-adjectives.

Creating nouns from verbs:
nominalizer の no and こと koto

To want + object, person:
X が欲しい ga hoshii

	NON-PAST AFFIRMATIVE	**NON-PAST NEGATIVE**	**PAST AFFIRMATIVE**	**PAST NEGATIVE**
Plain form	欲しい hoshii	欲しくない hoshiku nai	欲しかった hoshikatta	欲しくなかった hoshiku nakatta
Polite form	欲しいです hoshii desu	欲しく [ないです/ありません] hoshiku [nai desu/ arimasen]	欲しかったです hoshikatta desu	欲しく [なかったです/ありませんでした] hoshiku [nakatta desu/ arimasen deshita]

Let's look at how this expression is used. Please note that the direct object of 欲しい hoshii is marked by が ga instead of を o in affirmative sentences and questions with question words; you can use the particle は wa in yes/no questions and negative sentences as usual.

A: 今何か欲しいですか。

Ima nani ka hoshii desu ka.

Do you want anything now?

B: ええ、実は新しい車が欲しいんです。

Ee, jitsu wa atarashii kuruma ga hoshii n desu.

Yes, actually I want a new car.

B: いいえ、何も欲しく [ないです/ありません] 。

Iie, nani mo hoshiku [nai desu/arimasen].

No, I don't want anything.

A: 去年の誕生日に何が欲しかったですか。

Kyonen no tanjoobi (*birthday*) ni nani ga hoshikatta desu ka.

What did you want for your birthday last year?

B: カメラが欲しかったです。

Kamera ga hoshikatta desu.

I wanted a camera.

B: 特に何も欲しく [なかったです/ありませんでした]。

Toku ni nani mo hoshiku [nakatta desu/arimasen deshita].

I didn't want anything in particular.

Note that you can only use 欲しい hoshii when the subject is either the speaker or the addressee. If the subject is a third person not involved in the conversation, you have to use 欲しがっている hoshigatte iru.

> *Someone +* が/は X を 欲しがって [いる/います]
>
> *Someone +* ga/wa X o hoshigatte iru/imasu

欲しがっている Hoshigatte iru expresses someone's current desire; the direct object of 欲しがっている hoshigatte iru is marked by the direct object marker を o (in affiramtive sentences and questions with question words).

兄は新しい車を欲しがっています。

Ani wa atarashii kuruma o hoshigatte imasu.

My older brother wants a new car.

田中さんはガールフレンドを欲しがっています。

Tanaka san wa gaarufurendo o hoshigatte imasu.

Mr. Tanaka wants a girlfriend.

Question words
+ か ka and も mo

Potential form of verbs:
Can do and *be able to do*

Creating nouns from verbs:
nominalizer の no and こと koto

To want + object, person:
X が欲しい ga hoshii

ロペスさんは日本語の辞書を欲しがっています。

Ropesu san wa nihongo no jisho o hoshigatte imasu.

Mr./Ms. Lopez wants a Japanese dictionary.

When expressing someone's long-term, habitual desire, 欲しがる hoshigaru
is used.

妹はいつも私の物を欲しがります。

Imooto wa itsumo watashi no mono o hoshigarimasu.

My younger sister always wants my belongings.

✎ Work Out 2

Translate the following Japanese sentences into English.

1. 新しいコンピューターが欲しいですが、高いですから買えません。

   Atarashii konpyuutaa ga hoshii desu ga, takai desu kara kaemasen.

   _____

2. そのテレビは大きすぎますから、欲しくありません。

   Sono terebi wa ookisugimasu kara, hoshiku arimasen.

   _____

3. 中国語を勉強していますから、中国人の友達が欲しいです。

   Chuugokugo o benkyooshite imasu kara, chuugokujin no tomodachi ga hoshii

   desu.

   _____

4. この鞄は古いですから、新しいのが欲しいです。
かばん ふる   あたら   ほ

Kono kaban wa furui desu kara, atarashii no ga hoshii desu.

_____

5. 弟は新しいクラリネットを欲しがっています。
おとうと あたら   ほ

Otooto wa atarashii kurarinetto o hoshigatte imasu.

_____

ANSWER KEY

1. _I want a new computer, but I cannot buy one because it's expensive._ 2. _That television is too big, so I don't want it._ 3. _I'm studying Chinese, so I want Chinese friends._ 4. _This bag is old, so I want a new one._ 5. _My younger brother wants a new clarinet._

✎ Drive It Home

A. Fill in the blanks by choosing appropriate words from the word bank.
起きられます okiraremasu, 読めます yomemasu, 話せます hanasemasu

1. 日本語の本が _____。
   に ほん ご   ほん

   Nihongo no hon ga_____.

   I can read Japanese books.

2. 午前五時に _____。
   ご ぜん ご じ

   Gozen goji ni _____.

   I can get up at 5 a.m.

3. 英語とスペイン語が _____。
   えい ご   ご

   Eego to supeingo ga _____.

   I can speak English and Spanish.

Question words
+ か ka and も mo

Potential form of verbs:
Can do and *be able to do*

Creating nouns from verbs:
nominalizer の no and こと koto

To want + object, person:
X が欲しい ga hoshii

B. Fill in the blanks with appropriate words.

1. 日本語の本を読む _____。

   Nihongo no hon o yomu _____.

   I am able to read Japanese books.

2. 午前五時に起きる _____。

   Gozen goji ni okiru _____.

   I am able to get up at 5 a.m.

3. 英語とスペイン語を話す _____。

   Eego to supeingo o hanasu _____.

   I am able to speak English and Spanish.

C. Fill in the blanks with the appropriate form of 欲しい hoshii.

1. 新しい車が _____ です。

   Atarashii kuruma ga _____ desu.

   I want a new car.

2. 何も _____ です。

   Nani mo _____ desu.

   I don't want anything.

3. カメラが _____ です。

   Kamera ga _____ desu.

   I wanted a camera.

ANSWER KEY

A: 1. 読めます yomemasu; 2. 起きられます okiraremasu; 3. 話せます hanasemasu

B: 1.-3. all ことができます koto ga dekimasu

C: 1. 欲しい hoshii; 2. 欲しくない hoshiku nai; 3. 欲しかった hoshikatta

Tip!

List five things you can do and five things you cannot do in English. Try saying them in Japanese using both the potential form of verbs and ことができる **koto ga dekiru.** If you don't know the words you need, look them up in an English-Japanese dictionary. Having a bilingual dictionary handy as you go through the lessons is an excellent idea (or simply keep the glossary that appears in these coursebooks near at hand). You can look up words whenever you think of them; if you do this regularly, you will considerably expand your vocabulary—a key to communication.

How Did You Do?

Let's see how you did! By now, you should be able to:

☐ express *can do* and *be able to do* (Still unsure? Jump back to page 221)

☐ express *to want X* (Still unsure? Jump back to page 231)

✎ Word Recall

1. ジュース juusu   a. *two people* (polite)

2. 二名様 nimeesama   b. *juice, soft drink*

3. 寒い samui   c. *cold*

4. キャベツ kyabetsu   d. *food*

5. 涼しい suzushii		e. *onion*
6. 味噌汁 misoshiru		f. *cabbage*
7. じゃがいも jagaimo		g. *there is, to have, to exist* (polite)
8. ございます gozaimasu		h. *miso soup*
9. 食べ物 tabemono		i. *cool*
10. たまねぎ tamanegi		j. *potato*

ANSWER KEY

1. b; 2. a; 3. c; 4. f; 5. i; 6. h; 7. j; 8. g; 9. d; 10. e

Lesson 11: Sentences

In this lesson you'll learn how to:

☐ compare two items using *A is more X than B*

☐ compare three or more items using *A is the most X among D*

Sentence Builder 1

▶ 11A Sentence Builder 1 (CD 8, Track 23)

どんなスポーツが好きですか。

Donna supootsu ga suki desu ka.

What kind of sports do you like?

何かスポーツはしますか。

Nani ka supootsu wa shimasu ka.

Do you play any sports?

学生の時はバスケットボールをやっていました。

Gakusee no toki wa, basukettobooru o yatte imashita.

When I was a student, I played basketball.

学生の時は、柔道のクラブに入っていました。

Gakusee no toki wa, juudoo no kurabu ni haitte imashita.

When I was a student, I belonged to a judo club.

特に何も運動はしていません。

Toku ni nani mo undoo wa shite imasen.

I am not playing any sports in particular.

全然テニスはしませんか。

Zenzen tenisu wa shimasen ka.

Don't you play tennis at all?

よく家の近くのコートへ行って、二時間ぐらいテニスをします。

Yoku ie no chikaku no kooto e itte, nijikan gurai tenisu o shimasu.

I often go to the tennis court near my house and play tennis for about two hours.

テニスが上手なんでしょうね。

Tenisu ga joozu na n deshoo ne.

You are probably good at tennis, aren't you?

何度かテニスをしたことがありますけど、下手なんです。

Nando ka tenisu o shita koto ga arimasu kedo, heta na n desu.

I have played tennis several times, but I'm not good at it.

Creating nouns from verbs:
nominalizer の no and こと koto

To want + object, person:
X が欲しい ga hoshii

野球とサッカーを見るのが大好きです。

Yakyuu to sakkaa o miru no ga daisuki desu.

I like watching baseball and soccer very much.

試合がある時は、いつもテレビで見ています。

Shiai ga aru toki wa, itsumo terebi de mite imasu.

When there is a game, I am always watching it on TV.

野球とサッカーとどちらの方が好きですか。

Yakyuu to sakkaa to dochira no hoo ga suki desu ka.

Which do you like better, baseball or soccer?

野球の方が好きです。

Yakyuu no hoo ga suki desu.

I like baseball better.

柔道か剣道を習いたいんですけど、今は時間がないし・・・。

Juudoo ka kendoo o naraitai n desu kedo, ima wa jikan ga nai shi…

I want to take judo or kendo lessons, but I don't have time now, so…

もし習うんだったら、剣道より柔道の方がいいと思います。

Moshi narau n dattara, kendo yori juudoo no hoo ga ii to omoimasu.

If you take lessons, I think judo is better than kendo.

今度一緒にテニスをしませんか。

Kondo issho ni tenisu o shimasen ka.

Why don't we play tennis together sometime?

私もあまり上手にできませんから、大丈夫ですよ。

Watashi mo amari joozu ni dekimasen kara, daijoobu desu yo.

I cannot play it so well either, so it's okay.

平日使っているコートが会社の近くにあります。

Heejitsu tsukatteiru kooto ga kaisha no chikaku ni arimasu.

There's a tennis court near the office that I'm using on weekdays.

今度時間がある時にそこへ行きましょう。

Kondo jikan ga aru toki ni soko e ikimashoo.

Let's go there next time when we have time!

✎ Sentence Practice 1

Fill in the missing words in each of the following sentences.

1. _____ 運動をしていません。

_____ undoo o shite imasen.

I am not playing any sports in particular.

2. テニスが _____ ね。

Tenisu ga _____ ne.

You are probably good at tennis, aren't you?

3. 野球とサッカーを _____ です。

Yakyuu to sakkaa o _____ desu.

I like watching baseball and soccer very much.

4. _____ は、いつもテレビで見ています。

_____ wa, itsumo terebi de mite

imasu.

When there is a game, I am always watching it on TV.

Question words
+ か ka and も mo

Potential form of verbs:
Can do and *be able to do*

Creating nouns from verbs:
nominalizer の no and こと koto

To want + object, person:
X が欲しい ga hoshii

5. 野球<ruby>やきゅう</ruby>とサッカーと ＿＿＿＿＿＿＿＿＿ 好<ruby>す</ruby>きですか。

   Yakyuu to sakkaa to ＿＿＿＿＿＿＿＿＿＿＿ suki

   desu ka.

   Which do you like better, baseball or soccer?

6. ＿＿＿＿＿＿＿＿＿ 好<ruby>す</ruby>きです。

   ＿＿＿＿＿＿＿＿＿ **suki desu.**

   I like baseball better.

7. 柔道<ruby>じゅうどう</ruby>か剣道<ruby>けんどう</ruby>を習<ruby>なら</ruby>いたいんですけど、今<ruby>いま</ruby>は ＿＿＿＿＿＿＿ し・・・。

   Juudoo ka kendoo o naraitai n desu kedo, ima wa ＿＿＿＿＿＿＿＿

   ＿＿＿＿＿ shi...

   I want to take judo or kendo lessons, but I don't have time now, so...

8. 僕<ruby>ぼく</ruby>もあまり上手<ruby>じょうず</ruby>にできませんから、 ＿＿＿＿＿＿＿＿ よ。

   Boku mo amari joozu ni dekimasen kara, ＿＿＿＿＿＿＿＿

   ＿＿＿＿＿ yo.

   I cannot play it so well either, so it's okay.

ANSWER KEY
1. 特<ruby>とく</ruby>に何<ruby>なに</ruby>も Toku ni nani mo; 2. 上手<ruby>じょうず</ruby>なんでしょう joozu na n deshoo; 3. 見<ruby>み</ruby>るのが大好<ruby>だいす</ruby>き miru no
ga daisuki; 4. 試合<ruby>しあい</ruby>がある時<ruby>とき</ruby> Shiai ga aru toki; 5. どちらの方<ruby>ほう</ruby>が dochira no hoo ga; 6. 野球<ruby>やきゅう</ruby>の方<ruby>ほう</ruby>が
Yakyuu no hoo ga; 7. 時間<ruby>じかん</ruby>がない jikan ga nai; 8. 大丈夫<ruby>だいじょうぶ</ruby>です daijoobu desu

Grammar Builder 1

COMPARATIVES

▶ 11B Grammar Builder 1 (CD 8, Track 24)

You can compare two items (*A and B*) using the structure below.

| A は B より X。 | A wa B yori X. | A is more X than B. |

In this structure, X can be an adjective or the combination of an adverb and a verb, like たくさん食べます takusan tabemasu (*eat a lot*). Now, let's look at how this structure can be used in sentences.

アメリカは日本より大きいです。

Amerika wa nihon yori ookii desu.

The U.S.A. is bigger than Japan.

このアパートはあのアパートより便利です。

Kono apaato wa ano apaato yori benri desu.

This apartment is more convenient than that apartment.

本田さんは川田さんよりたくさん勉強します。

Honda san wa Kawada san yori takusan benkyooshimasu.

Mr./Ms. Honda studies more than Mr./Ms. Kawada.

When asking and answering questions comparing two items, the following structures are used.

| A と B とどちらの方が X か。 | A to B to dochira no hoo ga X ka. | Which is more X, A or B? |
| A/B の方が (B/A より) X. | A/B no hoo ga (B/A yori) X. | A/B is more X than B/A. |

Let's see how these expressions can be used. Please note that B より yori (*than B*) is often dropped when answering questions.

A: コーヒーと紅茶とどちらの方が好きですか。

Koohii to koocha to dochira no hoo ga suki desu ka.

Which do you like better, coffee or (black) tea?

Question words + か ka and も mo		Potential form of verbs: *Can do* and *be able to do*

	Creating nouns from verbs: nominalizer の no and こと koto		*To want* + object, person: X が欲しい ga hoshii

B: 紅茶の方がコーヒーより好きです。

Koocha no hooga koohii yori suki desu.

I like (black) tea more than coffee.

A: 佐藤さんと川村さんとどちらの方がたくさん食べますか。

Satoo san to Kawamura san to dochira no hoo ga takusan tabemasu ka.

Who eats more, Mr./Ms. Sato or Mr./Ms. Kawamura?

B: 川村さんの方がたくさん食べると思います。

Kawamura san no hoo ga takusan taberu to omoimasu.

I think Mr./Ms. Kawamura eats more.

A: すしとピザとどちらの方がおいしいと思いますか。

Sushi to piza to dochira no hoo ga oishii to omoimasu ka.

Which do you think is more delicious, sushi or pizza?

B: すしの方がおいしいと思います。

Sushi no hoo ga oishii to omoimasu.

I think sushi is more delicious.

✎ Work Out 1

A. Translate the following sentences into Japanese using the words given in parentheses. Make sure to use the structure A は wa B より yori X.

1. *The U.S. is bigger than England.*

   (アメリカ amerika, イギリス igirisu, 大きいです ookii desu)

2. *This park is more quiet than that park.*

   (あの公園 ano kooen, 静かです shizuka desu, この公園 kono kooen)

   _____

3. *This book is more interesting than that book.*

   (面白いです omoshiroi desu, あの本 ano hon, この本 kono hon)

   _____

4. *Mr. Watanabe exercises more (lit., does more exercises) than Mr. Kobayashi.*

   (渡辺さん Watanabe san, たくさん takusan, 小林さん Kobayashi san, 運動しま

   す undooshimasu)

   _____

5. *I think the subway is more convenient than the bus.*

   (バス basu, 地下鉄 chikatetsu, と to, 思います omoimasu, 便利だ benri da)

   _____

B. Form questions and answers using the words provided in parentheses. Make sure
   to use the structures A と B とどちらの方が X ですか。A to B to dochira no
   hoo ga X desu ka. and A/B の方が (B/A より) X。A/B no hoo ga (B/A yori) X.

1. (平日 heejitsu, 好きです suki desu, 週末 shuumatsu)

   Q. Which do you like better, weekends or weekdays?

   A. I like weekends better than weekdays.

   _____

2. (よく yoku, 日本茶 nihoncha, 飲みます nomimasu, 紅茶 koocha)

   Q. Which do you drink more often, Japanese tea or black tea?

Unit 3 Lesson 11: Sentences   **245**

Question words
+ か ka and も mo

Potential form of verbs:
Can do and *be able to do*

Creating nouns from verbs:
nominalizer の no and こと koto

To want + object, person:
X が欲しい ga hoshii

A. I drink black tea more often.

---

3. (大おおきいです ookii desu, 韓国かんこく kankoku, 中国ちゅうごく chuugoku)

Q. Which is bigger, China or Korea?

A. China is bigger than Korea.

---

4. (思おもいます omoimasu, 肉料理にくりょうり niku ryoori, おいしい oishii, 魚料理さかなりょうり sakana

ryoori, と to)

Q. Which do you think is more delicious, fish-based cuisine or meat-based cuisine?

A. I think fish-based cuisine is more delicious.

---

5. (たくさん takusan, ビール biiru, 飲のめます nomemasu, ワイン wain)

Q. Which can you drink more of, beer or wine?

A. I can drink beer more.

ANSWER KEY

A. 1. アメリカはイギリスより大おおきいです。Amerika wa igirisu yori ookii desu. 2. この公園こうえんはあの公園こうえんより静しずかです。Kono kooen wa ano kooen yori shizuka desu. 3. この本ほんはあの本ほんより面白おもしろいです。Kono hon wa ano hon yori omoshiroi desu. 4. 渡辺わたなべさんは小林こばやしさんよりたくさん運動うんどうします。Watanabe san wa Kobayashi san yori takusan undooshimasu. 5. 地下鉄ちかてつはバスより便利べんりだと思おもいます。Chikatetsu wa basu yori benri da to omoimasu.

B. 1. Q. 週末しゅうまつと平日へいじつとどちらの方ほうが好すきですか。Shuumatsu to heejitsu to dochira no hoo ga suki desu ka. A. 週末しゅうまつの方ほうが平日へいじつより好すきです。Shuumatsu no hoo ga heejitsu yori suki desu. 2. Q. 日本茶にほんちゃと紅茶こうちゃとどちらの方ほうがよく飲のみますか。Nihoncha to koocha to dochira no hoo ga yoku nomimasu ka. A. 紅茶こうちゃの方ほうがよく飲のみます。 Koocha no hoo ga yoku nomimasu. 3. Q. 中国ちゅうごくと韓国かんこくとどちらの方ほうが大おおきいですか。Chuugoku to kankoku to dochira no hoo ga ookii desu ka.

A. 中国の方が韓国より大きいです。Chuugoku no hoo ga kankoku yori ookii desu. 4. Q. 魚料理と肉料理とどちらの方がおいしいと思いますか。Sakana ryoori to niku ryoori to dochira no hoo ga oishii to omoimasu ka. A. 魚料理の方がおいしいと思います。Sakana ryoori no hoo ga oishii to omoimasu. 5. Q. ビールとワインとどちらの方がたくさん飲めますか。Biiru to wain to dochira no hoo ga takusan nomemasu ka. A. ビールの方がたくさん飲めます。Biiru no hoo ga takusan nomemasu.

Sentence Builder 2

▶ 11C Sentence Builder 2 (CD 9, Track 1)

何か趣味はありますか。

Nani ka shumi wa arimasu ka.

Do you have any hobbies?

何も趣味はありません。

Nani mo shumi wa arimasen.

I have no hobbies.

趣味は絵を描くことです。

Shumi wa e o kaku koto desu.

My hobby is painting.

絵を描くのが好きです。

E o kaku no ga suki desu.

I like painting.

写真を撮るのが好きです。

Shashin o toru no ga suki desu.

I like taking pictures.

Question words
+ か ka and も mo

Potential form of verbs:
Can do and *be able to do*

Creating nouns from verbs:
nominalizer の no and こと koto

To want + object, person:
X が欲しい ga hoshii

本を読むのも好きです。

Hon o yomu no mo suki desu.

I like reading books, too.

一週間に二冊ぐらい本を読みます。

Isshuukan ni nisatsu gurai hon o yomimasu.

I read about two books a week.

ロペスさんが描いた絵を見てみたいです。

Ropesu san ga kaita e o mite mitai desu.

I want to try seeing the paintings that Ms. Lopez painted.

週末よくカメラを持って出掛けます。

Shuumatsu yoku kamera o motte dekakemasu.

On weekend, I often go out and take a camera with me.

何か楽器は演奏できますか。

Nani ka gakki wa ensoodekimasu ka.

Can you play any musical instruments?

何も楽器は演奏できません。

Nani mo gakki wa ensoodekimasen.

I cannot play any musical instruments.

バイオリンとチェロとピアノが弾けます。

Baiorin to chero to piano ga hikemasu.

I can play the violin, the cello, and the piano.

フルートを習っていますけど、なかなか上手に吹けません。

Furuuto o naratte imasu kedo, nakanaka joozu ni fukemasen.

I am taking lessons in flute, but I cannot play it well so easily.

バイオリンとチェロとピアノの中でどれが一番得意ですか。

Baiorin to chero to piano no naka de dore ga ichiban tokui desu ka.

Which are you best at, the violin, the cello, or the piano?

もう二十年ぐらい習っていますから、バイオリンが一番得意です。

Moo nijuunen gurai naratte imasu kara, baiorin ga ichiban tokui desu.

Since I have been taking lessons for twenty years already, I am best at the violin.

今使っているバイオリンは古いので、新しいのが欲しいです。

Ima tsukatte iru baiorin wa furui node, atarashii no ga hoshii desu.

The violin I am using now is old, so I want a new one.

とても高いですから、買えません。

Totemo takai desu kara, kaemasen.

Since it's very expensive, I cannot buy it.

今までにコンサートで演奏したことはありますか。

Ima made ni konsaato de ensoooshita koto wa arimasu ka.

Have you ever performed at a concert?

今度の土曜日に銀座のレストランで演奏するんですけど、いらっしゃいませんか。

Kondo no doyoobi ni ginza no resutoran de ensoosuru n desu kedo,
irasshaimasen ka.

I will perform at a restaurant in Ginza this Saturday, so why don't you come?

Question words
+ か ka and も mo

Potential form of verbs:
Can do and *be able to do*

Creating nouns from verbs:
nominalizer の no and こと koto

To want + object, person:
X が欲しい ga hoshii

✎ Sentence Practice 2

Fill in the missing words in each of the following sentences.

1. 趣味(しゅみ)は _____ です。

   Shumi wa _____ **desu.**

   My hobby is painting.

2. _____ が好(す)きです。

   _____ **ga suki desu.**

   I like painting.

3. _____ 本(ほん)を読(よ)みます。

   _____ **hon**

   o yomimasu.

   I read about two books a week.

4. ロペスさんが _____ を見(み)てみたいです。

   Ropesu san ga _____ **o mite mitai desu.**

   I want to try seeing the paintings that Ms. Lopez painted.

5. バイオリンとチェロとピアノの中(なか)で _____ ですか。

   Baiorin to chero to piano no naka de _____

   _____ **desu ka.**

   Which are you best at, the violin, the cello, or the piano?

6. とても高(たか)いですから、 _____。

   Totemo takai desu kara, _____.

   Since it's very expensive, I cannot buy it.

7. 今<small>いま</small>までにコンサートで ＿＿＿＿＿＿＿＿＿＿＿＿ はありますか。

Ima made ni konsaato de ＿＿＿＿＿＿＿＿＿＿＿＿＿ wa

arimasu ka.

Have you ever performed at a concert?

8. 今度<small>こんど</small>の土曜日<small>どようび</small>に銀座<small>ぎんざ</small>のレストランで演奏<small>えんそう</small>するんですけど、＿＿＿＿＿＿＿＿

。

Kondo no doyoobi ni ginza no resutoran de ensoosuru n desu kedo,

＿＿＿＿＿＿＿＿＿＿＿＿＿＿＿＿＿.

I will perform at a restaurant in Ginza this Saturday, so why don't you come?

ANSWER KEY

1.絵を描くこと **e o kaku koto**; 2.絵<small>え</small>を描<small>か</small>くの **E o kaku no**; 3.一週間<small>いっしゅうかん</small>に二冊<small>にさつ</small>ぐらい **Isshuukan ni nisatsu gurai**; 4.描<small>か</small>いた絵<small>え</small> **kaita e**; 5.どれが一番得意<small>いちばんとくい</small> **dore ga ichiban tokui**; 6.買<small>か</small>えません **kaemasen**; 7.演奏<small>えんそう</small>したこと **ensoooshita koto**; 8.いらっしゃいませんか **irasshaimasen ka**

Grammar Builder 2

SUPERLATIVES

▶ 11D Grammar Builder 2 (CD 9, Track 2)

You can compare three or more items using the structures described below.

A と B と C の中<small>なか</small>で A が一番<small>いちばん</small> X です。	A to B to C no naka de A ga ichiban X desu.	*A is the most X among A, B, and C.*
D の中<small>なか</small>で A が一番<small>いちばん</small> X です。	D no naka de A ga ichiban X desu.	*Among D, A is the most X.*

Let's see now how these structures can be used.

Question words
+ か ka and も mo

Potential form of verbs:
Can do and *be able to do*

Creating nouns from verbs:
nominalizer の no and こと koto

To want + object, person:
X が欲しい ga hoshii

ピアノとバイオリンとフルートの中^{なか}でピアノが一番得意^{いちばんとくい}です。

Piano to baiorin to furuuto no naka de piano ga ichiban tokui desu.

Among the piano, the violin and the flute, I am the best at the piano.

楽器^{がっき}の中^{なか}でピアノが一番得意^{いちばんとくい}です。

Gakki no naka de piano ga ichiban tokui desu.

Among musical instruments, I'm the best at the piano.

高橋^{たかはし}さんと林^{はやし}さんと森^{もり}さんの中^{なか}で林^{はやし}さんが一番若^{いちばんわか}いです。

Takahashi san to Hayashi san to Mori san no naka de Hayashi san ga ichiban wakai (young) desu.

Among Mr./Ms. Takahashi, Mr./Ms. Hayashi and Mr./Ms. Mori, Mr./Ms. Hayashi is the youngest.

このクラスの学生^{がくせい}の中^{なか}で林^{はやし}さんが一番若^{いちばんわか}いです。

Kono kurasu no gakusee no naka de Hayashi san ga ichiban wakai desu.

Among the students in this class, Mr./Ms. Hayashi is the youngest.

You can ask and answer the questions comparing three or more items using the structures below.

AとBとCの中^{なか}で[どれ / 誰^{だれ} / どこ / いつ / etc.]が一番^{いちばん}Xですか。	A to B to C no naka de [dore/dare/doko/itsu/ etc.] ga ichiban X desu ka.	*[Which/Who/Where/ When/etc.] is the most X, A, B, or C?*
Dの中^{なか}で[何^{なに} / 誰^{だれ} / どこ / いつ /etc.]が一番^{いちばん}Xですか。	D no naka de [nani/ dare/doko/itsu/etc.] ga ichiban X desu ka.	*[What/Who/Where/ When/etc.] is the most X among D?*

Note that どれ **dore** is usually used when listing the items being compared, such as テニスとゴルフと野球の中で **tenisu to gorufu to yakyuu no naka de** (*among tennis, golf, and baseball*), while **nani** is usually used for items that are not listed, such as スポーツの中で **supootsu no naka de** (*among [all] sports*). Let's see how these structures can be used.

A: お茶と紅茶とコーヒーの中でどれが一番好きですか。

Ocha to koocha to koohii no naka de dore ga ichiban suki desu ka.

Which do you like best, Japanese tea, black tea, or coffee?

B: コーヒーが一番好きです。

Koohii ga ichiban suki desu.

I like coffee best.

A: 飲み物の中で何が一番好きですか。

Nomimono no naka de nani ga ichiban suki desu ka.

Among [all] beverages, what do you like best?

B: トマトジュースが一番好きです。

Tomato juusu ga ichiban suki desu.

I like tomato juice best.

A: 土曜日と日曜日と月曜日の中で何曜日が一番忙しいですか。

Doyoobi to nichiyoobi to getsuyoobi no naka de nan-yoobi ga ichiban isogashii desu ka.

Which day of the week are you busiest, Saturday, Sunday, or Monday?

B: 月曜日が一番忙しいです。

Getsuyoobi ga ichiban isogashii desu.

I am busiest on Monday.

Question words
+ か ka and も mo

Potential form of verbs:
Can do and *be able to do*

Creating nouns from verbs:
nominalizer の no and こと koto

To want + object, person:
X が欲しい ga hoshii

A: 一週間の中で何曜日が一番忙しいですか。

Isshuukan no naka de nan-yoobi ga ichiban isogashii desu ka.

On what day of the week are you busiest?

B: 金曜日が一番忙しいです。

Kin-yoobi ga ichiban isogashii desu.

I'm busiest on Friday.

✎ Work Out 2

Translate the following sentences into Japanese using the expressions given in parentheses. You'll also need to provide the appropriate particles in order to form complete sentences.

1. *Which do you like best, tennis, golf, or jogging?*

   (好きです suki desu, テニス tenisu, ジョギング jogingu, 一番 ichiban, ゴルフ gorufu, どれ dore, か ka, 中 naka)

   _____

2. *I am best at the violin among the musical instruments.*

   (バイオリン baiorin, 中 naka, 一番 ichiban, 楽器 gakki, 得意です tokui desu)

   _____

3. *Which country is the biggest, Japan, China, or Korea?*

   (大きいです ookii desu, 日本 nihon, どの国 dono kuni, 韓国 kankoku, 中国 chuugoku, 一番 ichiban, か ka, 中 naka)

   _____

4. *Who works the most among the employees* (shain)?

（たくさん takusan, 社員 shain, 誰 dare, 中 naka, 一番 ichiban, か ka, 働きます hatarakimasu）

_____

5. *December is the busiest month of the year* (lit., in a year).

（一年 ichinen, 十二月 juunigatsu, 忙しいです isogashii desu, 中 naka, 一番 ichiban）

_____

ANSWER KEY

1. テニスとゴルフとジョギングの中でどれが一番好きですか。Tenisu to gorufu to jogingu no naka de dore ga ichiban suki desu ka. 2. 楽器の中でバイオリンが一番得意です。Gakki no naka de baiorin ga ichiban tokui desu. 3. 日本と中国と韓国の中でどの国が一番大きいですか。Nihon to chuugoku to kankoku no naka de dono kuni ga ichiban ookii desu ka. 4. 社員の中でが一番たくさん働きますか。 Shain no naka de dare ga ichiban takusan hatarakimasu ka. 5. 一年の中で十二月が一番忙しいです。 Ichinen no naka de juunigatsu ga ichiban isogashii desu.

✎ Drive It Home

Fill in the blanks with the appropriate words.

1. アメリカと日本と_____が大きいですか。

Amerika to nihon to _____ ga ookii desu ka.

Which is bigger, the U.S.A. or Japan?

2. アメリカの ＿ が日本より大きいです。

Amerika no _____ ga nihon yori ookii desu.

The U.S.A. is bigger than Japan.

Question words
+ か ka and も mo

Potential form of verbs:
Can do and *be able to do*

Creating nouns from verbs:
nominalizer の no and こと koto

To want + object, person:
X が欲しい ga hoshii

3. このアパートとあのアパートと _____ が便利ですか。

   Kono apaato to ano apaato to _____ **ga**

   benri desu ka.

   Which is more convenient, this apartment or that apartment?

4. このアパートの ___ があのアパートより便利です。

   Kono apaato no _____ **ga ano apaato yori benri desu.**

   This apartment is more convenient than that apartment.

5. お茶と紅茶とコーヒーの中で _____ 好きですか。

   Ocha to koocha to koohii no naka de _____

   _____ **suki desu ka.**

   Which do you like best, Japanese tea, black tea, or coffee?

6. 飲み物の中で _____ 好きですか。

   Nomimono no naka de _____ **suki desu**

   ka.

   Among beverages, what do you like best?

7. コーヒーが _____ 好きです。

   Koohii ga _____ **suki desu.**

   I like coffee best.

ANSWER KEY

1. どちらの方 dochira no hoo; 2. 方 hoo; 3. どちらの方 dochira no hoo; 4. 方 hoo; 5. どれが一番 dore ga ichiban; 6. 何が一番 nani ga ichiban; 7. 一番 ichiban

💡 Tip!

Ask your Japanese friends, classmates, or colleagues what their hobbies are in Japanese. You can also ask them about their favorite sports and whether or not they have some other special skills, such as painting or playing instruments. You can extend the conversation by asking if there is something they are particularly good or bad at. These topics are easy to talk about, and people will most likely ask you the same questions in return. If there aren't any Japanese speakers around you, ask the same questions to your family, friends, or colleagues in English. Write down the information you collect, then try saying it in Japanese.

How Did You Do?

Let's see how you did! By now, you should be able to:

☐ compare two items using *A is more X than B* (Still unsure? Jump back to page 242)

☐ compare three or more items using *A is the most X among D* (Still unsure? Jump back to page 251)

✏️ Word Recall

1. レタス retasu   a. *amount*

2. ご飯 gohan   b. *lettuce*

3. きゅうり kyuuri   c. *tobacco, cigarette*

4. おかず okazu   d. *half*

5. ハム hamu   e. *bread*

6. 量 ryoo   f. *cooked rice, meal*

7. 卵 tamago   g. *ham*

Question words
+ か ka and も mo

Potential form of verbs:
Can do and *be able to do*

Creating nouns from verbs:
nominalizer の no and こと koto

To want + object, person:
X が欲しい ga hoshii

8. 半分 hanbun ^{はんぶん}

h. *dish eaten with cooked rice*

9. パン pan

i. *egg*

10. 煙草 tabako ^{たばこ}

j. *cucumber*

ANSWER KEY

1. b; 2. f; 3. j; 4. h; 5. g; 6. a; 7. i; 8. d; 9. e; 10. c

Lesson 12: Conversations

In this lesson you'll learn how to:

☐ talk about past experiences

☐ use relative clauses

Conversation 1

▶ 12A Conversation 1 (Japanese: CD 9, Track 3; Japanese and English: CD 9, Track 4)

Mr. Clark and Mr. Tanaka are talking about sports during a break at work.

田中/Tanaka:
クラークさんはどんなスポーツが好きですか。

Kuraaku san wa donna supootsu ga suki desu ka.

クラーク/Kuraaku:
大学生の時は、バスケットボールをやっていました。でも、今はテニスが好きで、週末はよく家の近くのテニスコートへ行って、二時間ぐらいテニスをします。

Daigakusee no toki wa, basukettobooru o yatte imashita.

Demo, ima wa tenisu ga suki de, shuumatsu wa yoku ie

no chikaku no tenisu kooto e itte, nijikan gurai tenisu o

shimasu.

田中/Tanaka: へえ、じゃあ、テニスが上手なんでしょうね。

Hee, jaa, tenisu ga joozu na n deshoo ne.

クラーク/Kuraaku: まあまあです。それから、野球とサッカーを見るのが大好きで、試合がある時は、いつもテレビで見ています。

Maa maa desu. Sorekara, yakyuu to sakkaa o miru no ga daisuki de, shiai ga aru toki wa, itsumo terebi de mite imasu.

田中/Tanaka: そうですか。野球とサッカーとどちらの方が好きですか。

Soo desu ka. Yakyuu to sakkaa to dochira no hoo ga suki desu ka.

クラーク/Kuraaku: ううん、やっぱり野球の方が好きですね。田中さんは何かスポーツはしますか。

Uun, yappari yakyuu no hoo ga suki desu ne. Tanaka san wa nanika supootsu wa shimasu ka.

田中/Tanaka: 僕は学生の時は柔道のクラブに入っていましたが、今は得に何も運動はしていません。

Boku wa gakusee no toki wa juudoo no kurabu ni haitte imashita ga, ima wa toku ni nanimo undoo wa shite imasen.

クラーク/Kuraaku: そうですか。でも、柔道はいいですね。僕も柔道か剣道を習いたいんですけど、今は時間がないし・・・。

Soo desu ka. Demo, juudoo wa ii desu ne. Boku mo juudoo ka kendoo o narai tai n desu kedo, ima wa jikan ga nai shi …

田中/Tanaka: もし習うんだったら、剣道より柔道の方がいいと思いますよ。

Moshi narau n dattara, kendoo yori juudoo no hoo ga ii to omoimasu yo.

Question words
+ か ka and も mo

Potential form of verbs:
Can do and *be able to do*

Creating nouns from verbs:
nominalizer の no and こと koto

To want + object, person:
X が欲しい ga hoshii

クラーク/Kuraaku:　そうですね。僕もそう思います。ところで、田中さんは全然テニスはしませんか。

Soo desu ne. Boku mo soo omoimasu. Tokoro de, Tanaka san wa zenzen tenisu wa shimasen ka.

田中/Tanaka:　何度かしたことがありますけど、下手なんです。

Nando ka shita koto ga arimasu kedo, heta na n desu.

クラーク/Kuraaku:　今度一緒にテニスをしませんか。

Kondo issho ni tenisu o shimasen ka.

田中/Tanaka:　でも、僕は下手ですから・・・。

Demo, boku wa heta desu kara…

クラーク/Kuraaku:　僕もあまり上手にできませんから、大丈夫ですよ。僕が平日たまに使っているコートが会社の近くにありますから、そこでしませんか。

Boku mo amari joozu ni dekimasen kara, daijoobu desu yo. Boku ga heejitsu tamani tsukatte iru kooto ga kaisha no chikaku ni arimasu kara, soko de shimasen ka.

田中/Tanaka:　ええ、じゃあ今度時間がある時にそこへ行きましょう。

Ee, jaa kondo jikan ga aru toki ni soko e ikimashoo.

Tanaka:	*What kind of sports do you like, Mr. Clark?*
Clark:	*I played basketball when I was a college student. But, now I like tennis and often go to the tennis court near my house and play tennis for about two hours on weekends.*
Tanaka:	*Well, then, you are probably good at tennis, aren't you?*
Clark:	*So-so. And, I also like watching baseball and soccer very much, so when there is a game, I am always watching it on TV.*
Tanaka:	*I see. And which do you like better, baseball, or soccer?*
Clark:	*Well, I like baseball better, after all. Mr. Tanaka, do you play any sports?*

Tanaka:	I was in the judo club when I was a student, but now I'm not excersizing in particular.
Clark:	I see. But, judo is good, isn't it? I also want to take lessons in judo or kendo, but I don't have time now, so...
Tanaka:	If you take lessons, I think judo is better than kendo.
Clark:	Yes. I think so, too. By the way, Mr. Tanaka, don't you play tennis at all?
Tanaka:	I have played several times, but I am bad at it.
Clark:	Why don't we play tennis together sometime?
Ken:	But, I'm bad at it, so ...
Clark:	I cannot play so well either, so it's alright. The tennis court that I use occasionally on weekdays is near the office, so why don't we play there?
Tanaka:	Yes, then next time when we have time, let's go there!

✎ Conversation Practice 1

Fill in the blanks in the following sentences. If you're unsure of the answer, listen to the conversation one more time.

1. クラークさんは大学生の時、＿＿＿＿＿＿＿＿＿＿＿＿ をやっていました。

   Kuraaku san wa daigakusee no toki,

   ＿＿＿＿＿＿＿＿＿＿＿＿＿＿ **o yatte imashita.**

2. クラークさんは週末によく家の近くの＿＿＿＿＿＿＿＿＿へ行って、二時間ぐらいテニスをします。

   Kuraaku san wa shuumatsu ni yoku ie no chikaku no ＿＿＿＿＿＿

   ＿＿＿＿＿＿ **e itte, nijikan gurai tenisu o shimasu.**

Creating nouns from verbs: nominalizer の no and こと koto

To want + object, person: X が欲しい ga hoshii

3. クラークさんは ＿＿＿＿＿＿ の方がサッカーより好きです。

Kuraaku san wa ＿＿＿＿＿＿＿＿ no hoo ga sakkaa yori suki desu.

4. 田中さんは学生の時、＿＿＿＿＿＿ のクラブに入っていました。

Tanaka san wa gakusee no toki, ＿＿＿＿＿＿＿＿ no kurabu ni haitte imashita.

5. 田中さんは ＿＿＿＿＿＿＿ を何度かしたことがありますが、下手です。

Tanaka san wa ＿＿＿＿＿＿＿ o nando ka shita koto ga arimasu ga, heta desu.

ANSWER KEY

1. バスケットボール basukettobooru; 2. テニスコート tenisu kooto; 3. 野球 yakyuu; 4. 柔道 juudoo;
5. テニス tenisu

Grammar Builder 1

TALKING ABOUT PAST EXPERIENCES

▶ 12B Grammar Builder 1 (CD 9, Track 5)

You can talk about your past experiences using the structure below.

> *Plain past tense form of a verb (た ta-form)* + ことがあります/ある koto ga
> arimasu/aru

日本へ行ったことがあります。

Nihon e itta koto ga arimasu.

I have been to Japan.

京都の写真を撮ったことがあります。

Kyooto no shashin o totta koto ga arimasu.

I have taken pictures of Kyoto.

コンサートで演奏したことがあります。

Konsaato de ensooshita koto ga arimasu.

I have performed at a concert.

When answering a question, you can just use あります arimasu or ありません arimasen without repeating what was already mentioned in the question, as shown in the following example.

A: この映画を見たことはありますか。

Kono eega o mita koto wa arimasu ka.

Have you seen this movie?

B: ええ、あります。/いいえ、ありません。

Ee, arimasu./Iie, arimasen.

Yes, I have./No, I haven't.

The following time expressions are often used with this structure.

今までに、 これまでに	ima made ni, kore made ni	*up to now*
一度	ichido	*once*
何度も	nando mo	*many times*
一度も + *negative*	ichido mo + *negative*	*never*
まだ + *negative*	mada + *negative*	*not yet*

A: 今までにポルトガル語を勉強したことはありますか。

Ima made ni porutogarugo o benkyooshita koto wa arimasu ka.

Have you ever studied Portuguese before?

Question words
+ か ka and も mo

Potential form of verbs:
Can do and *be able to do*

Creating nouns from verbs:
nominalizer の no and こと koto

To want + object, person:
X が欲しい ga hoshii

B: いいえ、一度もありません。

Iie, ichido mo arimasen.

No, I have never (studied it).

A: 図書館で本を借りたことはありますか。

Toshokan de hon o karita koto wa arimasu ka.

Have you ever borrowed books at the library?

B: はい、何度もあります。

Hai, nando mo arimasu.

Yes, I have (borrowed them) many times.

A: 日本語でレポートを書いたことはありますか。

Nihongo de repooto o kaita koto wa arimasu ka.

Have you ever written a report in Japanese?

B: いいえ、まだありません。

Iie, mada arimasen.

No, I haven't (written it) yet.

A: これまでにおすしを作ったことはありますか。

Kore made ni osushi o tsukutta koto wa arimasu ka.

Have you ever made sushi?

B: はい、一度あります。

Hai, ichido arimasu.

Yes, I have (made it) once.

✎ Work Out 1

Translate the following Japanese sentences into English.

1. 今までにその本を読んだことはありますか。

   Ima made ni sono hon o yonda koto wa arimasu ka.

   _____

2. 一度もピアノを弾いたことはありません。

   Ichido mo piano o hiita koto wa arimasen.

   _____

3. 一度大学のテニスコートでテニスをしたことがあります。

   Ichido daigaku no tenisu kooto de tenisu o shita koto ga arimasu.

   _____

4. まだ相撲をみたことはありませんから、今度是非見てみたいです。

   Mada sumoo o mita koto wa arimasen kara, kondo zehi mite mitai desu.

   _____

5. 駅の前のイタリア料理のレストランへ何度も行ったことがあります。

   Eki no mae no itaria ryoori no resutoran e nando mo itta koto ga arimasu.

   _____

ANSWER KEY

1. *Have you ever read that book before?* 2. *I have never played the piano even once.* 3. *I played tennis at the university tennis court once.* 4. *I haven't seen a sumo match yet, so I'd like to try and see one sometime by all means.* 5. *I have been to the Italian restaurant in front of the station many times.*

Creating nouns from verbs: *To want* + object, person:
nominalizer の no and こと koto   X が欲しい ga hoshii

🔊 Conversation 2

▶ 12C Conversation 2 (Japanese: CD 9, Track 6; Japanese and English: CD 9, Track 7)

Ms. Lopez and Ms. Yano are chatting about their interests and hobbies on their way home from the work.

矢野/Yano:	ロペスさんは何か趣味はありますか。
	Ropesu san wa nani ka shumi wa arimasu ka.
ロペス/Ropesu:	えっと、絵を描くのが好きです。それから、本を読むのも好きで、一週間に二冊ぐらい読むんですよ。
	Etto, e o kaku no ga suki desu. Sorekara, hon o yomu no mo suki de, isshuukan ni nisatsu gurai yomu n desu yo.
矢野/Yano:	へえ、絵を描くことと読書ですか。いいですねえ。今度、ロペスさんが書いた絵を見てみたいです。
	Hee, e o kaku koto to dokusho desu ka. Ii desu nee.
	Kondo, Ropesu san ga kaita e o mite mitai desu.
ロペス/Ropesu:	あまり上手じゃありませんけど。矢野さんは何か趣味はありますか。
	Amari joozu ja arimasen kedo. Yano san wa nani ka shumi wa arimasu ka.
矢野/Yano:	私は絵を描くことはできないけど、写真を撮るのが好きなんです。週末はよくカメラを持って出掛けるんですよ。
	Watashi wa e o kaku koto wa dekinai kedo, shashin o toru no ga suki na n desu. Shuumatsu wa yoku kamera o motte dekakeru n desu yo.
ロペス/Ropesu:	そうですか。
	Soo desu ka.
矢野/Yano:	ロペスさんは何か楽器は演奏できますか。
	Ropesu san wa nani ka gakki wa ensoodekimasu ka.

ロペス/Ropesu:

私は何も楽器は演奏できないんです。今フルートを習っていますけど、なかなか上手に吹けません。とても難しいです。矢野さんは？

Watashi wa nani mo gakki wa ensoodekinai n desu.

Ima furuuto o naratte imasu kedo, nakanaka joozu ni fukemasen. Totemo muzukashii desu. Yano san wa?

矢野/Yano:

私はバイオリンとチェロとピアノが弾けます。

Watashi wa baiorin to chero to piano ga hikemasu.

ロペス/Ropesu:

へえ、すごいですね。バイオリンとチェロとピアノの中でどれが一番得意ですか。

Hee, sugoi desu ne. Baiorin to chero to piano no naka de dore ga ichiban tokui desu ka.

矢野/Yano:

もう二十年ぐらい習っていますから、バイオリンが一番得意です。

Moo nijuunen gurai naratte imasu kara, baiorin ga ichiban tokui desu.

ロペス/Ropesu:

そうですか。

Soo desu ka.

矢野/Yano:

今使っているバイオリンは古いので、新しいのが欲しいんですけど、とても高いですから買えません。

Ima tsukatte iru baiorin wa furui node, atarashii no ga hoshii n desu kedo, totemo takai desu kara kaemasen.

ロペス/Ropesu:

今までにコンサートで演奏したことはありますか。

Ima made ni konsaato de ensooshita koto wa arimasu ka.

矢野/Yano:

ええ、何度かあります。実は今度の土曜日に銀座のレストランで演奏するんですけど、いらっしゃいませんか。

Ee, nando ka arimasu. Jitsu wa kondo no doyoobi ni ginza no resutoran de ensoosuru n desu kedo, irasshaimasen ka.

Question words
+ か ka and も mo

Potential form of verbs:
Can do and *be able to do*

Creating nouns from verbs:
nominalizer の no and こと koto

To want + object, person:
X が欲しい ga hoshii

ロペス/Ropesu:　　　　ええ、是非行きたいです。
　　　　　　　　　　　Ee, zehi ikitai desu.

Yano:	*Ms. Lopez, do you have any hobbies?*
Lopez:	*Well, I like painting. Besides, I like reading books, so I read about two books per week.*
Yano:	*Painting and reading books, I see. That's good. I'd like to see (lit., I want to try seeing) the paintings you've done some day.*
Lopez:	*I'm not so good at it, but… Ms. Yano, do you have any hobbies?*
Yano:	*I can't paint, but I like taking pictures. On weekends, I often go out with a camera.*
Lopez:	*I see.*
Yano:	*Ms. Lopez, can you play any musical instruments?*
Lopez:	*I cannot play any instruments. I am taking flute lessons now, but cannot play it well easily. It's very difficult. What about you, Ms. Yano?*
Yano:	*I can play the violin, the cello, and the piano.*
Lopez:	*Wow, that's amazing, isn't it? Which one are you best at, violin, cello, or piano?*
Yano:	*I've been taking lessons for about twenty years already, so I'm best at the violin.*
Lopez:	*I see.*
Yano:	*Since the violin which I am using now is old, I'd like to buy a new one, but it's very expensive, so I cannot buy it.*
Lopez:	*Have you ever performed at a concert?*
Yano:	*Yes, I performed several times. Actually, I will perform at a restaurant in Ginza next Saturday, so why don't you come?*
Lopez:	*Yes, by all means, I'd like to come.*

✎ Conversation Practice 2

Fill in the blanks in the following sentences with the missing words. If you're unsure of the answer, listen to the conversation one more time.

1. ロペスさんの趣味（しゅみ）は _____ と読書（どくしょ）です。

   Ropesu san no shumi wa _____ **to dokusho desu.**

2. ロペスさんは一週間（いっしゅうかん）に本（ほん）を _____ ぐらい読（よ）みます。

   Ropesu san wa isshuukan ni hon o _____ **gurai yomimasu.**

3. ロペスさんは今（いま） _____ を習（なら）っています。

   Ropesu san wa ima _____ **o naratte imasu.**

4. 矢野（やの）さんは楽器（がっき）の中（なか）で _____ が一番得意（いちばんとくい）です。

   Yano san wa gakki no naka de _____ **ga ichiban tokui desu.**

5. 矢野（やの）さんは今度（こんど）の土曜日（どようび）に銀座（ぎんざ）の _____ でバイオリンを演奏（えんそう）します。

   Yano san wa kondo no doyoobi ni ginza no _____ **de baiorin o ensooshimasu.**

ANSWER KEY
1. 絵（え）を描（か）くこと e o kaku koto; 2. 二冊（にさつ） nisatsu; 3. フルート furuuto; 4. バイオリン baiorin; 5. レストラン resutoran

Question words
+ か ka and も mo

Potential form of verbs:
Can do and *be able to do*

Creating nouns from verbs:
nominalizer の no and こと koto

To want + object, person:
X が欲しい ga hoshii

Grammar Builder 2

RELATIVE CLAUSES

▶ 12D Grammar Builder 2 (CD 9, Track 8)

Nouns are usually modified by adjectives, but nouns can also be modified by relative clauses. For instance, in the sentence *The book which I bought yesterday is interesting*, *which I bought yesterday* is a relative clause modifying *the book*.

There are two major differences between the English and the Japanese relative clause construction. First, unlike in English, in Japanese the relative clause precedes a noun just as adjectives do. Second, there are no relative pronouns (such as English *which*, *who*, *that*, or *whose*) in Japanese. The structure of relative clauses is described below; it differs depending on whether it contains a verb, an adjective + noun or a noun as a predicate.

> *plain form of a verb/*い *i-adjective*
> な na-*adjective* + な na *(non-past)/*だった datta *(past)* + *noun*
> *noun* + の no *(non-past)/*だった datta *(past)*

As for verbs and い i-adjectives, you have to use the plain form in relative clauses. The clauses enclosed in parentheses in the following examples are the relative clauses. Please also note that a subject inside a relative clause is usually marked by が ga rather than は wa.

(昨日見た) 映画はとても良かったです。
(**Kinoo mita**) **eega wa totemo yokatta desu.**
The movie (that I saw yesterday) was very good.

(鈴木さんが読んでいる) 本が読みたいです。
(**Suzuki san ga yonde iru**) **hon ga yomitai desu.**
I want to read the book (which Mr./Ms. Suzuki is reading).

（魚料理がおいしい）レストランへ行きたいです。

(Sakana ryoori ga oishii) resutoran e ikitai desu.

I want to go to a restaurant (where fish dishes are delicious).

（居間が広い）アパートを探しています。

(Ima ga hiroi) apaato o sagashite imasu.

I am looking for an apartment (whose living room is spacious).

As for な na-adjectives, a な na-adjective + な na (non-past) or な na-adjective + だった datta (past) appears at the end of a relative clause.

（ピアノとバイオリンが得意な）人は誰ですか。

(Piano to baiorin ga tokui na) hito wa dare desu ka.

Who is the person (who is good at the piano and violin)?

（朝きれいだった）部屋がもう汚いです。

(Asa kiree datta) heya ga moo kitanai desu.

The room (which was clean in the morning) is already dirty.

With nouns, a noun + の no (non-past) or noun + だった datta (past) also appears at the end of a relative clause.

（誕生日が一月の）人は何人いますか。

(Tanjoobi ga ichigatsu no) hito wa nannin imasu ka.

How many people are there (whose birthday is in January)?

（お父さんが弁護士だった）友達がいます。

(Otoosan ga bengoshi datta) tomodachi ga imasu.

I have a friend (whose father was a lawyer).

Question words
+ か ka and も mo

Potential form of verbs:
Can do and *be able to do*

Creating nouns from verbs:
nominalizer の no and こと koto

To want + object, person:
X が欲しい ga hoshii

✎ Work Out 2

A. Use the appropriate forms of the verbs, adjectives and copula given in parentheses
   to complete the sentences.

1. これは (私が今欲しいです) 車です。

   Kore wa (watashi ga ima hoshii desu) kuruma desu.

   This is the car which I want now.

   _____

2. (スミスさんが撮りました) 写真が見てみたいです。

   (Sumisu san ga torimashita) shashin ga mite mitai desu.

   I want to try seeing pictures that Mr./Ms. Smith took.

   _____

3. (週末も静かです) 公園はありますか。

   (Shuumatsu mo shizuka desu) kooen wa arimasu ka.

   Is there a park that is quiet on weekends, too?

   _____

4. (フルートがとても上手に吹けます) 友達がいます。

   (Furuuto ga totemo joozu ni fukemasu) tomodachi ga imasu.

   I have a friend who can play the flute very well.

   _____

5. (あそこでピアノを弾いています) 女の人は川村さんです。

   (Asoko de piano o hiite imasu) onna no hito wa Kawamura san desu.

The woman who is playing the piano there is Ms. Kawamura.

B. Translate the following Japanese sentences into English.

1. 田中さんと話している男の人は高橋さんのお兄さんです。

   Tanaka san to hanashite iru otoko no hito wa Takahashi san no oniisan desu.

2. お父さんが日本人でお母さんがアメリカ人の友達がいます。

   Otoosan ga nihonjin de okaasan ga amerikajin no tomodachi ga imasu.

3. 週末デパートで買ったセーターはちょっと高かったです。

   Shuumatsu depaato de katta seetaa wa chotto takakatta desu.

4. 台所が狭いアパートは不便だと思います。

   Daidokoro ga semai apaato wa fuben da to omoimasu.

5. 日曜日から土曜日までいつも暇な人はいますか。

   Nichiyoobi kara doyoobi made itsumo hima na hito wa imasu ka.

ANSWER KEY

A. 1. 私が今欲しい watashi ga ima hoshii; 2. スミスさんが撮った Sumisu san ga totta; 3. 週末も静かな Shuumatsu mo shizuka na; 4. フルートがとても上手に吹ける Furuuto ga totemo joozu ni fukeru; 5. あそこでピアノを弾いている Asoko de piano o hiite iru

B. 1. *The man who is talking with Mr./Ms. Tanaka is Mr./Ms. Takahashi's older brother.* 2. *I have a*

Question words
+ か ka and も mo

Potential form of verbs:
Can do and *be able to do*

Creating nouns from verbs:
nominalizer の no and こと koto

To want + object, person:
X が欲しい ga hoshii

friend whose father is Japanese and mother is American. 3. The sweater I bought at the department store on the weekend was a little expensive. 4. I think apartments with small kitchens (lit., whose kitchens are small) are inconvenient. 5. Are there people who have always a lot of free time from Sunday to Saturday?

✎ Drive It Home

A. Fill in the blanks with appropriate words from the word bank.

1. 日本へ行った _____ 。

   Nihon e itta _____.

   I have been to Japan.

2. 京都の写真を撮った _____ 。

   Kyooto no shashin o totta _____.

   I have taken pictures of Kyoto.

3. コンサートで演奏した _____ 。

   Konsaato de ensooshita _____.

   I have performed at a concert.

4. おすしを作った _____ 。

   Osushi o tsukutta _____.

   I have made sushi.

B. Fill in the blanks with the words in parentheses in their appropriate form.

1. 昨日 _____ 映画はとても良かったです。(見る)

   Kinoo _____ **eega wa totemo yokatta desu. (miru)**

   The movie that I saw yesterday was very good.

2. 魚料理が（さかなりょうり） _____ レストランへ行（い）きたいです。(おいしい)

Sakana ryoori ga _____ resutoran e ikitai desu. (oishii)

I want to go to a restaurant where fish dishes are delicious.

3. ピアノとバイオリンが_____ 人（ひと）は誰（だれ）ですか。(得意（とくい）)

Piano to baiorin ga _____ hito wa dare desu ka. (tokui)

Who is the person who is good at the piano and violin?

4. 誕生日（たんじょうび）が _____ 人（ひと）は何人（なんにん）いますか。(一月（いちがつ）)

Tanjoobi ga _____ hito wa nannin imasu ka.

(ichigatsu)

How many people are there whose birthdays are in January?

ANSWER KEY

A: 1. ことがあります koto ga arimasu; 2. ことがあります koto ga arimasu; 3. ことがあります koto ga arimasu; 4. ことがあります koto ga arimasu

B: 1. 見（み）た mita; 2. おいしい oishii; 3. 得意（とくい）な tokui na; 4. 一月（いちがつ）の ichigatsu no

How Did You Do?

Let's see how you did! By now, you should be able to:

☐ talk about past experiences (Still unsure? Jump back to page 262)

☐ use relative clauses (Still unsure? Jump back to page 270)

✎ Word Recall

1. 塩辛<ruby>塩辛<rt>しおから</rt></ruby>い shiokarai   a. *chance*

2. えび ebi   b. *to give*

3. <ruby>一度<rt>いちど</rt></ruby> ichido   c. *shellfish*

4. <ruby>和風<rt>わふう</rt></ruby> wafuu   d. *to order*

5. <ruby>注文<rt>ちゅうもん</rt></ruby>する chuumonsuru   e. *to receive*

6. いか ika   f. *shrimp*

7. あげる ageru   g. *salty*

8. <ruby>貝<rt>かい</rt></ruby> kai   h. *cuttlefish, squid*

9. もらう morau   i. *Japanese style*

10. <ruby>機会<rt>きかい</rt></ruby> kikai   j. *once*

ANSWER KEY

1. g; 2. f; 3. j; 4. i; 5. d; 6. h; 7. b; 8. c; 9. e; 10. a

Don't forget to practice and reinforce what you've learned by visiting **www.livinglanguage.com/languagelab** for flashcards, games, and quizzes for Unit 3!

Unit 3 Essentials

Vocabulary Essentials

Test your knowledge of the key material in this unit by filling in the blanks in the following charts. Once you've completed these pages, you'll have tested your retention, and you'll have your own reference for the most essential vocabulary.

SPORTS

	exercise(s)
	soccer
	volleyball
	swimming
	judo
	kendo
	tennis court
	club
	game (of sport)

MUSIC

	musical instrument
	piano
	violin
	cello
	flute

	clarinet
	concert

OTHER HOBBIES AND SKILLS

	like a lot
	skillful
	unskillful
	hobby
	special ability, special skill
	painting, drawing
	reading books
	seeing movies (lit., movie appreciation)
	photography

VERBS

	to be good at
	to be bad at
	to exercise
	to swim
	to take lessons in
	to do
	to own, to hold
	to perform (a musical instrument)
	to play (a string instrument)

	to play (a wind instrument)
	to play (a percussion instrument)
	to want

ADVERBS

	next time, this time, shortly
	especially
	several times
	up to now
	once
	many times
	never
	not yet

OTHER USEFUL EXPRESSONS

	after all, as expected
	So-so.
	That's amazing.

Grammar Essentials

Here is a reference of the key grammar that was covered in Unit 3. Make sure you understand the summary and can use all of the grammar it covers.

QUESTION WORDS + か KA AND も MO

<ruby>何<rt>なに</rt></ruby>か	nani ka	*something*
<ruby>誰<rt>だれ</rt></ruby>か	dare ka	*someone*
どこか	doko ka	*somewhere*
<ruby>何<rt>なに</rt></ruby>も + *negative*	nani mo + *negative*	*nothing*
<ruby>誰<rt>だれ</rt></ruby>も + *negative*	dare mo + *negative*	*no one, nobody*
どこも + *negative*	doko mo + *negative*	*nowhere*

CREATING NOUNS OUT OF VERBS: NOMINALIZER の NO AND こと KOTO

Plain form of verbs + の *no or* こと *koto*

POTENTIAL FORM OF VERBS

CAN DO

Class I (う u-verbs)

DICTIONARY FORM	POTENTIAL FORM OF VERBS (PLAIN FORM)			
	Non-past affirmative	Non-past negative	Past affirmative	Past negative
<ruby>書<rt>か</rt></ruby>く kaku *(to write)*	<ruby>書<rt>か</rt></ruby>ける kakeru	<ruby>書<rt>か</rt></ruby>けない kakenai	<ruby>書<rt>か</rt></ruby>けた kaketa	<ruby>書<rt>か</rt></ruby>けなかった kakenakatta
<ruby>読<rt>よ</rt></ruby>む yomu *(to read)*	<ruby>読<rt>よ</rt></ruby>める yomeru	<ruby>読<rt>よ</rt></ruby>めない yomenai	<ruby>読<rt>よ</rt></ruby>めた yometa	<ruby>読<rt>よ</rt></ruby>めなかった yomenakatta

DICTIONARY FORM	POTENTIAL FORM OF VERBS (PLAIN FORM)			
	Non-past affirmative	Non-past negative	Past affirmative	Past negative
聞く kiku (to listen)	聞ける kikeru	聞けない kikenai	聞けた kiketa	聞けなかった kikenakatta
使う tsukau (to use)	使える tsukaeru	使えない tsukaenai	使えた tsukaeta	使えなかった tsukaenakatta
行く iku (to go)	行ける ikeru	行けない ikenai	行けた iketa	行けなかった ikenakatta

Class II (る ru-verbs)

DICTIONARY FORM	POTENTIAL FORM OF VERBS (PLAIN FORM)			
	Non-past affirmative	Non-past negative	Past affirmative	Past negative
食べる taberu (to eat)	食べられる taberareru	食べられない taberarenai	食べられた taberareta	食べられなかった taberarenakatta
見る miru (to see)	見られる mirareru	見られない mirarenai	見られた mirareta	見られなかった mirarenakatta
起きる okiru (to get up)	起きられる okirareru	起きられない okirarenai	起きられた okirareta	起きられなかった okirarenakatta

DICTIONARY FORM	POTENTIAL FORM OF VERBS (PLAIN FORM)			
	Non-past affirmative	Non-past negative	Past affirmative	Past negative
寝る neru *(to sleep)*	寝られる nerareru	寝られない nerarenai	寝られた nerareta	寝られなかった nerarenakatta
教える oshieru *(to teach)*	教えられる oshierareru	教えられない oshierarenai	教えられた oshierareta	教えられなかった oshierarenakatta

Class III

DICTIONARY FORM	POTENTIAL FORM OF VERBS (PLAIN FORM)			
	Non-past affirmative	Non-past negative	Past affirmative	Past negative
する suru *(to do)*	できる dekiru	できない dekinai	できた dekita	できなかった dekinakatta
来る kuru *(to come)*	来られる korareru	来られない korarenai	来られた korareta	来られなかった korarenakatta

TO BE ABLE TO DO

Dictionary form of a verb + ことができる koto ga dekiru

TO WANT + OBJECT

X が欲しい (です) ga hoshii (desu).

	NON-PAST AFFIRMATIVE	NON-PAST NEGATIVE	PAST AFFIRMATIVE	PAST NEGATIVE
Plain form	欲しい hoshii	欲しくない hoshiku nai	欲しかった hoshikatta	欲しくなかった hoshiku nakatta
Polite form	欲しいです hoshii desu	欲しく [ないです/ありません] hoshiku [nai desu/ arimasen]	欲しかったです hoshikatta desu	欲しく [なかったです/ありませんでした] hoshiku [nakatta desu/ arimasen deshita]

Someone + が/は X を 欲しがって [いる/います]
Someone + ga/wa X o hoshigatte [iru/imasu]

COMPARATIVES

A は B より X。	A wa B yori X.	*A is more X than B.*

A と B とどちらの方が X か。	A to B to dochira no hoo ga X ka.	*Which is more X, A or B?*
A/B の方が (B/A より) X.	A/B no hoo ga (B/A yori) X.	*A/B is more X than B/A.*

SUPERLATIVE

A と B と C の中で A が 一番 X です。	A to B to C no naka de A ga ichiban X desu.	*A is the most X among A, B, and C.*
D の中で A が一番 X です。	D no naka de A ga ichiban X desu.	*Among D, A is the most X.*

A と B と C の中で [どれ/誰/どこ/いつ/etc.] が一番 X ですか。	A to B to C no naka de [dore/dare/doko/itsu/ etc.] ga ichiban X desu ka.	*[Which/Who/Where/ When/etc.] is the most X, A, B or C?*
D の中で [何/誰/どこ/ いつ/etc.] が一番 X で すか。	D no naka de [nani/ dare/doko/itsu/etc.] ga ichiban X desu ka.	*[What/Who/Where/ When/etc.] is the most X among D?*

TALKING ABOUT PAST EXPERIENCES

Plain past tense form of a verb (た ta-form) +
ことがあります/ある koto ga arimasu/aru

RELATIVE CLAUSES

*plain form of a verb/*い i-adjective
な na-adjective + な na *(non-past)/*だった datta *(past) + noun*
noun + の no *(non-past)/*だった datta *(past)*

Unit 3 Quiz

Let's put the most essential Japanese words and grammar points you've learned so far into practice with a few exercises. It's important to be sure that you've mastered this material before you move on. Score yourself at the end of the review and see if you need to go back for more practice, or if you're ready to move on to Unit 4.

A. Fill in the blanks with appropriate "question word + particle" combination.

1. ＿＿＿＿＿＿＿特技_{とくぎ}はありますか。

   ＿＿＿＿＿＿＿＿＿ tokugi wa arimasu ka.

   Do you have any special skills?

2. 昨日_{きのう} ＿＿＿＿＿＿＿ 来_きましたか。

   Kinoo ＿＿＿＿＿＿＿＿＿kimashita ka.

   Did anyone come yesterday?

3. ＿＿＿＿＿＿＿来_きませんでした。

   ＿＿＿＿＿＿＿＿＿ kimasen deshita.

   No one came.

B. Fill in the blanks by changing the verbs in the parentheses into nouns with the nominalizer の no.

1. ＿＿＿＿＿＿＿と ＿＿＿＿＿＿が好_すきです。(食_たべる、寝_ねる)

   ＿＿＿＿＿＿＿＿＿＿ to ＿＿＿＿＿＿＿＿＿ ga suki desu. (taberu, neru)

   I like eating and sleeping.

2. _____ はあまり好<ruby>き<rt>す</rt></ruby>じゃありません。(勉強<ruby><rt>べんきょう</rt></ruby>する)

_____ wa amari suki ja arimasen.

(benkyoosuru)

I don't like studying so much.

C. Fill in the blanks by changing the verbs in parentheses to their
   appropriate form.

1. 日本語<ruby><rt>にほんご</rt></ruby>の本<ruby><rt>ほん</rt></ruby>が _____。(読<ruby><rt>よ</rt></ruby>みます)

   Nihongo no hon ga _____. (yomimasu)

   I can read Japanese books.

2. 午前五時<ruby><rt>ごぜんごじ</rt></ruby>に _____。(起<ruby><rt>お</rt></ruby>きます)

   Gozen goji ni _____. (okimasu)

   I can get up at 5 a.m.

3. 英語<ruby><rt>えいご</rt></ruby>とスペイン語<ruby><rt>ご</rt></ruby>が _____。(話<ruby><rt>はな</rt></ruby>します)

   Eego to supeingo ga _____. (hanashimasu)

   I can speak English and Spanish.

D. Fill in the blanks with the appropriate words.

1. 私<ruby><rt>わたし</rt></ruby>は日本人<ruby><rt>にほんじん</rt></ruby>の友達<ruby><rt>ともだち</rt></ruby>が _____。

   Watashi wa nihonjin no tomodachi ga _____.

   I want Japanese friends.

2. スミスさんは日本人<ruby><rt>にほんじん</rt></ruby>の友達<ruby><rt>ともだち</rt></ruby>を _____。

   Sumisu san wa nihonjin no tomodachi o _____

   _____.

   Mr./Ms. Smith wants Japanese friends.

3. 誕生日にカメラが _____ 。

Tanjoobi ni kamera ga _____ .

I wanted a camera for my birthday.

E. Translate the following sentences into Japanese using the expressions given in parentheses. You'll also need to provide the appropriate particles in order to form complete sentences.

1. *Which is bigger, the U.S.A. or Japan?*

(大きい、アメリカ、です、方、日本、か、どちら)

(ookii, amerika, desu, hoo, nihon, ka, dochira)

_____

2. *The U.S.A. is bigger than Japan.*

(です、より、日本、方、アメリカ、大きい)

(desu, yori, nihon, hoo, amerika, ookii)

_____

3. *Among beverages, what do you like best?*

(何、一番、か、です、中、好き、飲み物)

(nani, ichiban, ka, desu, naka, suki, nomimono)

_____

4. *I like coffee best.*

(一番、です、コーヒー、好き)

(ichiban, desu, koohii, suki)

_____

F. Complete the sentences by using the verbs in parentheses.

1. 日本へ ＿＿＿＿＿＿＿＿＿＿＿＿＿＿＿＿ 。(行く)

   Nihon e ＿＿＿＿＿＿＿＿＿＿＿＿＿＿＿＿＿＿＿＿. (iku)

   I have been to Japan.

2. おすしを ＿＿＿＿＿＿＿＿＿＿＿＿＿＿ 。(作る)

   Osushi o ＿＿＿＿＿＿＿＿＿＿＿＿＿＿＿＿＿＿

   ＿＿＿＿＿＿＿＿＿＿. (tsukuru)

   I have made sushi.

G. Complete the following sentences containing relative clauses.

1. 昨日＿＿＿＿＿＿＿＿ はとても良かったです。

   Kinoo ＿＿＿＿＿＿＿＿＿＿＿wa totemo yokatta desu.

   The movie that I saw yesterday was very good.

2. ＿＿＿＿＿＿＿＿＿＿＿ レストランへ行きたいです。

   ＿＿＿＿＿＿＿＿＿＿＿＿＿resutoran e ikitai desu.

   I want to go to a restaurant where sushi is delicious.

3. ピアノが ＿＿＿＿＿＿＿＿ は誰ですか。

   Piano ga ＿＿＿＿＿＿＿＿＿＿＿＿＿ hito wa dare desu ka. (tokui)

   Who is the person who is good at the piano?

ANSWER KEY

A. 1. 何か Nani ka; 2. 誰か dare ka; 3. 誰も Dare mo

B. 1. 食べるの Taberu no, 寝るの neru no; 2. 勉強するの Benkyoosuru no

C. 1. 読めます yomemasu; 2. 起きられます okiraremasu; 3. 話せます hanasemasu

D. 1. 欲しいです hoshii desu; 2. 欲しがっています hoshigatte imasu; 3. 欲しかったです hoshikatta desu

E. 1. アメリカと日本とどちらの方が大きいですか Amerika to nihon to dochira no hoo ga ookii desu ka; 2. アメリカの方が日本より大きいです Amerika no hoo ga nihon yori ookii desu; 3. 飲み物の中

で何が一番好きですか Nomimono no naka de nani ga ichiban suki desu ka; 4. コーヒーが一番好きです Koohii ga ichiban suki desu
F. 1. 行ったことがあります itta koto ga arimasu; 2. 作ったことがあります tsukutta koto ga arimasu
G. 1. 見た映画 mita eega; 2. すしがおいしい Sushi ga oishii; 3. 得意な人 tokui na hito

How Did You Do?

Give yourself a point for every correct answer, then use the following key to tell whether you're ready to move on:

0-7 points: It's probably a good idea to go back through the lesson again. You may be moving too quickly, or there may be too much "down time" between your contact with Japanese. Remember that it's better to spend 30 minutes with Japanese three or four times a week than it is to spend two or three hours just once a week. Find a pace that's comfortable for you, and spread your contact hours out as much as you can.

8-12 points: You would benefit from a review before moving on. Go back and spend a little more time on the specific points that gave you trouble. Re-read the Grammar Builder sections that were difficult, and do the work out one more time. Don't forget about the online supplemental practice material, either. Go to **www.livinglanguage.com/languagelab** for games and quizzes that will reinforce the material from this unit.

13-17 points: Good job! There are just a few points that you could consider reviewing before moving on. If you haven't worked with the games and quizzes on **www.livinglanguage.com/languagelab**, please give them a try.

18-20 points: Great! You're ready to move on to the next unit.

points

Unit 4:
Doctors and Health

Welcome to the final Unit of *Advanced Japanese*. You've come a long way and you should be proud of yourself! In Unit 4, you will learn how to talk about your body and health, as well as how to speak to a doctor and describe your symptoms when you are sick. By the end of the unit, you'll be able to:

☐ use key vocabulary related to your body and health

☐ use key vocabulary related to visiting a doctor's office

☐ use pronouns

☐ describe actions taken before hand in preparation for some coming events

☐ use the て te-form of adjectives

☐ use giving and receiving verbs to express actions taken as a favor

☐ ask for permission

☐ make negative requests

☐ express obligation

☐ give advice

Lesson 13: Words

In this lesson you'll learn how to:

☐ use key vocabulary related to your body and health

☐ use key vocabulary related to visiting a doctor's office

☐ use pronouns

☐ describe actions taken before hand in preparation for some coming events

Word Builder 1

▶ 13A Word Builder 1 (CD 9, Track 9)

しんりょうじょ 診療所	shinryoojo	*clinic*
うけつけ 受付	uketsuke	*front desk*
しんさつしつ 診察室	shinsatsushitsu	*consulting room*
まちあいしつ 待合室	machiaishitsu	*waiting room*
しんさつ 診察	shinsatsu	*medical consultation*
しょしん 初診	shoshin	*the first medical consultation*
かんじゃ 患者	kanja	*patient*
ほけんしょう 保険証	hokenshoo	*health insurance card*
ようし 用紙	yooshi	*form*
からだ　　からだ 体 *or* 身体	karada	*body*

頭 (あたま)	atama	*head*
顔 (かお)	kao	*face*
目 (め)	me	*eye*
口 (くち)	kuchi	*mouth*
鼻 (はな)	hana	*nose*
耳 (みみ)	mimi	*ear*
腕 (うで)	ude	*arm*
足 (あし)	ashi	*foot*
脚 (あし)	ashi	*leg*
胸 (むね)	mune	*chest*
お腹、腹 (なか、はら)	onaka, hara	*belly, abdomen*
腰 (こし)	koshi	*waist, hip*
心臓 (しんぞう)	shinzoo	*heart*
脳 (のう)	noo	*brain*
胃 (い)	i	*stomach*
肺 (はい)	hai	*lung*
腸 (ちょう)	choo	*intestine*
毛 (け)	ke	*hair*
痛い (いた)	itai	*painful*
記入します / 記入する (きにゅう / きにゅう)	kinyuushimasu/ kinyuusuru	*to fill in*
呼びます / 呼ぶ (よ / よ)	yobimasu/yobu	*to call*

| すわ すわ
座ります / 座る | suwarimasu/suwaru | *to sit down* |

Take It Further

Note that the words that mean *leg* and *foot* have the identical pronunciation but are assigned different kanji, 脚 **ashi** is used to refer to a leg or legs, and 足 **ashi** is used to refer to a foot or feet. In fact, 足 is sometimes used as a general character referring to either feet or legs. The character 脚, however, can never be used to refer to just feet.

✎ Word Practice 1

Translate the following words into Japanese.

1. *clinic* _____

2. *front desk* _____

3. *waiting room* _____

4. *medical consultation* _____

5. *the first medical consultation* _____

6. *patient* _____

7. *health insurance card* _____

8. *head* _____

9. *eye* _____

10. *mouth* _____

ANSWER KEY

1. 診療所 shinryoojo; 2. 受付 uketsuke; 3. 待合室 machiaishitsu; 4. 診察 shinsatsu; 5. 初診 shoshin; 6. 患者 kanja; 7. 保険証 hokenshoo; 8. 頭 atama; 9. 目 me; 10. 口 kuchi

Grammar Builder 1

PRONOUNS

▶ 13B Grammar Builder 1 (CD 9, Track 10)

Let's look at the Japanese pronouns corresponding to English *I*, *you*, *he*, *she*, and *it*.

私 watashi	*I*
あなた anata	*you*
彼 kare	*he*
彼女 kanojo	*she*
それ sore	*it*

Japanese pronouns are not used as frequently as English pronouns. The pronoun あなた anata (*you*) in particular is seldom used—such direct address is considered impolite in many contexts, e.g., when speaking to a superior. The use of the addressee's name or title is preferred. Take a look at the following short dialogue between Division Manager Tanaka and his secretary Ms. Sato.

佐藤: 部長は明日の会議にお出になりますか。

Satoo: **Buchoo wa ashita no kaigi ni ode ni narimasu ka.**

Division Manager, are you going to attend the tomorrow's meeting?

田中: ええ、出ますよ。佐藤さんも出ますね?

Tanaka: **Ee, demasu yo. Satoo san mo demasu ne?**

Yes, I will. Ms. Sato, you will also attend, right?

佐藤: はい。

Satoo: **Hai.**

Yes.

It is also worth noting that pronouns 彼 **kare** and 彼女 **kanojo** can sometimes be used to mean *boyfriend* and *girlfriend* respectively. Now, let's look at the plural form of pronouns.

私達 **watashitachi**	*we*
あなた達 **anatatachi** あなた方 **anatagata**	*you*
彼ら **karera**	*they (m.)*
彼女ら **kanojora** 彼女達 **kanojotachi**	*they (f.)*

それら	*they (it)*
sorera	

Both あなた達 anatatachi and あなた方 anatagata are the plural forms of あなた anata, but あなた方 anatagata is more polite. Also, the plural form of 彼 kare (*he*) is 彼ら karera, whereas the plural form of 彼女 kanojo (*she*) is either 彼女ら kanojora or 彼女達 kanjotachi. 彼ら karera can also refer to a group of people consisting of both men and women.

The Japanese pronouns corresponding to the English possessive pronouns *my, your, his, her, its* are formed by using the possessive marker の no.

私の	*my*
watashi no	
あなたの	*your*
anata no	
彼の	*his*
kare no	
彼女の	*her*
kanojo no	
その	*its*
sono	

Note that the possessive form of それ sore is その sono and not それの sore no.

The Japanese indirect object pronouns corresponding to the English pronouns *(to) me, (to) you, (to) him, (to) her, (to) it* are formed by using the indirect object marker に ni.

私に わたし watashi ni	(to) me
あなたに anata ni	(to) you
彼に かれ kare ni	(to) him
彼女に かのじょ kanojo ni	(to) her
それに sore ni	(to) it

Finally, the Japanese direct object pronouns corresponding to *me, you, him, her, it* are formed by using the direct object marker を o.

私を わたし watashi o	*me*
あなたを anata o	*you*
彼を かれ kare o	*him*
彼女を かのじょ kanojo o	*her*
それを sore o	*it*

✎ Work Out 1

Fill in the blanks with the appropriate pronouns. Don't forget to include particles where necessary.

1. これは友達のジョン・スミスさんのカメラです。 ＿＿ は写真を撮るのが趣味で、たくさんカメラを持っています。

   Kore wa tomodachi no Jon Sumisu san no kamera desu. _____ wa shashin o toru no ga shumi de, takusan kamera o motte imasu.

2. 明日山田健さんと鈴木真理さんと一緒に映画を見ます。 ＿＿＿＿＿ は私のクラスメートです。

   Ashita Yamada Ken san to Suzuki Mari san to issho ni eega o mimasu.

   _____ wa watashi no kurasumeeto desu.

3. リサ・ホワイトさんは私の友達です。 ＿＿＿＿＿ お父さんはアメリカ人ですが、お母さんは中国人です。

   Risa Howaito san wa watashi no tomodachi desu. _____

   _____ otoosan wa amerikajin desu ga, okaasan wa chuugokujin desu.

4. (showing a picture) これは弟の弘です。＿＿＿＿ 特技はバスケットボールです。

   (showing a picture) Kore wa otooto no Hiroshi desu. _____
   tokugi wa basukettobooru desu.

5. ナンシー・チェンさんにこの鞄をもらったので、私は ＿＿＿＿ スカーフをあげました。

   Nansii Chen san ni kono kaban o moratta node, watashi wa

   _____ sukaafu o agemashita.

ANSWER KEY

1. 彼 Kare; 2. 彼ら Karera; 3. 彼女の Kanojo no; 4. 彼の Kare no; 5. 彼女に kanojo ni

Word Builder 2

▶ 13C Word Builder 2 (CD 9, Track 11)

熱	netsu	*fever*
風邪	kaze	*cold*
頭痛	zutsuu	*headache*
腹痛	fukutsuu	*stomachache*
吐き気	hakike	*nausea*
めまい	memai	*dizziness*
下痢	geri	*diarrhea*
食欲	shokuyoku	*appetite*
睡眠	suimin	*sleep*
アレルギー	arerugii	*allergy*
血圧	ketsuatsu	*blood pressure*
貧血	hinketsu	*anemia*
癌	gan	*cancer*
疲労	hiroo	*exhaustion, fatigue*
ストレス	sutoresu	*stress*
怪我	kega	*injury*
検査	kensa	*examination*

注射 ちゅうしゃ	chuusha	*injection, shot*
手術 しゅじゅつ	shujutsu	*operation, surgery*
薬 くすり	kusuri	*medicine*
ビタミン剤 ざい	bitaminzai	*vitamin supplement*
三十八度 さんじゅうはち ど	sanjuuhachi do	*38 degrees*
今朝 け さ	kesa	*this morning*
ひどい	hidoi	*terrible, severe*
早く はや	hayaku	*early, fast*
ちゃんと、きちんと	chanto (*colloquial*), kichinto	*properly, exactly, accurately*
注射します / 注射する ちゅうしゃ　ちゅうしゃ	chuushashimasu/ chuushasuru	*to give an injection*
手術します / 手術する しゅじゅつ　しゅじゅつ	shujutsushimasu/ shujutsusuru	*to operate*
入院します / 入院する にゅういん　にゅういん	nyuuinshimasu/ nyuuinsuru	*to be hospitalized*
退院します / 退院する たいいん　たいいん	taiinshimasu/taiinsuru	*to leave the hospital, to be released from hospital*
開けます / 開ける あ　あ	akemasu/akeru	*to open*
閉めます / 閉める し　し	shimemasu/shimeru	*to close*
残業します / 残業する ざんぎょう　ざんぎょう	zangyooshimasu/ zangyoo suru	*to work overtime*

休^{やす}みます / 休^{やす}む	yasumimasu/yasumu	to take some rest, to be absent, to take a day off
連絡^{れんらく}します / 連絡^{れんらく}する	renrakushimasu/ renrakusuru	to contact

✎ Word Practice 2

Translate the following words into Japanese.

1. *fever* _____

2. *cold* _____

3. *headache* _____

4. *stomachache* _____

5. *nausea* _____

6. *sleep* _____

7. *allergy* _____

8. *blood pressure* _____

9. *anemia* _____

10. *injury* _____

ANSWER KEY
1. 熱^{ねつ} netsu; 2. 風邪^{かぜ} kaze; 3. 頭痛^{ずつう} zutsuu; 4. 腹痛^{ふくつう} fukutsuu; 5. 吐^はき気^け hakike; 6. 睡眠^{すいみん} suimin;
7. アレルギー arerugii; 8. 血圧^{けつあつ} ketsuatsu; 9. 貧血^{ひんけつ} hinketsu; 10. 怪我^{けが} kega

Grammar Builder 2

VERB + ておきます TE OKIMASU

▶ 13D Grammar Builder 2 (CD 9, Track 12)

A special structure, shown below, can be used in Japanese to describe actions taken beforehand in preparation for future events.

> て te-*form of a verb* + おきます / おく okimasu/oku

Let's see how this structure is used.

来月カナダへ行きますから、新しいスーツケースを買っておきます。
Raigetsu kanada e ikimasu kara, atarashii suutsukeesu o katte okimasu.
I'm going to Canada next month, so I will buy a new suitcase beforehand.

明日家でパーティーをしますから、食べ物と飲み物をたくさん買っておきましょう。
Ashita uchi de paatii o shimasu kara, tabemono to nomimono o takusan katte okimashoo.
We're having a party at home tomorrow, so let's buy a lot of food and beverages beforehand.

今日友達と出掛けますから、昨日宿題をしておきました。
Kyoo tomodachi to dekakemasu kara, kinoo shukudai o shite okimashita.
I'm going out with my friend(s) today, so I did the homework yesterday in advance.

最近たまにめまいがするので、出張に行く前に一度検査を受けておきます。
Saikin tama ni memai ga suru node, shucchoo (business trip) ni iku mae ni ichido kensa o ukete okimasu.
Recently I've been feeling dizzy occasionally, so I will go see a doctor (lit., have a medical examination) in advance before I go on a business trip.

✎ Work Out 2

Using the て te-form of the verbs in parentheses, complete the sentences using the structure *verb* + ておきます te okimasu. Change おきます okimasu into its appropriate form as necessary.

1. 母はいつも父が帰る前に晩ご飯を _____。(作る)

   Haha wa itsumo chichi ga kaeru mae ni bangohan o _____

   _____. (tsukuru)

   My mother always makes dinner in advance, before my father comes home.

2. 日本に来る前に日本語を _____。(勉強する)

   Nihon ni kuru mae ni nihongo o _____

   _____. (benkyoosuru)

   I studied Japanese in advance, before I came to Japan.

3. ミーティングに出る前に昼ご飯を _____！(食べる)

   Miitingu ni deru mae ni hirugohan o _____

   _____！(taberu)

   Let's eat lunch in advance, before attending the meeting!

4. 明日コンサートでバイオリンを弾きますから、たくさん _____。
   (練習する)

   Ashita konsaato de baiorin o hikimasu kara, takusan

   _____.

   (renshuusuru)

   I will play the violin at a concert tomorrow, so I practiced a lot beforehand.

5. あのレストランは人気があるから、行く前に _____ !
（予約する）

Ano resutoran wa ninki ga aru kara, iku mae ni

_____ !

(yoyakusuru)

That restaurant is popular, so let's make a reservation in advance, before we go there.

ANSWER KEY
1. 作っておきます **tsukutte okimasu**; 2. 勉強しておきました **benkyooshite okimashita**;
3. 食べておきましょう **tabete okimashoo**; 4. 練習しておきました **renshuushite okimashita**;
5. 予約しておきましょう **yoyakushite okimashoo**

✎ Drive It Home

A. Fill in the blanks with the appropriate pronouns. Don't forget to include a particle where necessary.

1. ジョン・スミスさんは私の友達です。_____ は写真を撮るのが好きです。

   Jon Sumisu san wa watashi no tomodachi desu. _____ wa shashin o toru no ga suki desu.

   Mr. John Smith is my friend. He likes taking pictures.

2. ジョン・スミスさんと _____ お兄さんは大学生です。

   Jon Sumisu san to _____ oniisan wa daigakusee desu.

   Mr. John Smith and his older brother are college students.

3. 明日はジョン・スミスさんの誕生日です。_____ 新しいカメラをあげます。

Ashita wa Jon Sumisu san no tanjoobi desu. _____ atarashii

kamera o agemasu.

Tomorrow is Mr. John Smith's birthday. I'll give a new camera to him.

4. 今日カメラを買いました。明日 _____ をスミスさんにあげます。

Kyoo kamera o kaimashita. Ashita _____ o Sumisu san ni agemasu.

I bought a camera today. I'll give it to him tomorrow.

5. 昨日、ジョン・スミスさんとチャールズ・スミスさんに会いました。_____ は
兄弟です。

Kinoo, Jon Sumisu san to Chaaruzu Sumisu san ni aimashita.

_____ wa kyoodai desu._____

I saw Mr. John Smith and Mr. Charles Smith. They are brothers.

B. Fill in the blanks with appropriate words.

1. 来月カナダへ行きますから、新しいスーツケースを買っ _____。

Raigetsu kanada e ikimasu kara, atarashii suutsukeesu o kat _____

_____.

I will go to Canada next month, so I will buy a new suitcase beforehand.

2. 明日家でパーティーをしますから、食べ物と飲み物をたくさん

買っ _____。

Ashita uchi de paatii o shimasu kara, tabemono to nomimono o takusan kat

_____.

We will have a party at home tomorrow, so I'll buy a lot of food and beverages

beforehand.

3. 明日友達と出掛けますから、今日 宿 題をし ＿＿＿＿＿＿＿＿＿＿＿＿＿。

    Ashita tomodachi to dekakemasu kara, kyoo shukudai o shi ＿＿＿＿＿＿＿

    ＿＿＿＿＿＿＿＿＿＿＿＿.

I will go out with my friends tomorrow, so I'll do the homework today in advance.

4. たまにめまいがするので、 出張に行く前に一度検査を受け ＿＿＿＿＿＿＿＿。

    Tama ni memai ga suru node, shucchoo ni iku mae ni ichido kensa o uke ＿＿＿＿＿

    ＿＿＿＿＿＿＿＿＿＿＿＿.

I've been feeling dizzy occasionally, so I will go see a doctor (lit., have a medical

examination) in advance before I go on a business trip.

ANSWER KEY
A. 1. 彼 **Kare**; 2. 彼の **kare no**; 3. 彼に **Kare ni**; 4. それ **sore**; 5. 彼ら **Karera**
B. 1. ておきます **te okimasu**; 2. ておきます **te okimasu**; 3. ておきます **te okimasu**; 4. ておきます **te okimasu**

How Did You Do?

Let's see how you did! By now, you should be able to:

☐ use key vocabulary related to your body and health (Still unsure? Jump back to page 291)

☐ use key vocabulary related to visiting a doctor's office (Still unsure? Jump back to page 299)

☐ use pronouns (Still unsure? Jump back to page 294)

☐ describe actions taken before hand in preparation for some coming events (Still unsure? Jump back to page 302)

✎ Word Recall

1. ゆで卵 _{たまご} yudetamago — a. *salt*
2. 社長 _{しゃちょう} shachoo — b. *section manager*
3. 塩 _{しお} shio — c. *pepper*
4. 部長 _{ぶちょう} buchoo — d. *sugar*
5. 砂糖 _{さとう} satoo — e. *division manager*
6. 胡椒 _{こしょう} koshoo — f. *seasoning*
7. 課長 _{かちょう} kachoo — g. *president of a company*
8. 洋風 _{ようふう} yoofuu — h. *Western style*
9. 調味料 _{ちょうみりょう} choomiryoo — i. *to eat, to drink, to receive*
10. いただく itadaku — j. *boiled egg*

ANSWER KEY

1. j; 2. g; 3. a; 4. e; 5. d; 6. c; 7. b; 8. h; 9. f; 10. i

Lesson 14: Phrases

In this lesson you'll learn how to:

☐ use the て te-form of adjectives

☐ use giving and receiving verbs to express actions taken as a favor

Phrase Builder 1

▶ 14A Phrase Builder 1 (CD 9, Track 13)

髪、髪の毛	kami, kami no ke	*hair (on the head)*
頭が痛いです、頭痛がします	atama ga itai desu, zutsuu ga shimasu	*have a headache*
お腹が痛いです	onaka ga itai desu	*have a stomachache*
下痢をします / する	geri o shimasu/suru	*have diarrhea*
吐き気がします / する	hakike ga shimasu/suru	*feel like vomiting*
めまいがします / する	memai ga shimasu/suru	*feel dizzy*
めまいがひどいです	memai ga hidoi desu	*feel extremely dizzy*
寒気がします / する	samuke ga shimasu/suru	*have chills*
顔色が悪いです	kaoiro ga warui desu	*look pale*
医者に診てもらいます / もらう	isha ni mite moraimasu/morau	*be checked by a doctor*
病院で診てもらいます / もらう	byooin de mite moraimasu/morau	*be checked at a hospital*
診察を受けます / 受ける	shinsatsu o ukemasu/ukeru	*consult a physician*
医者に診てもらった方がいいです。	Isha ni mite moratta hoo ga ii desu.	*You'd better consult a doctor.*
診察を受けたことがあります / ある。	Shinsatsu o uketa koto ga arimasu/aru.	*I have consulted a doctor.*

用紙に記入します / する	yooshi ni kinyuushimasu/suru	*fill out a form*
用紙を持って来ます / 持って来る	yooshi o motte kimasu/ motte kuru	*bring the form*
初めてです	hajimete desu	*it's the first time*
これでいいです	kore de ii desu	*be okay with this*
アレルギーに関する	arerugii ni kansuru	*concerning (my) allergies*
アレルギーに関する質問	arerugii ni kansuru shitsumon	*questions concerning allergies*
質問の答え	shitsumon no kotae	*answers to questions*
今飲んでいる薬	ima nonde iru kusuri	*the medicine that I'm taking now*
他の薬	hoka no kusuri	*other medicine*

✎ Phrase Practice 1
Fill in the missing words below.

1. 頭が _____ です

   atama ga _____ desu

   have a headache

2. _____ がします

   _____ ga shimasu

   feel like vomiting

3. _____ がします

_____ ga shimasu

feel dizzy

4. _____ がします

_____ e ga shimasu

have chills

5. _____ が悪<small>わる</small>いです

_____ ga warui desu

look pale

6. _____ を受<small>う</small>けます

_____ o ukemasu

consult a physician

7. _____ です

_____ desu

it's the first time

8. _____ に関<small>かん</small>する

_____ ni kansuru

concerning (my) allergies

9. 他<small>ほか</small>の _____

hoka no _____

other medicine

ANSWER KEY

1. 痛い itai; 2. 吐き気 hakike; 3. めまい memai; 4. 寒気 samuke; 5. 顔色 kaoiro; 6. 診察 shinsatsu; 7. 初めて hajimete; 8. アレルギー arerugii; 9. 薬 kusuri

Grammar Builder 1

THE て TE-FORM OF ADJECTIVES

▶ 14B Grammar Builder 1 (CD 9, Track 14)

You have already learned the て te-form of the copula and several verbs. Next, we'll discuss the て te-form of adjectives. First, let's look at how the て te-form of い i-adjectives is formed.

> *Drop final* い i *and attach* くて kute

Let's see how this works with several い i-adjectives you're already familiar with.

大きい ookii (*big*)	大きくて ookikute
明るい akarui (*bright*)	明るくて akarukute
忙しい isogashii (*busy*)	忙しくて isogashikute
おいしい oishii (*delicious*)	おいしくて oishikute
暖かい atatakai (*warm*)	暖かくて atatakakute
痛い itai (*painful*)	痛くて itakute

Next, let's look at how the て te-form of な na-adjectives is formed.

---

stem of な na-adjectives + で de

Remember that で de is the て te-form of the copula です/だ desu/da. Let's see how this works with some な na-adjectives.

ゆうめい 有名 yuumee (*famous*)	ゆうめい 有名で yuumee de
しんせつ 親切 shinsetsu (*kind*)	しんせつ 親切で shinsetsu de
かんたん 簡単 kantan (*easy, simple*)	かんたん 簡単で kantan de
しず 静か shizuka (*quiet*)	しず 静かで shizuka de
にぎ 賑やか nigiyaka (*lively*)	にぎ 賑やかで nigiyaka de
きれい kiree (*beautiful, clean*)	きれいで kiree de

The て te-form of adjectives is used when connecting two or more adjectives. Just as is the case with verbs, the て te-form of adjectives cannot appear at the end of sentences. Also, the て te-form of adjectives does not express tense, which is determined by the adjective that appears at the end of the sentence.

かわ だ　　　いえ　あたら
川田さんの家は新しくてきれいです。

Kawada san no ie wa atarashikute kiree desu.

Mr./Ms. Kawada's house is new and clean.

六本木は賑やかで面白いです。

Roppongi wa nigiyaka de omoshiroi desu.

Roppongi is lively and interesting.

その公園は大きくて、きれいで、静かですから、よく行きます。

Sono kooen wa ookikute, kiree de, shizuka desu kara, yoku ikimasu.

That park is big, pretty and quiet, so I often go there.

昨日の宿題は短くて、簡単で、良かったです。

Kinoo no shukudai wa mijikakute, kantan de, yokatta desu.

Yesterday's homework was short, easy and good.

The て te-form of adjectives can also appear in a prenominal position as shown in the following examples.

上田さんは親切でいい人です。

Ueda san wa shinsetsu de ii hito desu.

Mr./Ms. Ueda is a kind and nice person.

安くておいしいレストランを知っていますか。

Yasukute oishii resutoran o shitte imasu ka.

Do you know of any restaurants which are cheap and delicious?

✎ Work Out 1

Fill in the blanks by choosing the appropriate adjective from the list below, and giving its て te-form.

短い mijikai, 長い nagai, 近い chikai, 遠い tooi, 難しい muzukashii, 簡単 kantan, 親切 shinsetsu, 古い furui, 新しい atarashii, 小さい chiisai, 大きい ookii, きれい kiree

1. 駅に _____ 便利なアパートに住みたいです。

   Eki ni _____ benri na apaato ni sumitai desu.

   I want to live in an apartment which is close to the station and convenient.

2. あの先生は _____ いいです。

   Ano sensee wa _____ ii desu.

   That teacher is kind and good.

3. その映画館は _____ 不便です。

   Sono eegakan (*movie theater*) wa _____

   _____ fuben desu.

   That movie theater is old, small, and inconvenient.

4. この本は _____ つまらなかったです。

   Kono hon wa _____

   _____ tsumaranakatta desu.

   This book was long, difficult and boring.

5. 三田さんの家は _____ いいですね。

   Mita san no ie wa _____

   ii desu ne.

   Mr./Ms. Mita's house is new, clean, and nice, isn't it?

ANSWER KEY

1. 近くて chikakute; 2. 親切で shinsetsu de; 3. 古くて小さくて furukute chiisakute;
4. 長くて難しくて nagakute muzukashikute; 5. 新しくてきれいで atarashikute kiree de

Phrase Builder 2

▶ 14C Phrase Builder 2 (CD 9, Track 15)

風邪をひきます / ひく	kaze o hikimasu/hiku	catch a cold
熱があります / ある	netsu ga arimasu/aru	have a fever
熱を測ります / 測る	netsu o hakarimasu/ hakaru	check one's temperature
喉が痛いです	nodo ga itai desu	have a sore throat
食欲があります / ある	shokuyoku ga arimasu/ aru	have an appetite
食欲がありません / ない	shokuyoku ga arimasen/nai	don't have an appetite
血圧が高いです	ketsuatsu ga takai desu	have high blood pressure
血圧が低いです	ketsuatsu ga hikui desu	have low blood pressure
睡眠をとります / とる	suimin o torimasu/toru	get some sleep
不眠症です	fuminshoo desu	suffer from insomnia
ストレスが溜まって います / いる	sutoresu ga tamatte imasu/iru	to be under a lot of stress (lit., stress has accumulated)
肩が凝っています / いる	kata ga kotte imasu/iru	have stiff shoulders
怪我をします / する	kega o shimasu/suru	get injured

骨を折ります / 折る、骨折します / する	hone o orimasu/oru, kossetsushimasu/suru	break a bone
捻挫します / する	nenzashimasu/suru	have a sprain
四時間しか寝ていません / 寝ていない	yojikan shika nete imasen/nete inai	had only four hours of sleep
私が知っている医者	watashi ga shitteiru isha	the doctor that I know
彼に連絡します / 連絡する	kare ni renrakushimasu/renrakusuru	contact him
彼に連絡しておきます / 連絡しておく	kare ni renrakushite okimasu/renrakushite oku	contact him beforehand
早く家に帰ります / 帰る	hayaku ie ni kaerimasu/kaeru	go home early
休んだ方がいいです	yasunda hoo ga ii desu	you'd better get some rest
会社を休みます / 休む	kaisha o yasumimasu/yasumu	take a day off (from work)
残業しないでください。	Zangyooshinaide kudasai.	Please don't work overtime.

✎ Phrase Practice 2

Fill in the missing words below.

1. ＿＿＿＿＿＿ をひきます

＿＿＿＿＿＿ o hikimasu

catch a cold

2. ＿＿＿＿＿＿ があります

＿＿＿＿＿＿ ga arimasu

have a fever

3. ＿＿＿＿＿＿ が痛いです

＿＿＿＿＿＿ ga itai desu

have a sore throat

4. ＿＿＿＿＿＿ があります

＿＿＿＿＿＿＿＿＿＿ ga arimasu

have an appetite

5. ＿＿＿＿＿＿ が高いです

＿＿＿＿＿＿＿＿＿＿ ga takai desu

have high blood pressure

6. ＿＿＿＿＿＿ をとります

＿＿＿＿＿＿＿ o torimasu

get some sleep

7. ＿＿＿＿＿＿ です

＿＿＿＿＿＿＿＿＿＿ desu

suffer from insomnia

8. _____ をします

_____ o shimasu

get injured

9. _____ しないでください。

_____ shinaide kudasai.

Please don't work overtime.

ANSWER KEY
1. 風邪 kaze; 2. 熱 netsu; 3. 喉 nodo; 4. 食欲 shokuyoku; 5. 血圧 ketsuatsu; 6. 睡眠 suimin;
7. 不眠症 fuminshoo; 8. 怪我 kega; 9. 残業 Zangyoo

Grammar Builder 2

GIVING AND RECEIVING VERBS 2

▶ 14D Grammar Builder 2 (CD 9, Track 16)

You learned the giving and receiving verbs あげます agemasu, もらいます moraimasu, くれます kuremasu, and their polite form さしあげます sashiagemasu, いただきます itadakimasu, くださいます kudasaimasu in Lesson 5, where you learned how to use them as the main verbs in sentences. These giving and receiving verbs can also attach to the て te-form of other verbs (marked as X below); in this case, their meaning is doing or receiving the favor of some action.

A が / は B に X てあげます / さしあげます。	A ga/wa B ni X te agemasu/ sashiagemasu.	A gives B the favor of doing something (X). (A does something – X – for B.)

A が / は B に X てもらいます / いただきます。	A ga/wa B ni X te moraimasu/ itadakimasu.	A receives a favor from B of having something done (X). (B does something – X – for A.)
A が / は B に X てくれます / くださいます。 (B = a speaker or his/her in-group member)	A ga/wa B ni X te kuremasu/ kudasaimasu. (B = a speaker or his/her in-group member)	A gives me/my in-group member the favor of doing something (X). (A does something – X – for me/ my in-group member.)

This is a very important construction and is commonly in use in everyday conversation.

In the case of 〜てもらいます … te moraimasu or 〜ていただきます … te itadakimasu, the doer of a favor can be marked only by に ni, whereas the giver of an object can be marked by either に ni or から kara when もらいます moraimasu or いただきます itadakimasu are used as main verbs.

私は林さん [に/から] 本をもらいました。
Watashi wa Hayashi san [ni/kara] hon o moraimashita.
I received a book from Mr./Ms. Hayashi.

私は林さんに本を貸してもらいました。
Watashi wa Hayashi san ni hon o kashite moraimashita.
I borrowed a book from Mr./Ms. Hayashi. (lit., I received a favor from Mr./Ms. Hayashi of his/her lending a book to me.)

In the first example, 林さん **Hayashi san**, the giver of the book, can be marked by either に ni or から kara, but in the second example, 林さん **Hayashi san**, the giver of a favor of lending a book, can be marked by only に ni.

母は妹に新しいセーターを買ってあげました。

Haha wa imooto ni atarashii seetaa o katte agemashita.

My mother bought a new sweater for my younger sister. (lit., My mother gave my younger sister a favor of buying her a new sweater.)

私は部長にレポートを読んでさしあげました。

Watashi wa buchoo ni repooto o yonde sashiagemashita.

I read a report to the division manager. (lit., I gave the division manager a favor of my reading a report to him.)

私は鈴木さんに彼が撮った写真を見せてもらいました。

Watashi wa Suzuki san ni kare ga totta shashin o misete moraimashita.

Mr. Suzuki showed me the pictures that he took. (lit., I received a favor from Mr. Suzuki of him showing me the pictures that he took.)

私はカンポス先生にスペイン語を教えていただきました。

Watashi wa Kanposu sensee ni supeingo o oshiete itadakimashita.

Professor Campos taught me Spanish. (lit., I received a favor from Professor Campos of his/her teaching me Spanish.)

ルームメートが部屋を掃除してくれました。

Ruumumeeto ga heya o soojishite kuremashita.

My roommate cleaned our room. (lit., My roommate gave me a favor of his/her cleaning our room.)

先生はいつも私達に面白い話をしてくださいます。

Sensee wa itsumo watashitachi ni omoshiroi hanashi o shite kudasaimasu.

The professor always tells us interesting stories. (lit., The professor always gives us a favor of his/her telling interesting stories.)

✎ Work Out 2

Choose the appropriate combination of the て te-form of the verb and the giving or receiving verb to fill in the blanks. Change the tense as necessary.

買ってくれます katte kuremasu, 撮ってあげます totte agemasu, 作ってもらいます tsukutte moraimasu, 見せてくださいます misete kudasaimasu, 教えていただきます oshiete itadakimasu, 読んでさしあげます yonde sashiagemasu

1. 今日はカレーが食べたかったので、母に _____。

   Kyoo wa karee ga tabetakatta node, haha ni _____

   _____.

   Today I wanted to eat curry, so my mother made it for me (lit., I received a favor from my mother of her making it).

2. 昨日私は部長にレポートを _____。

   Kinoo watashi wa buchoo ni repooto o _____

   _____.

   Yesterday I read a report for the division manager. (lit., I gave the division manager a favor of my reading a report.)

3. 両親は私と妹に新しいコンピューターを _____。

   Ryooshin wa watashi to imooto ni atarashii konpyuutaa o _____

   _____.

   My parents bought a new computer for me and my sister. (lit., My parents gave me and my younger sister a favor of their buying a new computer.)

4. 先生にその言葉の意味を _____。

Sensee ni sono kotoba no imi o _____

_____.

My teacher told me the meaning of that word. (lit., I received a favor from my

teacher of his/her telling me the meaning of that word.)

5. 週末公園で田中さんの写真を _____。

Shuumatsu kooen de Tanaka san no shashin o _____

_____.

On the weekend, let's take a picture of Mr./Ms. Tanaka at the park. (lit., On the

weekend, let's give Mr./Ms. Tanaka a favor of our taking her picture at the park.)

6. イタリア語の先生がローマの写真を _____。

Itariago no sensee ga rooma no shashin o _____

_____.

The Italian teacher showed me/us pictures of Rome. (lit., The Italian teacher gave

(me/us) a favor of his/her showing pictures of Rome.)

ANSWER KEY
1. 作ってもらいました tsukutte moraimashita; 2. 読んでさしあげました yonde sashiagemashita;
3. 買ってくれました katte kuremashita; 4. 教えていただきました oshiete itadakimashita;
5. 撮ってあげましょう totte agemashoo; 6. 見せてくださいました misete kudasaimashita

✎ Drive It Home

A. Fill in the blanks by inserting the て te-form of the adjectives given in
   parentheses.

1. _____ おいしいケーキですね。(大_{おお}きい)

   _____ oishii keeki desu ne. (ookii)

   It's a big and delicious cake, isn't it?

2. _____ 暖_{あたた}かい部屋_{へや}ですね。(明_{あか}るい)

   _____ atatakai heya desu ne. (akarui)

   It's a bright and warm room, isn't it?

3. _____ いい人_{ひと}ですね。(親切_{しんせつ})

   _____ ii hito desu ne. (shinsetsu)

   He/she is a kind and good person, isn't he/she?

4. _____ 賑_{にぎ}やかな町_{まち}ですね。(有名_{ゆうめい})

   _____ nigiyaka na machi desu ne. (yuumee)

   It's a famous and lively town, isn't it?

B. Fill in the blanks by inserting the words in parentheses in their appropriate form.

1. 私_{わたし}は姉_{あね}に本_{ほん}を貸_かして _____ 。(もらいます)

   Watashi wa ane ni hon o kashite _____.

   (moraimasu)

   I borrowed a book from my older sister. (lit., I received a favor from my older sister

   of her lending a book to me.)

2. 姉_{あね}が私_{わたし}に本_{ほん}を貸_かして _____ 。(くれます)

   Ane ga watashi ni hon o kashite _____.

   (kuremasu)

   My sister lent me a book. (lit., My sister gave me a favor of lending a book to me.)

3. 私_{わたし}は弟_{おとうと}に本_{ほん}を貸_かして _____。(あげます)

   Watashi wa otooto ni hon o kashite _____.

   (agemasu)

   I lent a book to my younger brother. (lit., I gave my younger brother a favor of

   lending a book to him.)

4. 母_{はは}は妹_{いもうと}に新_{あたら}しいセーターを買_かって _____。(あげます)

   Haha wa imooto ni atarashii seetaa o katte _____.

   (agemasu)

   My mother bought a new sweater for my younger sister. (lit., My mother gave my

   younger sister a favor of buying her a new sweater.)

5. 妹_{いもうと}は母_{はは}に新_{あたら}しいセーターを買_かって _____。(もらいます)

   Imooto wa haha ni atarashii seetaa o katte

   _____. (moraimasu)

   My mother bought a new sweater for my younger sister. (lit., My younger sister

   received a favor from my mother of buying her a new sweater.)

ANSWER KEY
A. 1. 大_{おお}きくて Ookikute; 2. 明_{あか}るくて Akarukute; 3. 親切_{しんせつ}で Shisetsu de; 4. 有名_{ゆうめい}で Yuumee de
B. 1. もらいました moraimashita; 2. くれました kuremashita; 3. あげました agemashita; 4. あげました agemashita; 5. もらいました moraimashita

⊕ Culture Note

While Western medicine is mainstream in Japan, Eastern medicine is still
well-accepted and popular there as well. For instance, some people prefer to
have acupuncture when they catch a cold or have some other medical problem.
Also, some people prefer taking herbal medicines, which are obtainable over

the counter. Taking vitamin supplements has become more common in Japan recently, but the number of people who take such supplements is still much lower compared to the United States.

How Did You Do?

Let's see how you did! By now, you should be able to:

☐ use the て te-form of adjectives (Still unsure? Jump back to page 311)

☐ use giving and receiving verbs to express actions taken as a favor (Still unsure? Jump back to page 318)

✎ Word Recall

1. 冷たい tsumetai   a. *price*

2. ダース daasu   b. *same*

3. 運動 undoo   c. *next time, this time, shortly*

4. 水泳 suiee   d. *swimming*

5. 値段 nedan   e. *prices (of commodities)*

6. 試合 shiai   f. *exercise(s)*

7. 物価 bukka   g. *dozen*

8. 今度 kondo   h. *game*

9. 同じ onaji   i. *cold*

10. 趣味 shumi   j. *hobby*

ANSWER KEY

1. i; 2. g; 3. f; 4. d; 5. a; 6. h; 7. e; 8. c; 9. b; 10. j

Lesson 15: Sentences

In this lesson you'll learn how to:

☐ ask for permission

☐ make negative requests

Sentence Builder 1

▶ 15A Sentence Builder 1 (CD 9, Track 17)

<ruby>保険証<rt>ほけんしょう</rt></ruby>は<ruby>お持<rt>も</rt></ruby>ちですか。

Hokenshoo wa omochi desu ka.

Do you have an insurance card? (polite)

これでいいですか。

Kore de ii desu ka.

Is this okay?

<ruby>予約<rt>よやく</rt></ruby>なさいましたか。

Yoyaku nasaimashita ka.

Did you make an appointment? (polite)

<ruby>予約<rt>よやく</rt></ruby>をしなくてはいけませんか。

Yoyaku o shinakute wa ikemasen ka.

Do I have to make an appointment?

<ruby>予約<rt>よやく</rt></ruby>していなかったら、ちょっと<ruby>お待<rt>ま</rt></ruby>ちになるかもしれません。

Yoyakushite inakattara, chotto omachi ni naru kamoshiremasen.

If you didn't make an appointment, you may have to wait for a little while. (polite)

今日はどうなさいましたか。

Kyoo wa doo nasaimashita ka.

What is wrong (with you) today? (polite)

頭が痛くて、吐き気がします。

Atama ga itakute, hakike ga shimasu.

I have a headache and feel like vomiting.

今朝はめまいもしました。

Kesa wa memai mo shimashita.

This morning I felt dizzy, too.

一度病院で診てもらった方がいいと思いました。

Ichido byooin de mite moratta hoo ga ii to omoimashita.

I thought I'd better get checked at a hospital for once.

以前にこの病院で診察を受けたことはありますか。

Izen ni kono byooin de shinsatsu o uketa koto wa arimasu ka.

Have you consulted a doctor at this hospital before?

あちらに座ってこの用紙に記入して持って来てください。

Achira ni suwatte kono yooshi ni kinyuushite motte kite kudasai.

Please sit down over there, fill out this form, and bring it back.

アレルギーに関する質問の答えも書いていただけますか。

Arerugii ni kansuru shitsumon no kotae mo kaite itadakemasu ka.

Could you write the answers to the questions concerning the allergies? (polite)

今飲んでいるお薬がございましたら、それも書いてください。

Ima nondeiru okusuri ga gozaimashitara, sore mo kaite kudasai.

If you have any medicine that you are currently taking, please write that, too. (polite)

アレルギーは特に何もありません。

Arerugii wa toku ni nani mo arimasen.

I don't have any allergies in particular.

ビタミン剤を飲んでいますが、他の薬は何も飲んでいません。

Bitaminzai o nonde imasu ga, hoka no kusuri wa nani mo nonde imasen.

I am taking a vitamin supplement, but I'm not taking any other medicine.

お名前をお呼びしますから、あちらでお待ちください。

Onamae o oyobishimasu kara, achira de omachi kudasai.

We will call your name, so please wait there. (polite)

Take It Further

どうしましたか。Doo shimashita ka. and its polite form どうなさいましたか。Doo nasaimashita ka. can have different translations in different contexts. Possible translations are *What's the matter?*, *What happened?* and *What's wrong?*

✎ Sentence Practice 1

Fill in the missing words in each of the following sentences.

1. これで _____ 。

   Kore de _____ .

   Is this okay?

2. 頭が痛くて、_____ 。
   <small>あたま</small> <small>いた</small>

   Atama ga itakute, _____ .

   I have a headache and feel like vomiting.

3. 一度病院で _____ と思いました。
   <small>いち ど びょういん</small> <small>おも</small>

   Ichido byooin de _____

   _____ to omoimashita.

   I thought I'd better get checked at a hospital right away.

4. 以前にこの病院で診察を _____ がありますか。
   <small>い ぜん</small> <small>びょういん しんさつ</small>

   Izen ni kono byooin de shinsatsu o _____ ga arimasu

   ka.

   Have you consulted a doctor at this hospital before?

5. あちらに座ってこの用紙に記入して _____ 。
   <small>すわ</small> <small>よう し きにゅう</small>

   Achira ni suwatte kono yooshi ni kinyuushite _____

   _____ .

   Please sit down over there, fill out this form, and bring it back.

6. _____ 質問の答えも書いていただけますか。
   <small>しつもん こた か</small>

   _____ shitsumon no kotae mo

   kaite itadakemasu ka.

   Could you write the answers to the questions concerning the allergies?

7. アレルギーは _____。

Arerugii wa _____

_____.

I don't have any allergies.

8. ビタミン剤を飲んでいますが、他の薬は _____。

Bitaminzai o nonde imasu ga, hoka no kusuri wa _____

_____.

I am taking a vitamin supplement, but I'm not taking any other medicine.

ANSWER KEY

1. いいですか ii desu ka; 2. 吐き気がします hakike ga shimasu; 3. 診てもらった方がいい mite moratta hoo ga ii; 4. 受けたこと uketa koto; 5. 持って来てください motte kite kudasai; 6. アレルギーに関する Arerugii ni kansuru; 7. 特に何もありません toku ni nani mo arimasen; 8. 何も飲んでいません nani mo nonde imasen

Grammar Builder 1

ASKING FOR PERMISSION

▶ 15B Grammar Builder 1 (CD 9, Track 18)

You can ask for a permission using the following structure.

て te-*form of a verb* + (も) いいですか。 (mo) ii desu ka.	*May I . . . ?*

The particle も mo is optional, but in most cases it is used. By using a different form of いいですか ii desu ka, you can change the level of politeness.

て te-*form of a verb* + (も) いい？ (mo) ii? *(with a rising intonation)*

て te-*form of a verb* + (も) いいですか。(mo) ii desu ka.

て te-*form of a verb* + (も) いいでしょうか。(mo) ii deshoo ka.

て te-*form of a verb* + (も) よろしいですか。(mo) yoroshii desu ka.

て te-*form of a verb* + (も) よろしいでしょうか。(mo) yoroshii deshoo ka.

The て te-form of a verb + (も) いい (mo) ii is the least polite, and is used only in informal situations, while the て te-form of a verb + (も) よろしいでしょうか。(mo) yoroshii deshoo ka is the most polite among these five expressions. You can also use かまいませんか kamaimasen ka instead of いいですか ii desu ka. This expression corresponds to the English *Do you mind … ?*

A: すみませんが、ここに座ってもいいですか。

Sumimasen ga, koko ni suwatte mo ii desu ka.

Excuse me, but may I sit down here?

B: ええ、どうぞ。

Ee, doozo.

Yes, please.

A: 先生、質問してもいいでしょうか。

Sensee, shitsumonshite mo ii deshoo ka.

Professor, may I ask a question?

B: ええ、どうぞ。

Ee, doozo.

Yes, please.

A: お母さん、このケーキ食べてもいい？

Okaasan, kono keeki tabete mo ii?

Mom, may I eat this cake?

B:晩ご飯の後食べたらどう？

Bangohan no ato tabetara doo?

What about if you eat it after the dinner?

A:社長、この本をお借りしてもよろしいでしょうか。

Shachoo, kono hon o okarishite mo yoroshii deshoo ka.

President, may I borrow this book?

B:ええ、どうぞ。

Ee, doozo.

Yes, please.

A:煙草を吸ってもかまいませんか。

Tabako o suttemo kamaimasen ka.

Do you mind if I smoke?

B:すみませんが、ちょっと …

Sumimasen ga, chotto …

Sorry, but a little …

✎ Work Out 1

Construct sentences asking for permission using the words provided in parentheses.

1. 課長、すみませんが、気分が悪いので、＿＿＿＿＿＿＿＿＿＿＿＿＿＿ 。
（家、も、でしょう、に、よろしい、帰って、か）

Kachoo, sumimasen ga, kibun ga warui node, ＿＿＿＿＿＿＿＿＿＿＿＿ .

(uchi, mo, deshoo, ni, yoroshii, kaette, ka)

2. お父さん、_____ ？
(車、買って、を、いい、新しい、も)

Otoosan, _____ ?

(kuruma, katte, o, ii, atarashii, mo)

3. クレジットカードで _____ 。
(も、でしょう、か、払って、いい)

Kurejitto kaado de _____ .

(mo, deshoo, ka, haratte, ii)

4. ちょっと寒いので、窓を _____ 。
(か、閉めて、かまいません、も)

Chotto samui node, mado (window) o _____ .

(ka, shimete, kamaimasen, mo)

5. この美術館の中で _____ 。
(を、いい、写真、か、撮って、です、も)

Kono bijutsukan (art museum) no naka de _____ .

(o, ii, shashin, ka, totte, desu, mo)

6. 先生、風邪をひいて熱があるので、_____ 。
(休んで、か、よろしい、午後のセミナー、も、でしょう、を)

Sensee, kaze o hiite netsu ga aru node, _____ .

(yasunde, ka, yoroshii, gogo no seminaa, mo, deshoo, o)

ANSWER KEY
1. 家に帰ってもよろしいでしょうか uchi ni kaette mo yoroshii deshoo ka；2. 新しい車を買ってもいい atarashii kuruma o katte mo ii；3. 払ってもいいでしょうか haratte mo ii deshoo ka；4. 閉めても

かまいませんか shimete mo kamaimasen ka; 5. 写真を撮ってもいいですか shashin o totte mo ii desu ka; 6. 午後のセミナーを休んでもよろしいでしょうか gogo no seminaa o yasunde mo yoroshii deshoo ka

Sentence Builder 2

▶ 15C Sentence Builder 2 (CD 9, Track 19)

ここに座ってください。

Koko ni suwatte kudasai.

Please sit down here.

頭痛と吐き気とめまいですか。

Zutsuu to hakike to memai desu ka.

A headache, nausea, and dizziness?

今もめまいはしますか。

Ima mo memai wa shimasu ka.

Do you still feel dizzy?

今朝はめまいがひどくて、びっくりしました。

Kesa wa memai ga hidokute, bikkurishimashita.

This morning I was extremely dizzy, which scared me.

熱を測ってみましょう。

Netsu o hakatte mimashoo.

Let's check the temperature.

三十八度ですから、少し熱もあります。

Sanjuuhachi do desu kara, sukoshi netsu mo arimasu.

It's thirty-eight degrees, so you have a little fever, too.

口を開けてください。

Kuchi o akete kudasai.

Please open your mouth.

喉は痛くありませんか。

Nodo wa itaku arimasen ka.

Do you have a sore throat?

下痢はしていませんか。

Geri wa shite imasen ka.

Do you have diarrhea?

お腹は痛くないし、下痢もしていません。

Onaka wa itakunai shi, geri mo shite imasen.

I don't have a stomach ache, and I don't have diarrhea either.

今仕事がとても忙しくて、毎晩残業しています。

Ima shigoto ga totemo isogashikute, maiban zangyooshite imasu.

I am very busy with my work now and am working overtime every night.

睡眠はちゃんととっていますか。

Suimin wa chanto totte imasu ka.

Are you getting enough sleep?

四時間ぐらいしか寝ていません。

Yojikan gurai shika nete imasen.

I'm getting only about four hours of sleep.

多分疲労でしょう。

Tabun hiroo deshoo.

Perhaps it's exhaustion.

一度検査してもらった方がいいです。

Ichido kensashite moratta hoo ga ii desu.

You'd better be examined for once.

大学病院に私が知っている医者がいますから、彼に連絡しておきます。

Daigakubyooin ni watashi ga shitte iru isha ga imasu kara, kare ni renrakushite okimasu.

There's a doctor who I know at the university hospital, so I will contact him beforehand.

今日は残業しないでください。

Kyoo wa zangyooshinaide kudasai.

Please don't work overtime today.

早く家に帰って休んだ方がいいです。

Hayaku ie ni kaette yasunda hoo ga ii desu.

You'd better go home early and get some rest.

✎ Sentence Practice 2

Fill in the missing words in each of the following sentences.

1. ここに ＿＿＿＿＿＿＿＿＿＿＿＿＿＿＿＿ 。

   Koko ni ＿＿＿＿＿＿＿＿＿＿＿＿＿＿＿＿＿＿＿.

   Please sit down here.

2. 今朝はめまいがひどくて、_____ 。

   Kesa wa memai ga hidokute,

   _____.

   This morning I was extremely dizzy, which scared me.

3. _____ みましょう。

   _____ mimashoo.

   Let's check the temperature.

4. 今仕事がとても忙しくて、毎晩 _____ 。

   Ima shigoto ga totemo isogashikute, maiban

   _____.

   I am very busy with my work now and am working overtime every night.

5. 睡眠はちゃんと _____ 。

   Suimin wa chanto _____.

   Are you getting enough sleep?

6. _____ 寝ていません。

   _____ nete imasen.

   I'm getting only about four hours of sleep.

7. 多分_____ 。

   Tabun _____.

   Perhaps it's exhaustion.

8. 早はやく家いえに帰かえって _____ 。

Hayaku ie ni kaette _____

_____.

You'd better go home early and get some rest.

ANSWER KEY

1. 座すわってください suwatte kudasai; 2. びっくりしました bikkurishimashita; 3. 熱ねつを測はかって Netsu o hakatte; 4. 残業ざんぎょうしています zangyooshite imasu; 5. とっていますか totte imasu ka; 6. 四時間よじかんぐらい しか Yojikan gurai shika; 7. 疲労ひろうでしょう hiroo deshoo; 8. 休やすんだ方がいいです yasunda hoo ga ii desu

Grammar Builder 2

NEGATIVE REQUEST

▶ 15D Grammar Builder 2 (CD 9, Track 20)

You learned how to make requests in *Intermediate Japanese*. Now, let's learn how to make negative requests—as in the English expression *Please don't do that.*

> *Plain non-past negative form of a verb* (ない *nai-form*) + で *de* + ください **kudasai**

クラスで寝ねないでください。

Kurasu de nenai de kudasai.

Please don't sleep during the class.

そこに入はいらないでください。

Soko ni hairanai de kudasai.

Please don't enter there.

熱があったら、お風呂に入らないでください。

Netsu ga attara, ofuro ni hairanai de kudasai.

If you have a fever, please don't take a bath.

このレストランで煙草は吸わないでください。

Kono resutoran de tabako wa suwanai de kudasai.

Please don't smoke in this restaurant.

美術館の中で写真は撮らないでください。

Bijutsukan (*art museum*) no naka de shashin wa toranai de kudasai.

Please don't take pictures in the art museum.

そのコンピューターは使わないでください。

Sono konpyuutaa wa tsukawanai de kudasai.

Please don't use that computer.

嘘はつかないでください。

Uso (*lie*) wa tsukanaide kudasai.

Please don't tell a lie.

ください Kudasai can be dropped when talking to friends and family members.

お母さん、私の部屋に入らないで。

Okaasan, watashi no heya ni hairanai de.

Mom, please don't enter my room.

誰にも言わないでね。

Dare ni mo iwanai de ne.

Please don't tell it to anyone.

✎ Work Out 2

Make negative requests using the expressions provided in parentheses. You will need to change the verbs to their appropriate form.

1. 勉強^{べんきょう}していますから、 ＿＿＿＿＿＿＿＿＿＿＿ ください。(テレビを見^みる)

   Benkyooshite imasu kara, ＿＿＿＿＿＿＿＿＿＿＿＿＿＿＿＿＿＿

   kudasai. (terebi o miru)

2. 日本語^{にほんご}のクラスで ＿＿＿＿＿＿＿＿ ください。(英語^{えいご}を話^{はな}す)

   Nihongo no kurasu de ＿＿＿＿＿＿＿＿＿＿＿＿＿＿＿＿＿＿＿

   ＿＿＿＿ **kudasai. (eego o hanasu)**

3. ＿＿＿＿＿＿＿＿＿＿＿＿＿＿＿ ください。(ミーティングを休^{やす}む)

   ＿＿＿＿＿＿＿＿＿＿＿＿＿＿＿＿＿＿＿ **kudasai.**

   (miitingu o yasumu)

4. あまりたくさん ＿＿＿＿＿＿＿＿＿ ください。(お酒^{さけ}を飲^のむ)

   Amari takusan ＿＿＿＿＿＿＿＿＿＿＿＿＿＿＿＿＿＿

   kudasai. (osake o nomu)

   ANSWER KEY

   1. テレビは見^みないで terebi wa minai de; 2. 英語^{えいご}は話^{はな}さないで eego wa hanasanai de; 3. ミーティングは休^{やす}まないで miitingu wa yasumanai de; 4. お酒^{さけ}は飲^のまないで osake wa nomanai de

✎ Drive It Home

A. Fill in the blanks by inserting the expressions below from least formal to most.

いい ii, いいですか ii desu ka, いいでしょうか ii deshoo ka, よろしいですか yoroshii desu ka, よろしいでしょうか yoroshii deshoo ka

1. ここに座^{すわ}っても _____ ？

   Koko ni suwatte mo _____?

   May I sit down here?

2. ここに座^{すわ}っても _____。

   Koko ni suwatte mo _____.

   May I sit down here?

3. ここに座^{すわ}っても _____ 。

   Koko ni suwatte mo _____.

   May I sit down here?

4. ここに座^{すわ}っても _____ 。

   Koko ni suwatte mo _____.

   May I sit down here?

5. ここに座^{すわ}っても _____ 。

   Koko ni suwatte mo _____.

   May I sit down here?

B. Fill in the blanks with the appropriate words.

1. クラスで寝^ね _____。

   Kurasu de ne _____.

   Please don't sleep during the class.

2. このレストランで煙草^{たばこ}は吸わ^す _____。

   Kono resutoran de tabako wa suwa _____.

   Please don't smoke in this restaurant.

3. 美術館の中で写真は撮ら _____。

Bijutsukan (*art museum*) no naka de shashin wa tora _____

_____.

Please don't take pictures in the art museum.

4. そのコンピューターは使わ _____。

Sono konpyuutaa wa tsukawa _____.

Please don't use that computer.

ANSWER KEY

A. 1. いい ii; 2. いいですか ii desu ka; 3. いいでしょうか ii deshoo ka; 4. よろしいですか yoroshii desu ka; 5. よろしいでしょうか yoroshii deshoo ka

B. 1. ないでください nai de kudasai; 2. ないでください nai de kudasai; 3. ないでください nai de kudasai; 4. ないでください nai de kudasai

🔅 Tip!

Suppose that you have a profession such as a teacher, flight attendant, policeman, landlord, or superintendent at a museum. Think of some situations where you would ask other people, such as students, customers, drivers, or tenants, not to do certain things. Try giving those negative requests in Japanese using ないでくだ さい nai de kudasai. You should try forming sentences using words you already know. If you need to use the words that have not been introduced yet, you can always look them up in a dictionary.

How Did You Do?

Let's see how you did! By now, you should be able to:

☐ ask for permission (Still unsure? Jump back to page 330)

☐ make negative requests (Still unsure? Jump back to page 338)

✎ Word Recall

1. 全部 zenbu   a. *to play (a percussion instrument)*

2. 召し上がる meshiagaru   b. *all*

3. お目にかかる ome ni kakaru   c. *to eat, to drink*

4. たたく tataku   d. *scallop*

5. 吹く fuku   e. *photography, photograph*

6. 弾く hiku   f. *to perform (a musical instrument)*

7. 演奏する ensoosuru   g. *special ability, special skill*

8. 帆立 hotate   h. *to see, to meet*

9. 特技 tokugi   i. *to play (a wind instrument)*

10. 写真 shashin   j. *to play (a string instrument)*

ANSWER KEY

1. b; 2. c; 3. h; 4. a; 5. i; 6. j; 7. f; 8. d; 9. g; 10. e

Lesson 16: Conversations

In this lesson you'll learn how to:

☐ express obligation

☐ give advice

🎧 Conversation 1

▶ 16A Conversation 1 (Japanese: CD 9, Track 21; Japanese and English: CD 9, Track 22)

Mr. Yamazaki does not feel well, so he is visiting the doctor's office close to his workplace.

受付係/Uketsukegakari: お名前は？

Onamae wa?

山崎/Yamazaki: 山崎です。

Yamazaki desu.

受付係/Uketsukegakari: えっと、予約なさいましたか。

Etto, yoyaku nasaimashita ka.

山崎/Yamazaki: いいえ。予約をしなくてはいけませんか。

Iie. Yoyaku o shinakute wa ikemasen ka.

受付係/Uketsukegakari: 予約していなかったら、ちょっとお待ちになるかも
しれませんけど、よろしいですか。

Yoyakushite inakattara, chotto omachi ni naru
kamoshiremasen kedo, yoroshii desu ka.

山崎/Yamazaki: はい、大丈夫です。

Hai, daijoobu desu.

受付係/Uketsukegakari: 今日はどうなさいましたか。

Kyoo wa doo nasaimashita ka.

山崎/Yamazaki: 昨日から頭が痛くて、吐き気がするんです。今朝は
めまいもしたので、一度病院で診てもらったほうが
いいと思いました。

Kinoo kara atama ga itakute, hakike ga suru n desu.
Kesa wa memai mo shita node, ichido byooin de
mite moratta hoo ga ii to omoimashita.

受付係/Uketsukegakari: そうですか。以前にこの病院で診察を受けたことは
ありますか。

Soo desu ka. Izen ni kono byooin de shinsatsu o
uketa koto wa arimasu ka.

山崎/Yamazaki:　　　　いいえ、初めてです。

Iie, hajimete desu.

受付係/Uketsukegakari:　それでは、あちらに座ってこの用紙に記入して持って
来てください。

Soredewa, achira ni suwatte kono yooshi ni

kinyuushite motte kite kudasai.

(Five minutes later.)

山崎/Yamazaki:　　　　これでいいですか。

Kore de ii desu ka.

受付係/Uketsukegakari:　えっと、アレルギーに関する質問の答えも書いていた
だけますか。それから、今飲んでいるお薬がございま
したら、それも書いてください。

Etto, arerugii ni kansuru shitsumon no kotae mo

kaite itadakemasu ka. Sorekara, ima nondeiru

okusuri ga gozaimashitara, sore mo kaite kudasai.

山崎/Yamazaki:　　　　アレルギーは特に何もありません。それから、ビタミン
剤を飲んでいますが、他の薬は何も飲んでいません。

Arerugii wa toku ni nani mo arimasen. Sorekara,

bitaminzai o nonde imasu ga, hoka no kusuri wa

nani mo nonde imasen.

受付係/Uketsukegakari:　分かりました。それから、保険証はお持ちですか。

Wakarimashita. Sorekara, hokenshoo wa omochi

desu ka.

山崎/Yamazaki:　　　　はい、これです。

Hai, kore desu.

受付係/Uketsukegakari:　それでは、お名前をお呼びしますから、あちらでお待
ちください。

Soredewa, onamae o oyobishimasu kara, achira de

omachi kudasai.

やまざき
山崎/**Yamazaki:**   はい。

                         Hai.

Receptionist: *What's your name?*

Yamazaki: *Yamazaki.*

Receptionist: *Well, did you make an appointment?*

Yamazaki: *No. Do I have to make an appointment?*

Receptionist: *If you haven't made an appointment, you may have to*
                         wait for a little while, but is it okay with you?

Yamazaki: *Yes, it's okay.*

Receptionist: *What's wrong with you today?*

Yamazaki: *I have a headache since yesterday and also feel like*
                         vomiting. I also felt dizzy this morning, so I thought I'd
                         better get checked at a hospital for once.

Receptionist: *I see. Have you ever consulted a doctor at this hospital*
                         before?

Yamazaki: *No, it's my first time.*

Receptionist: *Then, please have a seat there, fill out this form and*
                         bring it back here.

(Five minutes later.)

Yamazaki: *Is this okay?*

Receptionist: *Well, could you write the answer to the questions*
                         concerning allergies, too? And, if there's any medicine
                         that you are currently taking, please write that, too.

Yamazaki: *I don't have any allergies. And, I'm taking a vitamin*
                         supplement, but I'm not taking any other medicine.

Receptionist: *Okay. And, do you have your health insurance card?*

Yamazaki: *Yes, here it is.*

Receptionist: *Then, we will call your name, so please wait there.*

Yamazaki: *Okay.*

✎ Conversation Practice 1

Fill in the blanks in the following sentences with the missing words. If you're unsure of the answer, listen to the conversation one more time.

1. 山崎さんは昨日から頭が痛くて、＿＿＿＿＿がします。

    Yamazaki san wa kinoo kara atama ga itakute, ＿＿＿＿＿＿＿＿＿＿ga shimasu.

2. 山崎さんは今朝、＿＿＿＿＿＿＿＿ もしました。

    Yamazaki san wa kesa, ＿＿＿＿＿＿＿＿＿ mo shimashita.

3. 山崎さんはこの病院で診察を受けるのは ＿＿＿＿＿＿ です。

    Yamazaki san wa kono byooin de shinsatsu o ukeru no wa

    ＿＿＿＿＿＿＿＿＿＿＿ desu.

4. 山崎さんは＿＿＿＿＿＿＿＿＿＿＿は特に何もありません。

    Yamazaki san wa ＿＿＿＿＿＿＿＿＿＿＿ wa toku ni nani mo arimasen.

5. 山崎さんは＿＿＿＿＿＿＿＿＿＿＿を飲んでいます。

    Yamazaki san wa ＿＿＿＿＿＿＿＿＿＿＿＿＿ o nonde imasu.

ANSWER KEY

1. 吐き気 hakike; 2. めまい memai; 3. 初めて hajimete; 4. アレルギー arerugii; 5. ビタミン剤 bitaminzai

Grammar Builder 1

EXPRESSING OBLIGATION

▶ 16B Grammar Builder 1 (CD 9, Track 23)

Obligation (*to have to*) is expressed using the following structure.

> て te-*form of plain negative form of a verb* + は wa+ いけません / いけない
> **ikemasen/ikenai** *or* なりません / ならない **narimasen/naranai**

Before we look at how this structure is used, we first have to learn how to form
て te-form of plain negative form of a verb. Remember that the negative forms of
verbs such as 飲む nomu, 食べる taberu and する suru are 飲まない nomanai,
食べない tabenai and しない shinai respectively. Since the conjugation of ない
nai is the same as that of い i-adjectives, whose conjugation you learned in Lesson
14, the て te-form of ない nai would be なくて nakute. Consequently, the て te-
form of 飲まない nomanai, 食べない tabenai and しない shinai are 飲まなくて
nomanakute, 食べなくて tabenakute and しなくて shinakute respectively.
Either はいけません wa ikemasen or はなりません wa narimasen follows the
て te-form of the negative forms of verbs. Let's see how this structure is used in
a few example sentences.

明日経済学のテストがありますから、今日勉強しなくてはいけません。

**Ashita keezaigaku no tesuto ga arimasu kara, kyoo benkyooshinakute wa
ikemasen.**

Since I have an economics test tomorrow, I have to study today.

お客さんが来るので、居間を掃除しなくてはなりません。

Okyakusan ga kuru node, ima o soojishinakute wa narimasen.

We have (a) guest(s), so we have to clean the living room.

明日は朝早く起きなくてはなりませんから、今晩早く寝なくてはいけません。

Ashita wa asa hayaku okinakute wa narimasen kara, konban hayaku nenakute wa ikemasen.

I have to get up early tomorrow morning, so I have to go to bed early tonight.

今晩家でパーティーをするので、食べ物や飲み物を買っておかなくてはいけません。

Konban uchi de paatii o suru node, tabemono ya nomimono o katte okanakute wa ikemasen.

We will have a party at home tonight, so we have to buy food and beverages among other things beforehand.

Instead of なくてはいけません/なりません nakute wa ikemasen/narimasen, you can also use なければいけません/なりません nakereba ikemasen/narimasen. なければ Nakereba is the so-called ば ba-form of ない nai. You haven't yet learned the ば ba-form of verbs and adjectives; for now, just remember なければ nakereba as a fixed expression. Compare the following sentence groups.

ミーティングに出なくてはいけません。
Miitingu ni denakute wa ikemasen.

ミーティングに出なければいけません。
Miitingu ni denakereba ikemasen.
I have to attend the meeting.

もっと野菜を食べなくてはなりません。
Motto yasai o tabenakute wa narimasen.

もっと野菜を食べなければなりません。

Motto yasai o tabenakereba narimasen.

You have to eat more vegetables.

病気ですから、薬を飲まなくてはいけません。

Byooki desu kara, kusuri o nomanakute wa ikemasen.

病気ですから、薬を飲まなければいけません。

Byooki desu kara, kusuri o nomanakereba ikemasen.

I'm sick, so I have to take medicine.

✎ Work Out 1

Translate the following Japanese sentences into English.

1. アメリカに留学する前に英語を勉強しなくてはいけません。

    Amerika ni ryuugakusuru mae ni eego o benkyooshinakute wa ikemasen.

    _____

2. 晩ご飯を食べた後、宿題をしなくてはなりません。

    Bangohan o tabeta ato, shukudai o shinakute wa narimasen.

    _____

3. 三時に友達に会うので、二時半に家を出なければいけません。

    Sanji ni tomodachi ni au node, niji han ni uchi o denakereba ikemasen.

    _____

4. 会社で面接を受ける時、スーツを着なくてはいけませんか。

Kaisha de mensetsu o ukeru toki, suutsu (suit) o kinakute wa ikemasen ka.

5. 大学病院で検査を受ける時は、予約しておかなければなりません。

Daigakubyooin de kensa o ukeru toki wa, yoyakushite okanakereba

narimasen.

ANSWER KEY

1. You have to study English before going to study abroad in the U.S.A. 2. I have to do homework after eating dinner. 3. I will meet my friend(s) at three o'clock, so I have to leave home at two-thirty. 4. Do I have to wear a suit when I go to interview at a company? 5. When you have a medical exam at a university hospital, you have to make an appointment in advance.

🔊 Conversation 2

▶ 16C Conversation 2 (Japanese: CD 9, Track 24; Japanese and English: CD 9, Track 25)

Mr. Yamazaki enters the examination room.

山崎/Yamazaki:	失礼します。
	Shitsureeshimasu.
医者/Isha:	はい、じゃあここに座ってください。えっと、頭痛と吐き気とめまいですか。
	Hai, jaa koko ni suwatte kudasai. Etto, zutsuu to hakike to memai desu ka.
山崎/Yamazaki:	はい。
	Hai.
医者/Isha:	今もめまいはしますか。
	Ima mo memai wa shimasu ka.

山崎/Yamazaki: 今は大丈夫ですけど、今朝はめまいがひどくて、びっくりしました。

Ima wa daijoobu desu kedo, kesa wa memai ga hidokute,

bikkurishimashita.

医者/Isha: そうですか。ちょっと熱を測ってみましょう。*(after a little while)* 三十八度ですから、少し熱もありますね。口を開けてください。喉は痛くありませんか。

Soo desu ka. Chotto netsu o hakatte mimashoo. *(after*

a little while) Sanjuuhachi do desu kara, sukoshi netsu

mo arimasu ne. Kuchi o akete kudasai. Nodo wa itaku

arimasen ka.

山崎/Yamazaki: いいえ。

Iie.

医者/Isha: お腹はどうですか。下痢はしていませんか。

Onaka wa doo desu ka. Geri wa shite imasen ka.

山崎/Yamazaki: いいえ。お腹は痛くないし、下痢もしていません。

Iie. Onaka wa itaku nai shi, geri mo shite imasen.

医者/Isha: ううん、風邪じゃないですね。お仕事は忙しいですか。

Uun, kaze ja nai desu ne. Oshigoto wa isogashii desu ka.

山崎/Yamazaki: はい、今とても忙しくて、毎晩残業しています。

Hai, ima totemo isogashikute, maiban zangyooshite

imasu.

医者/Isha: 睡眠はちゃんととっていますか。

Suimin wa chanto totte imasu ka.

山崎/Yamazaki: 最近は毎晩四時間ぐらいしか寝ていません。

Saikin wa maiban yojikan gurai shika nete imasen.

医者/Isha: そうですか。多分疲労でしょう。でも、一度検査してもらった方がいいですね。

Soo desu ka. Tabun hiroo deshoo. Demo, ichido

kensashite moratta hoo ga ii desu ne.

山崎/Yamazaki:　検査ですか。

Kensa desu ka.

医者/Isha:　大学病院に私が知っている医者がいますから、彼に連絡しておきます。明日の午後二時頃は大丈夫ですか。

Daigakubyooin ni watashi ga shitte iru isha ga imasu kara, kare ni renrakushite okimasu. Ashita no gogo niji goro wa daijoobu desu ka.

山崎/Yamazaki:　はい、大丈夫です。今日は会社に戻って仕事をしてもいいですか。

Hai, daijoobu desu. Kyoo wa kaisha ni modotte shigoto o shite mo ii desu ka.

医者/Isha:　気分が悪くなかったら、仕事をしてもいいですけど、残業しないでくださいね。早く家に帰って休んだ方がいいですよ。

Kibun ga warukunakattara, shigoto o shite mo ii desu kedo, zangyooshinaide kudasai ne. Hayaku ie ni kaette yasunda hoo ga ii desu yo.

山崎/Yamazaki:　はい、そうします。

Hai, soo shimasu.

Yamazaki:	*May I come in? (lit., Excuse me.)*
Doctor:	*Yes, please sit down here. So, a headache, nausea and dizziness?*
Yamazaki:	*Yes.*
Doctor:	*Do you still feel dizzy now?*
Yamazaki:	*Now, I'm fine, but I felt extremely dizzy this morning, which scared me.*
Doctor:	*I see. Let's check your body temperature. It's thirty-eight degrees, so you have a little fever, too. Please open your mouth. Your throat doesn't hurt?*
Yamazaki:	*No.*

Doctor:	How's your stomach? Don't you have diarrhea?
Yamazaki:	No, I don't have a stomachache and don't have diarrhea either.
Doctor:	Well, it's not a cold. Are you busy at your work?
Yamazaki:	Yes, I'm very busy now and working overtime every night.
Doctor:	Are you having enough sleep?
Yamazaki:	Recently, I've been sleeping for only about four hours a night.
Doctor:	I see. Perhaps it's exhaustion. But, you'd better be examined for once.
Yamazaki:	An examination?
Doctor:	There's a doctor I know at the university hospital, so I will contact him beforehand. Is around 2:00 p.m. tomorrow okay?
Yamazaki:	Yes, that's fine. May I go back to the office and do my work today?
Doctor:	If you don't feel sick, you may work, but please don't work overtime today. You'd better go home early and get some rest.
Yamazaki:	Okay, I will do so.

✎ Conversation Practice 2

Fill in the blanks in the following sentences with the missing words. If you're unsure of the answer, listen to the conversation one more time.

1. 山崎さんは熱が _____ 度あります。

   Yamazaki san wa netsu ga _____ do arimasu.

2. 山崎さんは _____ とお腹は痛くありません。

   Yamazaki san wa _____ to onaka wa itaku arimasen.

3. 山崎さんは _____ が忙しいです。

   Yamazaki san wa _____ ga isogashii desu.

4. 山崎さんは毎晩 _____ ぐらいしか寝ていません。

   Yamazaki san wa maiban _____ gurai shika nete imasen.

5. 山崎さんは明日大学病院で _____ を受けます。

   Yamazaki san wa ashita daigaku byooin de _____ o ukemasu.

ANSWER KEY
1. 三十八 sanjuuhachi; 2. 喉 nodo; 3. 仕事 shigoto; 4. 四時間 yojikan; 5. 検査 kensa

Grammar Builder 2

GIVING ADVICE

▶ 16D Grammar Builder 2 (CD 9, Track 26)

When you want to give other people an advice (*You'd better ...*), you can use the structure below.

> *Plain past affirmative form (た ta/ だ da-form) of a verb*
> *+ がいいです hoo ga ii desu*

もっと野菜を食べた方いいですよ。

Motto yasai o tabeta hoo ga ii desu yo.

You'd better eat more vegetables.

熱があったら、病院へ行った方がいいでしょう。

Netsu ga attara, byooin e itta hoo ga ii deshoo.

If you have a fever, you'd probably better go to a hospital.

あのレストランはいつも混んでいるから、予約した方がいいと思います。

Ano resutoran wa itsumo konde iru kara, yoyakushita hoo ga ii to omoimasu.

That restaurant is always crowded, so I think you'd better make a reservation.

分からなかったら、先生に聞いた方がいいですよ。

Wakaranakattara, sensee ni kiita hoo ga ii desu yo.

If you don't understand, you'd better ask a teacher.

ビタミン剤を飲んだ方がいいと思いますか。

Bitaminzai o nonda hoo ga ii to omoimasu ka.

Do you think it's better to take vitamin supplements?

You can also advise people not to do something (*you'd better not … /it's better that …*) using the following structure.

> *Plain non-past negative form (* ない *nai-form) of a verb +* がいいです hoo ga ii desu

身体によくありませんから、あまり煙草は吸わない方がいいですよ。

Karada ni yoku arimasen kara, amari tabako wa suwanai hoo ga ii desu yo.

You'd better not smoke so much because it's not good for your health.

めまいがする時は、出掛けない方がいいと思います。

Memai ga suru toki wa, dekakenai hoo ga ii to omoimasu.

When you feel dizzy, I think that you'd better not go out.

お酒は飲みすぎない方がいいですよ。

Osake wa nomisuginai hoo ga ii desu yo.

You'd better not drink too much.

下痢をしていたら、晩ご飯は食べない方がいいでしょう。

Geri o shite itara, bangohan wa tabenai hoo ga ii deshoo.

If you have diarrhea, it's probably better for you not to eat dinner.

頭が痛かったら、パーティーに行かない方がいいと思います。

Atama ga itakattara, paatii ni ikanai hoo ga ii to omoimasu.

If you have a headache, I think it's better for you not to go to the party.

✎ Work Out 2

A. Using the words in parentheses, give advice using た/だ方がいいです ta/da hoo ga ii desu.

1. *You'd better attend the meeting.*

(ミーティングに出る miitingu ni deru)

_____

2. *You'd better read more books.*

(もっと本を読む motto hon o yomu)

_____

3. *You'd better talk with the division manager.*

(部長と話す buchoo to hanasu)

_____

4. *You'd better clean the room.*

(部屋を掃除する heya o soojisuru)

_____

5. *You'd better take a rest.*

(休<ruby>やす</ruby>む yasumu)

_____

B. Use the words in parentheses and the structure verb + ない方<ruby>ほう</ruby>がいいです nai hoo ga ii desu to give advice. Don't forget the particles!

_____

1. *You'd better not see this movie.*

(この映画<ruby>えいが</ruby>を見<ruby>み</ruby>る kono eega o miru)

_____

2. *You'd better not be absent from school.*

(学校<ruby>がっこう</ruby>を休<ruby>やす</ruby>む gakkoo o yasumu)

_____

3. *You'd better not drink coffee too much.*

(コーヒーを飲<ruby>の</ruby>みすぎる koohii o nomisugiru)

_____

4. *You'd better not do exercises today.*

(運動<ruby>うんどう</ruby>する undoosuru)

_____

5. *You'd better not spend (use) so much money.*

(お金<ruby>かね</ruby>を使<ruby>つか</ruby>う okane o tsukau)

_____

ANSWER KEY

A. 1. ミーティングに出た方がいいです。Miitingu ni deta hoo ga ii desu. 2. もっと本を読んだ方がい いです。Motto hon o yonda hoo ga ii desu. 3. 部長と話した方がいいです。Buchoo to hanashita hoo ga ii desu. 4. 部屋を掃除した方がいいです。Heya o soojishita hoo ga ii desu. 5. 休んだ方がいいです。 Yasunda hoo ga ii desu.

B. 1. この映画は見ない方がいいです。Kono eega wa minai hoo ga ii desu. 2. 学校は休まない方がい いです。 Gakkoo wa yasumanai hoo ga ii desu. 3. コーヒーは飲みすぎない方がいいです。Koohii wa nomisuginai hoo ga ii desu. 4. 今日 (は) 運動しない方がいいです。Kyoo (wa) undooshinai hoo ga ii desu. 5. お金はあまり使わない方がいいです。Okane wa amari tsukawanai hoo ga ii desu.

✎ Drive It Home

A. Fill in the blanks by choosing appropriate expressions from the word bank.

飲まなければいけません nomanakereba ikemasen, 食べなければなりません tabenakereba narimasen, 出なくてはいけません denakute wa ikemasen

1. ミーティングに _____ 。

   Miitingu ni _____

   I give a card to my father.

2. もっと野菜を _____ 。

   Motto yasai o _____

   _____.

   You have to eat more vegetables.

3. 病気ですから、薬を _____ 。

   Byooki desu kara, kusuri o _____

   _____.

   I'm sick, so I have to take medicine.

B. Fill in the blanks with the appropriate words.

1. もっとを野菜を食べ _____ ですよ。

   Motto yasai o tabe _____ **desu yo.**

   You'd better eat more vegetables.

2. 熱があったら、病院へ行っ _____ でしょう。

   Netsu ga attara, byooin e it _____ **deshoo.**

   If you have a fever, you'd better go to a hospital.

3. 分からなかったら、先生に聞い _____ ですよ。

   Wakaranakattara, sensee ni kii _____ **desu yo.**

   If you don't understand, you'd better ask a teacher.

C. Fill in the blanks with appropriate words.

1. めまいがする時は、出掛け _____ と思います。

   Memai ga suru toki wa, dekake _____ **to omoimasu.**

   When you feel dizzy, I think that you'd better not go out.

2. 下痢をしていたら、晩ご飯は食べ _____ でしょう。

   Geri o shite itara, bangohan wa tabe _____ **deshoo.**

   If you have diarrhea, it's probably better for you not to eat dinner.

3. 頭が痛かったら、パーティーに行か _____ と思います。

   Atama ga itakattara, paatii ni ika _____ **to**

omoimasu.

If you have a headache, I think it's better for you not to go to the party.

ANSWER KEY

A. 1. 出^でなくてはいけません denakute wa ikemasen; 2. 食^たべなければなりません tabenakereba narimasen; 3. 飲^のまなければいけません nomanakereba ikemasen

B. 1. た方^{ほう}がいい ta hoo ga ii; 2. た方^{ほう}がいい ta hoo ga ii; 3. た方^{ほう}がいい ta hoo ga ii

C. 1. ない方^{ほう}がいい nai hoo ga ii; 2. ない方^{ほう}がいい nai hoo ga ii; 3. ない方^{ほう}がいい nai hoo ga ii

 ## Tip!

To practice expressing obligation, try making a to-do list every evening for the following day. If you haven't yet learned the verbs you want to use, you can look them up in a dictionary and change them into their なくて nakute or なければ nakereba form. If you continue to do this task for a week, you'll probably start to see some repetition of tasks, but that's fine. Practice—and repetition—makes perfect!

How Did You Do?

Let's see how you did! By now, you should be able to:

☐ express obligation (Still unsure? Jump back to page 348)

☐ give advice (Still unsure? Jump back to page 355)

✎ Word Recall

1. 楽器 <ruby>楽器<rt>がっき</rt></ruby> gakki　　　　　　a. *be insufficient, be short*

2. <ruby>読書<rt>どくしょ</rt></ruby> dokusho　　　　b. *to own, to hold*

3. もし moshi　　　　　　c. *after all, as expected*

4. <ruby>苦手<rt>にがて</rt></ruby> nigate　　　　　d. *to be bad at*

5. やっぱり yappari　　　　e. *to be good at*

6. <ruby>上手<rt>じょうず</rt></ruby> joozu　　　　　f. *skillful*

7. <ruby>得意<rt>とくい</rt></ruby> tokui　　　　　g. *if, in case*

8. <ruby>作<rt>つく</rt></ruby>る tsukuru　　　　h. *reading books*

9. <ruby>持<rt>も</rt></ruby>つ motsu　　　　　i. *to make*

10. <ruby>足<rt>た</rt></ruby>りない tarinai　　　j. *musical instrument*

ANSWER KEY

1. j; 2. h; 3. g; 4. d; 5. c; 6. f; 7. e; 8. i; 9. b; 10. a

Don't forget to practice and reinforce what you've learned by visiting **www.livinglanguage.com/ languagelab** for flashcards, games, and quizzes for Unit 4!

Unit 4 Essentials

Vocabulary Essentials

Test your knowledge of the key material in this unit by filling in the blanks in the following charts. Once you've completed these pages, you'll have tested your retention, and you'll have your own reference for the most essential vocabulary.

BODY PARTS

	body
	head
	face
	eye
	mouth
	nose
	ear
	arm
	foot
	leg
	chest
	belly, abdomen
	waist, hip
	heart
	brain
	stomach
	lung

	intestine
	hair
	hair (on the head)

AT A CLINIC AND HOSPITAL

	clinic
	front desk
	consulting room
	waiting room
	medical consultation
	the first medical consultation
	patient
	health insurance card
	form
	examination
	injection, shot
	operation, surgery
	medicine
	vitamin supplement
	it's the first time
	What is wrong (with you) today? (polite)

PHYSICAL CONDITIONS

	painful
	terrible, severe
	38 degrees
	fever
	cold
	headache
	stomachache
	nausea
	dizziness
	diarrhea
	appetite
	sleep
	allergy
	blood pressure
	anemia
	exhaustion, fatigue
	stress
	injury
	cancer

VERBS

	to fill in
	to call
	to sit down

	to give an injection
	to operate
	to be hospitalized
	to leave the hospital, to be released from hospital
	to open
	to close
	to work overtime
	to take some rest, to be absent, to take a day off
	to contact
	to have a headache
	to have a stomachache
	to have diarrhea
	to feel like vomiting
	to feel dizzy
	to feel extremely dizzy
	to have chills
	to look pale
	to be checked by a doctor
	to catch a cold
	to have a fever
	to check the temperature
	to have a sore throat
	to have an appetite

	to have high blood pressure
	to have low blood pressure
	to get some sleep
	to suffer from insomnia
	to be under a lot of stress (lit., stress has accumulated)
	to have stiff shoulders
	to get injured
	to break a bone
	to have a sprain

ADVERBS

	this morning
	early, fast
	properly, exactly, accurately

Grammar Essentials

Here is a reference of the key grammar that was covered in Unit 4. Make sure you understand the summary and can use all of the grammar it covers.

SINGULAR PRONOUNS

私 watashi	I
あなた anata	you
彼 kare	he
彼女 kanojo	she

それ sore	*it*

PLURAL PRONOUNS

私達 watashitachi	*we*
あなた達 anatatachi あなた方 anatagata	*you*
彼ら karera	*they (m.)*
彼女ら kanojora 彼女達 kanojotachi	*they (f.)*
それら sorera	*they (it)*

POSSESSIVE PRONOUNS

私の watashi no	*my*
あなたの anata no	*your*
彼の kare no	*his*
彼女の kanojo no	*her*
その sono	*its*

INDIRECT OBJECT PRONOUNS

私に watashi ni	*(to) me*
あなたに anata ni	*(to) you*
彼に kare ni	*(to) him*

彼女に <ruby>かのじょ<rt></rt></ruby> kanojo ni	*(to) her*
それに sore ni	*(to) it*

DIRECT OBJECT PRONOUNS

私を <ruby>わたし<rt></rt></ruby> watashi o	*me*
あなたを anata o	*you*
彼を <ruby>かれ<rt></rt></ruby> kare o	*him*
彼女を <ruby>かのじょ<rt></rt></ruby> kanojo o	*her*
それを sore o	*it*

DO SOMETHING BEFOREHAND: VERB + ておきます TE OKIMASU

て te-*form of a verb* + おきます/おく okimasu/oku

THE て TE-FORM OF ADJECTIVES
い I-ADJECTIVES

Drop final い i *and attach* くて kute

大きい ookii *(big)*	大きくて okikute	おいしい oishii *(delicious)*	おいしくて ishikute
明るい akarui *(bright)*	明るくて akarukute	暖かい atatakai *(warm)*	暖かくて atatakakute
忙しい isogashii *(busy)*	忙しくて isogashikute	痛い itai *(painful)*	痛くて itakute

な NA-ADJECTIVES

stem of な na-*adjectives* + で de

<ruby>有名<rt>ゆうめい</rt></ruby> yuumee *(famous)*	<ruby>有名<rt>ゆうめい</rt></ruby>で yuumee de	<ruby>静<rt>しず</rt></ruby>か shizuka *(quiet)*	<ruby>静<rt>しず</rt></ruby>かで shizuka de
<ruby>親切<rt>しんせつ</rt></ruby> shinsetsu *(kind)*	<ruby>親切<rt>しんせつ</rt></ruby>で shinsetsu de	<ruby>賑<rt>にぎ</rt></ruby>やか nigiyaka *(lively)*	<ruby>賑<rt>にぎ</rt></ruby>やかで nigiyaka de
<ruby>簡単<rt>かんたん</rt></ruby> kantan *(easy, simple)*	<ruby>簡単<rt>かんたん</rt></ruby>で kantan de	きれい kiree *(beautiful, clean)*	きれいで kiree de

GIVING AND RECEIVING VERBS

A が/は B に X てあげます/さしあげます。	A ga/wa B ni X te agemasu/ sashiagemasu.	*A gives B the favor of doing something (X). (A does something – X - for B.)*
A が/は B に X てもらいます/いただきます。	A ga/wa B ni X te moraimasu/ itadakimasu.	*A receives a favor from B of having something done (X). (B does something – X - for A.)*
A が/は B に X てくれます/くださいます。 *(B = a speaker or his/her in-group member)*	A ga/wa B ni X te kuremasu/ kudasaimasu. *(B = a speaker or his/her in-group member)*	*A gives me/my in-group member the favor of doing something (X). (A does something – X - for me/ my in-group member.)*

ASKING FOR PERMISSION

て te-form of a verb + (も) いい? (mo) ii? *(with a rising intonation)*

て te-form of a verb + (も) いいですか。 (mo) ii desu ka.

て te-form of a verb + (も) いいでしょうか。 (mo) ii deshoo ka.

て te-form of a verb + (も) よろしいですか。 (mo) yoroshii desu ka.

て te-form of a verb + (も) よろしいでしょうか。 (mo) yoroshii deshoo ka.

NEGATIVE REQUEST

Plain non-past negative form of a verb (ない nai-form) + で de + ください kudasai

EXPRESSING OBLIGATION

て te-form of plain negative form of a verb + は wa + いけません/いけない ikemasen/ikenai *or* なりません/ならない narimasen/naranai

GIVING ADVICE

You'd better …

Plain past affirmative form (た ta/だ da-form) *of a verb* + 方がいいです hoo ga ii desu

You'd better not …

Plain non-past negative form (ない nai-form) *of a verb* + 方がいいです hoo ga ii desu

Unit 4 Quiz

Let's put the most essential Japanese words and grammar points you've learned so far to practice in a few exercises. Score yourself at the end of the review and see if you need to go back for more practice.

A. Fill in the blanks with appropriate pronouns.

1. _____は今日一緒に図書館で勉強します。

   _____ wa kyoo issho ni toshokan de

   benkyooshimasu.

   We are going to study at the library together today.

2. メアリー・クラークさんはピアニストです。明日、_____ のコンサートがあります。

   Mearii kuraaku san wa pianisuto desu. Ashita, _____ no

   konsaato ga arimasu.

   Ms. Mary Clerk is a pianist. Her concert will be tomorrow.

3. 田中さんの _____ はとてもいい人ですよ。

   Tanaka san no _____ wa totemo ii hito desu yo.

   Ms. Tanaka's boyfriend is a very nice person.

B. Fill in the blanks by using the verbs in parentheses.

1. 明日は母の誕生日ですからケーキを _____。(買います)

   Ashita wa haha no tanjoobi desukara keeki o _____

_____. (kaimasu)

Tomorrow is my mother's birthday, so I'll buy a cake in advance.

2. レストランへ行く前に_____。（予約をします）

Resutoran he iku mae ni _____

_____. (yoyaku o shimasu)

Before going to the restaurant, I'll make a reservation in advance.

C. Fill in the blanks by inserting the て te-form of the adjectives in parentheses.

1. 川田さんの家は_____きれいです。（新しい）

Kawada san no ie wa _____ kiree desu. (atarashii)

Mr./Ms. Kawada's house is new and clean.

2. その公園は_____、_____、静かですから、よく行きます。（大きい、きれい）

Sono kooen wa _____, _____, shizuka desu kara, yoku ikimasu. (ookii, kiree)

That park is big, pretty and quiet, so I often go there.

D. Fill in the blanks by choosing the appropriate expressions from the word bank.

もらいました moraimashita, くれました kuremashita, さしあげました sashiagemashita, いただきました itadakimashita

1. 私は部長にレポートを読んで_____。

Watashi wa buchoo ni repooto o yonde

_____.

I read a report to the division manager. (lit., I gave the division manager a favor of my reading a report to him.)

2. 私は鈴木さんに彼が撮った写真を見せて _____。

   Watashi wa Suzuki san ni kare ga totta shashin o misete

   _____.

   Mr. Suzuki showed me the pictures that he took. (lit., I received a favor from Mr. Suzuki of him showing me the pictures that he took.)

3. 私はカンポス先生にスペイン語を教えて _____。

   Watashi wa Kanposu sensee ni supeingo o oshiete

   _____.

   Professor Campos taught me Spanish. (lit., I received a favor from Professor Campos of his/her teaching me Spanish.)

4. ルームメートが部屋を掃除して _____。

   Ruumumeeto ga heya o soojishite _____.

   My roommate cleaned our room. (lit., My roommate gave me a favor of his/her cleaning our room.)

E. Construct sentences asking for permission using the words provided in parentheses.

1. (して、です、質問、も、か、よろしい)。

   (shite, desu, shitsumon, mo, ka, yoroshii).

   May I ask a question?

   _____

2. (か、部屋、いい、に、も、入って、です)。

(ka, heya, ii, ni, mo, haitte, desu).

May I enter your room?

_____

F. Fill in the blanks by giving the verbs in the parentheses in the appropriate form.

1. そこに_____ ください。(入る)

Soko ni _____ kudasai. (hairu)

Please don't enter there.

2. 誰にも _____ ください。(言う)

Dare ni mo _____ kudasai. (iu)

Please don't tell it to anyone.

G. Fill in the blanks by choosing the appropriate expressions from the word bank.

寝なくてはいけません nenakute wa ikemasen, 勉強しなくてはいけません benkyooshinakute wa ikemasen, 掃除しなくてはなりません soojishinakute wa narimasen

1. 明日経済学のテストがありますから、今日 _____

_____。

Ashita keezaigaku no tesuto ga arimasu kara, kyoo

_____

_____.

Since I have an economics test tomorrow, I have to study today.

2. お客^{きゃく}さんが来^くるので、居間^{いま}を _____ 。

Okyakusan ga kuru node, ima o _____

_____ .

We have (a) guest(s), so we have to clean the living room.

3. 明日^{あした}は朝早^{あさはや}く起^おきなくてはなりませんから、今晩早^{こんばんはや}く _____

_____ 。

Ashita wa asa hayaku okinakute wa narimasen kara, konban hayaku

_____ .

I have to get up early tomorrow morning, so I have to go to bed early tonight.

H. Using the words in parentheses, give advice with the expression た/だ方^{ほう}がいいです ta/da hoo ga ii desu or ない方^{ほう}がいいです nai hoo ga ii desu.

1. *You'd better take medicine.*

(薬^{くすり}を飲^のむ kusuri o nomu)

_____

2. *You'd better not buy this car.*

(この車^{くるま}を買^かう kono kuruma o kau)

_____

ANSWER KEY

A. 1. 私達^{わたしたち} Watashitachi; 2. 彼女^{かのじょ} kanojo; 3. 彼^{かれ} kare

B. 1. 買^かっておきます katte okimasu; 2. 予約^{よやく}をしておきます yoyaku o shite okimasu

C. 1. 新^{あたら}しくて atarashikute; 2. 大^{おお}きくて ookikute、きれいで kiree de

D. 1. さしあげました sashiagemashita; 2. もらいました moraimashita; 3. いただきました itadakimashita; 4. くれました kuremashita

E. 1. 質問^{しつもん}してもよろしいですか Shitsumonshite mo yoroshii desu ka; 2. 部屋^{へや}に入^{はい}ってもいいですか Heya ni haitte mo ii desu ka

F. 1. 入^{はい}らないで hairanai de; 2. 言^いわないで iwanai de

G. 1. 勉強^{べんきょう}しなくてはいけません benkyooshinakute wa ikemasen; 2. 掃除^{そうじ}しなくてはなりません

soojishinakute wa narimasen; 3. 寝なくてはいけません nenakute wa ikemasen
H. 1. 薬を飲んだ方がいいです。 Kusuri o nonda hoo ga ii desu. 2. この車は買わない方がいいです。
Kono kuruma wa kawanai hoo ga ii desu.

How Did You Do?

Give yourself a point for every correct answer, then use the following key to find
out how you did.

0-7 points: It's probably a good idea to go back through the lesson again. You
may be moving too quickly, or there may be too much "down time" between
your contact with Japanese. Remember that it's better to spend 30 minutes with
Japanese three or four times a week than it is to spend two or three hours just
once a week. Find a pace that's comfortable for you, and spread your contact
hours out as much as you can.

8-12 points: You would benefit from a review before moving on. Go back and
spend a little more time on the specific points that gave you trouble. Re-read
the Grammar Builder sections that were difficult, and do the work out one more
time. Don't forget about the online supplemental practice material, either. Go
to **www.livinglanguage.com/languagelab** for games and quizzes that will
reinforce the material from this unit.

13-17 points: Good job! There are just a few points that you could consider
reviewing before moving on. If you haven't worked with the games and quizzes
on **www.livinglanguage.com/languagelab**, please give them a try.

18-20 points: Great! Your Japanese has come a long way!

		points

Even though you've reached the end of this course, there's no reason to stop learning. Consider some of these activities to keep your Japanese fresh, and to continue learning.

☐ Watch Japanese language movies.

☐ Download (legally!) a few Japanese songs and pay attention to the lyrics or look up the lyrics online to read along.

☐ Bookmark an online Japanese language newspaper or magazine. Read a little bit every day.

☐ Buy a book in Japanese and try to read it every day.

☐ Check out chatrooms or other online communities in Japanese.

☐ Remember to visit **www.livinglanguage.com/languagelab** for further practice, and return to this book to review any time you want.

☐ Use your imagination! You can tailor your Japanese exposure to your interests—food, music, theater, music, sports: the path is up to you.

Glossary

Note that the following abbreviations will be used in this glossary: (m.) = masculine, (f.) = feminine, (sg.) = singular, (pl.) = plural, (fml.) = formal/polite, (infml.) = informal/familiar. If a word has two grammatical genders, (m./f.) or (f./m.) is used.

Japanese-English

A

aa ああ *ah, oh*

achira あちら *that, that way (far from both the speaker and the listener) (polite)*

ageru, agemasu あげる、あげます *to give*
... te ageru, ... te agemasu 〜てあげる、〜てあげます *to give a favor of ... ing*

(... to ... no) aida (〜と〜の)間 *between (... and ...)*

aisukuriimu アイスクリーム *ice cream*

aka 赤 *red (noun)*

aka wain 赤ワイン *red wine*

akai 赤い *red (adjective)*

akarui 明るい *bright*

akeru, akemasu 開ける、開けます *to open (transitive verb)*

aki 秋 *fall, autumn*

amai 甘い *sweet*

ame 雨 *rain*
Ame desu. 雨です。 *It's raining.*
Ame ga futte imasu. 雨が降っています。 *It's raining.*

amerika アメリカ *the United States*

amerikajin アメリカ人 *American (person)*

anata あなた *you (sg.) (subject pronoun)*
anatagata あなた方 *you (pl.) (subject pronoun)*
anata no あなたの *your (sg.)*
anatatachi あなた達 *you (pl.) (subject pronoun)*

ane 姉 *older sister (one's own)*

ani 兄 *older brother (one's own)*

a(n)mari (+ negative) あ（ん）まり *not so often, not so much*

ano あの *that (far from both the speaker and the listener)*
ano pen あのペン *that pen*

anoo あのう *Well ...*

ao 青 *blue (noun)*

aoi 青い *blue (adjective)*

apaato アパート *apartment*

arau, araimasu 洗う、洗います *to wash*

are あれ *that (far from both the speaker and the listener)*

arerugii アレルギー *allergy*

Arigatoo gozaimashita. ありがとうございました。 *Thank you.*
Arigatoo gozaimasu. ありがとうございます。 *Thank you.*
Doomo arigatoo gozaimashita. どうもありがとうございました。 *Thank you very much.*
Doomo arigatoo gozaimasu. どうもありがとうございます。 *Thank you very much.*

aru, arimasu ある、あります *there is ... / to have ... (inanimate)*

aruku, arukimasu 歩く、歩きます *to walk*
aruite gofun 歩いて五分 *five minute walk*

asa 朝 *morning*

asagohan 朝ご飯 *breakfast (infml.)*

asatte あさって *the day after tomorrow*

ashi 足 *foot*

ashi 脚 *leg*

ashisutanto アシスタント *assistant*

ashita 明日 *tomorrow*

asobu, asobimasu 遊ぶ、遊びます *to play (a game)*

asoko あそこ *there (far from both the speaker and the listener)*

asu 明日 *tomorrow*

atama 頭 *head*
atama ga itai, atama ga itai desu 頭が痛い、頭が痛いです *to have a headache*

atarashii 新しい *new*

atatakai 暖かい *warm*

atesaki 宛先 *(sent) to*

ato de 後で *later, after*

resutoran o deta ato de レストランを出た後で
  after leaving a restaurant
atsui 暑い *hot (weather, room temperature)*
atsui 熱い *hot (to the touch)*
au, aimasu 会う、会います *to meet*
au, aimasu 合う、合います *to match*
  jiinzu ni au ジーンズに合う *to match with jeans*
azukaru, azukarimasu 預かる、預かります
  to keep
baa バー *bar*
baggu バッグ *bag*
baiorin バイオリン *violin*
ban バン *van*
ban 晩 *evening, night*
  konban 今晩 *tonight*
  maiban 毎晩 *every night*
bareebooru バレーボール *volleyball*
basu バス *bus*
basukettobooru バスケットボール *basketball*
basutee バス停 *bus stop*
bataa バター *butter*
batto バット *bat*
beddo ベッド *bed*
bengoshi 弁護士 *lawyer*
benkyoosuru, benkyooshimasu 勉強する、
  勉強します *to study*
benri 便利 *convenient*
besuto ベスト *vest, best*
biichi ビーチ *beach*
biiru ビール *beer*
  biiru ken ビール券 *beer gift coupon*
bikkurisuru, bikkurishimasu びっくりする、
  びっくりします *to be surprised, to be scared*
bin 瓶 *bottle*
biru ビル *high-rise building*
bitaminzai ビタミン剤 *vitamin supplement*
biyooin 美容院 *beauty salon*
biyooshi 美容師 *hair dresser*
bojoreenuuboo ボジョレーヌーボー *Beaujolais
  nouveau*
boku (used only by male speakers) 僕 *I*
booeki 貿易 *trade, export and import business*
booekigaisha 貿易会社 *trading company*
booru ボール *ball*
boorupen ボールペン *ballpoint pen*
bu 部 *set, copy (counter for written materials)*
buchoo 部長 *division manager*
bukka 物価 *prices (of commodities)*

bungaku 文学 *literature*
buranchi ブランチ *brunch*
burausu ブラウス *blouse*
buta 豚 *pig*
butaniku 豚肉 *pork*
byakuya 白夜 *white night*
byooin 病院 *hospital*
byooki 病気 *illness*
canada カナダ *Canada*
chairo 茶色 *brown (noun)*
chairoi 茶色い *brown (adjective)*
… chaku ～着 *arriving…*
  Naha chaku 那覇着 *arriving in Naha*
chansu チャンス *chance*
chanto ちゃんと *properly, exactly, accurately
  (infml.)*
cheen チェーン *chain*
chero チェロ *cello*
chichi 父 *father (one's own)*
chichi no hi 父の日 *father's day*
chiisai 小さい *small*
chiizu チーズ *cheese*
chikai 近い *close*
chikaku 近く *nearby*
chikatetsu 地下鉄 *subway*
chikin sarada チキンサラダ *chicken salad*
chokoreeto チョコレート *chocolate*
choo 腸 *intestine*
choomiryoo 調味料 *seasoning*
chooshoku 朝食 *breakfast (fml.)*
chotto ちょっと *a little*
chuugakkoo 中学校 *junior high school*
chuugoku 中国 *China*
chuugokugo 中国語 *Chinese (language)*
chuugokujin 中国人 *Chinese (person)*
chuumon 注文 *order*
chuumonsuru, chuumonshimasu 注文する、
  注文します *to order*
chuusha 注射 *injection, shot*
chuushasuru, chuushashimasu 注射する、
  注射します *to give an injection*
chuushoku 昼食 *lunch (fml.)*
da, desu だ、です *to be*
daasu ダース *dozen*
dai 台 *counter for mechanical items*
daidokoro 台所 *kitchen*
daigaku 大学 *college, university*
daigakuin 大学院 *graduate school*

daigakuinsee 大学院生 *graduate school student*
daigakusee 大学生 *college student*
daijoobu 大丈夫 *all right*
daisuki da, daisuki desu 大好きだ、大好きです
  to like very much, to like a lot
dake だけ *only*
dansu ダンス *dance, dancing*
dare 誰 *who*
  dare ka 誰か *someone*
  dare mo (+ negative) 誰も *no one, nobody*
daroo, deshoo だろう、でしょう *will probably*
  ... te (mo) ii deshoo ka. 〜て(も)いいでしょ
   うか。 *May I ... ? (polite)*
  ... te (mo) yoroshii deshoo ka. 〜て(も)よろしい
   でしょうか。 *May I ... ? (polite)*
de で *particle (marks a place where some action
  takes place; marks means and instruments)*
dekakeru, dekakemasu 出掛ける、出掛けます *to
  go out*
  kamera o motte dekakemasu カメラを持って出
   掛けます *to go out with a camera*
dekiru, dekimasu できる、できます *can do*
demo でも *however, but*
... demo 〜でも *... or something like that*
  koohii demo コーヒーでも *coffee or something
   like that*
denki gishi 電気技師 *electrical engineer*
densha 電車 *train*
denshirenji 電子レンジ *microwave oven*
(o)denwa (お)電話 *telephone (polite with o)*
(o)denwabangoo (お)電話番号 *telephone number
  (polite with o)*
denwasuru, denwashimasu 電話する、電話し
  ます *to make a phone call*
depaato デパート *department store*
deru, demasu 出る、出ます *to leave, to attend*
  dete iru, dete imasu 出ている、出ています
   to have left
  ... ni deru 〜に出る *to attend ...*
  ... o deru 〜を出る *to leave ...*
  deshi 弟子 *disciple*
dewa では *then*
dezaato デザート *dessert*
dezain デザイン *design*
diizeru ディーゼル *diesel*
disupurei ディスプレイ *display*
do 度 *degree*
  sanjuuhachi do 三十八度 *38 degrees*

dochira どちら *where, which one, which way
  (polite)*
  dochira no hoo どちらの方 *which one*
doitsu ドイツ *Germany*
doitsugo ドイツ語 *German (language)*
doitsujin ドイツ人 *German (person)*
doko どこ *where*
  doko ka どこか *somewhere*
  doko mo (+ negative) どこも *nowhere*
doku 毒 *poison*
dokusho 読書 *reading books*
donata どなた *who (polite)*
donna どんな *what kind of*
dono どの *which (one)*
  dono pen どのペン *which pen*
dono gurai どのぐらい *how long, how much*
doo どう *how*
  Doo deshita ka. どうでしたか。 *How was it?*
  Doo desu ka. どうですか。 *How is it?/
   What about ... ?/How about ... ?*
  Doo nasaimashita ka. どうなさいましたか。
   What's the matter? (polite)
  Doo shimashita ka. どうしましたか。 *What's
   the matter?*
  doo yatte どうやって *how*
dooitsu 同一 *identical*
dookoo 同行 *accompaniment*
dooshite どうして *why*
Doozo. どうぞ。 *Here you go./Please.*
  Doozo yoroshiku. どうぞよろしく。 *Nice to
   meet you.*
dore どれ *which one*
doresshingu ドレッシング *dressing*
doyoobi 土曜日 *Saturday*
e 絵 *drawing, painting*
e へ *particle (marks the goal of movement)*
ebi えび *shrimp*
ee ええ *yes (infml.)*
eega 映画 *movie*
eega kanshoo 映画鑑賞 *seeing movies (lit., movie
  appreciation)*
eegakan 映画館 *movie theater*
eego 英語 *English (language)*
eegyoo hookokusho 営業報告書 *business report*
eki 駅 *station*
en 円 *yen*
  ichiman en 一万円 *10,000 yen*
  sen en 千円 *1,000 yen*

enjin エンジン *engine*

enjinia エンジニア *engineer*

enpitsu 鉛筆 *pencil*

ensoosuru, ensooshimasu 演奏する、演奏します
  to perform (music)

etto えっと *Well…*

fakkusu ファックス *fax*

fensu フェンス *fence*

finrando フィンランド *Finland*

fonto フォント *font*

fooku フォーク *fork*

fuben 不便 *inconvenient*

fujisan 富士山 *Mt. Fuji*

fukee 父兄 *fathers and eldest sons (fml.)*

fuku, fukimasu 吹く、吹きます *to play (a wind
  instruments)*

fukumu, fukumimasu 含む、含みます *to be
  included*

fukutsuu 腹痛 *stomachache*

fuminshoo 不眠症 *insomnia*

  fuminshoo da, fuminshoo desu 不眠症だ、
    不眠症です *to suffer from insomnia*

fumon 不問 *passing over a matter*

furansu フランス *France*

furansu ryoori フランス料理 *French cuisine*

furansugo フランス語 *French (language)*

furansujin フランス人 *French (person)*

furu, furimasu 降る、降ります *to fall,
  to come down*

  Ame ga futte imasu. 雨が降っています。
    It's raining.

  Yuki ga futte imasu. 雪が降っています。
    It's snowing.

furui 古い *old*

furuuto フルート *flute*

futa 蓋 *lid*

futari 二人 *two people*

futatsu 二つ *two (native Japanese number)*

futsuka 二日 *second (day of the month)*

futtobooru フットボール *football*

(go)fuufu （ご）夫婦 *married couple (polite
  with go)*

fuyu 冬 *winter*

ga が *particle (marks a subject)*

ga が *but*

ga 蛾 *moth*

gaarufurendo ガールフレンド *girlfriend*

gakki 楽器 *musical instrument*

gakkoo 学校 *school*

gakusee 学生 *student*

gan 癌 *cancer*

geemu ゲーム *game*

genkan 玄関 *entrance hall*

genki 元気 *vigorous*

  Genki desu. 元気です。 *I'm fine.*

  Ogenki desu ka. お元気ですか。 *How are you?*

genkin 現金 *cash*

geri 下痢 *diarrhea*

  geri o suru, geri o shimasu 下痢をする、
    下痢をします *to have diarrhea*

getsuyoobi 月曜日 *Monday*

ginkoo 銀行 *bank*

ginkooin 銀行員 *bank clerk*

gishi 技師 *engineer*

go 五 *five*

go 後 *later, after*

  sanjuppun go 三十分後 *30 minutes later*

gobyuu 誤びゅう *error (fml.)*

gofun 五分 *five minutes*

gogatsu 五月 *May*

gogo 午後 *afternoon, p.m.*

gohan ご飯 *cooked rice, meal*

goji 五時 *five o'clock*

gojitsu 後日 *later, some other day*

gojuu 五十 *fifty*

gokai 五階 *fifth floor*

gokyoodai ご兄弟 *siblings (someone else's)*

Gomennasai. ごめんなさい。 *I'm sorry.*

goran ni naru, goran ni narimasu ご覧になる、
  ご覧になります *to see, to look, to watch
  (honorific)*

goro 頃 *about, approximately*

gorufu ゴルフ *golf*

goshujin ご主人 *husband (someone else's)*

gozaimasu ございます *to exist, there is, to have
  (polite)*

  … de gozaimasu. ～でございます。 *to be …
    (polite)*

gozen 午前 *morning, a.m.*

gruupu happyoo グループ発表 *group
  presentation*

gurai ぐらい *about, approximately*

guree グレー *grey (noun)*

guriin sarada グリーンサラダ *green salad*

guuzen 偶然 *coincidence*

gyaku 逆 *opposite*

gyuuniku 牛肉 *beef*

ha 歯 *tooth*

haadowea ハードウェア *hardware*

haato ハート *heart*

hachi 八 *eight*

hachifun 八分 *eight minutes*

hachigatsu 八月 *August*

hachiji 八時 *eight o'clock*

hachijuu 八十 *eighty*

hade 派手 *showy, loud*

haha 母 *mother (one's own)*

hai はい *yes*

hai 杯 *counter for liquid in cups/glasses/bowls*

hai 肺 *lung*

haikensuru, haikenshimasu 拝見する、
拝見します *to see, to look, to watch (humble)*

hairu, hairimasu 入る、入ります *to enter, to join*

haitte iru, haitte imasu 入っている、
入っています *to have entered, to belong*

ofuro ni hairu, ofuro ni hairimasu お風呂に入
る、お風呂に入ります *to take a bath*

Hajimemashite. はじめまして。 *How do you do?*

hajimete 初めて *first time, for the first time*

hakaru, hakarimasu 測る、測ります *to measure*

netsu o hakaru, netsu o hakarimasu 熱を測
る、熱を測ります *to check one's temperature*

hakike 吐き気 *nausea*

hakike ga suru, hakike ga shimasu 吐き気がす
る、吐き気がします *to feel like vomiting*

hakka 発火 *ignition*

haku 泊 *staying over night*

nihaku 二泊 *two nights*

nihaku mikka 二泊三日 *two nights three days*

hamu ハム *ham*

han 半 *half, half past the hour*

goji han 五時半 *five thirty*

hana 花 *flower*

hana 鼻 *nose*

hanasu, hanashimasu 話す、話します *to speak*

hanbun 半分 *half*

hankachi ハンカチ *handkerchief*

hantoshi 半年 *half a year*

hantoshikan 半年間 *for half a year*

happun 八分 *eight minutes*

happyoo 発表 *presentation*

hara 腹 *belly, abdomen*

harau, haraimasu 払う、払います *to pay*

hare 晴れ *sunny*

Hare desu. 晴れです。 *It's sunny.*

Harete imasu. 晴れています。 *It's sunny.*

haru 春 *spring*

hashi 箸 *chopsticks*

hashiru, hashirimasu 走る、走ります *to run*

hataraku, hatarakimasu 働く、働きます
to work

… hasu 〜発 *leaving …*

Haneda hatsu 羽田発 *leaving Haneda*

hatsuka 二十日 *twentieth (day of the month)*

hayabaya 早々 *promptly*

hayai 早い *early*

hayaku 早く *early, quickly*

hayashi 林 *woods*

Hee. へえ。 *Well… /Wow./I see.*

heejitsu 平日 *weekday*

heta 下手 *unskillful, poor at*

heya 部屋 *room*

hi 日 *day*

hidari 左 *left*

hidarigawa 左側 *left side*

hidoi ひどい *terrible, severe*

higashigawa 東側 *east side*

hiki 匹 *counter for animal*

hikkosu, hikkoshimasu 引っ越す、引っ越します
to move (to a new location)

hikooki 飛行機 *airplane*

hiku, hikimasu 弾く、弾きます *to play (piano)*

hikui 低い *low*

hima 暇 *be free (having a lot of free time)*

hin 品 *dignity*

hinketsu 貧血 *anemia*

hippuhoppu ヒップホップ *hip-hop*

hiragana 平仮名 *hiragana characters*

hiroi 広い *spacious*

hiroo 疲労 *exhaustion, fatigue*

hiroshima 広島 *Hiroshima*

(o)hiru (お)昼 *noon (polite with o)*

hirugohan 昼ご飯 *lunch (infml.)*

hisabisa 久々 *long-absence*

Hisashiburi desu ne. 久しぶりですね。
Long time no see.

hito 人 *person*

onna no hito 女の人 *woman*

otoko no hito 男の人 *man*

hitori 一人 *one person*

hitorikko 一人っ子 *only child*

hitotsu 一つ *one (native Japanese number)*

hiyaku 飛躍 *leap*
hiyoo 費用 *cost, expense*
  kootsuuhi 交通費 *transportation costs*
hoka 他 *other*
hoken 保険 *insurance*
  shakaihoken 社会保険 *social insurance*
hokenshoo 保険証 *health insurance card*
hon 本 *book*
hon 本 *counter for long cylindrical objects*
hone 骨 *bone*
  hone o oru, hone o orimasu 骨を折る、骨を折り
  ます *to break a bone*
honkon 香港、ホンコン *Hong Kong*
hontoo 本当 *true*
  Hontoo desu ka. 本当ですか。 *Really?/Is that true?*
  hontoo ni 本当に *really*
hon-ya 本屋 *book store*
hoo 方 *direction, side*
  dochira no hoo どちらの方 *which one*
  ~ nai hoo ga ii desu. ～ない方がいいです。 *You'd better not …*
  … (ta/da) hoo ga ii desu. ～(た/だ)方がいい
  です。 *You'd better …*
hookoo 方向 *direction*
hooritsu 法律 *law*
hooritsu jimusho 法律事務所 *law firm*
hoshii, hoshii desu 欲しい、欲しいです *to want*
  hoshigatte iru, hoshigatte imasu 欲しがってい
  る、欲しがっています *(Someone) wants*
  hotate 帆立 *scallop*
hoteru ホテル *hotel*
hyaku 百 *hundred*
hyakupaasento 100パーセント *hundred percent*
  uuru hyakupaasento ウール100パーセント
  100% wool
hyoogen 表現 *expression*
i 胃 *stomach*
ichi 一 *one*
  ichiman 一万 *ten thousand*
  ichiman en 一万円 *ten thousand yen*
ichiban 一番 *number one, the most*
  ichiban ii 一番いい *the best*
ichido 一度 *once*
  ichido mo (+negative) 一度も *never*
  moo ichido もう一度 *once more*
ichigatsu 一月 *January*
ichiji 一時 *one o'clock*

ie 家 *house*
igirisu イギリス *England*
igirisujin イギリス人 *English (person)*
ii いい *good*
  emu de ii エムでいい *medium is okay*
  Junbi wa ii desu ka. 準備はいいですか。
  Are you ready?
  moshi yokattara もし良かったら *if it's okay, if you like*
  Sore wa yokatta. それはよかった。 *I'm glad to hear that.*
  … te (mo) ii?/ … te (mo) ii desu ka./ … te
  (mo) ii deshoo ka. ～て(も)いい?/～て(も)いい
  ですか。/～て(も)いいでしょうか。 *May I … ?*
iie いいえ *no*
iimeeru イーメール *e-mail*
ijoo 以上 *more than*
ika いか *cuttlefish, squid*
ikaga いかが *how (polite)*
  Ikaga deshita ka. いかがでしたか。 *How was it? (polite)*
  Ikaga desu ka. いかがですか。 *How is it? (polite)*
  … wa ikaga desu ka. ～はいかがですか。
  How about … ? (polite)
iku, ikimasu 行く、行きます *to go*
  itte iru, itte imasu 行っている、行っています
  to have gone
(o)ikura (polite with o) （お）いくら *how much*
(o)ikutsu (polite with o) （お）いくつ *how many, how old*
ima 今 *now*
ima 居間 *living room*
ima made ni 今までに *up to now*
imi 意味 *meaning*
imooto 妹 *younger sister (one's own)*
imootosan 妹さん *younger sister (someone else's)*
inchi インチ *inch*
indo インド *India*
intaanetto インターネット *internet*
inu 犬 *dog*
ippai 一杯 *full*
ipponjooshi 一本調子 *monotonous*
ippun 一分 *one minute*
Irasshaimase. いらっしゃいませ。 *Welcome (to our store).*

irassharu, irasshaimasu いらっしゃる、いらっしゃいます *to go, to come, to exist, there is (honorific)*
ireru, iremasu 入れる、入れます *to put into*
　sarada ni ireru, sarada ni iremasu サラダに入れる、サラダに入れます *to put into a salad*
iru, imasu いる、います *to have … /there is … (animate)*
　uchi ni iru, uchi ni imasu 家にいる、家にいます *to stay home*
isha 医者 *medical doctor*
isogashii 忙しい *busy*
issho ni 一緒に *together*
isu 椅子 *chair*
itadaku, itadakimasu いただく、いただきます *to eat, to drink, to receive (humble)*
　… te itadaku, … te itadakimasu 〜ていただく、〜ていただきます *to receive a favor of … ing (humble)*
itai 痛い *painful*
　atama ga itai, atama ga itai desu 頭が痛い、頭が痛いです *to have a headache*
　nodo ga itai, nodo ga itai desu 喉が痛い、喉が痛いです *to have a sore throat*
　onaka ga itai, onaka ga itai desu お腹が痛い、お腹が痛いです *to have a stomachache*
itaria イタリア *Italy*
itaria ryoori イタリア料理 *Italian cuisine*
itariago イタリア語 *Italian (language)*
itasu, itashimasu いたす、いたします *to do (humble)*
itoko 従兄弟 *cousin*
itsu いつ *when*
itsuka 五日 *fifth (day of the month)*
itsumo いつも *always*
itsutsu 五つ *five (native Japanese number)*
iu, iimasu 言う、言います *to say*
izen 以前 *before*
ja(a) じゃ(あ) *then*
jagaimo じゃがいも *potato*
jama 邪魔 *obstruction*
　Ojamashimasu. お邪魔します。 *Pardon the intrusion.*
jazu ジャズ *jazz*
jiinzu ジーンズ *jeans*
jikan 時間 *time, hour(s)*
　nijikan 二時間 *two hours*
jimi 地味 *sober, quiet (color)*

jimu 事務 *office (clerical) work*
jimusho 事務所 *office*
jinja 神社 *shrine*
jinjibu 人事部 *human resources department*
jisho 辞書 *dictionary*
jitsu wa 実は *actually*
jiyuu 自由 *freedom*
jiyuu 自由 *free*
　jiyuujikan 自由時間 *free time*
jogingu ジョギング *jog, jogging*
joozu 上手 *skillful, good at*
jugyoo 授業 *class*
junbi 準備 *preparation*
　Junbi wa ii desu ka. 準備はいいですか。 *Are you ready?*
juppun 十分 *ten minutes*
juu 十 *ten*
juu 銃 *gun*
juudoo 柔道 *judo*
juugatsu 十月 *October*
juugo 十五 *fifteen*
juuhachi 十八 *eighteen*
juuichi 十一 *eleven*
juuichigatsu 十一月 *November*
juuichiji 十一時 *eleven o'clock*
juuji 十時 *ten o'clock*
juuku 十九 *nineteen*
juukyuu 十九 *nineteen*
juunana 十七 *seventeen*
juuni 十二 *twelve*
juunigatsu 十二月 *December*
juuniji 十二時 *twelve o'clock*
juuroku 十六 *sixteen*
juusan 十三 *thirteen*
juushi 十四 *fourteen*
juushichi 十七 *seventeen*
juusu ジュース *juice, soft drink*
juuyon 十四 *fourteen*
ka か *particle (marks a question; used to express surprise)*
ka 蚊 *mosquito*
ka か *or*
kaado カード *card, credit card*
kaato カート *shopping cart*
kaban かばん *bag*
kabushikigaisha 株式会社 *joint-stock cooperation*
kachoo 課長 *section manager*

kado 角 *corner*

kaeru, kaerimasu 帰る、帰ります *to go back, to return, to go home, to come home*

kafeore カフェオレ *café au lait*

kagu 家具 *furniture*

kai 貝 *shellfish*

kaidan 階段 *stairs*

kaigi 会議 *meeting*

kaii moji 会意文字 *compound ideographic characters*

kaimono 買い物 *shopping*

kaisha 会社 *company*

kaishain 会社員 *office worker, company employee*

kakaru, kakarimasu かかる、かかります *to take (time)*

kakijun 書き順 *stroke order*

kaku 画 *stroke (for writing characters)*

kaku, kakimasu 書く、書きます *to write*

kakushu 各種 *various*

kakusuu 画数 *number of strokes*

kamau, kamaimasu 構う、構います *to mind*
  … te (mo) kamaimasen ka. 〜て(も)構いませんか。 *Do you mind … ing?*

kamera カメラ *camera*

kami 紙 *paper*

kami 髪 *hair (on the head)*

kami no ke 髪の毛 *hair (on the head)*

kamoshirenai, kamoshiremasen かもしれない、かもしれません *may (conjecture)*

… kana(a) 〜かな(あ) *I wonder …*

kanadajin カナダ人 *Canadian (person)*

kanai 家内 *wife (one's own)*

kanbi 完備 *fully furnished*

kangae 考え *idea*

kangoshi 看護師 *nurse*

kanja 患者 *patient*

kanji 漢字 *Chinese characters*

kankoku 韓国 *Korea*

kankoo 観光 *sightseeing*

kannu カンヌ *Cannes*

kanojo 彼女 *she*
  kanojo no 彼女の *her*
  kanojora 彼女ら *they (people, feminine)*
  kanojotachi 彼女達 *they (people, feminine)*

kansuru 関する *concerning, regarding*

kantan 簡単 *easy, simple*

kao 顔 *face*

kaoiro 顔色 *complexion*
  kaoiro ga warui, kaoiro ga warui desu 顔色が悪い、顔色が悪いです *to look pale*

kapuchiino カプチーノ *cappuccino*

kara から *from*
  … kara … made 〜から〜まで *from … to …*

kara から *because, so*

karaa カラー *hair dye, hair color*

karada 体、身体 *body*

karai 辛い *spicy*

kare 彼 *he*
  kare no 彼の *his*
  karera 彼ら *they (people)*

karee カレー *curry*

kariru, karimasu 借りる、借ります *to borrow*
  karate iru, karate imasu 借りている、借りています *to have borrowed*

karui 軽い *light*

Kashikomarimashita. かしこまりました。 *Certainly. (polite)*

… kashira. 〜かしら。 *I wonder …*

kashu 歌手 *singer*

kasu, kashimasu 貸す、貸します *to lend*
  kashite iru, kashite imasu 貸している、貸しています *to have lent*

kata 方 *person (polite)*

kata 肩 *shoulders*
  kata ga kotte iru, kata ga kotte imasu 肩が凝っている、肩が凝っています *to have stiff shoulders*

katakana 片仮名 *katakana characters*

katsu かつ *cutlet*

katsute かつて *formerly*

katte 勝手 *selfish*

katto カット *haircut*

kau, kaimasu 買う、買います *to buy*

kawa 川 *river*

kawaii かわいい *cute*

kawaru, kawarimasu 代わる、代わります *to replace (a person), to transfer (a phone line)*

kawaru, kawarimasu 変わる、変わります *to change*

kayoobi 火曜日 *Tuesday*

kaze 風 *wind*

kaze 風邪 *cold*
  kaze o hiku, kaze o hikimasu 風邪をひく、風邪をひきます *to catch a cold*

(go)kazoku (polite with go) （ご）家族 *family*

gonin kazoku 五人家族 *five people in a family*

ke 毛 *hair*

kedo けど *but*

kee-eegaku 経営学 *business management*

keekaku 計画 *plan*

keeken 経験 *experience*

keeki ケーキ *cake*

keeri 経理 *accounting*

keesatsu 警察 *police*

keesatsukan 警察官 *police officer*

keesee moji 形声文字 *phonetic-ideographic characters*

keetai (denwa) 携帯(電話) *cell phone*

keezai 経済 *economy*

keezaigaku 経済学 *economics*

kega 怪我 *injury*
  kega o suru, kega o shimasu 怪我をする、怪我をします *to get injured*

Kekkoo desu. 結構です。 *No, thank you.*

ken 件 *matter, case*

ken 券 *coupon, voucher*
  biiru ken ビール券 *beer gift coupon*

kendoo 剣道 *kendo*

kenmee 件名 *subject (letter, e-mail)*

kensa 検査 *examination*

kensasuru, kensashimasu 検査する、検査します *to examine*

kesa 今朝 *this morning*

ketsuatsu 血圧 *blood pressure*
  ketsuatsu ga takai, ketsuatsu ga takai desu 血圧が高い、血圧が高いです *to have high blood pressure*
  ketsuatsu ga hikui, ketsuatsu ga hikui desu 血圧が低い、血圧が低いです *to have low blood pressure*

ki 木 *tree*

kibun 気分 *feeling*
  kibun ga warui, kibun ga warui desu 気分が悪い、気分が悪いです *to feel sick*

kichinto きちんと *properly, exactly, accurately*

kiiboodo キーボード *keyboard*

kiiro 黄色 *yellow (noun)*

kiiroi 黄色い *yellow (adjective)*

kikai 機会 *chance*

kiku, kikimasu 聞く、聞きます *to listen, to inquire*

kiku, kikimasu 聴く、聴きます *to listen (with focus, such as listening to music)*

kinmu 勤務 *work (fml.)*
  kinmuchi 勤務地 *place of work*

kinoo 昨日 *yesterday*

kin-yoobi 金曜日 *Friday*

kinyuusuru, kinyuushimasu 記入する、記入します *to fill out (a form)*

kirai da, kirai desu 嫌いだ、嫌いです *to dislike*

kiree きれい *beautiful, pretty, clean*

kiru, kirimasu 切る、切ります *to cut*

kissaten 喫茶店 *coffee shop*

kitagawa 北側 *north side*

kitanai 汚い *dirty*

kiyaku 規約 *agreement, rules*

kiyoo 起用 *promotion, appointment*

kochira こちら *this, this way (polite)*

kodomo 子供 *child*

kodomosan 子供さん *child (somebody else's)*

kokage 木陰 *tree shadow*

koko ここ *here*

kokonoka 九日 *ninth (day of the month)*

kokonotsu 九つ *nine (native Japanese number)*

kokoro 心 *heart*

komu, komimasu 混む、混みます *to get crowded*
  konde iru, konde imasu 混んでいる、混んでいます *to be crowded*

komugi 小麦 *wheat*

konban 今晩 *tonight*

Konban wa. こんばんは。 *Good evening.*

konbini コンビニ *convenience store*

kondo 今度 *next time, this time, shortly*

Konnichi wa. こんにちは。 *Hello./Good afternoon.*

konnyaku こんにゃく *konnyaku potato*

kono この *this*
  kono hen ni この辺に *in this area*
  kono pen このペン *this pen*

konpyuutaa コンピューター *computer*

konsaato コンサート *concert*

konshuu 今週 *this week*

konshuumatsu 今週末 *this weekend*

kooban 交番 *police booth*

koobe 神戸 *Kobe*

koocha 紅茶 *black tea*

kooen 公園 *park*

koohii コーヒー *coffee*

kooka 効果 *effect*

kookoku 広告 *advertisement*

kookoo 高校 *high school*

kookoosee 高校生 *high school student*
koosaten 交差点 *intersection*
kootsuu 交通 *transportation*
   kootsuhi 交通費 *transportation costs*
kopii コピー *copy*
kopiisuru, kopiishimasu コピーする、コピーします *to copy*
kore これ *this*
kore made ni これまでに *up to now*
korokke コロッケ *croquette*
koru, korimasu 凝る、凝ります *to get stiff*
   kata ga kotte iru, kata ga kotte imasu 肩が凝っている、肩が凝っています *to have stiff shoulders*
koshi 腰 *waist, hip*
koshoo 胡椒 *pepper*
kossetsusuru, kossetsushimasu 骨折する、骨折します *to break a bone*
kotae 答え *answer*
koto こと *thing*
   … koto ga aru, … koto ga arimasu 〜ことがある、〜ことがあります *to have done … , to have an experience of … ing*
   taberu koto to nomu koto 食べることと飲むこと *eating and drinking*
kotoba 言葉 *word, language*
kotoshi 今年 *this year*
ku 九 *nine*
kubaru, kubarimasu 配る、配ります *to distribute*
kuchi 口 *mouth*
kudasaru, kudasaimasu くださる、くださいます *to give (honorific)*
   … naide kudasai 〜ないでください。 *Please don't …*
   … o kudasai. 〜をください。 *Please give me …*
   … te kudasai 〜てください。 *Please …*
   … te kudasaru, … te kudasaimasu 〜てくださる、〜てくださいます *to give a favor of … ing (honorific)*
kugatsu 九月 *September*
kuji 九時 *nine o'clock*
kukkii クッキー *cookie*
kumori 曇り *cloudy*
   Kumori desu. 曇りです。 *It's cloudy.*
kuni 国 *country, nation*
kurabu クラブ *club*
kurai 暗い *dark*

kurarinetto クラリネット *clarinet*
kurashikku クラシック *classical*
kurasu クラス *class*
kurasumeeto クラスメート *classmate*
kurejitto kaado クレジットカード *credit card*
kureru, kuremasu くれる、くれます *to give*
   … te kureru, … te kuremasu 〜てくれる、〜てくれます *to give a favor of … ing*
kurisumasu クリスマス *Christmas*
kuroi 黒い *black*
kuru, kimasu 来る、来ます *to come*
   kite iru, kite imasu 来ている、来ています *to have come, to be here*
kuruma 車 *car*
kuruujingu クルージング *cruise*
kusuri 薬 *medicine*
kutsu 靴 *shoes*
kuuki 空気 *air*
kyabetsu キャベツ *cabbage*
kyaku 客 *customer, guest*
kyappu キャップ *cap*
kyonen 去年 *last year*
kyoo 今日 *today*
kyoodai 兄弟 *siblings (one's own)*
   sannin kyoodai 三人兄弟 *three children in a family*
kyookasho 教科書 *textbook*
kyooshi 教師 *teacher*
kyooto 京都 *Kyoto*
kyuu 九 *nine*
kyuubo 急募 *immediate opening*
kyuufun 九分 *nine minutes*
kyuujin (kookoku) 求人(広告) *job posting*
kyuujuu 九十 *ninety*
kyuuri きゅうり *cucumber*
(o)kyuuryoo (polite with o) (お)給料 *salary*
kyuuyo 給与 *salary*
maa maa まあまあ *so so*
maaketingu マーケティング *marketing*
machi 町 *town*
machiaishitsu 待合室 *waiting room*
mada まだ *still, yet (in negative)*
made まで *until*
   … kara … made 〜から〜まで *from … to …*
mado 窓 *window*
(… no) mae (〜の)前 *in front of …*
   mae ni 前に *before*

paatii e iku mae ni パーティーへ行く前に *before going to the party*
magaru, magarimasu 曲がる、曲がります *to turn*
mai 枚 *counter for thin flat objects*
maiban 毎晩 *every night*
mainichi 毎日 *every day*
mairu, mairimasu 参る、参ります *to go, to come (humble)*
majime 真面目 *earnest*
maku, makimasu 蒔く、蒔きます *to plant (seeds)*
mannenhitsu 万年筆 *fountain pen*
manshon マンション *condominium*
… masen ka. ～ませんか。 *Why don't we … ?*
… mashoo. ～ましょう。 *Let's …*
… mashoo ka. ～ましょうか。 *Shall we … ?*
massugu まっすぐ *straight*
mata また *again*
mataseru, matasemasu 待たせる、待たせます *to keep someone waiting*
Omatase itashimashita. お待たせいたしました。 *I have kept you waiting. (polite)*
matsu, machimasu 待つ、待ちます *to wait*
Omachi kudasai. お待ちください。 *Please wait. (polite)*
Omachishite orimasu. お待ちしております。 *I/We will be waiting for you. (polite)*
matto マット *mat*
mausu マウス *mouse*
(… no) mawari (～の)まわり *around …*
mazui まずい *bad (taste)*
me 目 *eye*
… me ～目 *the … th/the … rd*
futatsume 二つ目 *second*
hitotsume 一つ目 *first*
ichinichime 一日目 *the first day*
mittsume 三つ目 *third*
medium エム *medium (size)*
emu de ii エムでいい *medium is okay*
mee 名 *counter for customers in restaurants, clubs, bars (polite)*
nimeesama 二名様 *two people (polite)*
meeru メール *e-mail*
meetoru メートル *meter*
mekishiko メキシコ *Mexico*
mekishiko ryoori メキシコ料理 *Mexican cuisine*
mekishikojin メキシコ人 *Mexican (person)*
memai めまい *dizziness*

memai ga suru, memai ga shimasu めまいがする、めまいがします *to feel dizzy*
men 綿 *cotton*
mensetsu 面接 *interview*
menyuu メニュー *menu*
meotojawan 夫婦茶碗 *"his and hers" rice bowl set*
meshiagaru, meshiagarimasu 召し上がる、召し上がります *to eat, to drink (honorific)*
michi 道 *street, road*
midori 緑 *green (noun)*
mieru, miemasu 見える、見えます *to be able to be seen, to be visible*
migaku, migakimasu 磨く、磨きます *to brush, to polish*
migi 右 *right*
migigawa 右側 *right side*
miitingu ミーティング *meeting*
mijikai 短い *short*
mikka 三日 *third (day of the month)*
mikkusu sarada ミックスサラダ *mixed salad*
mimi 耳 *ear*
minamigawa 南側 *south side*
minasan 皆さん *everyone (polite)*
minna みんな *everyone*
miru, mimasu 見る、見ます *to watch, to look*
miru, mimasu 診る、診ます *to check, to examine*
… te miru, … te mimasu ～てみる、～てみます *to try … ing*
miruku ミルク *milk*
mise 店 *store*
miso 味噌 *soy bean paste*
(o)misoshiru (polite with o) (お)味噌汁 *miso soup*
mittsu 三つ *three (native Japanese number)*
(o) mizu (polite with o) (お)水 *water*
mo も *also, too, both … and*
modoru, modorimasu 戻る、戻ります *to return*
modotte iru, modotte imasu 戻っている、戻っています *to have returned*
mokuyoobi 木曜日 *Thursday*
mondai 問題 *problem*
monitaa モニター *monitor*
mono 者 *person (humble)*
tantoo no mono 担当の者 *a person in charge*
moo もう *already*
moo ichido もう一度 *once more*
moo sukoshi もう少し *a little more*

Mooshiwake arimasen. 申し訳ありません。
I'm very sorry. (polite)

Mooshiwake gozaimasen. 申し訳ございません。
I'm very sorry. (polite)

moosu, mooshimasu 申す、申します *to say*
(humble)

morau, moraimasu もらう、もらいます *to receive*
… **te morau,** … **te moraimasu** 〜てもらう、〜て
もらいます *to receive a favor of … ing*

mori 森 *forest*

moshi もし *if, in case*
moshi yokattara もし良かったら *if it's okay, if
you like*

moshi moshi もしもし *hello (on the phone)*

motsu, mochimasu 持つ、持ちます *to hold,
to own*
**kamera o motte dekakeru, kamera o motte
dekakemasu** カメラを持って出掛ける、カメラを
持って出掛けます *to go out with a camera*
motte iru, motte imasu 持っている、持ってい
ます *to have*
omochi desu ka. お持ちですか。 *Do you have …
? (polite)*

motte iku, motte ikimasu 持って行く、持って行き
ます *to take something (inanimate object)*

motte kuru, motte kimasu 持って来る、持って来
ます *to bring something (inanimate object)*

motto もっと *more*

muika 六日 *sixth (day of the month)*

muji 無地 *solid (color)*

(… **no) mukai (gawa)** (〜の)向かい(側) *across
from …*

mukashimukashi 昔々 *once upon a time*

mune 胸 *chest*

musuko 息子 *son (one's own)*

musukosan 息子さん *son (someone else's)*

musume 娘 *daughter (one's own)*

musumesan 娘さん *daughter (someone else's)*

muttsu 六つ *six (native Japanese number)*

muurugai ムール貝 *mussel*

muzukashii 難しい *difficult*

myaku 脈 *pulse*

myoo 妙 *strange*

nagai 長い *long*

naifu ナイフ *knife*

(… **no) naka** (〜の)中 *inside …, among …*

nakanaka なかなか *not easily, not readily (in
negative); quite (in affirmative)*

nakanaka ii なかなかいい *quite good*

nakanaka konai, nakanaka kimasen なかなか来
ない、なかなか来ません *to not come readily*

… **nakereba ikenai,** … **nakereba ikemasen** 〜
なければいけない、〜なければいけません
to have to …

… **nakereba naranai,** … **nakereba narimasen**
〜なければならない、〜なければなりません *to
have to …*

… **nakute wa ikenai,** … **nakute wa ikemasen**
〜なくてはいけない、〜なくてはいけません *to have
to …*

… **nakute wa naranai,** … **nakute wa
narimasen** 〜なくてはならない、〜なくてはなりま
せん *to have to …*

(o)namae (polite with o) (お)名前 *name*
Onamae wa? お名前は？ *What's your name?*

nan(i) 何 *what*
nani ka 何か *something*
nani mo (+ negative) 何も *nothing*

nana 七 *seven*

nanafun 七分 *seven minutes*

nanajuu 七十 *seventy*

nanatsu 七つ *seven (native Japanese number)*

nande なんで *why (infml.)*

nando ka 何度か *several times*

nando mo 何度も *many times*

nanji 何時 *what time*

nanoka 七日 *seventh (day of the month)*

narau, naraimasu 習う、習います *to take lessons
on*

naru, narimasu なる、なります *to become*
natte iru, natte imasu なっている、なってい
ます *to have become*
oyasuku natte imasu お安くなっています *has
been priced down (polite)*

nasaru, nasaimasu なさる、なさいます *to do
(honorific)*

nasu なす *eggplant*

natsu 夏 *summer*

natsu yasumi 夏休み *summer vacation*

naze なぜ *why*

ne ね *particle (used to seek agreement; express
agreement; confirm information)*

nedan 値段 *price*

nekki 熱気 *hot air*

neko 猫 *cat*

nekutai ネクタイ *necktie*

nen 年 *year*
  ichinenkan 一年間 *for a year*
nenree 年齢 *age*
nenzasuru, nenzashimasu 捻挫する、捻挫します
  to have a sprain
neru, nemasu 寝る、寝ます *to go to sleep, to sleep*
netsu 熱 *fever*
  netsu ga aru, netsu ga arimasu 熱がある、熱が
    あります *to have a fever*
  netsu o hakaru, netsu o hakarimasu 熱を測
    る、熱を測ります *to check one's temperature*
netsuki 寝つき *wake-to-sleep transition*
ni 二 *two*
ni に *particle (marks a location; marks time, day,*
  month; marks a purpose, goal)
nichiyoobi 日曜日 *Sunday*
nifun 二分 *two minutes*
nigai 苦い *bitter*
nigate 苦手 *poor at*
nigatsu 二月 *February*
nigiyaka 賑やか *lively*
nihon 日本 *Japan*
nihongo 日本語 *Japanese (language)*
nihonjin 日本人 *Japanese (person)*
nihonshu 日本酒 *sake*
niji 二時 *two o'clock*
nijuu 二十 *twenty*
niku 肉 *meat*
nin 人 *counter for people*
ninki 人気 *popularity*
  ninki ga aru, ninki ga arimasu 人気がある、
    人気があります *to be popular*
nishigawa 西側 *west side*
niwa 庭 *garden, yard*
nizakana 煮魚 *boiled fish*
no の *particle (connects nouns)*
no の *one (indefinite pronoun)*
  amerika no アメリカの *the American one*
  muji no 無地の *the one in solid color*
node ので *because, since*
nodo 喉 *throat*
  nodo ga itai, nodo ga itai desu 喉が痛い、喉が
    痛いです *to have a sore throat*
nomimono 飲み物 *drink*
noo 脳 *brain*
nooto ノート *notebook*
noru, norimasu 乗る、乗ります *to ride, to get on*

noru, norimasu 載る、載ります *to get into, to be*
  put on
  notte iru, notte imasu 載っている、載ってい
    ます *to have been put on*
  nugu, nugimasu 脱ぐ、脱ぎます *to take off*
    (shoes, clothes)
nyoo 尿 *urine*
nyuugakusuru, nyuugakushimasu 入学する、
  入学します *to enter school*
nyuuinsuru, nyuuinshimasu 入院する、入院し
  ます *to be hospitalized*
nyuuyooku ニューヨーク *New York*
o を *particle (marks a direct object)*
obaasan おばあさん *grandmother (someone*
  else's)
ocha お茶 *Japanese tea*
odoru, odorimasu 踊る、踊ります *to dance*
ofisu オフィス *office*
ofuro お風呂 *bath*
  ofuro ni hairu, ofuro ni hairimasu お風呂に入
    る、お風呂に入ります *to take a bath*
ogawa 小川 *stream*
Ohayoo gozaimasu. おはようございます。 *Good*
  morning.
oishii おいしい *delicious*
ojiisan おじいさん *grandfather (someone else's)*
ojoosan お嬢さん *daughter (someone else's)*
okaasan お母さん *mother (someone else's)*
okaeshi お返し *return, change (polite)*
Okagesama de. おかげさまで。 *I'm fine. (polite)*
okaikee お会計 *check*
okane お金 *money*
okazu おかず *dish eaten with cooked rice*
okinawa 沖縄 *Okinawa*
okiru, okimasu 起きる、起きます *to get up*
okosan お子さん *child (someone else's)*
oku, okimasu 置く、置きます *to put*
  … te oku, … te okimasu 〜ておく、〜ておき
    ます *to do … beforehand*
okureru, okuremasu 遅れる、遅れます *to be late*
okusan 奥さん *wife (someone else's)*
okyakusan, okyakusama お客さん、お客さま
  customer, guest (polite)
ome ni kakaru, ome ni kakarimasu お目にかか
  る、お目にかかります *to see, to meet (humble)*
Omedetoo gozaimasu. おめでとうございます。
  Congratulations.
omoi 重い *heavy*

omoshiroi 面白い *interesting*
omou, omoimasu 思う、思います *to think*
onaji 同じ *same*
onaka お腹 *belly, abdomen*
   onaka ga itai, onaka ga itai desu お腹が痛い、
    お腹が痛いです *to have a stomachache*
oneesan お姉さん *older sister (someone else's)*
onegaisuru, onegaishimasu お願いする、お願いし
   ます *to ask for*
   Onegaishimasu. お願いします。 *Please. (asking*
    for a favor)
   … o onegaishimasu. 〜をお願いします。
    I'd like to have …
   ongaku 音楽 *music*
oniisan お兄さん *older brother (someone else's)*
onna 女 *female*
   onna no hito 女の人 *woman*
oobo 応募 *application*
ooi 多い *many, much, a lot*
ookii 大きい *big*
oosaka 大阪 *Osaka*
oosama 王様 *king*
opushonaru tsuaa オプショナルツアー *optional*
   tour
orenji オレンジ *orange*
oriru, orimasu 降りる、降ります *to get off*
   orite iru, orite imasu 降りている、降りています
    to have gotten off, to be off
oru, orimasu おる、おります *to exit, there is*
   (humble)
oshieru, oshiemasu 教える、教えます *to teach,*
   to tell
osoi 遅い *late*
ossharu, osshaimasu おっしゃる、おっしゃいます
   to say (honorific)
otearai お手洗い *restroom*
otoko 男 *male*
   otoko no hito 男の人 *man*
otoosan お父さん *father (someone else's)*
otooto 弟 *younger brother (one's own)*
otootosan 弟さん *younger brother (someone*
   else's)
ototoi おととい *the day before yesterday*
otsuri お釣り *change*
otto 夫 *husband (one's own)*
Oyasuminasai. おやすみなさい。 *Good night.*
oyogu, oyogimasu 泳ぐ、泳ぎます *to swim*
paama パーマ *perm*

paatii パーティー *party*
pan パン *bread*
panda パンダ *panda*
pantsu パンツ *pants*
pasokon パソコン *personal computer*
pen ペン *pen*
piano ピアノ *piano*
pin ピン *pin*
pinku ピンク *pink (noun)*
piza ピザ *pizza*
poppusu ポップス *pop*
porutogarugo ポルトガル語 *Portuguese*
   (language)
puuru プール *pool*
rainen 来年 *next year*
raishuu 来週 *next week*
raito ライト *light*
rajio ラジオ *radio*
ree 零 *zero*
reezooko 冷蔵庫 *refrigerator*
renrakusuru, renrakushimasu 連絡する、連絡し
   ます *to contact*
renshuusuru, renshuushimasu 練習する、練習し
   ます *to practice*
repooto レポート *report*
resutoran レストラン *restaurant*
retasu レタス *lettuce*
ringo りんご *apple*
rinku リンク *link, rink*
rirakkususu, rirakkusushimasu リラックスす
   る、リラックスします *to relax*
rirekisho 履歴書 *curriculum vitae, resume*
riyuu 理由 *reason*
rokku ロック *rock*
roku 六 *six*
rokugatsu 六月 *June*
rokuji 六時 *six o'clock*
rokujuu 六十 *sixty*
rooka 廊下 *hallway*
rooma ローマ *Rome*
roosoku 蝋燭 *candle*
roppun 六分 *six minutes*
ryakugo 略語 *abbreviation*
ryokoo 旅行 *travel*
ryokoosha 旅行社 *travel company*
ryoo 量 *amount*
ryoori 料理 *cooking, cuisine*

ryoori o suru, ryoori o shimasu 料理をする、料理をします *to cook*

(go)ryooshin (polite with go) (ご)両親 *parents*

ryuu 竜 *dragon*

ryuugakusuru, ryuugakushimasu 留学する、留学します *to study abroad*

sagasu, sagashimasu 探す、探します *to look for*

saikin 最近 *recently*

saizu サイズ *size*

sakana 魚 *fish*

(o)sake (polite with o) (お)酒 *alcoholic beverage*

sakkaa サッカー *soccer*

sama 様 *Mr., Ms. (polite)*

samui 寒い *cold (weather, room temperature)*

samuke 寒気 *chill*

　samuke ga suru, samuke ga shimasu 寒気がする、寒気がします *to have chills*

san さん *Mr., Ms.*

san 三 *three*

sangatsu 三月 *March*

sanji 三時 *three o'clock*

sanjuppun 三十分 *thirty minutes*

sanjuu 三十 *thirty*

sanpun 三分 *three minutes*

sarada サラダ *salad*

sashiageru, sashiagemasu さしあげる、さしあげます *to give (humble)*

　… te sashiageru, … te sashiagemasu ～てしあげる、～てさしあげます *to give a favor of … ing (humble)*

sashimi 刺身 *sliced raw fish*

satoo 砂糖 *sugar*

satsu 冊 *counter for bound objects*

Sayoonara. さようなら。 *Goodbye.*

seekatsu 生活 *everyday life*

seetaa セーター *sweater*

seeyakugaisha 製薬会社 *pharmaceutical company*

semai 狭い *narrow*

seminaa セミナー *seminar*

sen 千 *thousand*

　sen en 千円 *thousand yen*

senjitsu 先日 *the other day*

senmenjo 洗面所 *area with a wash stand*

sensee 先生 *teacher*

　Tanaka sensee 田中先生 *Prof./Dr. Tanaka*

senshuu 先週 *last week*

sentakuki 洗濯機 *washing machine*

setsumee 説明 *description*

shaabetto シャーベット *sherbet*

shachoo 社長 *president of a company*

shain 社員 *company employee*

shakai 社会 *society*

　shakaihoken 社会保険 *social insurance*

shakoo dansu 社交ダンス *ballroom daincing*

shashin 写真 *photograph, photography*

shatsu シャツ *shirt*

shawaa シャワー *shower*

　shawaa o abiru, shawaa o abimasu シャワーを浴びる、シャワーを浴びます *to take a shower*

sheedo シェード *shade*

shepaado シェパード *Shepherd*

shi 四 *four*

shiai 試合 *game (of sport)*

shibaraku しばらく *for a while*

shichi 七 *seven*

shichigatsu 七月 *July*

shichiji 七時 *seven o'clock*

shigatsu 四月 *April*

(o)shigoto (polite with o) (お)仕事 *job, work*

(o)shiharai (polite with o) (お)支払い *payment*

shiifuudo sarada シーフードサラダ *seafood salad*

shiji moji 指示文字 *indicative characters*

shika (+ negative) しか *only*

shikago シカゴ *Chicago*

shikaku 資格 *qualification*

shiken 試験 *exam*

shikyuusuru, shikyuushimasu 支給する、支給します *to provide, to cover*

shima 縞 *stripes*

… te shimau, … te shimaimasu ～てしまう、～てしまいます *to finish … ing, to have done …*

shimeru, shimemasu 閉める、閉めます *to close (transitive verb)*

shinbun 新聞 *newspaper*

shingoo 信号 *traffic light*

　shingoo no temae 信号の手前 *before the traffic light*

shinkansen 新幹線 *Japanese bullet train*

shinrigaku 心理学 *psychology*

shinryoojo 診療所 *clinic*

shinsatsu 診察 *medical consultation*

shinsatsushitsu 診察室 *medical consulting room*

(go)shinseki (polite with go) (ご)親戚 *relatives*

shinsetsu 親切 *kind, generous*

shinshitsu 寝室 *bedroom*

shinu, shinimasu 死ぬ、死にます *to die*
shinde iru, shinde imasu 死んでいる、死んでいます *to be dead*
shinzoo 心臓 *heart*
shio 塩 *salt*
shiokarai 塩辛い *salty*
shiro wain 白ワイン *white wine*
shiroi 白い *white*
shiru, shirimasu 知る、知ります *to know*
shitteimasu 知っています *I know*
shirimasen 知りません *I don't know*
(… no) shita (〜の)下 *under …*
shitee 師弟 *teacher and student*
shitee 子弟 *children (fml.)*
shitsumon 質問 *question*
shitsuree 失礼 *impoliteness, rudeness*
Shitsuree itashimasu 失礼いたします。 *Good-bye. (polite)*
Shitsureeshimasu. 失礼します。 *Good-bye. (polite)*
shizuka 静か *quiet*
shokugyoo 職業 *occupation*
shokuji 食事 *meal*
shokuyoku 食欲 *appetite*
shokuyoku ga aru, shokuyoku ga arimasu 食欲がある、食欲があります *to have an appetite*
shoobooshi 消防士 *firefighter*
shoogakkoo 小学校 *elementary school*
shookee moji 象形文字 *pictorial characters*
shookyuu 昇給 *salary increase*
shoorai 将来 *future*
shoosetsu 小説 *novel*
shooshoo 少々 *a few, a little*
shooto keeki ショートケーキ *shortcake*
shooyo 賞与 *bonus, reward*
shooyu 醤油 *soy sauce*
shoshin 初診 *the first medical consultation*
shucchoo 出張 *business trip*
shufu 主婦 *housewife*
shujin 主人 *husband (one's own)*
shujutsu 手術 *operation, surgery*
shujutsusuru, shujutsushimasu 手術する、手術します *to operate*
shukudai 宿題 *homework*
shumi 趣味 *hobby*
(go)shusshin (polite with go) (ご)出身 *place of origin, hometown*
shuu 週 *week*

isshuukan 一週間 *a week*
shuumatsu 週末 *weekend*
sobo 祖母 *grandmother (one's own)*
sochira そちら *that, that way (far from the speaker but close to the listener) (polite)*
sofaa ソファー *sofa*
sofu 祖父 *grandfather (one's own)*
sofuto ソフト *software*
sofutowea ソフトウェア *software*
soko そこ *there (far from the speaker but close to the listener)*
sono その *that (far from the speaker but close to the listener); its*
sono pen そのペン *that pen*
soo そう *so*
Soo da naa. そうだなあ。 *Let me see.*
Soo desu. そうです。 *That's right.*
Soo desu ka. そうですか。 *Is that so?/Really? (rising intonation)/I see. (falling intonation)*
Soo desu ne. そうですね。 *Yes, it is./Let me see./That's right. (falling intonation)/Right? (rising intonation)*
Soo desu yo. そうですよ。 *That's right.*
Soo ka. そうか。 *I see.*
Soo shimashoo! そうしましょう! *Let's do that!*
soo suru, soo shimasu そうする、そうします *to do so*
soojisuru, soojishimasu 掃除する、掃除します *to clean*
sooshinsha 送信者 *(sent) from*
soosoo 早々 *promptly*
sora 空 *sky*
sore それ *that (far from the speaker but close to the listener); it (subject pronoun)*
sorera それら *they (inanimate)*
sorede それで *so, for that reason*
sorede wa それでは *then*
Sorede wa mata. それではまた。 *See you then./See you later.*
sore ja(a) それじゃ(あ) *then (infml.)*
Sore ja(a) mata. それじゃ(あ)また。 *See you then./See you later. (infml.)*
sorekara それから *and then*
soshite そして *and, and then*
sotsugyoo 卒業 *graduation*
sotsugyoosuru, sotsugyooshimasu 卒業する、卒業します *to graduate*
sugiru, sugimasu すぎる、すぎます *too, too much*

sugoi すごい *amazing*

suiee 水泳 *swimming*

suimin 睡眠 *sleep*

suimin o toru, suimin o torimasu 睡眠をとる、睡眠をとります *to get some sleep*

suiyoobi 水曜日 *Wednesday*

sukaafu スカーフ *scarf*

sukaato スカート *skirt*

sukejuuru スケジュール *schedule*

suki da, suki desu 好きだ、好きです *to like*

sukii スキー *ski, skiing*

sukoshi 少し *a little*

moo sukoshi もう少し *a little more*

Sumimasen. すみません。 *Excuse me./I'm sorry./ Sorry for the trouble.*

sumoo 相撲 *sumo wrestling*

supagetti スパゲッティ *spaghetti*

supein スペイン *Spain*

supein ryoori スペイン料理 *Spanish cuisine*

supeingo スペイン語 *Spanish (language)*

supeinjin スペイン人 *Spanish (person)*

supootsu スポーツ *sport*

suppootsu o suru, supootsu o shimasu スポーツをする、スポーツをします *to play sports*

suppai すっぱい *sour*

supuun スプーン *spoon*

suru, shimasu する、します *to do*

… ni suru, … ni shimasu 〜にする、〜にします *to decide on …*

sushi 寿司 *sushi*

sutoresu ストレス *stress*

sutoresu ga tamatte iru, sutoresu ga tamatte imasu ストレスが溜まっている、ストレスが溜まっています *to be under a lot of stress*

suu, suimasu 吸う、吸います *to inhale*

tabako o suu, tabako o suimasu 煙草を吸う、煙草を吸います *to smoke a cigarette*

suugaku 数学 *mathematics*

suupaa スーパー *supermarket*

suutsukeesu スーツケース *suitcase*

suwaru, suwarimasu 座る、座ります *to sit down*

suzushii 涼しい *cool*

tabako 煙草 *tobacco, cigarette*

tabako o suu, tabako o suimasu 煙草を吸う、煙草を吸います *to smoke a cigarette*

tabemono 食べ物 *food*

taberu, tabemasu 食べる、食べます *to eat*

tabun 多分 *perhaps, probably*

tai, tai desu たい、たいです *to want to*

taiboku 大木 *big tree*

taifuu 台風 *typhoon*

taiguu 待遇 *treatment, labor conditions*

taihen 大変 *hard, very*

taiinsuru, taiinshimasu 退院する、退院します *to leave the hospital, to be released from hospital*

taimuzu sukuea タイムズスクエア *Times Square*

taisetsu 大切 *important*

takai 高い *high, tall, expensive*

tako たこ *octopus*

takusan たくさん *a lot, many, much*

takushii タクシー *taxi*

tamago 卵 *egg*

tamanegi たまねぎ *onion*

tamani たまに *once in a while*

tamaru, tamarimasu 溜まる、溜まります *to accumulate*

sutoresu ga tamatte iru, sutoresu ga tamatte imasu ストレスが溜まっている、ストレスが溜まっています *to be under a lot of stress*

tane 種 *seed*

tanjoobi 誕生日 *birthday*

tanoshii 楽しい *enjoyable, fun*

tanoshimi ni suru, tanoshimi ni shimasu 楽しみにする、楽しみにします *to look forward*

tansu たんす *chest of drawers*

tantoo 担当 *being in charge*

tantoo no mono 担当の者 *a person in charge*

tara たら *if, when (conjunction)*

tarinai, tarimasen 足りない、足りません *to be insufficient, to be short*

tataku, tatakimasu たたく、たたきます *to play (a percussion instrument)*

tatemono 建物 *building*

tatsu, tachimasu 立つ、立ちます *to stand up*

tazuneru, tazunemasu 訪ねる、訪ねます *to visit*

te 手 *hand*

teeburu テーブル *table*

teeshoku 定食 *prefix meal*

tegami 手紙 *letter*

temae 手前 *before, this side*

shingoo no temae 信号の手前 *before the traffic light*

ten-in 店員 *store clerk*

tenisu テニス *tennis*

tenisu kooto テニスコート *tennis court*

tenjoo 天井 *ceiling*

tenjooin 添乗員 *tour guide*
tenpura 天ぷら *tempura*
tenpusuru, tenpushimasu 添付する、添付します *to attach (a document)*
(o)tera (polie with o) (お)寺 *temple*
terebi テレビ *television*
tiishatsu ティーシャツ（Tシャツ） *T-shirt*
to と *and, with; when, if; that (conjunction)*
tochi 土地 *land*
(o)toiawase (polite wih o) (お)問い合わせ *inquiry*
toire トイレ *toilet*
tokee 時計 *watch, clock*
toki 時 *when (conjunction)*
tokidoki 時々 *sometimes*
tokoro 所 *place*
toku 徳 *virtue*
toku ni 特に *especially*
tokugi 特技 *special ability, special skill*
tokui 得意 *good at*
tomato トマト *tomato*
tomodachi 友達 *friend*
(... no) tonari (〜の)隣 *next to ...*
tonneru トンネル *tunnel*
too 十 *ten (native Japanese number)*
tooi 遠い *far*
tooka 十日 *tenth (day of the month)*
tookushoo トークショー *talk show*
Tookyoo 東京 *Tokyo*
toonyuu 豆乳 *soy milk*
toriniku 鶏肉 *chicken*
toru, torimasu 撮る、撮ります *to take (photos)*
toshokan 図書館 *library*
totemo とても *very, very much*
tsuaagaido ツアーガイド *tour guide*
tsuchi 土 *soil*
tsuitachi 一日 *first (day of the month)*
(... ni) tsuite (〜に)ついて *about ...*
tsukau, tsukaimasu 使う、使います *to use*
tsukeru, tsukemasu 点ける、点けます *to light*
tsuki 月 *moon*
tsuku, tsukimasu 着く、着きます *to arrive*
tsukue 机 *desk*
tsukuru, tsukurimasu 作る、作ります *to make*
tsuma 妻 *wife (one's own)*
tsumaranai つまらない *boring*
tsumetai 冷たい *cold (to the touch)*

tsurete iku, tsurete ikimasu 連れて行く、連れて行きます *to take someone or animal*
tsurete kuru, tsurete kimasu 連れて来る、連れて来ます *to bring someone or animal*
tsuyoi 強い *strong*
uchi 家 *house, one's home, one's family*
　uchi ni iru, uchi ni imasu 家にいる、家にいます *to stay home*
ude 腕 *arm*
(... no) ue (〜の)上 *on, above ...*
ueru, uemasu 植える、植えます *to plant*
ukeru, ukemasu 受ける、受けます *to take*
　shinsatsu o ukeru, shinsatsu o ukemasu 診察を受ける、診察を受けます *to take a medical consultation, to consult a physician*
uketsuke 受付 *reception desk, information desk, front desk*
uketsukegakari 受付係 *receptionist*
umi 海 *ocean*
un うん *yes (infml.)*
unagi うなぎ *eel*
unajuu うな重 *broiled eel on rice*
undoo 運動 *exercise*
undoosuru, undooshimasu 運動する、運動します *to exercise*
urusai うるさい *noisy*
(... no) ushiro (〜の)後ろ *behind ...*
uso 嘘 *lie*
　uso o tsuku, uso o tsukimasu 嘘をつく、嘘をつきます *to tell a lie*
uun ううん *Well ...*
uuru ウール *wool*
　uuru hyakupaasento ウール100パーセント *100% wool*
wa は *particle (marks a topic)*
waapuro ワープロ *word processor*
wafuu 和風 *Japanese style*
wain ワイン *wine*
　aka wain 赤ワイン *red wine*
　shiro wain 白ワイン *white wine*
wakai 若い *young*
wakaru, wakarimasu 分かる、分かります *to understand*
　Wakarimashita. 分かりました。 *I got it.*
warui 悪い *bad*
wataru, watarimasu 渡る、渡ります *to cross*
watashi 私 *I*
　watashi no 私の *my*

watashitachi 私達 *we*

webudezainaa ウェブデザイナー *web designer*

weeruzu ウェールズ *Wales*

weitoresu ウエイトレス *waitress*

windooshoppingu ウィンドーショッピング
window shopping

ya や *and*

yakizakana 焼き魚 *broiled fish*

yakyuu 野球 *baseball*

yama 山 *mountain*

yappari やっぱり *after all, as expected*

yaru, yarimasu やる、やります *to give (to a plant, an animal), to do (infml.)*

yasai 野菜 *vegetable*

yasashii 易しい *easy*

yasashii 優しい *kind, gentle*

yasui 安い *cheap*

oyasuku nattte imasu お安くなっています *has been priced down (polite)*

yasumi 休み *day off, holiday, vacation*

yasumu, yasumimasu 休む、休みます *to take some rest, to be absent, to take a day off*

kaisha o yasumu, kaisha o yasumimasu 会社を休む、会社を休みます *to take a day off from work*

yattsu 八つ *eight (native Japanese number)*

yo よ *particle (used to make an assertion)*

yobu, yobimasu 呼ぶ、呼びます *to call*

yoji 四時 *four o'clock*

yokka 四日 *fourth (day of the month)*

(… no) yoko (〜の)横 *the side of …*

yoku よく *often, well*

Yoku dekimashita. よくできました。 *Well done.*

yokushitsu 浴室 *bathroom*

yomu, yomimasu 読む、読みます *to read*

yon 四 *four*

yonfun 四分 *four minutes*

yonjuu 四十 *forty*

yonpun 四分 *four minutes*

yoochien 幼稚園 *kindergarden*

yoofuu 洋風 *Western style*

yooi 用意 *preparation*

yooka 八日 *eighth (day of the month)*

Yookoso. ようこそ。 *Welcome.*

yooshi 用紙 *form (to fill out)*

… yori … 〜より〜 *more … than …*

yorokonde … 喜んで〜 *to be glad to …*

yoroshii よろしい *good (polite)*

… te (mo) yoroshii deshoo ka. 〜て(も)よろしいでしょうか。 *May I … ? (polite)*

… te (mo) yoroshii desu ka. 〜て(も)よろしいですか。 *May I … ? (polite)*

yoroshii desu ka. よろしいですか。 *Is it okay? (polite)*

yoroshikattara よろしかったら *if it's okay, if you like (polite)*

yoru 夜 *evening, night*

yottsu 四つ *four (native Japanese number)*

yoyaku 予約 *appointment, reservation*

yoyakusuru, yoyakushimasu 予約する、予約します *to make an appointment, to make a reservation*

yudetamago ゆで卵 *boiled egg*

yuki 雪 *snow*

Yuki desu. 雪です。 *It's snowing.*

Yuki ga futte imasu. 雪が降っています。 *It's snowing.*

yukkuri ゆっくり *slowly*

yuubinkyoku 郵便局 *post office*

yuugata 夕方 *early evening*

yuugohan 夕ご飯 *dinner (infml.)*

yuuhan 夕飯 *dinner*

yuujin 友人 *friend (fml.)*

yuumee 有名 *famous*

yuushoku 夕食 *dinner (fml.)*

yuusoosuru, yuusooshimasu 郵送する、郵送します *to mail*

zangyoosuru, zangyooshimasu 残業する、残業します *to work overtime*

zasshi 雑誌 *magazine*

zehi 是非 *by all means, at any cost*

zen 禅 *zen*

zenbu 全部 *all*

zenbu de 全部で *all together*

zenzen (+ negative) 全然 *not at all*

zero ゼロ *zero*

zubon ズボン *pants*

zutsu ずつ *each*

zutsuu 頭痛 *headache*

zutsuu ga suru, zutsuu ga shimasu 頭痛がする、頭痛がします *to have a headache*

English-Japanese

A

a few *shooshoo* 少々

a little *chotto, shooshoo, sukoshi* ちょっと、少々、少し

a little more *moo sukoshi* もう少し

a lot *ooi, takusan* 多い、たくさん

a.m. *gozen* 午前

abbreviation *ryakugo* 略語

abdomen *hara, onaka* 腹、お腹

able (to be) *mieru, miemasu* 見える、見えます

about *goro, gurai* 頃、ぐらい

about… (… *ni) tsuite* (〜に)ついて

above… (… *no) ue* (〜の)上

absent (to be) *yasumu, yasumimasu* 休む、休みます

accompaniment *dookoo* 同行

accounting *keeri* 経理

accumulate (to) *tamaru, tamarimasu* 溜まる、溜まります

across from… (… *no) mukai (gawa)* (〜の)向かい(側)

actually *jitsu wa* 実は

advertisement *kookoku* 広告

after *ato de, go* 後で、後

 after leaving a restaurant *resutoran o deta ato de* レストランを出た後で

after all *yappari* やっぱり

afternoon *gogo* 午後

again *mata* また

age *nenree* 年齢

agreement *kiyaku* 規約

ah *aa* ああ

air *kuuki* 空気

 hot air *nekki* 熱気

airplane *hikooki* 飛行機

alcoholic beverage *(o)sake (polite with o)* (お)酒

all *zenbu* 全部

 all together *zenbu de* 全部で

 not at all *zenzen (+ negative)* 全然

 all right *daijoobu* 大丈夫

allergy *arerugii* アレルギー

already *moo* もう

also *mo* も

always *itsumo* いつも

amazing *sugoi* すごい

American *amerikajin (person)* アメリカ人

among… (… *no) naka* (〜の)中

amount *ryoo* 量

and *soshite, to, ya* そして、と、や

and then *sorekara, soshite* それから、そして

anemia *hinketsu* 貧血

answer *kotae* 答え

apartment *apaato* アパート

appetite *shokuyoku* 食欲

 have an appetite (to): *shokuyoku ga aru, shokuyoku ga arimasu* 食欲がある、食欲があります

apple *ringo* りんご

application *oobo* 応募

appointment *kiyoo, yoyaku* 起用、予約

 make an appointment (to) *yoyakusuru, yoyakushimasu* 予約する、予約します

approximately *goro, gurai* 頃、ぐらい

April *shigatsu* 四月

arm *ude* 腕

around… (… *no) mawari* (〜の)まわり

arrive (to) *tsuku, tsukimasu* 着く、着きます

arriving… … *chaku* 〜着

 arriving in Naha *naha chaku* 那覇着

as expected *yappari* やっぱり

ask for (to) *onegaisuru, onegaishimasu* お願いする、お願いします

assistant *ashisutanto* アシスタント

at any cost *zehi* 是非

attach (a document) (to) *tenpusuru, tenpushimasu* 添付する、添付します

attend (to) *deru, demasu* 出る、出ます

 attend… (to) … *ni deru* 〜に出る

August *hachigatsu* 八月

autumn *aki* 秋

bad *warui, mazui (taste)* 悪い、まずい

bag *baggu, kaban* バッグ、かばん

ball *booru* ボール

ballpoint pen *boorupen* ボールペン

ballroom dancing *shakoo dansu* 社交ダンス

bank *ginkoo* 銀行

bank clerk *ginkooin* 銀行員

bar *baa* バー

baseball *yakyuu* 野球

basketball *basukettobooru* バスケットボール

bat *batto* バット

bath *ofuro* お風呂

take a bath (to) *ofuro ni hairu, ofuro ni hairimasu* お風呂に入る、お風呂に入ります

bathroom *yokushitsu* 浴室

be (to) *da, desu ;… de gozaimasu. (polite)* だ、です;〜でございます。

beach *biichi* ビーチ

Beaujolais nouveau *bojoreenuuboo* ボジョレーヌーボー

beautiful *kiree* きれい

beauty salon *biyooin* 美容院

because *node, kara* ので、から

become (to) *naru, narimasu* なる、なります

have become (to) *natte iru, natte imasu* なっている、なっています

bed *beddo* ベッド

bedroom *shinshitsu* 寝室

beef *gyuuniku* 牛肉

beer *biiru* ビール

beer gift coupon *biiru ken* ビール券

before *izen, mae ni, temae* 以前、前に、手前

before going the party *paatii e iku mae ni* パーティーへ行く前に

before the traffic light: *shingoo no temae* 信号の手前

behind … (*… no) ushiro* (〜の)後ろ

being in charge *tantoo* 担当

a person in charge *tantoo no mono* 担当の者

belly *hara, onaka* 腹、お腹

belong (to) *haitte iru, haitte imasu* 入っている、入っています

best *besuto* ベスト

the best *ichiban ii* 一番いい

You'd better … *… (ta/da) hoo ga ii desu.* 〜(た/だ)方がいいです。

You'd better not … *… nai hoo ga ii desu.* 〜ない方がいいです。

between (… and …) (*… to … no) aida* (〜と〜の)間

big *ookii* 大きい

big tree *taiboku* 大木

birthday *tanjoobi* 誕生日

bitter *nigai* 苦い

black *kuroi* 黒い

black tea *koocha* 紅茶

blood pressure *ketsuatsu* 血圧

have high blood pressure (to) *ketsuatsu ga takai, ketsuatsu ga takai desu* 血圧が高い、血圧が高いです

have low blood pressure (to) *ketsuatsu ga hikui, ketsuatsu ga hikui desu* 血圧が低い、血圧が低いです

blouse *burausu* ブラウス

blue *aoi (adjective), ao (noun)* 青い、青

body *karada* 体、身体

boiled egg *yudetamago* ゆで卵

boiled fish *nizakana* 煮魚

bone *hone* 骨

break a bone (to) *hone o oru, hone o orimasu* 骨を折る、骨を折ります

bonus *shooyo* 賞与

book *hon* 本

book store *hon-ya* 本屋

boring *tsumaranai* つまらない

borrow (to) *kariru, karimasu* 借りる、借ります

have borrowed (to) *karate iru, karate imasu* 借りている、借りています

both … and *mo* も

bottle *bin* 瓶

brain *noo* 脳

bread *pan* パン

break a bone (to) *hone o oru, hone o orimasu; kossetsusuru, kossetsushimasu* 骨を折る、骨を折ります;骨折する、骨折します

breakfast *chooshoku (fml.), asagohan (infml.)* 朝食、朝ご飯

bright *akarui* 明るい

bring (to) *tsurete kuru, tsurete kimasu (animate); motte kuru, motte kimasu (inanimate)* 連れて来る、連れて来ます;持って来る、持って来ます

broiled eel on rice *unajuu* うな重

broiled fish *yakizakana* 焼き魚

brown *chairoi (adjective), chairo (noun)* 茶色い、茶色

brunch *buranchi* ブランチ

brush (to) *migaku, migakimasu* 磨く、磨きます

building *tatemono* 建物

high-rise building *biru* ビル

bullet train *shinkansen* 新幹線

bus *basu* バス

bus stop *basutee* バス停

business management *kee-eegaku* 経営学

business report *eegyoo hookokusho* 営業報告書

business trip *shucchoo* 出張

busy *isogashii* 忙しい

but *demo, ga, kedo* でも、が、けど

butter *bataa* バター

buy (to) *kau, kaimasu* 買う、買います

by all means *zehi* 是非

cabbage *kyabetsu* キャベツ

café au lait *kafeore* カフェオレ

cake *keeki* ケーキ

call (to) *yobu, yobimasu* 呼ぶ、呼びます

camera *kamera* カメラ

can do *dekiru, dekimasu* できる、できます

Canada *canada* カナダ

Canadian *kanadajin (person)* カナダ人

cancer *gan* 癌

candle *roosoku* 蝋燭

Cannes *kannu* カンヌ

cap *kyappu* キャップ

cappuccino *kapuchiino* カプチーノ

car *kuruma* 車

card *kaado* カード

  health insurance card *hokenshoo* 保険証

case *ken* 件

cash *genkin* 現金

cat *neko* 猫

catch a cold (to) *kaze o hiku, kaze o hikimasu* 風邪をひく、風邪をひきます

ceiling *tenjoo* 天井

cell phone *keetai (denwa)* 携帯(電話)

cello *chero* チェロ

Certainly. *Kashikomarimashita. (polite)* かしこまりました。

chain *cheen* チェーン

chair *isu* 椅子

chance *chansu, kikai* チャンス、機会

change *otsuri, okaeshi (polite)* お釣り、お返し

change (to) *kawaru, kawarimasu* 変わる、変わります

cheap *yasui* 安い

check *okaikee* お会計

check (to) *miru, mimasu* 診る、診ます

  check one's temperature (to) *netsu o hakaru, netsu o hakarimasu* 熱を測る、熱を測ります

cheese *chiizu* チーズ

chest *mune* 胸

chest of drawers *tansu* たんす

Chicago *shikago* シカゴ

chicken *toriniku* 鶏肉

chicken salad *chikin sarada* チキンサラダ

child *kodomo, kodomosan (somebody else's), okosan (somebody else's)* 子供、子供さん、お子さん

children *shitee (fml.)* 子弟

  three children in a family *sannin kyoodai* 三人兄弟

chill *samuke* 寒気

  have chills (to) *samuke ga suru, samuke ga shimasu* 寒気がする、寒気がします

China *chuugoku* 中国

Chinese *chuugokugo (language), chuugokujin (person)* 中国語、中国人

Chinese characters *kanji* 漢字

chocolate *chokoreeto* チョコレート

chopsticks *hashi* 箸

Christmas *kurisumasu* クリスマス

cigarette *tabako* 煙草

  smoke a cigarette (to) *tabako o suu, tabako o suimasu* 煙草を吸う、煙草を吸います

clarinet *kurarinetto* クラリネット

class *jugyoo, kurasu* 授業、クラス

classical *kurashikku* クラシック

classmate *kurasumeeto* クラスメート

clean *kiree* きれい

clean (to) *soojisuru, soojishimasu* 掃除する、掃除します

clinic *shinryoojo* 診療所

clock *tokee* 時計

close *chikai* 近い

close (to) *shimeru, shimemasu (transitive verb)* 閉める、閉めます

cloudy *kumori* 曇り

  It's cloudy. *Kumori desu.* 曇りです。

club *kurabu* クラブ

coffee *koohii* コーヒー

coffee shop *kissaten* 喫茶店

coincidence *guuzen* 偶然

cold *kaze* 風邪

  catch a cold (to) *kaze o hiku, kaze o hikimasu* 風邪をひく、風邪をひきます

cold *tsumetai (to the touch), samui (weather, room temperature)* 冷たい、寒い

college *daigaku* 大学

college student *daigakusee* 大学生

come (to) *kuru, kimasu; irassharu, irasshaimasu (honorific); mairu, mairimasu (humble)* 来る、来ます；いらっしゃる、いらっしゃいます；参る、参ります

have come (to) *kite iru, kite imasu* 来ている、来ています

not come readily (to) *nakanaka konai, nakanaka kimasen* なかなか来ない、なかなか来ません

come down (to) *furu, furimasu* 降る、降ります

come home (to) *kaeru, kaerimasu* 帰る、帰ります

company *kaisha* 会社

company employee *kaishain, shain* 会社員、社員

complexion *kaoiro* 顔色

compound ideographic characters *kaii moji* 会意文字

computer *konpyuutaa* コンピューター

concerning *kansuru* 関する

concert *konsaato* コンサート

condominium *manshon* マンション

Congratulations. *Omedetoo gozaimasu.* おめでとうございます。

consult a physician (to) *shinsatsu o ukeru, shinsatsu o ukemasu* 診察を受ける、診察を受けます

contact (to) *renrakusuru, renrakushimasu* 連絡する、連絡します

convenience store *konbini* コンビニ

convenient *benri* 便利

cook (to) *ryoori o suru, ryoori o shimasu* 料理をする、料理をします

cooked rice *gohan* ご飯

cookie *kukkii* クッキー

cooking *ryoori* 料理

cool *suzushii* 涼しい

copy *kopii* コピー

copy (counter for written materials) *bu* 部

copy (to) *kopiisuru, kopiishimasu* コピーする、コピーします

corner *kado* 角

cost *hiyoo* 費用

at any cost *zehi* 是非

transportation costs *kootsuuhi* 交通費

cotton *men* 綿

country *kuni* 国

coupon *ken* 券

beer gift coupon *biiru ken* ビール券

cousin *itoko* 従兄弟

cover (to) *shikyuusuru, shikyuushimasu* 支給する、支給します

credit card *kaado, kurejitto kaado* カード、クレジットカード

croquette *korokke* コロッケ

cross (to) *wataru, watarimasu* 渡る、渡ります

crowded (to be) *konde iru, konde imasu* 混んでいる、混んでいます

get crowded (to) *komu, komimasu* 混む、混みます

cruise *kuruujingu* クルージング

cucumber *kyuuri* きゅうり

cuisine *ryoori* 料理

curriculum vitae *rirekisho* 履歴書

curry *karee* カレー

customer *kyaku, okyakusan (polite), okyakusama (polite)* 客、お客さん、お客さま

cut (to) *kiru, kirimasu* 切る、切ります

cute *kawaii* かわいい

cutlet *katsu* かつ

cuttlefish *ika* いか

dance, dancing *dansu* ダンス

dance (to) *odoru, odorimasu* 踊る、踊ります

dark *kurai* 暗い

daughter *musume (one's own), musumesan (someone else's), ojoosan (someone else's)* 娘、娘さん、お嬢さん

day *hi* 日

some other day *gojitsu* 後日

the day after tomorrow *asatte* あさって

the day before yesterday *ototoi* おととい

the first day *ichinichime* 一日目

the other day *senjitsu* 先日

day off *yasumi* 休み

take a day off (to) *yasumu, yasumimasu* 休む、休みます

take a day off from work (to) *kaisha o yasumu, kaisha o yasumimasu* 会社を休む、会社を休みます

dead (to be) *shinde iru, shinde imasu* 死んでいる、死んでいます

December *juunigatsu* 十二月

decide on … (to) *… ni suru, … ni shimasu* 〜にする、〜にします

degree *do* 度

38 degrees *sanjuuhachi do* 三十八度

delicious *oishii* おいしい

department store *depaato* デパート

description *setsumee* 説明

design *dezain* デザイン

desk *tsukue* 机

dessert *dezaato* デザート

diarrhea *geri* 下痢
  have a diarrhea (to) *geri o suru, geri o shimasu* 下痢をする、下痢をします
dictionary *jisho* 辞書
die (to) *shinu, shinimasu* 死ぬ、死にます
diesel *diizeru* ディーゼル
difficult *muzukashii* 難しい
dignity *hin* 品
dinner *yuuhan, yuushoku (fml.), yuugohan (infml.)* 夕飯、夕食、夕ご飯
direction *hoo, hookoo* 方、方向
dirty *kitanai* 汚い
disciple *deshi* 弟子
dish eaten with cooked rice *okazu* おかず
dislike (to) *kirai da, kirai desu* 嫌いだ、嫌いです
display *disupurei* ディスプレイ
distribute (to) *kubaru, kubarimasu* 配る、配ります
division manager *buchoo* 部長
dizziness *memai* めまい
do (to) *suru, shimasu; yaru, yarimasu (infml.); itasu, itashimasu (humble); nasaru, nasaimasu (honorific)* する、します; やる、やります; いたす、いたします; なさる、なさいます
  do so *soo suru, soo shimasu* そうする、そうします
  do ... beforehand (to) *... te oku, ... te okimasu* 〜ておく、〜ておきます
  have done ... (to) *... te shimau, ... te shimaimasu; ... koto ga aru, ... koto ga arimasu* 〜てしまう、〜てしまいます; 〜ことがある、〜ことがあります
  Please don't ... *... naide kudasai* 〜ないでください。
dog *inu* 犬
dozen *daasu* ダース
dragon *ryuu* 竜
drawing *e* 絵
dressing *doresshingu* ドレッシング
drink *nomimono* 飲み物
drink (to) *meshiagaru, meshiagarimasu (honorific); itadaku, itadakimasu (humble)* 召し上がる、召し上がります; いただく、いただきます
each *zutsu* ずつ
ear *mimi* 耳
early *hayai, hayaku* 早い、早く
early evening *yuugata* 夕方
earnest *majime* 真面目
(not) easily *nakanaka (+ negative)* なかなか

east side *higashigawa* 東側
easy *kantan, yasashii* 簡単、易しい
eat (to) *taberu, tabemasu; meshiagaru, meshiagarimasu (honorific); itadaku, itadakimasu (humble)* 食べる、食べます; 召し上がる、召し上がります; いただく、いただきます
economics *keezaigaku* 経済学
economy *keezai* 経済
eel *unagi* うなぎ
effect *kooka* 効果
egg *tamago* 卵
eggplant *nasu* なす
eight *hachi, yattsu (native Japanese number)* 八、八つ
eight minutes *hachifun, happun* 八分
eight o'clock *hachiji* 八時
eighteen *juuhachi* 十八
eighth (day of the month) *yooka* 八日
eighty *hachijuu* 八十
electrical engineer *denki gishi* 電気技師
elementary school *shoogakkoo* 小学校
eleven *juuichi* 十一
eleven o'clock *juuichiji* 十一時
e-mail *iimeeru, meeru* イーメール、メール
engine *enjin* エンジン
engineer *enjinia* エンジニア
engineer *gishi* 技師
England *igirisu* イギリス
English *eego (language), igirisujin (person)* 英語、イギリス人
enjoyable *tanoshii* 楽しい
enter (to) *hairu, hairimasu* 入る、入ります
  have entered (to) *haitte iru, haitte imasu* 入っている、入っています
enter school (to) *nyuugakusuru, nyuugakushimasu* 入学する、入学します
entrance hall *genkan* 玄関
error *gobyuu (fml.)* 誤びゅう
especially *toku ni* 特に
evening *ban, yoru* 晩、夜
  early evening *yuugata* 夕方
every day *mainichi* 毎日
every night *maiban* 毎晩
everyday life *seekatsu* 生活
everyone *minna, minasan (polite)* みんな、皆さん
exactly *kichinto, chanto (infml.)* きちんと、ちゃんと
exam *shiken* 試験

examination *kensa* 検査

examine (to) *kensasuru, kensashimasu; miru, mimasu* 検査する、検査します; 診る、診ます

Excuse me. *Sumimasen.* すみません。

exercise *undoo* 運動

exercise (to) *undoosuru, undooshimasu* 運動する、運動します

exhaustion *hiroo* 疲労

exist (to) *irassharu, irasshaimasu (honorific); gozaimasu (polite); oru, orimasu (humble)* いらっしゃる、いらっしゃいます; ございます; おる、おります

expense *hiyoo* 費用

expensive *takai* 高い

experience *keeken* 経験
　　have an experience of ... ing (to) *... koto ga aru, ... koto ga arimasu* 〜ことがある、〜ことがあります

export and import business *booeki* 貿易

expression *hyoogen* 表現

eye *me* 目

face *kao* 顔

fall *aki* 秋

fall (to) *furu, furimasu* 降る、降ります

family *(go)kazoku (polite with go)* （ご）家族
　　five people in a family *gonin kazoku* 五人家族
　　one's family *uchi* 家

famous *yuumee* 有名

far *tooi* 遠い

father *chichi (one's own), otoosan (someone else's)* 父、お父さん

father's day *chichi no hi* 父の日

fathers and eldest sons *fukee (fml.)* 父兄

fatigue *hiroo* 疲労

fax *fakkusu* ファックス

February *nigatsu* 二月

feel dizzy (to) *memai ga suru, memai ga shimasu* めまいがする、めまいがします

feel like vomiting (to) *hakike ga suru, hakike ga shimasu* 吐き気がする、吐き気がします

feel sick (to) *kibun ga warui, kibun ga warui desu* 気分が悪い、気分が悪いです

feeling *kibun* 気分

female *onna* 女

fence *fensu* フェンス

fever *netsu* 熱
　　have a fever (to) *netsu ga aru, netsu ga arimasu* 熱がある、熱があります

fifteen *juugo* 十五

fifth (day of the month) *itsuka* 五日

fifth floor *gokai* 五階

fifty *gojuu* 五十

fill out (a form) (to) *kinyuusuru, kinyuushimasu* 記入する、記入します

I'm fine. *Genki desu./Okagesama de. (polite)* 元気です。/おかげさまで。

finish ... ing (to) *... te shimau, ... te shimaimasu* 〜てしまう、〜てしまいます

Finland *finrando* フィンランド

firefighter *shoobooshi* 消防士

first *hitotsume* 一つ目
　　first (day of the month) *tsuitachi* 一日
　　first time, for the first time *hajimete* 初めて
　　the first day *ichinichime* 一日目
　　the first medical consultation *shoshin* 初診

fish *sakana* 魚
　　sliced raw fish *sashimi* 刺身

five *go, itsutsu (native Japanese number)* 五、五つ

five minutes *gofun* 五分

five o'clock *goji* 五時

flower *hana* 花

flute *furuuto* フルート

font *fonto* フォント

food *tabemono* 食べ物

foot *ashi* 足

football *futtobooru* フットボール

for a while *shibaraku* しばらく

forest *mori* 森

fork *fooku* フォーク

form (to fill out) *yooshi* 用紙

formerly *katsute* かつて

forty *yonjuu* 四十

fountain pen *mannenhitsu* 万年筆

four *shi, yon, yottsu (native Japanese number)* 四、四、四つ

four minutes *yonfun, yonpun* 四分

four o'clock *yoji* 四時

fourteen *juushi, juuyon* 十四

fourth (day of the month) *yokka* 四日

France *furansu* フランス

free *jiyuu* 自由
　　free time *jiyuujikan* 自由時間

free (to be) (having a lot of free time) *hima* 暇

freedom *jiyuu* 自由

French　furansugo (language), furansujin
　(person) フランス語、フランス人
French cuisine　furansu ryoori フランス料理
Friday　kin-yoobi 金曜日
friend　tomodachi, yuujin (fml.) 友達、友人
from　kara から
　(sent) from　sooshinsha 送信者
　from … to …　… kara … made 〜から〜まで
front desk　uketsuke 受付
full　ippai 一杯
fully furnished　kanbi 完備
fun　tanoshii 楽しい
furniture　kagu 家具
future　shoorai 将来
game　geemu, shiai (of sport) ゲーム、試合
garden　niwa 庭
generous　shinsetsu 親切
gentle　yasashii 優しい
German　doitsugo (language), doitsujin (person)
　ドイツ語、ドイツ人
Germany　doitsu ドイツ
get off (to)　oriru, orimasu 降りる、降ります
　have gotten off (to)　orite iru, orite imasu 降り
　ている、降りています
get on (to)　noru, norimasu 乗る、乗ります
get up (to)　okiru, okimasu 起きる、起きます
girlfriend　gaarufurendo ガールフレンド
give (to)　ageru, agemasu; kureru, kuremasu;
　yaru, yarimasu (to a plant, an animal);
　kudasaru, kudasaimasu (honorific); sashiageru,
　sashiagemasu (humble) あげる、あげます; くれ
　る、くれます; やる、やります; くださる、くださいま
　す; さしあげる、さしあげます
　give a favor of … ing (to)　… te ageru, … te
　　agemasu; … te kureru, … te kuremasu; … te
　　kudasaru, … te kudasaimasu (honorific); …
　　te sashiageru, … te sashiagemasu (humble) 〜
　　てあげる、〜てあげます; 〜てくれる、〜てくれま
　　す; 〜てくださる、〜てくださいます; 〜てさしあげ
　　る、〜てさしあげます
　give an injection (to)　chuushasuru,
　　chuushashimasu 注射する、注射します
glad to … (to be)　yorokonde … 喜んで〜
　I'm glad to hear that.　Sore wa yokatta. それは
　　よかった。
go (to)　iku, ikimasu; irassharu, irasshaimasu
　(honorific); mairu, mairimasu (humble) 行く、

行きます; いらっしゃる、いらっしゃいます; 参る、
参ります
　have gone (to)　itte iru, itte imasu 行っている、
　行っています
go back (to)　kaeru, kaerimasu 帰る、帰ります
go home (to)　kaeru, kaerimasu 帰る、帰ります
go out (to)　dekakeru, dekakemasu 出掛ける、出
掛けます
　go out with a camera (to)　kamera o motte
　　dekakemasu カメラを持って出掛けます
go to sleep (to)　neru, nemasu 寝る、寝ます
golf　gorufu ゴルフ
good　ii, yoroshii (polite) いい、よろしい
　good at　joozu, tokui 上手、得意
　quite good　nakanaka ii なかなかいい
Good afternoon.　Konnichi wa. こんにちは。
Good evening.　Konban wa. こんばんは。
Good morning.　Ohayoo gozaimasu. おはようご
ざいます。
Good night.　Oyasuminasai. おやすみなさい。
Goodbye.　Sayoonara./Shitsuree itashimasu.
(polite)/Shitsureeshimasu. (polite) さようなら。/
失礼いたします。/失礼します。
(I) got it.　Wakarimashita. 分かりました。
graduate (to)　sotsugyoosuru, sotsugyooshimasu
卒業する、卒業します
graduate school　daigakuin 大学院
graduate school student　daigakuinsee 大学院生
graduation　sotsugyoo 卒業
grandfather　sofu (one's own), ojiisan (someone
else's) 祖父、おじいさん
grandmother　sobo (one's own), obaasan
(someone else's) 祖母、おばあさん
green　midori (noun) 緑
green salad　guriin sarada グリーンサラダ
grey　guree (noun) グレー
group presentation　gruupu happyoo グループ
発表
guest　kyaku, okyakusan (polite), okyakusama
(polite) 客、お客さん、お客さま
gun　juu 銃
hair　ke, kami (on the head), kami no ke (on the
head) 毛、髪、髪の毛
hair dresser　biyooshi 美容師
hair dye　karaa カラー
haircut　katto カット
half　han, hanbun 半、半分
　for half a year　hantoshikan 半年間

half a year *hantoshi* 半年
half past the hour *han* 半
hallway *rooka* 廊下
ham *hamu* ハム
hand *te* 手
handkerchief *hankachi* ハンカチ
hard *taihen* 大変
hardware *haadowea* ハードウェア
have (to) *motte iru, motte imasu* 持っている、
持っています

Do you have ... ? *aru, arimasu (inanimate);*
iru, imasu (animate); gozaimasu (polite);
omochi desu ka. (polite) ある、あります; いる、い
ます; ございます; お持ちですか。

have to ... (to) *... nakereba ikenai, ... nakereba*
ikemasen; ... nakereba naranai, ... nakereba
narimasen; ... nakute wa ikenai, ... nakute wa
ikemasen; ... nakute wa naranai, ... nakute wa
narimasen ～なければいけない、～なければいけま
せん; ～なければならない、～なければなりません;
～なくてはいけない、～なくてはいけません; ～なく
てはならない、～なくてはなりません

he *kare* 彼
headache *zutsuu* 頭痛

have a headache (to) *atama ga itai, atama ga*
itai desu; zutsuu ga suru, zutsuu ga shimasu
頭が痛い、頭が痛いです; 頭痛がする、頭痛がし
ます

health insurance card *hokenshoo* 保険証
heart *haato, kokoro, shinzoo* ハート、心、心臓
heavy *omoi* 重い
Hello. *Konnichi wa.; moshi moshi (on the phone)*
こんにちは。; もしもし
her *kanojo no* 彼女の
here *koko* ここ

here (to be) *kite iru, kite imasu* 来ている、来て
います

Here you go. *Doozo.* どうぞ。

high *takai* 高い
high school *kookoo* 高校
high school student *kookoosee* 高校生
high-rise building *biru* ビル
hip *koshi* 腰
hip-hop *hippuhoppu* ヒップホップ
hiragana characters *hiragana* 平仮名
Hiroshima *hiroshima* 広島
his *kare no* 彼の

"his and hers" rice bowl set *meotojawan* 夫
婦茶碗
hobby *shumi* 趣味
hold (to) *motsu, mochimasu* 持つ、持ちます
holiday *yasumi* 休み
home (one's) *uchi* 家

stay home (to) *uchi ni iru, uchi ni imasu* 家にい
る、家にいます

hometown *(go)shusshin (polite with go)* (ご)出身
homework *shukudai* 宿題
Hong Kong *honkon* 香港、ホンコン
hospital *byooin* 病院
hospitalized (to be) *nyuuinsuru,*
nyuuinshimasu 入院する、入院します
hot *atsui (to the touch), atsui (weather, room*
temperature) 熱い、暑い
hot air *nekki* 熱気
hotel *hoteru* ホテル
hour(s) *jikan* 時間

two hours *nijikan* 二時間

house *ie, uchi* 家
housewife *shufu* 主婦
how *doo, doo yatte, ikaga (polite)* どう、どうやっ
て、いかが

How about ... ? *Doo desu ka.* どうですか。
How are you? *... wa ikaga desu ka. (polite)*
～はいかがですか。
How do you do? *Ogenki desu ka.* お元気です
か。
How is it? *Hajimemashite.; Doo desu ka.;*
Ikaga desu ka. (polite) はじめまして。; どうです
か。; いかがですか。
How was it? *Doo deshita ka.; Ikaga deshita ka.*
(polite) どうでしたか。; いかがでしたか。

how long *dono gurai* どのぐらい
how many *(o)ikutsu (polite with o)* (お)いくつ
how much *(o)ikura (polite with o); dono gurai*
(お)いくら; どのぐらい
how old *(o)ikutsu (polite with o)* (お)いくつ
however *demo* でも
human resources department *jinjibu* 人事部
hundred *hyaku* 百

hundred percent *hyakupaasento* 100パーセ
ント
100% wool *uuru hyakupaasento* ウール100
パーセント

husband *otto (one's own), shujin (one's own),*
goshujin (someone else's) 夫、主人、ご主人

I *watashi, boku (used only by male speakers)* 私、僕

ice cream *aisukuriimu* アイスクリーム

idea *kangae* 考え

identical *dooitsu* 同一

if *moshi, tara, to* もし、たら、と

  if it's okay, if you like *moshi yokattara, yoroshikattara (polite)* もし良かったら、よろしかったら

ignition *hakka* 発火

illness *byooki* 病気

immediate opening *kyuubo* 急募

impoliteness *shituree* 失礼

important *taisetsu* 大切

in case *moshi* もし

in front of … *(… no) mae* (〜の)前

inch *inchi* インチ

included (to be) *fukumu, fukumimasu* 含む、含みます

inconvenient *fuben* 不便

India *indo* インド

indicative characters *shiji moji* 指示文字

information desk *uketsuke* 受付

inhale (to) *suu, suimasu* 吸う、吸います

injection *chuusha* 注射

injury *kega* 怪我

  get injured (to) *kega o suru, kega o shimasu* 怪我をする、怪我をします

inquire (to) *kiku, kikimasu* 聞く、聞きます

inquiry *(o)toiawase (polite wih o)* (お)問い合わせ

inside … *(… no) naka* (〜の)中

insomnia *fuminshoo* 不眠症

  suffer from insomnia (to) *fuminshoo da, fuminshoo desu* 不眠症だ、不眠症です

insufficient (to be) *tarinai, tarimasen* 足りない、足りません

insurance *hoken* 保険

  social insurance *shakaihoken* 社会保険

interesting *omoshiroi* 面白い

Internet *intaanetto* インターネット

intersection *koosaten* 交差点

interview *mensetsu* 面接

intestine *choo* 腸

it *sore* それ

Italian *itariago (language)* イタリア語

Italian cuisine *itaria ryoori* イタリア料理

Italy *itaria* イタリア

its *sono* その

January *ichigatsu* 一月

Japan *nihon* 日本

Japanese *nihongo (language), nihonjin (person)* 日本語、日本人

Japanese style *wafuu* 和風

jazz *jazu* ジャズ

jeans *jiinzu* ジーンズ

job *o(shigoto) (polite with o)* (お)仕事

job posting *kyuujin (kookoku)* 求人(広告)

jog, jogging *jogingu* ジョギング

join (to) *hairu, hairimasu* 入る、入ります

joint-stock cooperation *kabushikigaisha* 株式会社

judo *juudoo* 柔道

juice *juusu* ジュース

July *shichigatsu* 七月

June *rokugatsu* 六月

junior high school *chuugakkoo* 中学校

katakana characters *katakana* 片仮名

keep (to) *azukaru, azukarimasu* 預かる、預かります

  keep someone waiting (to) *mataseru, matasemasu* 待たせる、待たせます

  I have kept you waiting. *Omatase itashimashita. (polite)* お待たせいたしました。

kendo *kendoo* 剣道

keyboard *kiiboodo* キーボード

kind *shinsetsu, yasashii* 親切、優しい

kindergarten *yoochien* 幼稚園

king *oosama* 王様

kitchen *daidokoro* 台所

knife *naifu* ナイフ

know (to) *shiru, shirimasu* 知る、知ります

  I know *shitteimasu* 知っています

  I don't know *shirimasen* 知りません

Kobe *koobe* 神戸

konnyaku potato *konnyaku* こんにゃく

Korea *kankoku* 韓国

Kyoto *kyooto* 京都

labor conditions *taiguu* 待遇

land *tochi* 土地

language *kotoba* 言葉

last week *senshuu* 先週

last year *kyonen* 去年

late *osoi* 遅い

late (to be) *okureru, okuremasu* 遅れる、遅れます

later *ato de, go, gojitsu* 後で、後、後日

See you later. *Sorede wa mata./Sore ja(a) mata. (infml.)* それではまた。/それじゃ(あ)また。

30 minutes later *sanjuppun go* 三十分後

law *hooritsu* 法律

law firm *hooritsu jimusho* 法律事務所

lawyer *bengoshi* 弁護士

leap *hiyaku* 飛躍

leave (to) *deru, demasu* 出る、出ます

  have left (to) *dete iru, dete imasu* 出ている、出ています

  leave … (to) *… o deru, … o demasu* 〜を出る、〜を出ます

  leave the hospital (to) *taiinsuru, taiinshimasu* 退院する、退院します

leaving … *… hasu* 〜発

  leaving Haneda *Haneda hatsu* 羽田発

left *hidari* 左

left side *hidarigawa* 左側

leg *ashi* 脚

lend (to) *kasu, kashimasu* 貸す、貸します

  have lent (to) *kashite iru, kashite imasu* 貸している、貸しています

Let me see. *Soo da naa./Soo desu ne.* そうだなあ。/そうですね。

Let's … *… mashoo.* 〜ましょう。

  Let's do that! *Soo shimashoo!* そうしましょう!

letter *tegami* 手紙

lettuce *retasu* レタス

library *toshokan* 図書館

lid *futa* 蓋

lie *uso* 嘘

  tell a lie (to) *uso o tsuku, uso o tsukimasu* 嘘をつく、嘘をつきます

light *karui (adjective), raito (noun)* 軽い、ライト

light (to) *tsukeru, tsukemasu* 点ける、点けます

like (to) *suki da, suki desu* 好きだ、好きです

  like very much (to), like a lot (to) *daisuki da, daisuki desu* 大好きだ、大好きです

  I'd like to have … *… o onegaishimasu.* 〜をお願いします。

  if you like *moshi yokattara, yoroshikattara (polite)* もし良かったら、よろしかったら

link *rinku* リンク

listen (to) *kiku, kikimasu ; kiku, kikimasu (with focus, such as listening to music)* 聞く、聞きます;聴く、聴きます

literature *bungaku* 文学

lively *nigiyaka* 賑やか

living room *ima* 居間

long *nagai* 長い

  Long time no see. *Hisashiburi desu ne.* 久しぶりですね。

long-absence *hisabisa* 久々

look (to) *miru, mimasu* 見る、見ます

  look for (to) *goran ni naru, goran ni narimasu (honorific); haikensuru, haikenshimasu (humble)* ご覧になる、ご覧になります;拝見する、拝見します

  look forward (to) *sagasu, sagashimasu; tanoshimi ni suru, tanoshimi ni shimasu* 探す、探します;楽しみにする、楽しみにします

  look pale (to) *kaoiro ga warui, kaoiro ga warui desu* 顔色が悪い、顔色が悪いです

loud *hade* 派手

low *hikui* 低い

lunch *chuushoku (fml.), hirugohan (infml.)* 昼食、昼ご飯

lung *hai* 肺

magazine *zasshi* 雑誌

mail (to) *yuusoosuru, yuusooshimasu* 郵送する、郵送します

make (to) *tsukuru, tsukurimasu* 作る、作ります

  make a phone call (to) *denwasuru, denwashimasu* 電話する、電話します

  make a appointment/reservation (to) *yoyakusuru, yoyakushimasu* 予約する、予約します

male *otoko* 男

man *otoko no hito* 男の人

many *ooi, takusan* 多い、たくさん

  how many *(o)ikutsu (polite with o)* (お)いくつ

  many times *nando mo* 何度も

March *sangatsu* 三月

marketing *maaketingu* マーケティング

married couple *(go)fuufu (polite with go)* (ご)夫婦

mat *matto* マット

match (to) *au, aimasu* 合う、合います

match with jeans (to) *jiinzu ni au* ジーンズに合う

mathematics *suugaku* 数学

matter *ken* 件

May *gogatsu* 五月

may (conjecture) *kamoshirenai, kamoshiremasen* かもしれない、かもしれません

May I … ? … *te (mo) ii?; … te (mo) ii desu ka.; … te (mo) ii deshoo ka. (polite); … te (mo) yoroshii desu ka. (polite); … te (mo) yoroshii deshoo ka. (polite)* ～て(も)いい?；～て(も)いいですか。；～て(も)いいでしょうか。；～て(も)よろしいですか。；～て(も)よろしいでしょうか。

meal *gohan (infml.), shokuji (fml.)* ご飯、食事

meaning *imi* 意味

measure (to) *hakaru, hakarimasu* 測る、測ります

meat *niku* 肉

medical consultation *shinsatsu* 診察

　the first medical consultation *shoshin* 初診

medical consulting room *shinsatsushitsu* 診察室

medical doctor *isha* 医者

medicine *kusuri* 薬

medium (size) *medium* エム

　medium is okay *emu de ii* エムでいい

meet (to) *au, aimasu; ome ni kakaru, ome ni kakarimasu (humble)* 会う、会います; お目にかかる、お目にかかります

meeting *kaigi, miitingu* 会議、ミーティング

menu *menyuu* メニュー

meter *meetoru* メートル

Mexican *mekishikojin (person)* メキシコ人

Mexican cuisine *mekishiko ryoori* メキシコ料理

Mexico *mekishiko* メキシコ

microwave oven *denshirenji* 電子レンジ

milk *miruku* ミルク

mind (to) *kamau, kamaimasu* 構う、構います

　Do you mind … ing? … *te (mo) kamaimasen ka.* ～て(も)構いませんか。

miso soup *(o)misoshiru (polite with o)* (お)味噌汁

mixed salad *mikkusu sarada* ミックスサラダ

Monday *getsuyoobi* 月曜日

money *okane* お金

monitor *monitaa* モニター

monotonous *ipponjooshi* 一本調子

moon *tsuki* 月

more *motto* もっと

　a little more *moo sukoshi* もう少し

　more than *ijoo* 以上

　more … than … … *yori* … ～より～

　once more *moo ichido* もう一度

morning *asa, gozen* 朝、午前

　this morning *kesa* 今朝

mosquito *ka* 蚊

(the) most *ichiban* 一番

moth *ga* 蛾

mother (one's own) *haha (one's own), okaasan (someone else's)* 母、お母さん

mountain *yama* 山

mouse *mausu* マウス

mouth *kuchi* 口

move (to a new location) (to) *hikkosu, hikkoshimasu* 引っ越す、引っ越します

movie *eega* 映画

movie theater *eegakan* 映画館

Mr., Ms. *san, sama (polite)* さん、様

Mt. Fuji *fujisan* 富士山

much *ooi, takusan* 多い、たくさん

　how much *(o)ikura (polite with o)* (お)いくら

　not so much *a(n)mari (+ negative)* あ(ん)まり

music *ongaku* 音楽

musical instrument *gakki* 楽器

mussel *muurugai* ムール貝

my *watashi no* 私の

name *(o)namae (polite with o)* (お)名前

　What's your name? *Onamae wa?* お名前は？

narrow *semai* 狭い

nation *kuni* 国

nausea *hakike* 吐き気

nearby *chikaku* 近く

necktie *nekutai* ネクタイ

never *ichido mo (+negative)* 一度も

new *atarashii* 新しい

New York *nyuuyooku* ニューヨーク

newspaper *shinbun* 新聞

next time *kondo* 今度

next to … (… *no) tonari* (～の)隣

next week *raishuu* 来週

next year *rainen* 来年

Nice to meet you. *Doozo yoroshiku.* どうぞよろしく。

night *ban, yoru* 晩、夜

　every night *maiban* 毎晩

　two nights *nihaku* 二泊

　two nights three days *nihaku mikka* 二泊三日

nine *ku, kyuu, kokonotsu (native Japanese number)* 九、九、九つ

nine minutes *kyuufun* 九分

nine o'clock *kuji* 九時

nineteen *juuku, juukyuu* 十九

ninety *kyuujuu* 九十

ninth (day of the month) *kokonoka* 九日

no *iie* いいえ

no one *dare mo (+ negative)* 誰も

No, thank you. *Kekkoo desu.* 結構です。

nobody *dare mo (+ negative)* 誰も

noisy *urusai* うるさい

noon *(o)hiru (polite with o)* (お)昼

north side *kitagawa* 北側

nose *hana* 鼻

not at all *zenzen (+ negative)* 全然

not so much *a(n)mari (+ negative)* あ(ん)まり

not so often *a(n)mari (+ negative)* あ(ん)まり

notebook *nooto* ノート

nothing *nani mo (+ negative)* 何も

novel *shoosetsu* 小説

November *juuichigatsu* 十一月

now *ima* 今

nowhere *doko mo (+ negative)* どこも

number one *ichiban* 一番

nurse *kangoshi* 看護師

obstruction *jama* 邪魔

occupation *shokugyoo* 職業

ocean *umi* 海

October *juugatsu* 十月

octopus *tako* たこ

off (to be), have gotten off (to) *orite iru, orite imasu* 降りている、降りています

office *jimusho, ofisu* 事務所、オフィス

office (clerical) work *jimu* 事務

office worker *kaishain* 会社員

often *yoku* よく

  not so often *a(n)mari (+ negative)* あ(ん)まり

oh *aa* ああ

okay (good) *ii, yoroshii (polite)* いい、よろしい

  if it's okay *moshi yokattara, yoroshikattara (polite)* もし良かったら、よろしかったら

  Is it okay? *Yoroshii desu ka. (polite)* よろしいですか。

  medium is okay *emu de ii* エムでいい

Okinawa *okinawa* 沖縄

old *furui* 古い

  how old *(o)ikutsu (polite with o)* (お)いくつ

older brother *ani (one's own), oniisan (someone else's)* 兄、お兄さん

older sister *ane (one's own), oneesan (someone else's)* 姉、お姉さん

on *(… no) ue* (〜の)上

once *ichido* 一度

  once in a while *tamani* たまに

  once more *moo ichido* もう一度

once upon a time *mukashimukashi* 昔々

one (number) *ichi, hitotsu (native Japanese number)* 一、一つ

  one (indefinite pronoun) *no* の

  the American one *amerika no* アメリカの

  the one in solid color *muji no* 無地の

one minute *ippun* 一分

one o'clock *ichiji* 一時

one person *hitori* 一人

onion *tamanegi* たまねぎ

only *dake, shika (+ negative)* だけ、しか

  only child *hitorikko* 一人っ子

open (to) *akeru, akemasu (transitive verb)* 開ける、開けます

operate (to) *shujutsusuru, shujutsushimasu* 手術する、手術します

operation *shujutsu* 手術

opposite *gyaku* 逆

optional tour *opushonaru tsuaa* オプショナルツアー

or *ka* か

  … or something like that … *demo* 〜でも

  coffee or something like that *koohii demo* コーヒーでも

orange *orenji* オレンジ

order *chuumon* 注文

order (to) *chuumonsuru, chuumonshimasu* 注文する、注文します

Osaka *oosaka* 大阪

other *hoka* 他

  the other day *senjitsu* 先日

own (to) *motsu, mochimasu* 持つ、持ちます

p.m. *gogo* 午後

painful *itai* 痛い

painting *e* 絵

panda *panda* パンダ

pants *pantsu, zubon* パンツ、ズボン

paper *kami* 紙

Pardon the intrusion. *Ojamashimasu.* お邪魔します。

parents *(go)ryooshin (polite with go)* (ご)両親

park *kooen* 公園

party *paatii* パーティー

passing over a matter *fumon* 不問

patient *kanja* 患者

pay (to) *harau, haraimasu* 払う、払います

payment *(o)shiharai (polite with o)* (お)支払い

pen *pen* ペン

pencil *enpitsu* 鉛筆

pepper *koshoo* 胡椒

perform (to) (music) *ensoosuru, ensooshimasu* 演奏する、演奏します

perhaps *tabun* 多分

perm *paama* パーマ

person *hito* 人

person *mono (humble), kata (polite)* 者、方

  a person in charge *tantoo no mono (humble)* 担当の者

  one person *hitori* 一人

  two people *futari, nimeesama (polite)* 二人、二名様

personal computer *pasokon* パソコン

pharmaceutical company *seeyakugaisha* 製薬会社

phonetic-ideographic characters *keesee moji* 形声文字

photograph, photography *shashin* 写真

piano *piano* ピアノ

pictorial characters *shookee moji* 象形文字

pig *buta* 豚

pin *pin* ピン

pink *pinku (noun)* ピンク

pizza *piza* ピザ

place *tokoro* 所

  place of origin *(go)shusshin (polite with go)* (ご)出身

  place of work *kinmuchi* 勤務地

plan *keekaku* 計画

plant (to) *ueru, uemasu* 植える、植えます

plant (to) (seeds) *maku, makimasu* 蒔く、蒔きます

play (to) *asobu, asobimasu (a game); fuku, fukimasu (a wind instruments); hiku, hikimasu (piano); tataku, tatakimasu (a percussion instrument)* 遊ぶ、遊びます;吹く、吹きます;弾く、弾きます; たたく、たたきます

  play sports (to) *suppootsu o suru, supootsu o shimasu* スポーツをする、スポーツをします

Please. *Doozo.* どうぞ。

  Please. (asking for a favor) *Onegaishimasu.* お願いします。

  Please... *... te kudasai.* ～てください。

  Please don't... *... naide kudasai.* ～ないでください。

  Please give me... *... o kudasai.* ～をください。

poison *doku* 毒

police *keesatsu* 警察

police booth *kooban* 交番

police officer *keesatsukan* 警察官

polish (to) *migaku, migakimasu* 磨く、磨きます

pool *puuru* プール

poor at *heta, nigate* 下手、苦手

pop *poppusu* ポップス

popular (to be) *ninki ga aru, ninki ga arimasu* 人気がある、人気があります

popularity *ninki* 人気

pork *butaniku* 豚肉

Portuguese *porutogarugo (language)* ポルトガル語

post office *yuubinkyoku* 郵便局

potato *jagaimo* じゃがいも

practice (to) *renshuusuru, renshuushimasu* 練習する、練習します

prefix meal *teeshoku* 定食

preparation *junbi, yooi* 準備、用意

presentation *happyoo* 発表

  group presentation *gruupu happyoo* グループ発表

president of a company *shachoo* 社長

pretty *kiree* きれい

price *nedan* 値段

  prices (of commodities) *bukka* 物価

  have been priced down (to) *oyasuku natte imasu (polite)* お安くなっています

probably *tabun* 多分

  will probably *daroo, deshoo* だろう、でしょう

problem *mondai* 問題

promotion *kiyoo* 起用

promptly *hayabaya, soosoo* 早々

properly *kichinto, chanto (infml.)* きちんと、ちゃんと

provide (to) *shikyuusuru, shikyuushimasu* 支給する、支給します

psychology *shinrigaku* 心理学

pulse *myaku* 脈

put (to) *oku, okimasu* 置く、置きます

  put into (to) *ireru, iremasu* 入れる、入れます

  put into a salad (to) *sarada ni ireru, sarada ni iremasu* サラダに入れる、サラダに入れます

  put on (to be) *noru, norimasu* 載る、載ります

  have been put on (to) *notte iru, notte imasu* 載っている、載っています

qualification *shikaku* 資格

question *shitsumon* 質問

quickly *hayaku* 早く

quiet *shizuka, jimi (color)* 静か、地味

quite *nakanaka* なかなか

　quite good *nakanaka ii* なかなかいい

radio *rajio* ラジオ

rain *ame* 雨

　It's raining. *Ame desu./Ame ga futte imasu.* 雨です。/雨が降っています。

read (to) *yomu, yomimasu* 読む、読みます

　reading books *dokusho* 読書

not readily (in negative) *nakanaka* なかなか

　not come readily *nakanaka konai, nakanaka kimasen* なかなか来ない、なかなか来ません

　Are you ready? *Junbi wa ii desu ka.* 準備はいいですか。

really *hontoo ni* 本当に

　Really? *Hontoo desu ka./Soo desu ka.* 本当ですか。/そうですか。

reason *riyuu* 理由

　for that reason *sorede* それで

receive (to) *morau, moraimasu; itadaku, itadakimasu (humble)* もらう、もらいます；いただく、いただきます

　receive a favor of … ing (to) … *te morau, … te moraimasu; … te itadaku, … te itadakimasu (humble)* 〜てもらう、〜てもらいます；〜ていただく、〜ていただきます

recently *saikin* 最近

reception desk *uketsuke* 受付

receptionist *uketsukegakari* 受付係

red *akai (adjective), aka (noun)* 赤い、赤

red wine *aka wain* 赤ワイン

refrigerator *reezooko* 冷蔵庫

regarding *kansuru* 関する

relatives *(go)shinseki (polite with go)* （ご）親戚

relax (to) *rirakkususuru, rirakkusushimasu* リラックスする、リラックスします

released from hospital (to be) *taiinsuru, taiinshimasu* 退院する、退院します

replace (a person) (to) *kawaru, kawarimasu* 代わる、代わります

report *repooto* レポート

reservation *yoyaku* 予約

　make a reservation (to) *yoyakusuru, yoyakushimasu* 予約する、予約します

restaurant *resutoran* レストラン

restroom *otearai* お手洗い

resume *rirekisho* 履歴書

return *okaeshi (polite)* お返し

return (to) *kaeru, kaerimasu ; modoru, modorimasu* 帰る、帰ります；戻る、戻ります

　have returned (to) *kaette iru, kaette imasu; modotte iru, modotte imasu* 帰っている、帰っています；戻っている、戻っています

reward *shooyo* 賞与

ride (to) *noru, norimasu* 乗る、乗ります

right *migi* 右

　Right? *Soo desu ne. (rising intonation)* そうですね。

　That's right. *Soo desu.; Soo desu ne.; Soo desu yo.* そうです。；そうですね。；そうですよ。

right side *migigawa* 右側

rink *rinku* リンク

river *kawa* 川

road *michi* 道

rock *rokku* ロック

Rome *rooma* ローマ

room *heya* 部屋

rudeness *shitsuree* 失礼

rules *kiyaku* 規約

run (to) *hashiru, hashirimasu* 走る、走ります

sake *nihonshu* 日本酒

salad *sarada* サラダ

　chicken salad *chikin sarada* チキンサラダ

　green salad *guriin sarada* グリーンサラダ

　mixed salad *mikkusu sarada* ミックスサラダ

　seafood salad *shiifuudo sarada* シーフードサラダ

salary *(o)kyuuryoo (polite with o), kyuuyo (お)* 給料、給与

　salary increase *shookyuu* 昇給

salt *shio* 塩

salty *shiokarai* 塩辛い

same *onaji* 同じ

Saturday *doyoobi* 土曜日

say (to) *iu, iimasu; moosu, mooshimasu (humble); ossharu, osshaimasu (honorific)* 言う、言います；申す、申します；おっしゃる、おっしゃいます

scallop *hotate* 帆立

scared (to be) *bikkurisuru, bikkurishimasu* びっくりする、びっくりします

scarf *sukaafu* スカーフ

schedule *sukejuuru* スケジュール

school *gakkoo* 学校

seafood salad *shiifuudo sarada* シーフードサラダ

seasoning *choomiryoo* 調味料

second *futatsume* 二つ目

second (day of the month) *futsuka* 二日

section manager *kachoo* 課長

see (to) *goran ni naru, goran ni narimasu (honorific); haikensuru, haikenshimasu (humble); ome ni kakaru, ome ni kakarimasu (humble)* ご覧になる、ご覧になります; 拝見する、拝見します; お目にかかる、お目にかかります

I see. *Hee.; Soo desu ka.; Soo ka.* へえ。; そうですか。; そうか。

See you later/then. *Sorede wa mata./Sore ja(a) mata. (infml.)* それではまた。/それじゃ (あ)また。

seeing movies *eega kanshoo (lit., movie appreciation)* 映画鑑賞

seen (to be) *mieru, miemasu* 見える、見えます

seed *tane* 種

selfish *katte* 勝手

seminar *seminaa* セミナー

September *kugatsu* 九月

set (counter for written materials) *bu* 部

seven *nana, shichi, nanatsu (native Japanese number)* 七、七、七つ

seven minutes *nanafun* 七分

seven o'clock *shichiji* 七時

seventeen *juunana, juushichi* 十七

seventh (day of the month) *nanoka* 七日

seventy *nanajuu* 七十

several times *nando ka* 何度か

severe *hidoi* ひどい

shade *sheedo* シェード

Shall we … ? *… mashoo ka.* 〜ましょうか。

she *kanojo* 彼女

shellfish *kai* 貝

Shepherd *shepaado* シェパード

sherbet *shaabetto* シャーベット

shirt *shatsu* シャツ

shoes *kutsu* 靴

shopping *kaimono* 買い物

shopping cart *kaato* カート

short *mijikai* 短い

short (to be) *tarinai, tarimasen* 足りない、足りません

shortcake *shooto keeki* ショートケーキ

shortly *kondo* 今度

shot *chuusha* 注射

shoulders *kata* 肩

have stiff shoulders (to) *kata ga kotte iru, kata ga kotte imasu* 肩が凝っている、肩が凝っています

shower *shawaa* シャワー

take a shower (to) *shawaa o abiru, shawaa o abimasu* シャワーを浴びる、シャワーを浴びます

showy *hade* 派手

shrimp *ebi* えび

shrine *jinja* 神社

siblings *kyoodai (one's own), gokyoodai (someone else's)* 兄弟、ご兄弟

side *hoo* 方

the side of … *(… no) yoko* (〜の)横

this side *temae* 手前

sightseeing *kankoo* 観光

simple *kantan* 簡単

since *node* ので

singer *kashu* 歌手

sit down (to) *suwaru, suwarimasu* 座る、座ります

six *roku, muttsu (native Japanese number)* 六、六つ

six minutes *roppun* 六分

six o'clock *rokuji* 六時

sixteen *juuroku* 十六

sixth (day of the month) *muika* 六日

sixty *rokujuu* 六十

size *saizu* サイズ

ski, skiing *sukii* スキー

skillful *joozu* 上手

skirt *sukaato* スカート

sky *sora* 空

sleep *suimin* 睡眠

get some sleep (to) *suimin o toru, suimin o torimasu* 睡眠をとる、睡眠をとります

sleep (to) *neru, nemasu* 寝る、寝ます

sliced raw fish *sashimi* 刺身

slowly *yukkuri* ゆっくり

small *chiisai* 小さい

smoke a cigarette (to) *tabako o suu, tabako o suimasu* 煙草を吸う、煙草を吸います

snow *yuki* 雪

It's snowing. *Yuki desu./Yuki ga futte imasu.* 雪です。/雪が降っています。

so *kara (conjunction), sorede (conjunction), soo (pronoun)* から、それで、そう

do so (to) *soo suru, soo shimasu* そうする、そうします

Is that so? *Soo desu ka.* そうですか。
so-so *maa maa* まあまあ
sober (color) *jimi* 地味
soccer *sakkaa* サッカー
social insurance *shakaihoken* 社会保険
society *shakai* 社会
sofa *sofaa* ソファー
soft drink *juusu* ジュース
software *sofuto, sofutowea* ソフト、ソフトウェア
soil *tsuchi* 土
solid (color) *muji* 無地
some other day *gojitsu* 後日
someone *dare ka* 誰か
something *nani ka* 何か
sometimes *tokidoki* 時々
somewhere *doko ka* どこか
son *musuko* (one's own), *musukosan* (someone else's) 息子、息子さん
Sorry for the trouble. *Sumimasen.* すみません。
　I'm sorry. *Gomennasai./Sumimasen.* ごめんなさい。/すみません。
　I'm very sorry. *Mooshiwake arimasen.* (polite)/*Mooshiwake gozaimasen.* (polite) 申し訳ありません。/申し訳ございません。
sour *suppai* すっぱい
south side *minamigawa* 南側
soy bean paste *miso* 味噌
soy milk *toonyuu* 豆乳
soy sauce *shooyu* 醤油
spacious *hiroi* 広い
spaghetti *supagetti* スパゲッティ
Spain *supein* スペイン
Spanish *supeingo* (language), *supeinjin* (person) スペイン語、スペイン人
Spanish cuisine *supein ryoori* スペイン料理
speak (to) *hanasu, hanashimasu* 話す、話します
special ability/skill *tokugi* 特技
spicy *karai* 辛い
spoon *supuun* スプーン
sport *supootsu* スポーツ
　play sports (to) *suppootsu o suru, supootsu o shimasu* スポーツをする、スポーツをします
sprain *nenza* 捻挫
　have a sprain (to) *nenzasuru, nenzashimasu* 捻挫する、捻挫します
spring *haru* 春
squid *ika* いか
stairs *kaidan* 階段

stand up (to) *tatsu, tachimasu* 立つ、立ちます
station *eki* 駅
stay home (to) *uchi ni iru, uchi ni imasu* 家にいる、家にいます
staying over night *haku* 泊
stiff (to get) *koru, korimasu* 凝る、凝ります
　have stiff shoulders (to) *kata ga kotte iru, kata ga kotte imasu* 肩が凝っている、肩が凝っています
still *mada* まだ
stomach *i* 胃
stomachache *fukutsuu* 腹痛
　have a stomachache (to) *onaka ga itai, onaka ga itai desu* お腹が痛い、お腹が痛いです
store *mise* 店
store clerk *ten-in* 店員
straight *massugu* まっすぐ
strange *myoo* 妙
stream *ogawa* 小川
street *michi* 道
stress *sutoresu* ストレス
　under a lot of stress (to be) *sutoresu ga tamatte iru, sutoresu ga tamatte imasu* ストレスが溜まっている、ストレスが溜まっています
stripes *shima* 縞
stroke (for writing characters) *kaku* 画
　number of strokes *kakusuu* 画数
　stroke order *kakijun* 書き順
strong *tsuyoi* 強い
student *gakusee* 学生
　college student *daigakusee* 大学生
　graduate school student *daigakuinsee* 大学院生
　high school student *kookoosee* 高校生
　teacher and student *shitee* 師弟
study (to) *benkyoosuru, benkyooshimasu* 勉強する、勉強します
　study abroad (to) *ryuugakusuru, ryuugakushimasu* 留学する、留学します
subject (letter, e-mail) *kenmee* 件名
subway *chikatetsu* 地下鉄
sugar *satoo* 砂糖
suitcase *suutsukeesu* スーツケース
summer *natsu* 夏
　summer vacation *natsu yasumi* 夏休み
sumo wrestling *sumoo* 相撲
Sunday *nichiyoobi* 日曜日
sunny *hare* 晴れ

It's sunny. *Hare desu./Harete imasu.* 晴れです。/晴れています。

supermarket *suupaa* スーパー

surgery *shujutsu* 手術

surprised (to be) *bikkurisuru, bikkurishimasu* びっくりする、びっくりします

sushi *sushi* 寿司

sweater *seetaa* セーター

sweet *amai* 甘い

swim (to) *oyogu, oyogimasu* 泳ぐ、泳ぎます

swimming *suiee* 水泳

table *teeburu* テーブル

take (to) *ukeru, ukemasu* 受ける、受けます

take (photos) (to) *toru, torimasu* 撮る、撮ります

take (time) (to) *kakaru, kakarimasu* かかる、かかります

take a bath (to) *ofuro ni hairu, ofuro ni hairimasu* お風呂に入る、お風呂に入ります

take a day off (to) *yasumu, yasumimasu* 休む、休みます

take a day off from work (to) *kaisha o yasumu, kaisha o yasumimasu* 会社を休む、会社を休みます

take a medical consultation (to) *shinsatsu o ukeru, shinsatsu o ukemasu* 診察を受ける、診察を受けます

take a shower (to) *shawaa o abiru, shawaa o abimasu* シャワーを浴びる、シャワーを浴びます

take lessons on (to) *narau, naraimasu* 習う、習います

take off (shoes, clothes) (to) *nugu, nugimasu* 脱ぐ、脱ぎます

take some rest (to) *yasumu, yasumimasu* 休む、休みます

take (someone or animal) (to) *tsurete iku, tsurete ikimasu* 連れて行く、連れて行きます

take (something) (to) *motte iku, motte ikimasu* 持って行く、持って行きます

talk show *tookushoo* トークショー

tall *takai* 高い

taxi *takushii* タクシー

tea (Japanese kind) *ocha* お茶

teach (to) *oshieru, oshiemasu* 教える、教えます

teacher *kyooshi, sensee* 教師、先生

Prof./Dr. Tanaka *Tanaka sensee* 田中先生

teacher and student *shitee* 師弟

telephone *(o)denwa (polite with o)* (お)電話

telephone number *(o)denwabangoo (polite with o)* (お)電話番号

television *terebi* テレビ

tell (to) *oshieru, oshiemasu* 教える、教えます

tell a lie (to) *uso o tsuku, uso o tsukimasu* 嘘をつく、嘘をつきます

(check one's) temperature *netsu o hakaru, netsu o hakarimasu* 熱を測る、熱を測ります

temple *(o)tera (polie with o)* (お)寺

tempura *tenpura* 天ぷら

ten *juu, too (native Japanese number)* 十、十

ten thousand *ichiman* 一万

ten thousand yen *ichiman en* 一万円

ten minutes *juppun* 十分

ten o'clock *juuji* 十時

tennis *tenisu* テニス

tennis court *tenisu kooto* テニスコート

tenth (day of the month) *tooka* 十日

terrible *hidoi* ひどい

textbook *kyookasho* 教科書

the ... th ... *me* ～目

Thank you. *Arigatoo gozaimasu./Arigatoo gozaimashita.* ありがとうございます。/ありがとうございました。

Thank you very much. *Doomo arigatoo gozaimasu./Doomo arigatoo gozaimashita.* どうもありがとうございます。/どうもありがとうございました。

No, thank you. *Kekkoo desu.* 結構です。

that (conjunction) *to* と

that (demonstrative) *sono (far from the speaker but close to the listener) ; sore (far from the speaker but close to the listener); ano (far from both the speaker and the listener); are (far from both the speaker and the listener)* その;それ;あの;あれ

that pen *sono pen (far from the speaker but close to the listener); ano pen (far from both the speaker and the listener)* そのペン; あのペン

that way *sochira (far from the speaker but close to the listener) (polite); achira (far from both the speaker and the listener) (polite)* そちら; あちら

then *dewa, ja(a) (infml.), sorede wa, sore ja(a) (infml.)* では、じゃ(あ) 、それでは、それじゃ(あ)

and then *sorekara, soshite* それから、そして

See you then. *Sorede wa mata./Sore ja(a) mata. (infml.)* それではまた。/それじゃ(あ)また。

there *asoko (far from both the speaker and the listener) ; soko (far from the speaker but close to the listener)* あそこ;そこ

There is … *aru, arimasu (inanimate); iru, imasu (animate); gozaimasu (polite); irassharu, irasshaimasu (honorific); oru, orimasu (humble)* ある、あります; いる、います; ございます; いらっしゃる、いらっしゃいます; おる、おります

they *karera (people) ; kanojora (people, feminine) ; kanojotachi (people, feminine) ; sorera (inanimate)* 彼ら; 彼女ら; 彼女達; それら

thing *koto* こと

think (to) *omou, omoimasu* 思う、思います

third *mittsume* 三つ目

third (day of the month) *mikka* 三日

thirteen *juusan* 十三

thirty *sanjuu* 三十

five thirty *goji sanjuppun* 五時三十分

thirty minutes *sanjuppun* 三十分

this *kore, kono, kochira (polite)* これ、この、こちら

this morning *kesa* 今朝

this pen *kono pen* このペン

this time *kondo* 今度

this way *kochira (polite)* こちら

this week *konshuu* 今週

this weekend *konshuumatsu* 今週末

this year *kotoshi* 今年

thousand *sen* 千

ten thousand *ichiman* 一万

ten thousand yen *ichiman en* 一万円

thousand yen *sen en* 千円

three *san, mittsu (native Japanese number)* 三、三つ

three minutes *sanpun* 三分

three o'clock *sanji* 三時

throat *nodo* 喉

have a sore throat (to) *nodo ga itai, nodo ga itai desu* 喉が痛い、喉が痛いです

Thursday *mokuyoobi* 木曜日

time *jikan* 時間

this time *kondo* 今度

Times Square *taimuzu sukuea* タイムズスクエア

(sent) to *atesaki* 宛先

from … to … *… kara … made* ～から～まで

tobacco *tabako* 煙草

today *kyoo* 今日

together *issho ni* 一緒に

all together *zenbu de* 全部で

toilet *toire* トイレ

Tokyo *Tookyoo* 東京

tomato *tomato* トマト

tomorrow *ashita, asu* 明日

the day after tomorrow *asatte* あさって

tonight *konban* 今晩

too (also) *mo* も

too, too much *sugiru, sugimasu* すぎる、すぎます

tooth *ha* 歯

tour guide *tenjooin, tsuaagaido* 添乗員、ツアーガイド

town *machi* 町

trade *booeki* 貿易

trading company *booekigaisha* 貿易会社

traffic light *shingoo* 信号

before the traffic light *shingoo no temae* 信号の手前

train *densha* 電車

transfer (a phone line) (to) *kawaru, kawarimasu* 代わる、代わります

transportation *kootsuu* 交通

transportation costs *kootsuuhi* 交通費

travel *ryokoo* 旅行

travel company *ryokoosha* 旅行社

treatment *taiguu* 待遇

tree *ki* 木

big tree *taiboku* 大木

tree shadow *kokage* 木陰

true *hontoo* 本当

Is that true? *Hontoo desu ka.* 本当ですか。

try … ing (to) *… te miru, … te mimasu* ～てみる、～てみます

T-shirt *tiishatsu* ティーシャツ（Tシャツ）

Tuesday *kayoobi* 火曜日

tunnel *tonneru* トンネル

turn (to) *magaru, magarimasu* 曲がる、曲がります

twelve *juuni* 十二

twelve o'clock *juuniji* 十二時

twentieth (day of the month) *hatsuka* 二十日

twenty *nijuu* 二十

two *ni, futatsu (native Japanese number)* 二、二つ

two minutes *nifun* 二分

two o'clock *niji* 二時
two people *futari, nimeesama (polite)* 二人、二名様
typhoon *taifuu* 台風
under . . . *(. . . no) shita* (〜の)下
under a lot of stress (to be) *sutoresu ga tamatte iru, sutoresu ga tamatte imasu* ストレスが溜まっている、ストレスが溜まっています
understand (to) *wakaru, wakarimasu* 分かる、分かります
United States (the) *amerika* アメリカ
university *daigaku* 大学
unskillful *heta* 下手
until *made* まで
up to now *ima made ni, kore made ni* 今までに、これまでに
urine *nyoo* 尿
use (to) *tsukau, tsukaimasu* 使う、使います
vacation *yasumi* 休み
summer vacation *natsu yasumi* 夏休み
van *ban* バン
various *kakushu* 各種
vegetable *yasai* 野菜
very *totemo, taihen* とても、大変
very much *totemo* とても
vest *besuto* ベスト
vigorous *genki* 元気
violin *baiorin* バイオリン
virtue *toku* 徳
visible (to be) *mieru, miemasu* 見える、見えます
visit (to) *tazuneru, tazunemasu* 訪ねる、訪ねます
vitamin supplement *bitaminzai* ビタミン剤
volleyball *bareebooru* バレーボール
voucher *ken* 券
waist *koshi* 腰
wait (to) *matsu, machimasu* 待つ、待ちます
I/We will be waiting for you. *Omachishite orimasu. (polite)* お待ちしております。
Please wait. *Omachi kudasai. (polite)* お待ちください。
waiting room *machiaishitsu* 待合室
waitress *weitoresu* ウェイトレス
wake-to-sleep transition *netsuki* 寝つき
Wales *weeruzu* ウェールズ
walk (to) *aruku, arukimasu* 歩く、歩きます
five minute walk *aruite gofun* 歩いて五分
want (to) *hoshii, hoshii desu* 欲しい、欲しいです
(Someone) wants *hoshigatte iru, hoshigatte imasu* 欲しがっている、欲しがっています
want to (to) *tai, tai desu* たい、たいです
warm *atatakai* 暖かい
wash (to) *arau, araimasu* 洗う、洗います
washing machine *sentakuki* 洗濯機
watch *tokee* 時計
watch (to) *miru, mimasu; goran ni naru, goran ni narimasu (honorific); haikensuru, haikenshimasu (humble)* 見る、見ます; ご覧になる、ご覧になります; 拝見する、拝見します
water *(o) mizu (polite with o)* (お)水
we *watashitachi* 私達
web designer *webudezainaa* ウェブデザイナー
Wednesday *suiyoobi* 水曜日
week *shuu* 週
a week *isshuukan* 一週間
last week *senshuu* 先週
next week *raishuu* 来週
this week *konshuu* 今週
weekday *heejitsu* 平日
weekend *shuumatsu* 週末
this weekend *konshuumatsu* 今週末
Welcome. *Yookoso.* ようこそ。
Welcome (to our store). *Irasshaimase.* いらっしゃいませ。
well *yoku* よく
well . . . *anoo, etto, hee, uun* あのう、えっと、へえ、ううん
Well done. *Yoku dekimashita.* よくできました。
west side *nishigawa* 西側
Western style *yoofuu* 洋風
what *nan(i)* 何
What about . . . ? *Doo desu ka.* どうですか。
what kind of *donna* どんな
what time *nanji* 何時
What's the matter? *Doo shimashita ka./Doo nasaimashita ka. (polite)* どうしましたか。/どうなさいましたか。
wheat *komugi* 小麦
when *itsu (question); tara, to, toki (conjunction)* いつ; たら、と、時
where *doko, dochira (polite)* どこ、どちら
which (one) *dono* どの
which one *dore, dochira, dochira no hoo* どれ、どちら、どちらの方
which pen *dono pen* どのペン
which way *dochira (polite)* どちら

white *shiroi* 白い

white night *byakuya* 白夜

white wine *shiro wain* 白ワイン

who *dare, donate (polite)* 誰、どなた

why *dooshite, naze, nande (infml.)* どうして、なぜ、なんで

  Why don't we … ? *… masen ka.* 〜ませんか。

wife *kanai (one's own), tsuma (one's own), okusan (someone else's)* 家内、妻、奥さん

wind *kaze* 風

window *mado* 窓

window shopping *windooshoppingu* ウィンドーショッピング

wine *wain* ワイン

  red wine *aka wain* 赤ワイン

  white wine *shiro wain* 白ワイン

winter *fuyu* 冬

with *to* と

woman *onna no hito* 女の人

(I) wonder … *… kana(a)./ … kashira.* 〜かな(あ)。/〜かしら。

woods *hayashi* 林

wool *uuru* ウール

  100% wool *uuru hyakupaasento* ウール100パーセント

word *kotoba* 言葉

word processor *waapuro* ワープロ

work *o(shigoto) (polite with o), kinmu (fml.)* (お)仕事、勤務

  place of work *kinmuchi* 勤務地

  take a day off from work (to) *kaisha o yasumu, kaisha o yasumimasu* 会社を休む、会社を休みます

work (to) *hataraku, hatarakimasu* 働く、働きます

  work overtime (to) *zangyoosuru, zangyooshimasu* 残業する、残業します

Wow. *Hee.* へえ。

write (to) *kaku, kakimasu* 書く、書きます

yard *niwa* 庭

year *nen* 年

  for a year *ichinenkan* 一年間

  next year *rainen* 来年

  this year *kotoshi* 今年

yellow *kiiroi (adjective), kiiro (noun)* 黄色い、黄色

yen *en* 円

  ten thousand yen *ichiman en* 一万円

  thousand yen *sen en* 千円

yes *hai, ee (infml.), un (infml.)* はい、ええ、うん

  Yes, it is. *Soo desu ne.* そうですね。

yesterday *kinoo* 昨日

  the day before yesterday *ototoi* おととい

yet *mada (+negative)* まだ

you (subject pronoun) *anata (sg.), anatagata (pl.), anatatachi (pl.)* あなた、あなた方、あなた達

young *wakai* 若い

younger brother *otooto (one's own), otootosan (someone else's)* 弟、弟さん

younger sister *imooto (one's own), imootosan (someone else's)* 妹、妹さん

your (sg.) *anata no* あなたの

zen *zen* 禅

zero *ree, zero* 零、ゼロ